Object-Oriented Programming Using C++
Second Edition

Joyce Farrell
University of Wisconsin
Stevens Point

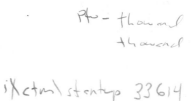

**COURSE
TECHNOLOGY**
™
THOMSON LEARNING

Australia • Canada • Mexico • Singapore • Spain • United Kingdom • United States

COURSE TECHNOLOGY
™
THOMSON LEARNING

Object-Oriented Programming Using C++, Second Edition is published by Course Technology.

Managing Editor Jennifer Normandin	**Production Editor** Anne Valsangiacomo	**Associate Marketing Manager** Meagan Walsh
Product Manager Margarita Donovan	**Developmental Editor** Lisa Ruffolo, The Software Resource	**Editorial Assistant** Janet Aras
Acquisitions Editor Christine Guivernau	**Associate Product Manager** Tricia Coia	**Cover Designer** Efrat Reis

BRIEF
Contents

TABLE OF
Contents

CHAPTER SIX
Class Features and Design Issues   195

CHAPTER SEVEN
Understanding Friends   233

CHAPTER ELEVEN
Using Templates   405

CHAPTER TWELVE
Handling Exceptions   443

Preface

Object-Oriented Programming Using C++, Second Edition is designed for many levels of programming students and a variety of programming teaching styles. Readers who are new to programming will find the basics of programming logic and the C++ programming language covered thoroughly and clearly. Clear, thorough explanations, multiple programming examples, and step-by-step programming lessons provide beginning readers with a solid C++ background. Users who know some C++ syntax, but are new to object-oriented programming, will find objects explored thoroughly from the first chapters. Objects are introduced early, so those who want to learn objects at the start of their programming experience can do so. Users who want to postpone objects can simply omit the later sections of each chapter and cover the basic programming structures with simple data types before returning to the more complex objects later on.

Organization and Coverage

Object-Oriented Programming Using C++ contains 13 chapters that present clear text explanation interspersed with hands-on instruction. In these chapters, readers learn about programming logic in general, C++ syntax in particular, and gain an appreciation for and understanding of the object-oriented approach. When readers complete the book, they will have an understanding of object-oriented concepts as they apply to programming, and the ability to use these concepts to develop C++ programs.

Approach

Object-Oriented Programming Using C++ teaches object-oriented concepts using C++ as a tool to demonstrate these concepts. This book teaches programming concepts using a task-driven rather than a command-driven approach. By working through the tutorials, students learn how to apply concepts in a concrete fashion.

Features

Object-Oriented Programming Using C++ is an exceptional textbook because it also includes the following features:

- **Objectives** A brief list of objectives appears at the beginning of each chapter so the student has an overview of the main topics to be covered.

- **Step-by-Step Methodology** The unique Course Technology methodology keeps students on track. Students read about a concept, then enter code within the context of solving a problem and using the concepts just presented.

- **Tips** provide additional information about a procedure or topic, such as an alternative method of performing a procedure.

- **Summaries** Following each lesson is a summary that recaps the programming concepts and commands covered in the lesson.

- **Questions and Exercises** Each lesson concludes with meaningful questions that test students' understanding of what they learned in the lesson, and exercises that provide students with the opportunity to apply the concepts they have mastered.

- **Debugging Exercises** Each lesson ends with debugging exercises—programs with a few syntax or logical errors. The student can find the errors and fix them, developing crucial skills of reading others' programs, analyzing probable cause of errors, and solving problems.

- **Running Case** The book contains a running case in which the student develops a large class, adding appropriate features as each new concept is introduced. By the end of the book the student has created a substantial working class.

Teaching Tools

The following teaching tools are available when this book is used in a classroom setting. All of the teaching tools available with this book are provided to the instructor on a single CD-ROM.

- **Instructional Material** Additional instructional material to assist in class preparation, including suggestions for lecture topics.

- **Solution Files** Solutions to all end-of-chapter materials. (Due to the nature of programming, students' solutions may differ from these solutions and still be correct.)

- **Data Files** Data files, containing all of the data that students will use for the tutorials and exercises in this book, are provided through Course Technology's Online Companion and on the Instructor's Resource Kit CD-ROM. See the "Read This Before You Begin" section preceding the Overview for more information on Data Files.

Course Test Manager 1.2 Accompanying this book is a powerful assessment tool known as the Course Test Manager. Designed by Course Technology, this cutting-edge Windows-based testing software helps instructors design and administer tests and pre-tests. In addition to being able to generate tests that can be printed and administered, this full featured program also has an outline testing component that allows students to take tests at the computer and have their exams graded automatically.

PowerPoint Presentations This book comes with Microsoft PowerPoint slides for each chapter. These are included as a teaching aid for classroom presentation, to make available to students on the network for chapter review, or to be printed for classroom distribution. Instructors can add their own slides for additional topics they introduce to the class.

MyCourse.com MyCourse.com is an online syllabus builder and course enhancement tool. Hosted by Course Technology, MyCourse.com adds value to your course by providing additional content that reinforces what students are learning.

Most importantly, MyCourse.com is flexible. You can choose how you want to organize the material—by date, by class session, or by using the default organization, which organizes content by chapter. MyCourse.com allows you to add your own materials, including hyperlinks, school logos, assignments, announcements, and other course content. If you are using more than one textbook, you can even build a course that includes all of your Course Technology texts in one easy-to-use site!

Start building your own course today! Just go to **www.mycourse.com/instructor**.

ACKNOWLEDGMENTS

I would like to thank all of the people who have this book a reality, especially Lisa Ruffolo, my Developmental Editor who remained patient and flexible as I changed jobs, moved to a new state, launched a child in college, and otherwise tried to have a normal life during the half year it took to write this book. I truly appreciate all of your hard work. Thanks also to Margarita Donovan, Product Manager; Anne Valsangiacomo, Production Editor; John Bosco, Quality Assurance Manager; and Nicole Ashton and Jeff Schwartz, Quality Assurance Engineers.

Thank you to the reviewers who provided helpful and insightful comments during the development of this book, including Ram Choppa, University of Houston – West Houston Institute; Lee Cottrell, Bradford School; Sandra Madison, University of Wisconsin-Stevens Point; Tim Reeves, San Juan College; Deborah Shapiro, Computer Learning Center; Paul Turnage, Schoolcraft College; and Catherine Wyman, DeVry Phoenix.

Thank you to my husband and best friend, Geoffrey. I never would have taught a class nor written a book if you had not encouraged and supported me.

Finally, this book is dedicated to the memory of my father, Elvin Bussell.

Read This Before You Begin

To the User

Using Your Own Computer:

■ Computer System and Software This text was written so that any C++ compiler can be used. The programs used in this book (except in Chapter 10, see Appendix) were written on a Borland C++ Compiler, version 5.0, and tested on Borland C++ 5.0 and 5.5, and Microsoft Visual C++, version 6.0. Additionally, most programs will work in Borland C++ version 3.0. No special memory or hard disk requirements apply. If you use Visual C++ to compile your programs, you will have to store the programs on your hard drive rather than on a diskette. Older compilers may not support templates as discussed in Chapter 10.

■ The Borland C++ 5.5 compiler can be downloaded from the World Wide Web at *www.borland.com*. The following system requirements apply:

  ■ Intel Pentium class processor or higher (P166 recommended)

  ■ Microsoft Windows 95 or later or Windows NT 4.0 or later

  ■ 32 MB of RAM (64Mb recommended)

  ■ Hard disk space: 50 Mb of available hard disk space

■ Microsoft Visual C++ Introductory Edition is an optional item with your book. The following system requirements apply:

  ■ Personal computer with a 486 or higher processor

  ■ Microsoft Windows 95 or later or Windows NT 4.0 or later

  ■ 32 MB of RAM

  ■ VGA or higher-resolution monitor (Super VGA recommended)

  ■ 225 MB hard disk space for installation

  ■ CD-ROM drive with 32-bit protected mode CD-ROM drivers

Data Files

You will not be able to complete all the exercises in this book using your own computer until you have Data Files. You can get the files for your Data Files from your instructor. The files also may be obtained electronically through the Internet at *www.course.com*.

TO THE INSTRUCTOR

To complete the chapters in this book, your students must use a set of Data Files. These files are included in the Instructor's Resource Kit. They may also be obtained electronically through the Internet. Go to *www.course.com* to download the Data Files that accompany this book.

Course Technology Data Files

You are granted a license to copy the data files to any computer or computer network used by students who have purchased the book.

CHAPTER

1

AN OVERVIEW OF OBJECT-ORIENTED PROGRAMMING AND C++

In this chapter, you will learn:

- ♦ About the task of programming
- ♦ About programming universals
- ♦ About procedural programming
- ♦ About object-oriented programming
- ♦ About the C++ programming environment
- ♦ How to create a main() function
- ♦ How to work with variables and the const qualifier
- ♦ How to create comments
- ♦ How to use libraries and preprocessor directives
- ♦ How to use cout and cin
- ♦ How to work with classes

Whether you are new to programming or have already had a class in logic or a programming language other than C++, this chapter introduces you to the fundamental concepts of programming, including procedural and object-oriented programming. After learning or reviewing what it means to program, you examine the characteristics of procedural programs and consider a few examples. Then you compare procedural and object-oriented programs and learn the additional features object-orientation provides.

In the rest of the chapter, you consider the basic principles behind object-oriented programming techniques, including objects, classes, inheritance, and polymorphism. Then you get started in the C++ programming environment by applying what you have learned. For example, you learn how to create a main() function, work with variables and constants, and create comments. Finally, you learn how to produce output and process input with C++, and you learn how to create your first classes and objects.

1

THE TASK OF PROGRAMMING

Programming a computer involves writing instructions that enable a computer to carry out a single task or a group of tasks. Writing these sets of instructions, which are known as **programs** or **software**, requires using a computer programming language and resolving errors in the instructions so that the programs work correctly.

As with any language, learning a computer **programming language** requires learning both vocabulary and syntax. Humans speak a variety of languages, such as English and Japanese, and programmers use many different programming languages, including BASIC, Pascal, COBOL, RPG, and **C++**.

The rules of any language make up its **syntax**. Writing in a programming language requires correct use of that language's syntax. In English, using incorrect syntax—that is, committing a **syntax error**—might make communication more difficult but usually does not prevent it altogether. If you ask, "Name yours what is?", most people can still figure out what you mean. If you are vague or spell a word wrong when writing, most people will nevertheless understand your message. Computers are not nearly as smart as most humans, nor as flexible. As a result, using correct syntax in a computer program is not just important—it's essential.

 An interpreter is a program that translates instructions one line at a time; a compiler works by translating the entire program at one time. C++ is a compiled language.

Most of today's programming languages follow syntax rules that are close enough to human language to make them accessible to anyone willing to learn and practice them. The statements you write in an English-like programming language must subsequently be translated into machine language. **Machine language** is the language that computers can understand; it consists of 1s and 0s. A translator (called either a compiler or an interpreter) checks your program for syntax errors. If there are no errors, the translator changes your written program statements into machine language. Therefore, syntax errors are not a big problem; you always have an opportunity to fix them before you actually run the program. For example, if you write a computer program in C++ but spell a word incorrectly or reverse the required order of two words, the compiler informs you of such errors and will not let you run the program until you have corrected them.

Much more time consuming to a programmer than syntax errors are logical errors. A **logical error** occurs when you use a statement that, although syntactically correct, doesn't do what you intended. For a program that is supposed to add two numbers and show the sum, logical errors arise when multiplication is used instead of addition, or when the sum is given before the arithmetic occurs. The language compiler will not tell you when you have committed a logical error; only running and testing your program will enable you to find inappropriate statements. You **run** a program by issuing a command to execute the program statements. You **test** a program by using sample data to determine whether the program results are correct.

Selecting data for testing is an art in itself. For example, imagine that you write a program to add two numbers, and test the program with the values 2 and 2. You cannot be sure that the program is free of logical errors just because the answer is 4. Perhaps you used the multiplication symbol rather than the addition symbol. You can confirm your program's accuracy by testing the program several times using a variety of data.

PROGRAMMING UNIVERSALS

All modern programming languages share common characteristics. For example, all programming languages provide methods for directing **output**—the information produced by a program—to a desired object, such as a monitor screen, printer, or file. Similarly, all programming languages provide methods for sending **input**—the data provided by an outside source such as a keyboard, scanner, or file—into the computer program so that it can be manipulated.

In addition, all programming languages provide for naming locations in computer memory. These locations commonly are called **variables** (or **attributes**). For example, if a person asks, "What is yourAge?", yourAge is considered a variable for two reasons: yourAge has different (varied) values for different people, and any person can have a change in age. When writing a computer program, yourAge becomes the name of a position or location in computer memory; the *value at* that location or the *state of* that location might be 18 or 80, or it might be unknown.

A variable or attribute is also an object, although it is a much simpler object than a monitor or file.

When discussing the variable yourAge, the separate words "your" and "Age" are run together on purpose. All modern programming languages require that variable names be one word; that is, they cannot include any embedded spaces. Each programming language has other specific rules as to which characters are not allowed, how many characters may be used in the variable name, and whether capitalization makes a difference.

Ideally, variables have meaningful names, although no programming language actually requires that they meet this standard. A payroll program, for example, is easier to read if a variable that is meant to hold your salary is called yourSalary, but it is legal, that is, okay, to call the variable ImHungry or jqxBr.

A variable may have only one value at a time, but it is the ability of memory variables to *change* in value that makes computers and programming worthwhile. Because one memory location, or variable, can be used repeatedly with different values, program instructions can be written once and then used for thousands of problems. Thus, one set of payroll instructions at your company might produce thousands of individual paychecks each week, and a variable for hourly wage, perhaps called hourlyWage, can be reused for each employee, holding a different value as each individual employee's paycheck is calculated.

In many computer programming languages, including C++, variables must be explicitly **declared**, or given a data type as well as a name, before they can be used. The **type** determines what kind of values may be stored in a variable. Most computer languages allow at least two types: one for numbers and one for characters. **Numeric variables** hold values like 13 or -6. **Character variables** hold values like 'A' or '&'. Many languages include even more specialized types, such as **integer** (for storing whole numbers) or **floating point** (for storing numbers with decimal places). Some languages, including C++, also let you create your own types. The distinction between variable types is important because computers handle the various types of data differently; each type of variable requires a different amount of storage and answers to different rules for manipulation. When you declare a variable with a type, you aren't merely naming it, you are giving it a set of characteristics and allowable values.

 Numeric values like 13 and -6 are called numeric constants; they always appear without quotes. Character values like 'A' and '&' are character constants, and always appear within single quotes.

PROCEDURAL PROGRAMMING

For most of the history of computer programming, which now covers roughly 60 years, most programs were written procedurally. **Procedural programs** consist of a series of steps or procedures that take place one after the other. The programmer determines the exact conditions under which a procedure takes place, how often it takes place, and when the program stops.

Programmers write procedural programs in many programming languages, such as COBOL, BASIC, FORTRAN, and RPG. You can also write procedural programs in C++. Although each language has a different syntax, they all share many elements.

Over the years, as programmers have sought better ways to accommodate the way people work best on computers, procedural programming techniques have evolved into object-oriented techniques. Some older languages do not support object-oriented techniques, but several newer languages do, including Visual Basic, Java, and C++.

Early Procedural Programs

When programming languages were first used, the programmer's job was to break a task into small, specific steps. Each step was then coded in an appropriate language.

Consider a program that creates customer bills for a small business. Assume that the business sells only one product that costs exactly $7.99. Each customer order must contain the desired quantity of the item, and the customer's name and address. If you could write the program in English rather than in a programming language, a simple version of the program might look something like Figure 1-1.

```
Declare variables quantityOrdered, customerName,
  customerAddress,and balanceDue
Read in quantityOrdered, customerName, and customerAddress
  from disk
Print "From:"
Print "ABC Company"
Print "Stevens Point, WI"
Print "Send To:"
Print customerName
Print customerAddress
Multiply quantityOrdered by 7.99 giving balanceDue
Print balanceDue
```

Figure 1-1   English language version of a simple procedural billing program

The programmer creates every step needed to produce a bill. He or she also chooses unique, descriptive variable names, such as customerName and balanceDue.

In a real-life program, often called a production program, the data stored in variables such as customerName and customerAddress most likely would be divided into appropriate subfields. Most companies would store firstName and lastName in separate fields, but use both on a customer bill. Similarly, streetAddress, city, state, and zipCode are likely to be separate variables. The example in Figure 1-1 uses customerName and customerAddress to limit the number of statements.

Three basic control structures are used in procedural programming. In the first structure, a **sequence**, program steps execute one after another, without interruption. The order of some of the statements is important; you must determine the balanceDue before you can print it out. For some other statements, however, order is unimportant. You can print the "From:" and "Send To:" information, compute the balanceDue, and then print the balanceDue as shown in Figure 1-1, but you also can compute the balanceDue first, print the "From:" and "To:" information, and then print the balanceDue with no difference in the resulting bill.

Procedural programs also can include a second control structure called **selection**, which you use to perform different tasks based on a condition. Perhaps you give a $5 discount to any customer who orders more than a dozen of an item. Figure 1-2 shows how this is accomplished. The selection occurs in the second line from the bottom of the program.

Programmers also call a selection a decision or an if-then.

```
Declare variables quantityOrdered, customerName,
  customerAddress,and balanceDue
Read in quantityOrdered, customerName, and customerAddress
  from disk
Print "From:"
Print "ABC Company"
Print "Stevens Point, WI"
Print "Send To:"
Print customerName
Print customerAddress
Multiply quantityOrdered by 7.99 giving balanceDue
If quantityOrdered is greater than 12 then
  subtract 5 from balanceDue
Print balanceDue
```

Figure 1-2   Adding a selection structure to the simple procedural billing

In the example shown in Figure 1-2, $5 is deducted from the balanceDue if—and only if—
the customer orders more than 12 items. The actual program that produces bills for a company might have many more selection statements than this example and usually is far more
detailed. What if you're out of stock? What about taxes? What if the customer has a credit
balance that should be applied to this order? What if one of the data items like quantityOrdered
or customerAddress has been left blank? Some programs contain dozens or even hundreds of
selection statements.

The third control structure used in computer programs is the **loop**. When companies bill customers, they usually bill many customers at one time. The relevant program accesses a customer
record from an input file, produces a bill, and continues to repeat the same steps until no more
customers remain in the file. The example in Figure 1-3 shows a program that loops.

```
Declare variables quantityOrdered, customerName,
  customerAddress,and balanceDue
Repeat until there are no more input records on the disk
  Read in quantityOrdered, customerName,
    and customerAddress from disk
  Print "From:"
  Print "ABC Company"
  Print "Stevens Point, WI"
  Print "Send To:"
  Print customerName
  Print customerAddress
  Multiply quantityOrdered by 7.99 giving balanceDue
  If quantityOrdered is greater than 12 then
    subtract 5 from balanceDue
  Print balanceDue
```

Figure 1-3   Adding a loop to a simple procedural billing program

Some programmers call the loop structure a repetition or iteration structure.

The indentation shown in the code in Figure 1-3 indicates that all nine statements, from "Read" until "Print balanceDue", occur repeatedly "until there are no more input records on the disk."

In reality, production programmers structure their loops a little differently to avoid printing one useless customer bill after the last data record is read from the disk. You will become comfortable with this concept after you learn about writing C++ loops.

The billing program shown in Figure 1-3 does not contain nearly as many sequential steps, selections, or loops as a full-blown production program would, but even as it stands, the billing program contains quite a few statements. As programs grow more complicated, they can contain many hundreds or even thousands of separate statements, and are difficult to follow. Luckily, all modern programming languages allow programmers to break their programs into smaller, easier-to-follow modules.

Modularity and Abstraction

Programming in the oldest procedural languages had two major disadvantages:

- The programming process involved so much detail that the programmer (and any person reading the program) lost sight of the big picture.

- Similar statements required in various parts of the program had to be rewritten in more than one place.

Writing programs became easier when programming languages began to allow the programmer to write methods. Using methods allows programmers to group statements together into modules, which are known in various programming languages as functions, procedures, methods, subprograms, subroutines, or simply routines. For example, you can create a module named printReturnAddress, as shown in the sample code in Figure 1-4.

```
module printReturnAddress
        Print "From:"
        Print "ABC Company"
        Print "Stevens Point, WI"
```

Figure 1-4   The printReturnAddress module

You then can change the customer billing program so it looks like the sample code in Figure 1-5.

```
Declare variables quantityOrdered, customerName,
     customerAddress,and balanceDue
Repeat until there are no more input records on the disk
  Read in quantityOrdered, customerName,
    and customerAddress from disk
  printReturnAddress
  Print "Send To:"
  Print customerName
  Print customerAddress
  Multiply quantityOrdered by 7.99 giving balanceDue
  If quanitityOrdered is greater than 12 then
     subtract 5 from balanceDue
  Print balanceDue
```

Figure 1-5   Billing program that uses the printReturnAddress module

The program that includes the printReturnAddress module is slightly shorter than the original program because three separate statements are summarized by a single module name. The use of the module name in the program represents a **call** to the module.

Modular programs are easier to read because one descriptive name represents an entire series of detailed steps. If more modules are created, the main program changes, as shown in Figure 1-6.

```
Declare variables quantityOrdered, customerName,
 customerAddress,and balanceDue
Repeat until there are no more input records on the disk
        Read in quantityOrdered, customerName,
            and customerAddress from disk
        printReturnAddress
        printSendToAddress
        computeBalance
        Print balanceDue
```

Figure 1-6   The procedural billing program containing several module calls

The new program is more concise and more understandable; it is also more abstract. Abstraction is the process of paying attention to important properties while ignoring details. Of course, you must attend to the details at some point; the individual modules must eventually be written in a step-by-step process. However, the main program can be written by using abstract concepts to represent sets of finer details.

Programming in the oldest programming languages—machine language and assembly language—is called low-level programming because you must deal with the details of how the machine physically works. In contrast, programming languages such as COBOL and BASIC are called high-level because the programmer need not worry about hardware details. Although C++ is a high-level language, it is sometimes referred to as mid-level because it contains features that allow you to use it on either a high or low level.

When you work with real-world objects, you take abstraction for granted. For example, you talk on the telephone without considering how the signals are transmitted. If you had to worry about every low-level detail, from how the words are formed in your mouth, to how the signals are transmitted across the phone lines, to how the phone charges are billed to your account, you would never complete a call.

Programming in a high-level programming language allows you to take advantage of abstraction. When you write a command to send output to a printer, you don't instruct the printer how to actually function—how to form-feed the paper, dispense ink, and print each character. Instead, you simply write an instruction such as Print balanceDue, and the hardware operations are carried out automatically. Every programming language contains a print command that takes care of the low-level printing details. You simply carry abstraction one step further when you create a command like printReturnAddress that takes care of the lower level return address details.

Besides the advantage of abstraction, modular programs can be written more quickly because different programmers can be assigned to write different modules. If the program contains four modules, four programmers can work simultaneously, with each handling one-fourth of the job.

Finally, a well-written module may be called from another place within the same program or from another program. Many applications can use the module that prints a company's return address, for example. Whether you are preparing job estimates, year-end tax returns, or stockholder reports, you need to print the company name and address.

Encapsulation

Modules or procedures act somewhat like relatively autonomous mini-programs. Not only can modular routines contain their own sets of instructions, but most programming languages allow them to contain their own variables as well. The variables and instructions within a module are hidden and contained—that is, **encapsulated**—which helps to make the module independent of all other modules, and therefore reusable.

You can find many real-world examples of encapsulation. When you build a house, you don't invent plumbing fixtures and heating systems. Rather, you reuse previously designed and tested systems. You don't need to know the fine details of how the systems work; they are self-contained units you incorporate in your house by plugging them in through some standard **interface**, such as an electrical outlet. This type of encapsulation certainly reduces the time and effort necessary to build a house. Assuming the plumbing fixtures and heating systems you choose are already in use in other houses, using existing systems also improves your house's **reliability**. Besides not needing to know how your furnace works, if you replace one model with another, you don't care if its internal operations differ. The result—a warm house—is what's important.

Similarly, reusable software saves time and money and enhances reliability. If the printReturnAddress routine in Figure 1-6 has been tested before, you can be confident that it will produce correctly spaced and aligned output. If another programmer creates a new and improved printReturnAddress routine, you don't care how it works as long as it prints the data correctly.

When you use modules within procedural programs, you are still limited in your programming. You must know the names of the modules to call, and you can't reuse those names for other modules within the same program. If you need a similar but slightly different procedure, you must create a new module with a different name, and use the new name when you call the similar module. The technique called object-oriented programming greatly reduces these limitations.

OBJECT-ORIENTED PROGRAMMING

Object-oriented programs use all the features of procedural programs you just read about: they contain variables that are operated on by instructions written in sequence, selection, and loop statements. However, object-oriented programming requires a different way of thinking and adds several new concepts to programming:

- You analyze the objects with which you are working—both the attributes of those objects and the tasks that need to be performed with and on those objects.
- You pass messages to objects, requesting the objects to take action.
- The same message works differently (and appropriately) when applied to the various objects.
- A method can work appropriately with different types of data it receives, without the need for separate method names.
- Objects can share or **inherit** traits of previously created objects, thereby reducing the time it takes to create new objects.
- Information hiding is more complete than in procedural programs.

The basic principles behind using object-oriented programming techniques involve:

- Objects
- Classes
- Inheritance
- Polymorphism

Each of these principles is complex. As you work through the lessons and exercises in this text, you will gain mastery of these concepts as they apply to C++. For now, the following sections provide a brief overview of each.

Objects and Classes

It is hard to discuss objects without mentioning classes; it is equally difficult to discuss classes without bringing up objects. An **object** is any *thing*. A **class** consists of a *category* of things. An object is a specific item that belongs to a class; it is called an **instance** of a class. A class defines the characteristics of its objects and the methods that can be applied to its objects.

For example, Dish is a class. You know that you can hold a Dish object in your hand, that you can eat from a Dish, and that you can wash it. Dishes have attributes like size and color. They also have methods like fill and wash. myDilbertMugWithTheChip is an object and a member of—or a specific instance of—the Dish class. This situation is considered an **is-a** relationship because you can say, "myDilbertMugWithTheChip is a Dish." For example, yourBlueCerealBowl is another instance of the Dish class. Because both myDilbertMugWithTheChip and yourBlueCerealBowl are examples of a Dish, they share characteristics. Each has a size and color; each can be filled and washed.

If I tell you I am buying my grandmother a scarletWindsor, you probably have no way of organizing its characteristics in your brain. Is it something you eat? Is it a piece of clothing? If I tell you a scarletWindsor "is a" Dish, you have a beginning frame of reference because of your knowledge of the Dish class in general. If it "is a" Dish, you assume it has a size and color and that it can be filled and washed.

Similarly, each button on the toolbar of a word-processing program is an instance of a Button class, and each button shares some general characteristics that all buttons possess.

In a program used to manage a hotel, thePenthouse and theBridalSuite are specific instances of HotelRoom. Organizing program components into classes and objects reflects a natural way of thinking.

 It is conventional, but not required, to begin object names with a lowercase letter, and to begin class names with an uppercase letter.

Inheritance

The concept of using classes provides a useful way to organize objects; it is especially useful because classes are reusable or **extensible**. You can create new classes that extend or are **descendants** of existing classes. The descendent classes can **inherit** all the attributes of the original (or **parent**) class, or they can override inappropriate attributes.

In geometry, a Cube is a descendent of a Square. A Cube has all Square attributes, plus one additional characteristic: depth. A Cube, however, has a different method of calculating totalArea (or volume) than does a Square. A DisposableDish class has all the characteristics of a Dish, plus some special ones. In business, a PartTimeEmployee contains all the attributes of an Employee, plus more specialized attributes.

Because object-oriented programming languages allow inheritance, you can build classes that are extensions of existing classes; you don't have to start fresh each time you want to create a class.

Polymorphism

Programming modules might occasionally need to change the way they operate depending on the context. Object-oriented programs use **polymorphism** to carry out the same operation in a manner customized to the object. Such differentiation is never allowed in languages that aren't object-oriented.

Without polymorphism you would have to use a separate module or method name for a method that multiplies two numbers and one that multiplies three numbers. Without polymorphism you would have to create separate module names for a method that cleans a Dish object, one that cleans a Car object, and one that cleans a Baby object. Just as your blender can produce juice regardless of whether you insert two fruits or three vegetables, using a polymorphic, object-oriented multiplication function will produce a correct product whether it receives two integers or three floating-point numbers. Furthermore, using a polymorphic, object-oriented clean method will operate correctly and appropriately on a Dish, a Car, or a Baby. This is how the English language works; you understand words based on their context. When you master polymorphism in an object-oriented programming language, you take a big step toward producing objects that function like their real-world counterparts.

Getting Started in the C++ Programming Environment

Depending on your C++ installation, you can access the compiler (the program that translates your C++ statements into machine language) by clicking an icon, selecting from a menu, or typing a command.

The main work area in any C++ programming environment is the editor. An **editor** is a simplified version of a word processor in which you type your program statements, or **source code**. When you save what you have written on a disk, you typically save C++ source code files with a filename that has a .cpp extension.

After you enter the source code for a program, you must compile the program. When you **compile**, the code you have written is transformed into machine language—the language that the computer can understand. The output from the compilation is **object code**. When a C++ program is compiled, a file is created that has the same filename as the source code, but has the extension .obj.

 In some programming environments, the file extensions might vary or not appear at all.

If you open a file with the .obj extension in an editor, the file will not be readable. Machine language code appears to be random and garbled. Rest assured your C++ statements have been translated into something the computer can use.

A runnable, or **executable**, program needs the object code as well as code from any outside sources (other files) to which it refers. The process of integrating these outside references is called **linking**. An executable file contains the same filename as the source code and the object code, but carries the extension .exe to distinguish it as a program.

When you compile a C++ program, **error messages** and/or **warnings** might appear. A C++ program with errors will not execute; you must eliminate all error messages before you can run the program. Although a warning will not prevent a program from executing, it's important that you examine every warning closely, as each probably indicates a problem. For example, if you try to display a variable that does not exist, C++ will issue an error message, such as "Undefined symbol", and you cannot run the program. If you attempt to display a variable that exists but has not been assigned a valid value, C++ will not issue an error message, but will issue a warning, such as "Possible use of variable before definition." You can run the program, but the variable value that is given will be meaningless.

If you have purposely included statements within a program that produce warning messages, for example, to experiment with what will happen, then it's OK to ignore warnings and run your program. However, in professional production programs, you should eliminate all warnings.

Creating a main() Function

C++ programs consist of modules called **functions**. Every statement within every C++ program is contained in a function.

Every function consists of two parts: a function header and a function body. The initial line of code in a C++ function makes up the **function header**, which always has three parts:

- Return type of the function
- Name of the function
- Types and names of any variables enclosed in parentheses, and which the function receives

A C++ program may contain many functions, but every C++ program contains at least one function, and that function is called **main()**. If the main function does not pass values to other programs or receives values from outside the program, then main() receives and returns a void type. (**Void** simply means nothing.) Many C++ programs begin with the header `void main(void)` or, for simplicity, `void main( )`.

You do not need to understand the terms void or return type to successfully run C++ programs. The purpose of these components will become apparent when you learn to write your own functions. For now, you can begin each program with the header void main().

In various C++ books and manuals, you might see the program header written as int main(), which means that the main program will return an integer (often 0) to the operating system in which the program is running. You might also see main() by itself. When no type is given, the function becomes an integer function by default; thus, the program returns an integer.

The body of every function in a C++ program is contained in curly braces, also known as curly brackets. Therefore, the simplest program you can write has the form shown in Figure 1-7. It contains the header void main() and an empty body.

```
void main()
   {
   }
```

Figure 1-7   The simplest C++ program

Placing the main() header and the pair of braces on three separate lines is a matter of style. The program void main() { } works as well as one written on three lines. As a matter of style, however, most C++ programmers give void main() a line of its own. They then give each brace a line of its own, and indent each bracket a few spaces.

The program shown in Figure 1-7 doesn't actually do anything because it contains no C++ statements. To create a program that does something, you must place one or more C++ statements between the opening and closing braces.

Every complete C++ statement ends with a semicolon. Often several statements must be grouped together, as when several statements must occur in a loop. In such a case, the statements have their own set of opening and closing braces within the main braces, forming a **block**. One universal C++ truth: Every C++ program must contain exactly the same number of opening braces as closing braces.

Don't block statements unless you have a reason to do so. Place statements in a block within a function only if they form a unit whose execution depends on a selection or a loop.

Working with Variables

In C++, you must name and give a type to variables (sometimes called **identifiers**) before you can use them.

Names of C++ variables can include letters, numbers, and underscores, but must begin with a letter or underscore. No spaces or other special characters are allowed within a C++ variable name. Age, lastName, tax_2002, ready2go, salary, Salary, and SALARY are all valid variable names. Note that salary, Salary, and SALARY all could be used within the same C++ function without conflict because C++ is case-sensitive. C++ programmers typically use all lowercase letters for variable names, or else capitalize only the first letter of each new word (after the first word) in a variable name, as in lastYearGross.

Every programming language contains a few vocabulary words, or **keywords**, that you need in order to use the language. A C++ keyword cannot be used as a variable name. Common C++ keywords are listed in Table 1-1. Keywords vary for each C++ compiler, so some of the terms listed in Table 1-1 might not be keywords in your system. It is best to not use any of these terms as variables. That way, your code will be portable to other compilers.

Table 1-1   Common C++ Keywords

and	continue	if	public	try
and_eq	default	inline	register	typedef
asm	delete	int	reinterpret_cast	typeid
auto	do	long	return	typename
bitand	double	mutable	short	uchar_t
bitor	dynamiccast	namespace	signed	union
bool	else	new	sizeof	unsigned
break	enum	not	state_cast	using
case	explicit	not_eq	static	virtual
catch	extern	operator	struct	void
char	false	or	switch	volatile
class	float	or_eq	template	wchar_t
compl	for	overload	this	while
const	friend	private	throw	xor
constcast	goto	protected	true	xor_eq

On some computer systems, only the first 31 characters of a variable name are actually used. Thus, variable names should be limited to 31 characters, or at least be unique within the first 31 characters.

Each named variable must have a type. C++ supports three simple types: integer, floating point, and character.

An **integer** is a whole number, either positive or negative. Examples are 4, 15, +5000, and -10. Integers do not include decimal points, and they cannot be written with commas, dollar signs, or any symbols other than a leading + or -. (Of course, if a + symbol is not used, the integer is assumed to be positive.)

When an integer is stored in two bytes, the 16 bits used can form only 65,536 combinations; thus, only 65,536 different integer values can be stored. One bit indicates whether the value is positive or negative; the other 15 bits can represent values from -32,768 through +32,767. Problems arise when a programmer forgets those limits. If you store a value of 60000 in an integer named salary and then print it out, C++ will not produce any error message, but will show -5536 rather than 60,000. Because 60,000 is larger than 32,767, C++ misinterprets salary as a negative number.

An integer value may be stored in an **integer variable** declared with the keyword **int**. You can also declare an integer variable using short int and long int. The amount of memory required by short int and long int depends on the computer system, but the integer types are meant to be relative. Therefore, a short int might take less memory than an int, and a long int might take more than an int. (But maybe not! The amount of memory used depends on your system.)

You can determine the size of variables in your system with the sizeof() operator. For example, to find out how much memory an integer uses, you can place the following statement in a program:

```
cout<<"Integer size is " <<sizeof(int)<<" on this computer";
```

Output might then be: Integer size is 2 on this computer.

Real or **floating-point numbers** are numbers that include decimal positions, such as 98.6, 1000.0002, and -3.85. They may be stored in variables with types **float**, **double**, and **long double**. The amount of storage required for each of these types varies from computer to computer. Usually a double occupies more memory space than a float (allowing a double to provide greater precision), but not necessarily. A long double typically uses more memory space than a double. A double never takes less storage space than a float, and a long double invariably requires no less space than a double.

Characters may be stored in variables declared with the keyword **char**. (Some people pronounce this keyword "care" because it comes from "character"; others pronounce it "char" because of the way it is spelled.) A **character** may hold any single symbol in the ASCII character set. Often it contains a letter of the alphabet, but it could include a space, digit, punctuation mark, arithmetic symbol, or other special symbol. In C++, a character value is always expressed in single quotes, such as 'A' or '&'.

A single character, such as 'D', is contained in single quotes. A string value such as "Donna" uses double quotes.

To declare a variable, you list its type and its name. In addition, a variable declaration is a C++ statement, so it must end with a semicolon. For example, int myTestScore is a complete C++ statement that declares an integer variable named myTestScore. Remember, C++

allows any one-word identifier to be used as a variable name, but your programs will be clearer and your work will be considered more professional if you use descriptive names like myTestScore instead of cryptic variable names such as x.

If you write a function that contains variables of diverse types, each variable must be declared in a statement of its own. If you want to declare two or more variables of the same type, you may declare them in the same statement. A declaration statement may include only one type. You must declare variables of different types in separate statements.

Variables may be declared anywhere in a C++ program, but are often declared just after the opening curly braces in a function. This traditional format makes the variables easier to locate when reading the function later. The code following this paragraph shows the beginning of a typical C++ program that will use variables of several types.

```
void main()
  {
      int myAge;
      int yourAge;
      char myMiddleInitial;
      double myMoney, yourMoney;
  }
```

Notice the integer variables myAge and yourAge are each declared in a separate statement. On the other hand, the two doubles, myMoney and yourMoney, are declared in the same statement. When you declare two variables within the same statement, you separate the variable names with a comma and place the semicolon at the end of the list of all the variables of that type. Either style of variable declaration (separate statements or a shared statement) is acceptable when you declare multiple variables of the same type.

Explicitly stating the value of a variable is called **assignment**, and is achieved with the assignment operator =. You can assign a value to a variable in the same statement that declares the variable, or assign the value later in another statement. For instance, in Figure 1-8, the variable midtermScore is declared in one statement, and assigned a value in a separate statement. The variable finalScore is declared and assigned a value at the same time. Assigning a value to a variable upon creation is often referred to as **initializing** the variable.

```
int midtermScore;
int finalScore = 100;
midtermScore = 76;
int quiz1Score = 10,
    quiz2Score = 5;
```

Figure 1-8   Declaring, initializing, and assigning values to variables

Unlike most other programming languages, C++ allows you to assign values to several variables in one statement. For example, tot = sum = amount = 0; assigns a value of 0 to all three variables listed in the statement.

Assignment always takes place from right to left; that is, a value on the right side of the assignment operator is stored in the memory location (variable) on the left side of the assignment operator. Although midtermScore = 76 and 76 = midtermScore are equivalent statements in algebra, C++ does not allow the second statement. C++ refers to locations where values may be stored as **Lvalues** because these values are located on the left side of assignment statements.

Figure 1-8 also shows two integer variables, quiz1Score and quiz2Score, being declared and initialized in the same statement. After C++ programmers become used to placing a semicolon at the end of each statement, they sometimes get carried away and put a semicolon at the end of every line. However, sometimes a statement extends across several lines. A declaration is complete only when you have listed as many variables as you want for that type; use a semicolon only when the entire statement is complete.

You also might have noticed that semicolons never follow function headers such as void main(). Function headers are not C++ statements. You can think of C++ statements as full actions, so you do not place a semicolon at the end of a function header, nor at the end of any line with a statement that continues on the next line.

The const Qualifier

A variable that does not change in a program should not be declared as a variable. (After all, it won't vary.) Instead, it should be a constant. The statement `const double MINIMUM_WAGE = 5.75;` declares a constant named MINIMUM_WAGE that can be used like a variable, but cannot be changed during a program. For example, if you declare `const double MINIMUM_WAGE = 5.75;` within a program, then it is illegal to write the statement `MINIMUM_WAGE = 6.00;` later in the same program. The keyword const is called a qualifier because it qualifies, or restricts, the ordinary capabilities of the named type (such as double). C++ programmers usually use all uppercase letters for a constant name; then constants are easily identified in a program and not mistaken for variables. However, such capitalization is not required.

Creating Comments

Comments are statements that do not affect the compiling or running of a program. That is, they do not show up when the program runs. Comments are simply explanatory remarks that the programmer includes in a program to clarify what is taking place. These remarks are useful to later program users because they might help explain the intent of a particular statement or the purpose of the entire program. In addition, comments could indicate who wrote the program and when. They might even help the programmer remember why something was done a certain way when the program was written weeks or months earlier.

C++ supports both line comments and block comments. A **line comment** begins with two slashes (//) and continues to the end of the line on which it is placed. It might take up an entire line, or it might begin after some executable C++ code and take up the rest of the line. A **block comment** begins with a single slash and an asterisk (/*) and ends with an asterisk and a slash (*/); it might be contained on a single line or continued across many lines. Like a line comment, a block comment might take up an entire line, or it might occur on a line along with executable code, either before or after the code. Figure 1-9 shows a program that contains only one executable statement: the highlighted statement that declares the variable myAge.

```
// this is a comment on one line
/* this comment is on a different line */
/* this is in front */   int myAge;     //this is in back
/* this comment runs across
     three lines of code just to show
     that it can be done !      */
```

Figure 1-9   Demonstrating comments

When using block comments, don't start a comment that never ends. Using /* without a corresponding end */ makes everything from /* on in the program a nonexecuting comment.

Throughout this text, comments are used to point out features in code examples. Sometimes a comment even indicates that a statement is invalid. This type of comment is for instruction only; you wouldn't use such comments in professional programs.

Using Libraries and Preprocessor Directives

C++ programs often refer to variables and code that lie outside the source code the programmer actually writes. C++ is powerful in part because many of its functions have already been written for you. For example, finding the square root of a number can be a fairly complicated mathematical task, but the creators of C++ have written a function that calculates square roots. You can include this function, sqrt(), in your own C++ programs—but only if the programs can find it when you link to outside files to create executable files.

Header files are files that contain predefined values and routines, such as sqrt(). Their filenames usually end in .h. In order for your C++ program to use these predefined routines, you must include a **preprocessor directive**, a statement that tells the compiler what to do before compiling the program. In C++, all preprocessor directives begin with a pound sign (#), which is also called an **octothorp**.

The **#include** preprocessor directive tells the compiler to include a file as part of the finished product. In any program, you might include a special-purpose file you wrote, or you might include a file that is packaged with your C++ compiler. For example, to use the sqrt() function, you need to use **#include<math.h>**. You will need another include directive to use C++ input and output statements.

The angle brackets in #include<math.h> indicate that the math.h file is found in the standard folder that holds include files.

C++ Output

C++ provides several objects for producing output. The simplest object is called **cout**, pronounced "see out." The name comes from Console OUTput, and cout shows whatever is passed to it. When contained in a complete C++ program, the statement cout<<"Hi there"; places the phrase "Hi there" on the monitor. The insertion symbol (<<) says "insert whatever is to my right into the object cout."

If you think like a computer (rather than a person), the direction of the brackets used with cout makes sense. In the statement cout<<"Hi there"; the phrase is being sent to the output device, so the insertion symbol points to the cout object.

The object cout is contained in the header file iostream.h. The term iostream is short for Input Output STREAM. The preprocessor directive #include<iostream.h> must appear at the top of any program that uses cout. A complete program that prints "Hi there" is shown in Figure 1-10. If you type this program into a C++ editor, compile it, and run it, the words "Hi there" will appear on the monitor.

```
#include<iostream.h>
void main()
   {
     cout<<"Hi there";
   }
```

Figure 1-10   A program that uses cout

With some compilers, the screen output appears, but is gone so quickly that you don't get a chance to read the output message. If this happens to you, include the line #include<conio.h> as the first line in your file, and include the line getch(); immediately after the statement cout<<"Hi there". This pauses the execution of your program and waits for one character to be input from the keyboard before the output screen closes down.

You could replace the cout statement in Figure 1-10 with two cout statements:

```
cout<<"Hi ";
cout<<"there";
```

Even though this version of the program uses two cout statements, nothing indicates that any output should be placed on a new line. The character string "Hi " (notice the space included before the last quotation mark) would print on the monitor, followed immediately by the character string "there". To indicate a **newline** character, you can use the **escape sequence \n**. The backslash removes the usual meaning of the letter *n*, (which is simply to produce the letter *n*, as in the statement cout<<'n';) and causes the output to move to a new line. The statement `cout<<"Hi\nthere";` shows "Hi" and "there" on two separate lines.

 Other commonly used escape sequences are \t for Tab, \" for a double quote, and \' for a single quote. To actually show a backslash, use \\.

Another way to advance output to a new line is to use the end line manipulator **endl**. Inserting endl into the output stream causes a new line plus all waiting output to become visible, a process called **flushing the buffer**. The following code produces "Hi" and "there" on two separate lines:

```
cout<<"Hi";
cout<<endl;
cout<<"there";
```

A single cout object might show more than one item, as long as each item is preceded by its own insertion symbol. For example, `cout<<"Hi"<<endl<<"there";` displays "Hi", goes to a new line, and displays "there" on the next line.

In the steps that follow, you will create your first executable C++ program.

To create a program that declares two variables, assigns values to them, and creates output:

1. Open your C++ editor. Type the comment shown below to explain the purpose of the program.

   // A first C++ program demonstrating variable use

2. On the next line, type the preprocessor directive that you need to use cout.

   #include<iostream.h>

3. As shown below, type the main() function header. Press **Enter** to move to a new line. Indent two or three spaces, and type the opening curly brace of the main() function. Then press the **Enter** key again.

   void main()
   {

4. Indent two or three spaces to the right of the opening curly brace on the previous line. Declare two variables. One variable is an integer named creditHours, and the other is a double variable named gradePointAverage.

   int creditHours;
   double gradePointAverage;

5. Press **Enter** to start a new line. Then assign values to the two declared variables.

   creditHours = 15;
   gradePointAverage = 3.25;

6. Add statements that show the assigned values with an explanation on two separate lines.

   cout<<"The number of credit hours is "<<creditHours<<endl;
   cout<<"The grade point average is "<<gradePointAverage<<endl;

7. Add a closing curly brace as the last line in the program. Align it vertically with the opening curly brace seven lines above it. The complete program is shown in Figure 1-11.

```
// A first C++ program demonstrating variable use
#include<iostream.h>

void main()
 {

   int creditHours;

   double gradePointAverage;
   creditHours = 15;
   gradePointAverage = 3.25;
   cout<<"The number of credit hours is "<<creditHours<<endl;
   cout<<"The grade point average is "<<gradePointAverage<<endl;
 }
```

Figure 1-11   Program listing for Output1.cpp

8. Save the file as **Output1.cpp**.

9. Compile the program. If you receive any error messages, correct the errors.

10. Run the program and observe the output.

    If the program runs, but the output screen vanishes before you can read the results, insert **#include<conio.h>** before or after the other #include statement at the top of the file, and then insert the statement **getch();** just after the last executable statement in the file **(cout<<"The grade point average is "<<gradePointAverage<<endl;)**. Compile the program, run it again, and press any key when you finish viewing the results.

    The output should look like Figure 1-12.

11. Change the values assigned to the variables creditHours and gradePointAverage. Run the program again. Confirm that the new output shows the new values you assigned to the variables.

```
OUTPUT1
The number of credit hours is 15
The grade point average is 3.25
```

Figure 1-12   Output of Output1.cpp

C++ INPUT

A program in which the programmer predetermines all variable values is not very useful. Many programs rely on input from a user. These are called **interactive programs** because the user interacts with the program statements. The program must provide a way the user can enter responses to program prompts. You create prompts by using the cout object; you retrieve user responses by using the cin object. The **cin** (pronounced see in) object fetches values from the keyboard. It is used with the **extraction operator** >>. Like cout, cin is contained in the iostream.h header file.

 According to computer logic, the direction of the brackets in cin makes sense. For example, the statement `cin>>quantity;` places a value into the variable quantity.

Prior to a cin statement, it is almost always necessary to provide the user with a **prompt**, or a short explanation of what is expected. You might confirm that the data was actually entered and stored by echoing it, or showing it in an unaltered form, soon after input. Figure 1-13 shows a program that declares a variable that stores a price, prompts the user for the price, and then echoes, or represents, the user input.

```cpp
#include<iostream.h>
void main ()
{
   double price;
   cout<<"Please enter the price ";
   cin>>price;
   cout<<"The price you entered is "<<price<<endl;
}
```

Figure 1-13   A program with a prompt and input

A space often appears within the quotes at the end of a prompt. The purpose of the space is cosmetic. As the program user enters a data value, that value appears on the monitor immediately to the right of the prompt. A space after the prompt, yet before the data, makes the screen easier to read.

In the program shown in Figure 1-13, after the prompt is given, the program pauses until a user types a price and presses Enter. Then the price is echoed. Similarly to cout, one cin object may be used to enter more than one value, as in the following example:

```
int score1, score2, score3;
cout<<"Please enter three scores. Use a space between them. ";
cin>>score1>>score2>>score3;
```

At the prompt "Please enter three scores. Use a space between them.", the user may enter three integers with any white space between them. **Whitespace** consists of any number of spaces, tabs, and Enter characters.

Although the previous code segment allows the user to enter three scores, it is almost always a better practice to ask a user for one value at a time. That is, first provide a prompt, then add a cin statement to read the first value. Provide the second prompt and its cin; and finally provide a third prompt and its cin.

In the next steps, you will add prompts and interactive input to the Output1.cpp program.

1. Open the **Output1.cpp** file if it is not already open on your system.

2. Delete the two lines:

   creditHours = 15;
   gradePointAverage = 3.25;

3. In place of the two deleted statements, insert a prompt for the creditHours variable.

   cout<<"Please enter your credit hours ";

4. On the next line, type the following statement that reads the creditHours in from the keyboard.

   cin>>creditHours;

5. On the next line, add the statements below that prompt for and read the gradePointAverage.

   cout<<"Please enter your grade point average ";
   cin>>gradePointAverage;

6. Save the file as **Output2.cpp**.

7. Compile the program and correct any errors. Remember that C++ is case-sensitive; some of your errors might be due to incorrect capitalization. When you have corrected any errors, save the file and compile it again.

8. Run the program. Enter data at the prompts, for example, **26** for the creditHours variable, and **3.78** for the gradePointAverage variable. The output should look like Figure 1-14.

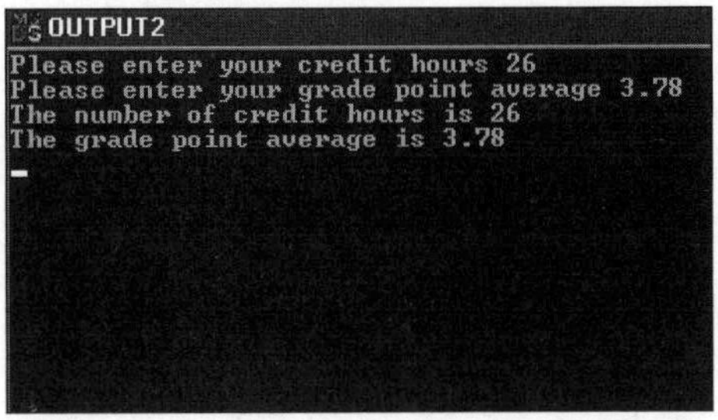

Figure 1-14   Output of Output2.cpp

C++ CLASSES AND OBJECTS

When you use data types like int, char, and double within a program, you are using the C++ built-in, **primitive** or **scalar** data types. A major feature of object-oriented languages is the ability to create your own new, complex data types. These new types are called **classes**.

Classes can become quite complex. A class can contain many simpler data types within it, as well as any number of functions. For example, you might create an Employee class with components such as firstName, lastName, hourlySalary, numberOfDependents, and hireDate. The relationship between these components, or **fields**, of the Employee class is often called a **has-a relationship** because every Employee "has a" firstName, lastName, and so on.

Consider a very simple Employee class that contains only two components: idNumber and hourlySalary. You could define such a class as shown in Figure 1-15. You use the C++ keyword **class** and follow it with a class name you choose. Between curly braces, you name the individual fields that will be part of the class. Each field type and identifier ends with a semicolon, and the class definition itself ends with a semicolon after the closing curly brace.

```
class Employee
   {
      int idNumber;
      double hourlySalary;
   };
```

Figure 1-15   A simple Employee class

The Employee class definition shown in Figure 1-15 indicates that an Employee has two components: an integer idNumber and a double hourlySalary. If you declare an integer within a C++ program, it can hold only a whole number value, such as 2345. If you declare a double within a C++ program, it can contain only a floating point number value, such as 12.95. However, if you create an Employee object, it can hold two values: an integer and a double. Figure 1-16 shows a program that declares two objects: an integer and an Employee. Note that whether you declare a primitive type variable or a class object, the syntax is the same: type, identifier, semicolon.

```
void main()
  {
   int companyStaffSize;
   Employee oneStaffMember;
  }
```

Figure 1-16 A program that declares an integer and an Employee

After you declare an Employee named oneStaffMember, you refer to the individual fields of oneStaffMember by using the object name, a dot operator (or period), and the field name. For example, the idNumber of the oneStaffMember is referenced with the identifier oneStaffMember.idNumber. However, if you include a new statement such as oneStaffMember.idNumber = 2345; within the program shown in Figure 1-16, then you will receive an error message that indicates the idNumber is not accessible from within your program. The reason is that by default, all class fields are private. That means they are not available for use outside the class. When you create a class, you can declare some fields to be private and some to be public, or available outside the class. For example, in the real world, you might want your name to be public knowledge, but your Social Security number, salary, or age to be private.

As you continue your study of C++, you will learn that most class fields are made private the majority of the time. You also will learn how to access these private fields. For now, you can include a statement that indicates that you want your fields to be public, or readily accessible outside their class. Figure 1-17 shows a complete program that declares a class with public fields, and uses that class within a main() function. Within the Employee class, the access modifier, public, and a colon have been inserted before the data fields.

```
// The Employee class and
// a main() function that declares and uses an Employee object
// Note that in most programs the data fields are not public
// Usually they are private
// The data fields are public here until you learn
// more about accessing private data
#include<iostream.h>
class Employee
   {
        public:
           int idNumber;
           double hourlySalary;
   };
void main()
  {
    Employee oneStaffMember;
    oneStaffMember.idNumber = 2345;
    oneStaffMember.hourlySalary = 12.95;
    cout<<"ID number is "<<oneStaffMember.idNumber<<endl;
    cout<<"Hourly rate is "<<oneStaffMember.hourlySalary<<endl;
  }
```

Figure 1-17 A complete class definition and a main() method that uses a class object

In the next steps you will create a Student class, and then create a program that uses a Student class object.

1. Open a new file in your C++ compiler. Type the comment below:

   // Demonstrating a Student class

2. Type the preprocessor directives to include iostream.h so that cout and cin will work correctly. Also type the directive to include conio.h if you will use the getch() function call at the end of the program to hold the output screen.

   #include<iostream.h>
   #include<conio.h>

3. Type a Student class that will contain two public fields: one that holds credit hours, and another that holds the grade point average.

   class Student
   {
   ** public:**
   **   int creditHours;**
   **   double gradePointAverage;**
   };

4. Next begin the main() function, and declare a Student object identified as oneSophomore.

   void main()
   {
     Student oneSophomore;

5. Write the statements that prompt for and allow entry of the Student's data.

   cout<<"Please enter a student's credit hours ";
   cin>>oneSophomore.creditHours;
   cout<<"Please enter the student's grade point average ";
   cin>>oneSophomore.gradePointAverage;

6. Add the statements that echo the data just entered.

   cout<<"The number of credit hours is " <<
     oneSophomore.creditHours<<endl;
   cout<<"The grade point average is "<<
     oneSophomore.gradePointAverage<<endl;

7. Add the getch(); statement if you need to hold the output screen.

8. Add the closing curly bracket for the program, and then save the file as **Student.cpp**.

9. Compile the program. When it is error-free, run the program. Depending on the data you use for input, the output should look similar to Figure 1-18.

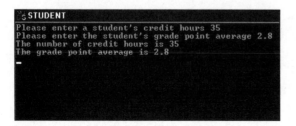

```
STUDENT
Please enter a student's credit hours 35
Please enter the student's grade point average 2.8
The number of credit hours is 35
The grade point average is 2.8
```

Figure 1-18   Output from Student.cpp

Creating a class provides a means to group data fields together in a logical way. When you think of an Employee, you think of an actual employee as encapsulating, or encompassing, an ID number and a salary (and usually even more fields). Similarly, a Student encapsulates a credit hour field as well as a grade point average field. Creating entities that mimic their real-world counterparts is a hallmark of object-oriented programming. As you continue your studies of C++ (or other object-oriented languages) you will learn how to encapsulate more fields and even actions, or functions, into a class.

CHAPTER SUMMARY

❐ Programming a computer involves learning the syntax of a computer programming language and resolving logical errors. To achieve a working program, you first write the program, and then compile it and test it.

❐ All programming languages provide methods for input and output of variable values. You declare a variable by providing it with a name and a type.

❐ Procedural programs consist of a series of steps or procedures that take place one after the other. Procedural programs use control structures named sequence, selection, and loop. Within programs, you can call modules or subroutines.

❐ Object-oriented programming adds several new programming concepts including objects, classes, inheritance, and polymorphism. An object is an instance of a class. Inheritance provides a means of extending a class to make more specific classes. Polymorphism is the feature that allows program modules to operate appropriately based on the context.

❐ You write a C++ program by typing source code into an editor and compiling the program. When you compile a program, the compiler might issue warnings or errors, which you must rectify before you can run the program.

❐ C++ modules are called functions, and each function contains a header and a body. Every C++ program contains a main() function.

❐ C++ variables must be given a type and a name. Simple types include integer for whole numbers, double and float for floating-point values, and character for any character. Variables must be given a one-word name that is not a C++ keyword. You can assign a value to a variable using the assignment operator, the equal sign. Values that do not vary are called constants.

❐ Comments are nonexecuting program statements. C++ supports line comments and block comments.

❐ A preprocessor directive tells the compiler to do something, such as to include a header file, before compiling the program.

❐ The cout statement (along with an insertion operator) is used to display values. The cin statement (along with an extraction operator) is used to read values into variables.

❐ When you create a class, you create your own C++ data type, which is a complex type composed of simpler types. When you create a class object, you access its fields with a dot operator.

REVIEW QUESTIONS

1. Writing instructions that enable a computer to carry out a task or group of tasks is known as _____.

   a. processing

   b. programming

   c. editing

   d. compiling

2. The physical components of a computer system are called _____.

   a. hardware

   b. software

   c. firmware

   d. programs

3. Another term for programs is _____.

   a. input

   b. floppy disks

   c. hardware

   d. software

4. C++, BASIC, Pascal, COBOL, and RPG are all _____.

   a. operating systems

   b. codes

   c. programming languages

   d. hardware

5. The rules of any programming language are its _____.

   a. syntax

   b. interpretation

   c. logic

   d. customs

6. A translator that notes whether you have used a language correctly might be called a _____.

   a. thesaurus

   b. compiler

   c. coder

   d. decoder

7. Using a correctly written statement at the wrong time creates a(n) _____ error.

   a. logical

   b. syntax

   c. object-oriented

   d. language

8. When a programmer determines the exact sequence in which events will take place, the program is said to be _____.

   a. compiled

   b. interpreted

   c. procedural

   d. object-oriented

9. Which type of statement does not occur in computer programs?

   a. sequence

   b. loop

   c. denial

   d. selection

10. Paying attention to the important properties while ignoring unessential details is known as _____.

   a. selectiveness

   b. polymorphism

   c. abstraction

   d. summarizing

11. Object-oriented programmers primarily focus on _____.

   a. procedures to be performed

   b. the step-by-step statements needed to solve a problem

   c. objects and the tasks that must be performed with those objects

   d. the physical orientation of objects within a program

12. An object is _____.

   a. a category of classes

   b. a name given to a class

   c. an instance of a class

   d. the same as a class

13. Object is to class as _____.

    a. library is to book

    b. mother is to daughter

    c. Plato is to philosopher

    d. president is to Lincoln

14. The feature that allows the same operations to be carried out differently depending on the context is _____.

    a. polymorphism

    b. polygamy

    c. inheritance

    d. multitasking

15. Which English language example best represents polymorphism?

    a. taking a nap as opposed to taking a bribe

    b. killing time as opposed to killing a bug

    c. ordering a pizza as opposed to ordering a soldier

    d. all of the above

16. All of the following are C++ data types except _____.

    a. letter

    b. double

    c. char

    d. int

17. All the following are program control structures except _____.

    a. sequence

    b. loop

    c. perpetuation

    d. selection

18. The symbol used with the cout object << is called the _____ operator.

    a. insertion

    b. extraction

    c. modification

    d. dot

19. When you create a class object, you access the object's fields using the
_____ operator.

   a. insertion

   b. extraction

   c. modification

   d. dot

20. If you create a class named Luggage and an object named myBlueOvernightBag, which of the following could output your overnight bag's price?

   a. `cout>>Luggage.price;`

   b. `cout>>price.myBlueOvernightBag;`

   c. `cout<<Luggage.myBlueOvernightBag;`

   d. `cout<<myBlueOvernightBag.price;`

EXERCISES

1. List the steps to perform each of the following tasks. Include at least one example of a loop and one example of a selection in this process.

   a. shopping for new shoes

   b. filling a customer's catalog order

   c. computing the amount of federal income tax you owe

2. Many systems are modular. Name some modules within each of the following systems:

   a. a stereo

   b. a college

   c. a payroll system

3. Name a class that contains each of these objects:

   a. William Shakespeare

   b. a customer letter indicating that an item has been back ordered

   c. a refund check to a customer who has overpaid

4. Name three objects in each of these classes:

   a. musical group

   b. business transaction

   c. year-end report

5. Write a C++ program that displays your name on the output screen.

6. Write a C++ program that displays your name, street address, and city and state on three separate lines on the screen.

7. Write a C++ program that declares a variable that can hold the amount of money in your pocket right now. Assign a value to the variable. Display the value, with explanation, on the screen. For example, the output might be "In my pocket, I have $4.36."

8. Write a C++ program that declares a value that can hold the price of a lunch. Prompt a user to enter the amount he or she spent on lunch. Read in the value, and display it with explanation.

9. Write a program that declares a variable that can hold the letter grade a student will receive in this class. Prompt the user to enter the letter. Then read it in, and echo it with explanation.

10. Write a program that declares two integer variables that can hold the ages of two people. Prompt a user to enter the ages of his or her two best friends and echo the numbers with explanation.

11. Create a class named Car that contains two public fields: an integer field for model year and a double field for miles per gallon. Write a program that declares a Car object. Assign values to the car's two data fields, and display the values with explanation.

12. Create a class named College that contains three public fields: the year the college was founded, the current student population, and the annual tuition. Write a program that declares a College object. Prompt the user for values for the fields, and echo them.

13. Create a class named Computer. Decide on at least three fields that you want to include within your Computer class. Each of the fields must be an int or a double. Write a program that declares two Computer objects. Prompt the user for values for the fields for each Computer, and echo them.

14. Each of the following files in the Chapter01 folder of your Data Disk contains syntax and/or logical errors. Determine the problem in each case, and fix the program.

    a. DEBUG1-1

    b. DEBUG1-2

    c. DEBUG1-3

    d. DEBUG1-4

CASE PROJECT

Teacher's Pet is a software firm that specializes in children's educational programs. The firm has decided to develop a series of products that will help children discover the properties of fractions. As you plan the program series, you realize that a fraction contains at least two data properties: a numerator and a denominator. Therefore, you begin to think of specific fractions as objects that belong to the class called Fraction. Develop the class Fraction so that it contains public data fields that hold the integer numerator and denominator. Write a main() function that declares a Fraction object and allows you to enter data values for the two Fraction fields. Echo the input.

2

USING C++ ARITHMETIC OPERATORS AND CONTROL STRUCTURES

In this chapter, you will learn:

♦ About C++ arithmetic operators

♦ About shortcut arithmetic operators

♦ How to evaluate boolean expressions

♦ How to use the if and if-else statements

♦ How to use the switch statement

♦ How to use the conditional operator

♦ How to use the logical AND and the logical OR

♦ How to use the while loop to repeat statements

♦ How to use the for statement

♦ How to use control structures with class object fields

When you write a program, you use variable names to create locations where you can store data. You can use assignment and input statements to provide values for the variables, and you can use output statements to display those values on the screen. In most programs that you write, you want to do more than input and output variable values. You also might want to perform arithmetic with values, or base decisions on values that users input.

In this chapter, you learn to use the C++ operators to create arithmetic expressions and study the results they produce. You also learn about the valuable shortcut arithmetic operators in C++. Then you concentrate on boolean expressions you can use to control C++ decisions and loops.

C++ Binary Arithmetic Operators

Often after data values are input, you perform calculations with them. C++ provides five simple arithmetic operators for creating arithmetic expressions: addition (+), subtraction (−), multiplication (*), division (/), and modulus (%). Each of these arithmetic operators is a **binary operator**; each takes two operands, one on each side of the operator, as in 12 + 9 or 16.2 * 1.5.

 Do not confuse binary operators with the binary numbering system. Binary operators take two operands; the binary numbering system is a system that uses only two values, −0 and 1.

The results of an arithmetic operation can be stored in memory. For example, each cout statement in the program shown in Figure 2-1 produces the value 21 as output. In the first statement within the main() function, the result, 21, is calculated within the cout statement. In the second cout statement, the value of a variable is shown. The advantage to this approach is that the result of the addition calculation is stored in the variable named sum, and can be accessed again later within the same program, if necessary. For example, you might need sum again if its value is required as part of a subsequent calculation.

```
#include<iostream.h>
void main()
    {
        cout<<12+9<<endl;    // displays the value 21
        int sum=12+9;        // calculates sum whose value becomes 21
        cout<<sum<<endl;     // displays the value of sum
    }
```

Figure 2-1   Program that uses two ways to produce 21

Addition, subtraction, multiplication, or division of any two integers results in an integer. For example, the expression 7 + 3 results in 10, and the expression 7 / 3 results in 2. When two integers are divided, the result is an integer, so any fractional part of the result is lost.

If either or both of the operands in addition, subtraction, multiplication, or division is a floating-point number, that is, a float or a double, then the result is also a floating-point number. For example, the value of the expression 3.2 * 2 is the floating-point value 6.4 because at least one of the operands is a floating-point number.

When you mix data types in a binary arithmetic expression, the result is always the same type as the one that takes the most memory to store. Therefore, any binary arithmetic expression that contains a double results in a double, and any binary arithmetic expression that does not contain a double but does contain a float results in a float. Figure 2-2 shows some arithmetic examples and explains the computed results.

```
// Using arithmetic expressions
//   Note that a, b, c, and so on are not very good
//   descriptive variable names
//   They are used here simply to hold values
void main()
{
   int a = 2, b = 4, c = 10, intResult;
   double d = 2.0, e = 4.4, f = 12.8, doubleResult;
   float g = 2.0, h = 4.4, i = 12.8, floatResult;
   intResult = a + b;  // result is 6, an int
                       // because both operands are int
   intResult = a * b;  // result is 8, an int
                       // because both operands are int
   intResult = c / a;  // result is 5, an int
                       // because both operands are int
   intResult = c / b;  // result is 2
                       // (losing the decimal fraction),
                       // an int because both operands are int
   floatResult = g / a; // result is 1.0, a float,
                       // because the operands are int and float
   floatResult = h / g; // result is 2.2, a float,
                       // because both operands are floats
   doubleResult = a * d;  // result is 4.0, a double
                       // because the operands are int and
double
   doubleResult = f / a; // result is 6.4, a double
                       // because the operands are int and
double
   doubleResult = e + h; // result is 8.8, a double,
                       // because operands are float and double

}
```

Figure 2-2   The resulting values of some arithmetic expressions

 As you continue to study C++, you will learn about additional C++ data types. In binary arithmetic expressions, the order of precedence from lowest to highest is as follows: char, short, int, unsigned int, long, unsigned long, float, double, long double.

In Figure 2-2, each operation is assigned to a result variable of the correct type. Note that the expression **a + b** has an integer result because both a and b are integers, *not* because their sum is stored in the intResult variable. If the program contained the statement **doubleResult = a + b;** the expression a + b would still have an integer value, but the value would be **cast**, or transformed, into a double when the sum is assigned to doubleResult. Whenever you assign a value to a variable type that is higher in the order of precedence, that value is automatically cast to the type that requires more memory. For example, the declaration **double moneyAmount = 8;** uses the constant integer 8, but actually assigns the value 8.0 to moneyAmount.

The automatic cast that occurs when you assign a value of one type to another is called an implicit cast. You also can perform an explicit cast by using a type name within parentheses in front of an expression. For example, the statement doubleResult = (double) a; explicitly converts an integer to a double before assigning its value to doubleResult.

The modulus operator (%), which gives the remainder of integer division, can be used only with integers. The expression 7 / 3 results in 2 because 3 "goes into" 7 two whole times. The expression 7 % 3 results in 1, because when 3 "goes into" 7 two times, there is 1 remaining. Similarly, the value of 12 % 5 is 2, and the value of 25 % 11 is 3.

When more than one arithmetic operator is included in an expression, then multiplication, division, and modulus operations always occur before addition or subtraction. Multiplication, division, and modulus are said to have **higher precedence**. When two operations with the same precedence appear in an expression, the operations are carried out from left to right. For example, the expression 2 + 3 * 4 results in 14 (not 20) because the multiplication of 3 and 4 takes place before 2 is added. All precedence rules can be overridden with parentheses. Thus, the expression (2 + 3) * 4 results in 20 (not 14) because the expression within the parentheses is evaluated first.

The same order of precedence (multiplication and division before addition and subtraction) is used not only in mathematics and C++, but in all programming languages.

In the following steps, you create a program that demonstrates some arithmetic operators used in C++.

1. Open your C++ editor. Type a line comment that explains that this program demonstrates arithmetic.

2. Type the include statement that allows you to use cout. Also type the include statement that supports getch() if it is necessary for you to use getch() to hold the C++ output on the screen.

   #include<iostream.h>
   #include<conio.h>

3. Begin the main function by typing its header and the opening curly brace.

   void main()
   {

4. Declare some integer and double variables, and then assign values to them.

```
int a,b,c;
double x,y,z;
a = 13;
b = 4;
x = 3.3;
y = 15.78;
```

5. Type the statement that calculates c as the sum of a and b. Then type the statement that shows the value of c on the screen, with an explanation.

```
c = a + b;
cout<<"a + b is "<<c<<endl;
```

6. Perform several more arithmetic calculations and display the results.

```
z = x + y;
cout <<"x + y is "<<z<<endl;
c = a / b;
cout<<"a / b is "<<c<<endl;
c = a % b;
cout<<"a % b is "<<c<<endl;
```

7. Include the **getch( )**; statement if you need it to hold the output screen. Then add the closing curly brace for the program.

8. Save the file as **Numberdemo.cpp** in the Chapter02 folder on your Student Data Disk or the Student Data folder on your hard drive. Compile, correct any errors, and execute the program. The results should look like Figure 2-3.

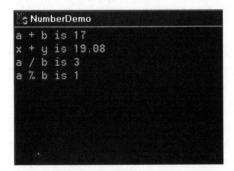

Figure 2-3   Output of Numberdemo.cpp

9. Change the values for the variables within the program. Try to predict the results and then run the program again. Change some of the operations to multiply and subtract. Continue to modify and run the program until you are confident you can predict the outcome of every arithmetic operation.

SHORTCUT ARITHMETIC OPERATORS

In addition to the standard binary arithmetic operators for addition, subtraction, multiplication, division, and modulus, C++ employs several shortcut operators.

When you add two variable values and store the result in a third variable, the expression takes the form `result = firstValue + secondValue`. When you use an expression like this, both firstValue and secondValue retain their original values; only the result is altered. When you want to increase a value, the expression takes the form `firstValue = firstValue + secondValue`. This expression results in firstValue being increased by the value stored in secondValue; secondValue remains unchanged, but firstValue takes on a new value. For example, if firstValue initially holds 5 and secondValue initially holds 2, then after the statement `firstValue = firstValue + secondValue` executes, the value of firstValue increases to 7. Because increasing a value by another value is such a common procedure, C++ provides a shortcut. The statement `firstValue += secondValue` produces results identical to `firstValue = firstValue + secondValue`.

Each expression means "Take the value in secondValue, add it to firstValue, and store the result in firstValue," or "Replace the value of firstValue with the new value you get when you add secondValue to firstValue." When you use the `+=` operator, you must *not* insert a space between the + and the =.

Similarly, C++ provides the `-=` operator for subtracting one value from another, the `*=` operator for multiplying one value by another, and the `/=` operator for dividing one value by another. As with the `+=` operator, you must not insert a space within the subtraction, multiplication, or division shortcut operators.

 The operators +=, -=, *=, and /= are all valid; the operators =+, =-, =*, and =/ are not. The assignment operator equal sign (=) always appears second.

Another common programming task is to add 1 to a variable—for example, when keeping count of how many times an event has occurred. C++ provides four ways to add 1 to a variable, shown in the short program in Figure 2-4.

Each of the options shown in Figure 2-4 means replace the current value of count with the value that is 1 more than count, or simply **increment** count. As you might expect, you can use two minus signs (`--`) before or after a variable to **decrement** it.

```
void main()
  {
    int count = 0;
     count = count + 1; // count becomes 1
     count += 1; // count becomes 2
     ++count;   // count becomes 3
       // This ++ is called a prefix increment operator
     count++;   // count becomes 4
       // This ++ is called a postfix increment operator
  }
```

Figure 2-4   Some sample selection statements within a C++ Program

The prefix and postfix increment and decrement operators are examples of unary operators. **Unary operators** (as opposed to binary operators) are those that require only one operand, such as num in the expression ++num.

When an expression includes a prefix operator (as in ++num), the mathematical operation takes place before the expression is evaluated. For example, the following code segment gives the result 7.

```
int num = 6;
result = ++num;
cout<<result;   // result is 7
cout<<num;      // num is 7
```

When an expression includes a postfix operator (as in num++), the mathematical operation takes place after the expression is evaluated. For example, the following code segment gives the result 6. The variable num is not increased until after it is evaluated, so it is evaluated as 6, 6 is assigned to result, and then num increases to 7.

```
num = 6;
result = num++;
cout<<result;   // result is 6
cout<<num;      // num is 7
```

The difference between the results produced by the prefix and postfix operators can be subtle, but the outcome of a program can vary greatly depending on which increment operator you use in an expression. If you use either the prefix or postfix increment in a standalone statement that simply adds 1 to, or subtracts 1 from a value, then it does not matter which one you use.

In the next steps you will add increment operator statements to the Numberdemo.cpp program so that you can become comfortable with the differences between prefix and postfix operators.

1. If necessary, open the **Numberdemo.cpp** program that you created earlier in this chapter.

2. Move your insertion point to the beginning of the last executable line of the program (getch();), and press the **Enter** key to start a new line. Type the following statements on their own line to give a value to a and to assign ++a to c.

a = 2;
c = ++a;

3. Add a statement to display the results.

cout<<"a is "<<a<<" and c is "<<c<<endl;

4. Now add statements that are similar, but that use the postfix increment operator with a.

a = 2;
c = a++;
cout<<"a is "<<a<<" and c is "<<c<<endl;

5. Save the modified program as **Numberdemo2.cpp** in the Chapter02 folder on your Student Data Disk or the Student folder on your hard drive. Compile and run the program. The output should look like Figure 2-5.

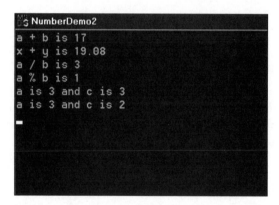

Figure 2-5   Output of Numberdemo2.cpp

6. Modify the values for the variables in the program, and continue to run it until you are confident you can predict the values that will be output.

Evaluating Boolean Expressions

Determining the value of an arithmetic expression like 2 + 3 * 4 is straightforward. However, C++ also evaluates many other expressions that have nothing to do with arithmetic.

C++ employs the six relational binary operators listed in Table 2-1. You use these relational operators to evaluate boolean expressions. A **boolean expression** is one that evaluates as true or false.

2

George Boole was a nineteenth-century mathematician who approached logic more simply than his predecessors did, so logical true/false expressions are named for him.

Table 2-1 Relational operators

Relational operator	Description
==	equivalent to
>	greater than
>=	greater than or equal to
<	less than
<=	less than or equal to
!=	not equal to

The operators >=, <=, and != are all valid; the operators =>, =<, and =! are not recognized by C++. The assignment operator (equal sign) always appears second.

All false relational expressions are evaluated as 0. Thus, an expression such as $2 > 9$ has the value 0. You can prove that $2 > 9$ is evaluated as 0 by entering the statement `cout<<(2>9);` into a C++ program. A 0 appears on output.

All true relational expressions are evaluated as 1. Thus, the expression $9 > 2$ has the value 1. You can prove this by entering the statement `cout<<(9>2);` into a C++ program. A 1 appears on output.

The unary operator **!** means **not**, and essentially reverses the true/false value of an expression. For example, `cout<<(9>2);` displays a 1 because "9 is greater than 2" is true. In contrast, `cout<<!(9>2);` displays a 0 because "not 9 greater than 2," is grammatically awkward, as well as a false statement. Table 2-2 shows how the ! (not) operator is evaluated.

Table 2-2 Values of expressions and !expressions

Value of expression	Value of !expression
True	False
False	True

A table like Table 2-2 is often called a truth table.

The comparison operator == deserves special attention. Suppose two variables, q and r, have been declared, and q = 7 and r = 8. The statement cout<<(q==r); produces 0 (false) because the value of q is not equivalent to the value of r. The statement cout<<(q=r);, however, produces 8. The single equal sign does not compare two variables; instead, it assigns the value of the rightmost variable to the variable on the left. Because r is 8, q becomes 8, and the value of the entire expression is 8. In several other programming languages, such as BASIC and COBOL, a single equal sign is used as the comparison operator, but this is not the case with C++. A common C++ programming error is to use the assignment operator (=) when you should use the comparison operator (==).

Selection

Computer programs seem smart because of their ability to use selections or make decisions. C++ lets you perform selections in a number of ways.

The if Statement

Computer programs use the selection structure to choose one of two possible courses of action. The selection structure (along with sequence and looping structures) is one of the three basic logical control structures used in programming. The primary C++ selection structure statement is an if statement. The single-alternative if takes the form:

Syntax Example

if (*boolean expression*)
    statement;

Syntax Dissection

- A *boolean expression* is any C++ expression that can be evaluated, and *statement* is any C++ statement or block of statements that you want to execute when the boolean expression evaluates as true, that is, not 0. When you write an if statement, you use the keyword if, a boolean expression within parentheses, and any statement that is the action that occurs if the boolean expression is true. The if statement is often written on two lines to visually separate the decision from its resulting action; however, only one semicolon follows the desired action.

Consider the program shown in Figure 2-6. An insurance policy base premium is set as $75.32. After the program prompts for and receives values for the driver's age and number of traffic tickets, several decisions are made.

```
#include<iostream.h>
void main()
  {
    int driverAge, numTickets;
    double premiumDue =   75.32;
    cout<<"Enter driver's age ";
    cin>>driverAge;
    cout<<"Enter traffic tickets issued ";
    cin>>numTickets;
    if(driverAge<26)
       premiumDue+=100;
    if(driverAge>50)
       premiumDue-=50;
    if(numTickets==2)
       premiumDue +=60.25;
    cout<<"Premium due is "<<premiumDue;
  }
```

Figure 2-6 Some sample selection statements within a C++ program

If the expression in the parentheses is true, then the statement following the if executes; if the driverAge is less than 26, then 100 is added to the premiumDue. Remember, the parentheses surrounding the evaluated expression are essential.

Do not inadvertently insert a semicolon prior to the end of the if statement. For example, consider the if statement in Figure 2-7. The expression driverAge < 26 is evaluated as true or false. Because the semicolon immediately follows the boolean expression, the code is interpreted as if driverAge < 26 then do nothing. The next statement, which adds 100 to the premium, is a new standalone statement, and does not depend on the decision regarding the driver's age. All drivers, whether under 26 or not, have 100 added to their premium variable. The example in Figure 2-7 is misleading, because the indentation of the addition statement makes it appear as though the addition depends on the if. However, C++ ignores your indentation because a semicolon indicates a statement's completion.

```
if(driverAge<26);     // Notice the semicolon
       premiumDue+=100;
```

Figure 2-7 A do-nothing if statement

If the execution of more than one statement depends on the selection, then the statements must be blocked with curly braces as shown in the code segment in Figure 2-8.

```
if(driverAge<26) // When driverAge < 26 evaluates as true,
                 // that is, 1
   {             // two things happen:
     premiumDue+=100;                 // the premium increases
     cout<<"Driver is under 26"<<endl;   // AND the output displays
   }
```

Figure 2-8   Multiple statements that depend on an if

The curly braces in the code segment in Figure 2-8 are very important. If they are removed, then only one statement depends on the if comparison, and the other statement becomes a standalone statement. Examine the code segment in Figure 2-9. If the driverAge is set to 35, then the boolean expression in the if evaluates as false (or 0) and the premium is not increased by 100. However, the "Driver is under 26" message is written on the screen because it is a new statement and not part of the if. The indentation in Figure 2-9 is misleading because it makes it appear that the execution of the cout statement depends on the if, but it does not. The C++ compiler ignores any indentations you make; only curly braces can indicate which statements are performed as a block.

```
if(driverAge<26) // When driverAge < 26 evaluates as true,
     premiumDue+=100;          // then the premium increases
     cout<<"Driver is under 26"<<endl;
     // Whether the driver is under 26 or not,
     // this message displays
```

Figure 2-9   An if with one dependent statement and misleading indents

The **dual-alternative if** uses an **else** to determine the action to take when an if expression is evaluated as false. For example, Figure 2-10 shows a program that uses an if-else structure. When you use an if-else structure, you identify one statement (or block of statements) that will execute when a boolean expression is true, and another statement (or block of statements) that will execute when the same boolean expression evaluates as false. In the program in Figure 2-10, after the user enters a character, the character is tested to see if it is equivalent to the character F. If it is, the output is the word Female, if it is not, the output is Male.

The semicolon that occurs after cout<<"Female" and before the else is required.

2

```
#include<iostream.h>
void main()
   {
     char genderCode;
     cout<<"Enter F for female or M for male ";
     cin>>genderCode;
     if(genderCode=='F')
            cout<<"Female"<<endl;
     else
            cout<<"Male"<<endl;
   }
```

Figure 2-10   An if-else statement

An else must always be associated with an if. You can have an if without an else, but you can't have an else without an if.

Note that in the program shown in Figure 2-10, the output will be the word "Male" if the user enters any character other than 'F'. The selection tests only whether the genderCode is an 'F', not whether it is an 'M' or any other character. Figure 2-11 shows a program that is slightly more sophisticated than the one in Figure 2-10. This one tests for the character 'M' as well as the character 'F'.

```
#include<iostream.h>
void main()
   {
     char genderCode;
     cout<<"Enter F for female or M for male ";
     cin>>genderCode;
     if(genderCode=='F')
        cout<<"Female"<<endl;
     else
        if(genderCode == 'M')
           cout<<"Male"<<endl;
         else
           cout<<"You entered an invalid code."<<endl;
   }
```

Figure 2-11   A nested if-else statement

The code in Figure 2-11 that compares the genderCode to 'M' is known as a **nested if**, or sometimes an **if-else-if**. If the genderCode is 'F', one action results. If the genderCode is not an 'F', then another if-else testing for genderCode 'M' occurs within the else portion of the original selection.

Note that the program code in Figure 2-11 is case-sensitive and does not check for genderCode 'm' or 'f' Each lowercase character has a different value from its uppercase counterpart.

As with an if, you also can block several statements in the else portion of a selection. Figure 2-12 shows the C++ code you could use if females pay a premium of $99.95, and males pay a premium that is $40.00 higher.

```cpp
#include<iostream.h>
void main()
    {
        char genderCode;
        double premium = 99.95;
        cout<<"Enter F for female or M for male ";
        cin>>genderCode;
        if(genderCode=='F')
            cout<<"Female. Premium is "<<<<premium<<endl;
        else
          {
            premium += 40.00;
            cout<<"Male. Premium is "<<premium<<endl;
          }
    }
```

Figure 2-12   Multiple executable statement in an if-else

Any C++ statements can appear in the block associated with an if, and any C++ statements can appear in the block associated with an else. Those statements can include, but are not limited to, variable declarations, output statements, and other ifs and elses.

Any C++ expression can be evaluated as part of an if statement. If the expression is evaluated as 0, it is considered false, and the statements following the if are not executed. If the expression is evaluated as 0 and an else exists, then the statements in the else block are executed. If the expression in an if statement is evaluated as *anything* other than 0, it is considered to be true. In that case, any statement associated with the if executes.

Examine the code in Figure 2-13. At first glance, it appears that the output will read, "No vacation days left". However, the programmer has mistakenly used the single equal sign in the expression within the if statement. The result is that 0 is assigned to vacationDays, the value of the expression is 0, and the expression is determined to be false. Therefore, the else portion of the if is the portion that executes and the message received is "You have vacation days coming".

```
#include<iostream.h>
void main()
   {
      int vacationDays = 0;
      if(vacationDays = 0)
          cout<<"No vacation days left"<<endl;
      else
          cout<<"You have vacation days coming"<<endl;
   }
```

Figure 2-13   An if statement that produces an unexpected result

 Any value other than 0, even a negative value, evaluates as true. Thus, the statement if(-5) cout<<"OK"; would print "OK".

The switch Statement

When you want to create different outcomes depending on specific values of a variable, you can use a series of ifs as shown in the program statement in Figure 2-14.

```
if(dept==1)
      cout<<"Human Resources";
else
      if(dept==2)
      cout<<"Sales";
      else
         if(dept==3)
            cout<<"Information Systems";
         else
      cout<<"No such department";
```

Figure 2-14   Multiple nested ifs

As an alternative to the long string of ifs shown in Figure 2-14, you can use the **switch statement**. For an example of a switch statement, see Figure 2-15.

 The switch can contain any number of cases in any order. The values in the case statements do not have to occur in descending order, nor do they have to be consecutive.

```
switch(dept)
   {
         case 1:
          cout<<"Human Resources";
          break;
         case 2:
          cout<<"Sales";
          break;
         case 3:
          cout<<"Information Systems";
          break;
         default:
          cout<<"No such department";
   }
```

Figure 2-15   Using the switch statement

The keyword **switch** identifies the beginning of the statement. Then the variable in parentheses is evaluated. Each case following the opening curly braces is compared with the variable dept. As soon as a case that equals the value of dept is found, all statements from that point on execute until either a break statement or the final curly brace in the switch is encountered. For example, when the dept variable holds the value 2, then case 1 is ignored, case 2 executes, printing "Sales", and then the break statement executes. The break causes the logic to continue with any statements beyond the closing curly brace of the switch statement.

If you remove the break statements from the code shown in Figure 2-15, then all four cout statements (those that print "Human Resources", "Sales", "Information Systems", and "No such department") execute when dept is 1. Without the break statements, the last three cout statements execute when the department is 2, and the last two execute when the department is 3. The default option executes when no cases are equivalent to the value of dept.

The if Operator

Another alternative to the if statement involves the **if operator** (also called the **conditional operator**), which is represented by a question mark (?). The if operator provides a concise way to express two alternatives. Consider the statements cout<<((driverAge<26) ? "Driver is under 26" : "Driver is at least 26");. If the driverAge is less than 26, the first message appears; if the driverAge is not less than 26, the second message appears. The question mark is necessary after the evaluated expression, and a colon must be included between the two alternatives. The advantage of using the if operator is the ability to place a decision and its two possible outcomes in an abbreviated format.

 The conditional operator is an example of a ternary operator, one that takes three operands instead of just one or two. As a matter of fact, the conditional operator is the only ternary operator used in C++.

2

Logical AND and Logical OR

In some programming situations, two or more conditions must be true to initiate an action. For example, you want to display the message "Discount should apply" if a customer visits your store more than five times a year and spends at least $1000 during the year. Assuming the variables are declared and have been assigned reasonable values, the code in Figure 2-16 works correctly using a **nested if**—that is, one if statement within another if statement.

```
if(numVisits>5)
      if (annualSpent>=1000)
         cout<<"Discount should apply";
```

Figure 2-16   A nested if in which two conditions must be true

If numVisits is not greater than 5, the statement is finished—the second comparison does not even take place. Alternatively, a **logical AND (&&)** can be used, as shown in Figure 2-17. A logical AND is a compound boolean expression in which two conditions must be true for the entire expression to evaluate as true.

```
if(numVisits>5 && annualSpent>=1000)
      cout<<"Discount should apply";
```

Figure 2-17   Using a logical AND

Do not enter a space between the ampersands (&&) in a logical AND. Likewise, do not enter a space between the pipes (||) in a logical OR (discussed later in this chapter).

You read the code in Figure 2-17 as "if numVisits is greater than 5 *and* annualSpent is greater than or equal to 1000, display Discount should apply". As with the nested ifs, if the first expression (numVisits > 5) is not evaluated as true, then the second expression (annualSpent >= 1000) is not evaluated.

When you use the logical AND, you must include a complete boolean expression on each side of the &&. For example, suppose you want to indicate that a salary is valid if it is at least $6.00 but no more than $12.00. You might be tempted to write the following:

```
if(salary >= 6.00 && <= 12.00)
      cout>>"Salary is valid"<<endl;
```

The preceding example won't compile, because the expression to the right of the &&, <= 12.00, is not a complete boolean expression that can evaluate as 0 or not 0. You must include the salary variable on both sides of the && as follows:

```
if(salary >= 6.00 && salary <= 12.00)
      cout>>"Salary is valid"<<endl;
```

Table 2-3 shows how an expression using && is evaluated. An entire expression is true only when the expression on each side of the && is true.

Table 2-3   Truth table for the && (logical AND) operator

Value of expression1	Value of expression2	Value of expression1 && expression2
True	True	True
True	False	False
False	True	False
False	False	False

Using the Logical OR

In certain programming situations, only one of two alternatives must be true for some action to take place. Perhaps a store delivers merchandise if a sale amounts to at least $300, or if the customer lives within the local area code, even if the sale total isn't $300. Two if statements could be used to display a "Delivery available" message, as shown in Figure 2-18.

```
if (saleAmt >= 300)
   cout<<"Delivery available";
else
   if(areaCode==localCode)
     cout<<"Delivery available";
```

Figure 2-18   A nested if in which one of two conditions must be true

If the saleAmt is at least $300, the conditions for delivery are established, and the areaCode is not evaluated. Only if the saleAmt is less than $300 is the area code evaluated. A **logical OR (||)** could also be used, as shown in Figure 2-19. A logical OR is a compound boolean expression in which either of two conditions must be true for the entire expression to evaluate as true.

```
if(saleAmt >=300 || areaCode==localCode)
   cout<<"Delivery available";
```

Figure 2-19   Using a logical OR

Read the statement in Figure 2-19 as "If the saleAmt is greater than or equal to 300 or the areaCode is equivalent to the localCode, then display Delivery available".

With an AND (&&), if the first boolean expression to the left of && is false, the second expression is not evaluated. With an OR (||), if the first expression is true, the second expression is not evaluated. As with code using the two ifs, if the first condition in the or expression is evaluated as true, then the second expression is not evaluated.

Table 2-4 shows how C++ evaluates any expression that uses the || operator. When either expression1 or expression2 is true (or both are true), the entire expression is true.

Table 2-4   Truth table for the || (logical OR) operator

Value of expression1	Value of expression2	Value of expression1 || expression2
True	True	True
True	False	True
False	True	True
False	False	False

In the next set of steps, you write a program that makes several decisions.

1. Open your C++ editor and type identifying comment lines. Then type the following include statements:

   #include<iostream.h>
   #include<conio.h>

2. Begin the main() function and declare three integer variables.

   void main()
   {
     int first, response, bigger;

3. Prompt for, and allow the user to enter a value for first. Notice the space within the quotation mark after the word "value." This means a space will appear on the screen just to the left of the value the user types.

   cout<<"Enter an integer value ";
   cin>> first;

4. Echo the user's choice to the screen, then prompt the user to enter any value that is larger than the entered number. The extra space in the cout statement after the first variable provides a space on the screen just before the user's answer. Read in the user's response.

   cout<<"You entered "<<first<<endl;
   cout<<"Enter any number bigger than "<<first<<" ";
   cin>>response;

5. Test the user's answer against the variable named first. If the user enters a value larger than first, congratulate the user. However, if the user enters a value that is not larger than first, use two statements to explain the problem.

   if(response>first)
       cout<<"Good job"<<endl;
   else
     {

```
            cout<<"You did not follow directions"<<endl;
            cout<<response<<" is not bigger than "<<first<<endl;
      }
```

6. Next, calculate the value of the number that is 6 larger than the user's number. Prompt the user to enter a value between the base number and the number that is 6 larger. Read in the user's response.

```
bigger = first + 6;
cout<<"Enter any number between "<<first<<" and "<<bigger<<" ";
cin>>response;
```

7. Decide if the response is between the base number and the number that is 6 larger, and then print an appropriate response.

```
if(response > first && response < bigger)
   cout<<"Good job "<<endl;
else
   cout<<"No "<<response<<" isn't between those numbers"<<endl;
```

8. Add the **getch( )**; statement that holds the screen output. Then add the closing curly brace for the program.

9. Save the program as **Decisions.cpp** in the Chapter02 folder on your Student Data Disk or Student Data folder on your hard drive. Compile and run the program. Enter any values you choose at each prompt. Depending on the values you choose, your output looks similar to Figure 2-20.

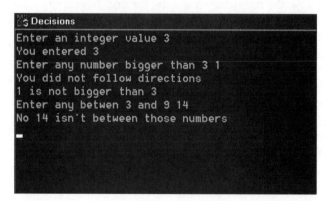

Figure 2-20   A typical run of the Decisions.cpp program

10. After you run the program several times, supplying different values each time, change the program so that it correctly prompts the user and tests for each of the following:

   ▪ Entering a number smaller than first
   ▪ Entering a number equal to first
   ▪ Entering a number smaller than first or larger than bigger

The while Loop

Loops provide a mechanism with which to perform statements repeatedly and, just as important, to stop that performance when warranted. It usually is decision-making that makes computer programs seem smart, but it is looping that makes programs powerful. By using loops, you can write one set of instructions that executes thousands or even millions of times.

Syntax Example

while(boolean expression)
  statement;

Syntax Dissection

- In a while loop, a boolean expression is evaluated as true or false. If it is false, the loop is over, and program execution continues with the next statement. If the expression is true, the *statement* (which can be a block of statements) executes, and the boolean expression is tested again. The cycle of execute-test-execute-test continues as long as the boolean expression continues to be evaluated as true.

In C++, the **while** statement can be used to loop. For example, the program shown in Figure 2-21 shows a loop that produces the numbers 1, 2, 3, and 4.

```
#include<iostream.h>
void main()
  {
     int count = 1;
     while(count<5)
        {
           cout<<count;
           ++count;
        }
  }
```

Figure 2-21   A while loop

In the program shown in Figure 2-21, a variable named count is initialized to the value 1. Then the value of count is compared to 5. Because the expression count < 5 is evaluated as true, the body of the loop, enclosed in curly braces, is executed. The value of count is output, and count is incremented to 2. Then the expression count < 5 is evaluated again. Because the expression is still true, the loop body executes again—the value 2 prints and count is incremented once more. When count becomes 5, the expression count < 5 becomes false and the loop stops executing.

The variable count, shown in the program in Figure 2-21, is often called a **loop-control variable**, because it is the value of count that controls whether the loop body continues to execute.

Any C++ expression can be placed inside the required parentheses in the while statement. As with the if statement, if the expression evaluates to zero, then the expression is false and the loop body is not entered. If the expression within the parentheses evaluates to non–zero, it is considered true, and the loop body executes. With a while statement, when the expression is evaluated as true, the statements that follow execute repeatedly as long as the expression remains true.

When creating loops in a computer program, you always run the risk of creating an **infinite loop**, or a never-ending loop. Figure 2-22 shows an infinite loop.

```
int e = 1;
while (e < 2)
    cout<<"Help! I can't stop! ";
```

Figure 2-22   An infinite loop

In Figure 2-22, because e is initially evaluated as less than 2, and the statement in the body of the loop does nothing to change the value of e, the expression e < 2 infinitely continues to be evaluated as true. As a result, "Help! I can't stop!" appears again and again.

 If you inadvertently execute an infinite loop on your computer, hold down the Control key and press the Pause/Break key to stop executing the program.

Figure 2-23 shows another infinite loop. As you learned with the if statement, C++ does not acknowledge any indenting you provide in your code. The program segment in Figure 2-23 sets e to 1. Then, while e remains less than 2, the program segment continues to print "Help! I can't stop". The statement ++e is not part of the while loop, and never executes. Figure 2-24 shows the corrected version of the program segment.

```
int e = 1;
while (e < 2)
    cout<<"Help! I can't stop! ";
    ++e;   // Although this line is indented,
      // it is not part of the while loop
```

Figure 2-23   An infinite loop with indented code

```
int e = 1;
while (e < 2)
   {
      cout<<"I do stop as soon as e becomes 2";
      ++e;
   }
```

Figure 2-24 A non-infinite loop

C++ also provides a do statement. It takes the form

```
do
   statement;
while (expression);
```

The do statement is used when the statements in the body of the loop must execute at least once. In a do loop, the expression that you are testing is not evaluated until the bottom of the loop. (With a while loop, programmers say that the expression you are testing is evaluated at the top of the loop, or prior to executing any loop body statements.)

You can use any C++ expression within the parentheses of a while loop. As long as the expression evaluates to any non-zero value, the loop continues to execute. For example, programmers often use while loops to validate data entry. Validating data entry means a data value is required to fall within a specific range of values before it is accepted into a program. Suppose a user is asked to respond to a question with a 1 or a 2. You want to make sure that the user enters a 1 or a 2 before the program proceeds. Beginning programmers often erroneously write the code as follows:

```
int response;
cout<<"Please enter a 1 or a 2 ";
cin>>response;
if (response < 1 || response > 2)
   {
      cout<<"Value must be 1 or 2. Please reenter. "<<endl;
      cin>>response;
   }
```

The code above correctly checks the response and issues the error message when the response is less than 1 or more than 2. However, if the user enters an invalid response the second time, the program does not check the second response; it simply continues with the next executable statement. The following code is superior:

```
int response;
cout<<"Please enter a 1 or a 2 ";
cin>>response;
while (response < 1 || response > 2)
   {
      cout<<"Value must be 1 or 2. Please reenter. "<<endl;
      cin>>response;
   }
```

The loop above continues to execute indefinitely until the user's response falls within the range of allowed values.

A common logical error often occurs when beginning programmers use the not (!) operator. Consider the following code:

```
int response = 0;
cout<<"Please enter a 1 or a 2 ";
cin>>response;
while (response != 1 || response != 2)
    {
        cout<<"Value must be 1 or 2. Please reenter. "<<endl;
        cin>>response;
    }
```

In the preceding program segment, suppose the user enters 2 at the first prompt. This is a correct response, and the error message should not appear. However, when the while statement tests the expression `response != 1`, it is evaluated as a true expression; it is true that response is not equal to 1. Because the expression is true, the while loop body executes, and an error message asks users to reenter the value. Similarly, when the user enters 1, the expression `response ! = 1` is false, but the expression `response != 2` is true.

Remember that when you use the logical OR, only one of the two involved expressions needs to be true for the whole expression to be true. Again, the user is presented with the error message when, in fact, no error was committed. The user is caught in an infinite loop because *every* value that can be entered is either not 1 or not 2, including 1 and 2. The correct solution is shown in the following code:

```
int response = 0;
cout<<"Please enter a 1 or a 2 ";
cin>>response;
while (response != 1 && response != 2)
    {
        cout<<"Value must be 1 or 2. Please reenter. "<<endl;
        cin>>response;
    }
```

With the preceding code segment, the error message correctly appears only when the user's response is *both* not 1 and not 2.

In the next set of steps you use a while loop to ensure that a user is entering an appropriate value.

1. Open a new file in your C++ editor.

2. Type comments to identify the program, and the include statements that you need.

    #include<iostream.h>
    #include<conio.h>

2

3. Start the main() function. Declare a variable to hold the user's response. Then prompt for and read in the response.

```
void main()
{
  int response;
  cout<<"Enter an ID number between 111 and 999 inclusive "<<endl;
  cin>> response;
```

4. Write the loop that continues to both prompt the user and read in new values while the user enters numbers that are out of range.

```
while(response<111 || response > 999)
  {
  cout<<"Invalid ID number"<<endl;
  cout<<"Please enter a number from 111 through 999"<<endl;
  cin>>response;
  }
```

5. When the user enters a valid ID number, the loop ends. Write a cout statement that notifies the user that the entered ID number is a valid one.

```
cout<<"Thank you. Your valid ID is "<<response<<endl;
```

6. Add a **getch();** statement if you need it. Add the closing curly brace.

7. Save the file as **ValidID.cpp** in the Chapter02 folder on your Student Data Disk or Student Data folder on your hard drive. Then compile and run the program. Confirm that the program continues to loop until your entered response is within the requested range. Figure 2-25 shows a sample run.

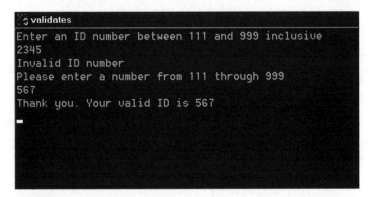

```
validates
Enter an ID number between 111 and 999 inclusive
2345
Invalid ID number
Please enter a number from 111 through 999
567
Thank you. Your valid ID is 567
```

Figure 2-25   Sample run of a program that validates user's response

The for Statement

The **for statement** represents an alternative to the while statement. It is most often used in a **definite loop**, or a loop that must execute a definite number of times. It takes the form

---

Syntax Example

for(*intialize;evaluate;alter*)
    statement;

Syntax Dissection

- Inside the parentheses, semicolons separate the three items—initialize, evaluate, and alter. *Initialize* represents any steps you want to take at the beginning of the statement. Most often, this includes initializing a loop control variable, but the initialize portion can consist of any C++ statement or even several C++ statements separated with commas.

- *Evaluate* represents any C++ expression that is evaluated as zero or non-zero. Most often, the evaluate part of the for statement compares the loop control variable with a limit, but evaluate can include any C++ expression. If the evaluation is true (not 0), any statements in the for loop are executed. If the evaluation is false (0), the for statement is completed, and program execution continues with the next statement, bypassing the body of the for statement.

- If the evaluation of the expression between the semicolons is true, and the statements in the body of the loop are executed, then the final portion of the for loop, represented by *alter*, takes place after the statements are complete. In the alter part of the loop, most often you use statements that change the value of the loop control variable. However, you can use any C++ statements in the alter part of the for loop if you want those statements to execute after the loop body and before the evaluate part executes again.

- Any C++ for statement can be rewritten as a while statement, and vice versa; sometimes one form of the loop suits your needs better than others. For example, Figure 2-26 shows two loops that produce identical results: the output **1 2 3**.

```
int num;
num = 1;
while(num < 4)
   {
      cout<<num;
      ++num;
   }
for(num = 1; num < 4; ++num)
   cout<<num;
```

Figure 2-26   Two loops that produce 1 2 3

Although the code used in the for loop in Figure 2-26 is more concise than that in the while loop, the execution is the same. With the for statement, you are less likely to make common looping mistakes, such as not initializing the variable that controls the loop, or not changing the value of the loop control variable during loop execution. Those mistakes remain possibilities, however, because C++ allows you to leave empty any of the three items inside the for loop parentheses. (The two semicolons are still required).

 C++ programmers usually prefer to declare variables at the beginning of a function. This is because of tradition and because all variables are located in one place, thus making it easier to implement later changes. One common exception arises when declaring the variable used to control a for loop. The variable is often declared and initialized inside the for statement, as in the following example:

```
// Notice that the variable a is declared right here
for(int a=1; a<5; ++a)
   {
      //statements
   }
```

Using Control Structures with Class Object Fields

When you create classes and subsequently create objects that are instantiations of those classes, you use the individual class fields the same way you use variables of the same type. For example, you can use any numeric class field in an arithmetic expression, or as part of the conditional test in a selection or a loop.

Consider the BaseballPlayer class in Figure 2-27. It contains two public fields: a player number and the number of hits. As you continue to study C++, you seldom make class fields public; usually you make them private. For simplicity, this example makes the fields public.

```
class BaseballPlayer
   {
     public:
       int playerNumber;
       int hits;
   };
```

Figure 2-27   A BaseballPlayer class with two public fields

A program that instantiates a BaseballPlayer object named ourShortStop is shown in Figure 2-28. The program uses a loop to ensure that the player number entered by the user is not larger than 99. The program also uses a nested decision to display one of three messages about the player's performance. The program is straightforward; examine it so that you understand that class object fields are simply variables like any other. Although their identifiers might be long, class object fields still control decisions and loops as simple non-class variables do.

```
#include<iostream.h>
#include<conio.h>
void main()
{
   BaseballPlayer ourShortStop;
   cout<<"Enter player number ";
   cin>>ourShortStop.playerNumber;
   while(ourShortStop.playerNumber > 99)
      {
        cout<<"Player numbers must be 1 or 2 digits"<<endl;
        cout<<"Please reenter the player number ";
        cin>>ourShortStop.playerNumber;
      }
   cout<<"Enter hits made by this player ";
   cin>>ourShortStop.hits;
   cout<<"Player #"<<ourShortStop.playerNumber<<
       " has "<<ourShortStop.hits<<" hits"<<endl;
   if(ourShortStop.hits < 5)
     cout<<"This player needs more playing time!"<<endl;
   else
      if(ourShortStop.hits < 20)
        cout<<"This player plays regularly"<<endl;
      else
        cout<<"Wow!"<<endl;
  getch();
}
```

Figure 2-28   A program that instantiates and uses a BaseballPlayer object

In the next steps, you create the BaseballPlayer class and program.

1. Open a new file in your C++ editor. Enter beginning comments and appropriate include statements.

2. Enter the BaseballPlayer class, as shown in Figure 2-27.

3. Enter the main() function, as shown in Figure 2-28.

4. Save the program as **Baseball.cpp**. Compile and run the program. Enter any data you like, being sure to include invalid player numbers so that you can test the loop. Run the program several times, using different values for the hits field so that you can test each branch of the nested selection. Figure 2-29 shows the results of a typical execution.

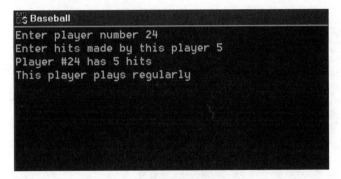

Figure 2-29   Output of Baseball.cpp

5. Next, you add atBats and average fields so you can calculate a BaseballPlayer's batting average. Move the insertion point to after the hits field declaration in the Baseball-Player class and press the **Enter** key to start a new line. Add these two fields:

   int atBats;
   double average;

6. Within the main() function, insert a prompt and a cin statement for the atBats, just after the entry for the hits.

   cout<<"Enter times at bat for this player ";
   cin>>ourShortStop.atBats;

7. Just before the getch() call at the end of main(), insert the calculation of the average and a cout statement to display the average. Remember that if you divide an integer by an integer, the result is an integer value that loses decimal places. One way to convert the player average to a decimal number that retains the fraction is to multiply the hits field by 1.0. This will convert the hits field to a floating-point number during the calculation.

   ourShortStop.average = ourShortStop.hits * 1.0 / ourShortStop.atBats;
   cout<<"Batting average is "<<ourShortStop.average<<endl;

8. Save the file as **Baseball2.cpp** in the Chapter02 folder on your Student Data Disk or in the Student Data folder on your hard drive. Compile and run the program. Confirm that the average calculation works correctly. A typical program execution is shown in Figure 2-30.

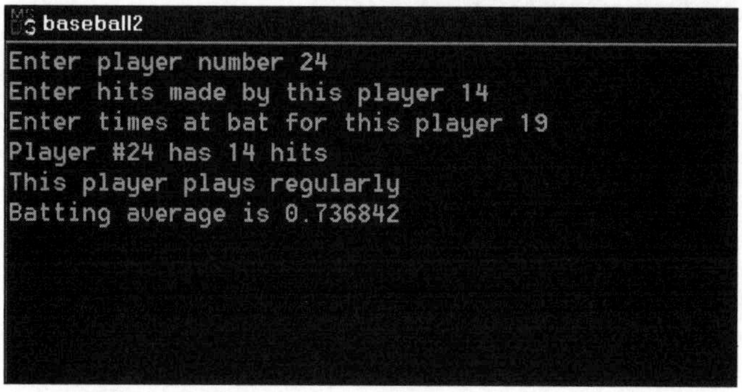

Figure 2-30   Output of Baseball2.cpp

CHAPTER SUMMARY

❑ C++ provides five simple binary arithmetic operators for creating arithmetic expressions: addition (+), subtraction (–), multiplication (*), division (/), and modulus (%).

❑ When you mix data types in a binary arithmetic expression, the result is always the same type as the type that takes the most memory to store.

❑ C++ employs several shortcut operators for arithmetic, such as +=, prefix ++, and postfix ++.

❑ A boolean expression is one that evaluates as true or false. In C++, the value 0 is always interpreted as false; all other values are interpreted as true.

❑ C++ uses the if, if-else, switch, and conditional operator statements to make selections.

❑ You can use the logical AND and OR to combine boolean evaluations.

❑ C++ uses the while statement, the do statement, and the for loop to create loops.

❑ Statements that depend on the boolean evaluation in a decision or a loop are blocked by using curly braces.

❑ Fields contained within class objects are used in arithmetic and boolean expressions in the same manner as are primitive variables.

REVIEW QUESTIONS

1. Arithmetic operations, such as addition (+), subtraction (–), multiplication (*), division (/), and modulus (%) that take two arguments use _____ operators.

   a. unary

   b. summary

c. binary

d. boolean

2. In C++, what is the result of 5 + 4 * 3 + 2?

a. 14

b. 19

c. 29

d. 54

3. In C++, what is the result of 19 % 2?

a. 0

b. 1

c. 9

d. 19

4. If a and b are integers, and a = 10 and b = 30, if you use the statement a += b, what is the resulting value of a?

a. 10

b. 20

c. 30

d. 40

5. If c is an integer, and c = 34, what is the value of ++c?

a. 0

b. 1

c. 34

d. 35

6. If d is an integer, and d = 34, what is the value of d++?

a. 0

b. 1

c. 34

d. 35

7. If e and f are integers, and d = 16 and e = 17, then what is the value of d == --e?

a. 0

b. 1

c. 16

d. 17

8. An expression that evaluates as true or false is known as a(n) _____ expression.

   a. unary

   b. binary

   c. boolean

   d. honest

9. All false relational expressions are evaluated as _____.

   a. 0

   b. 1

   c. negative

   d. positive

10. What is the output produced by the following code?

```
x = 7;
if(x > 10)
   cout<<"High";
else
   cout<<"Low";
```

   a. High

   b. Low

   c. HighLow

   d. nothing

11. What is the output produced by the following code?

```
x = 7;
if(x > 10)
    cout<<"High";
    cout<<"Low";
```

   a. High

   b. Low

   c. HighLow

   d. nothing

12. What is the output produced by the following code?

```
x = 15;
if(x > 10)
  {
    cout<<"High";
    cout<<"Low";
  }
```

    a. High

    b. Low

    c. HighLow

    d. nothing

13. A selection within a selection is known as a _____.

    a. nested if

    b. double whammy

    c. dual–alternative selection

    d. binary operator

14. If g and h are integers, and g = 20 and h = 30, then the value of the expression g > 5 && h < 5 is _____.

    a. 0

    b. 1

    c. 20

    d. 30

15. If i and j are integers, and i = 75 and j = 2, then the value of the expression i == 2 || j == 75 is _____.

    a. 0

    b. 1

    c. 2

    d. 75

16. Which of the following types of statements is never used to produce a loop?

    a. do

    b. switch

    c. while

    d. for

17. Which of the following types of statements is never used to produce a selection?

    a. if

    b. switch

    c. ?:

    d. while

18. A never-ending loop is _____.

   a. common in most C++ programs

   b. a tool used in highly mathematical C++ programs

   c. called an infinite loop

   d. impossible to effect in a C++ program

19. How many times is the word "Hello" printed by the following code?

```
for(k = 0; k < 6; ++k)
   cout<<"Hello";
```

   a. 0

   b. 1

   c. 6

   d. 7

20. How many times is the word "Goodbye" printed by the following code?

```
for(m = 0; m > 3; ++m)
   cout<<"Goodbye";
```

   a. 0

   b. 1

   c. 2

   d. 3

EXERCISES

1. Assume a, b, and c are integers, and that a = 0, b = 1, and c = 5. What is the value of each of the following? (Do not assume the answers are cumulative; evaluate each expression using the original values for a, b, and c.)

   a. a + b   f. b <= c

   b. a > b   g. a > 5 || b < 5

   c. 3 + b * c   h. a > 5 && b < 5

   d. ++b   i. b != c

   e. b++   j. b == c

2. Write a C++ program in which you declare a variable that holds an hourly wage. Prompt the user to enter an hourly wage. Multiply the wage by 40 hours and print the standard weekly pay.

3. Write a C++ program in which you declare variables that will hold an hourly wage, a number of hours worked, and a withholding percentage. Prompt the user to enter values for each of these fields. Compute and display net weekly pay, which is calculated as hours times rate, minus the percentage of the gross pay that is withholding.

2

4. Write a program that allows the user to enter two values. Display the results of adding the two values, subtracting them from each other, multiplying them, and dividing them.

5. Write a program that allows the user to enter two double values. Display one of two messages: "The first number you entered is larger", or "The first number you entered is not larger".

6. Write a program that allows the user to enter two double values. Display one of three messages: "The first number you entered is larger", "The second number you entered is larger", or "The numbers are equal".

7. Write a program that allows the user to enter two values. Then let the user enter a single character as the desired operation: 'a' for add, 's' for subtract, and so on. Perform the operation that the user selects and display the results.

8. Write a program that allows the user to enter two integer values. Display every whole number that falls between these values.

9. Write a program that asks a user to enter an integer between 1 and 10. Continue to prompt the user while the value entered does not fall within this range. When the user is successful, display a congratulatory message.

10. Write a program that asks a user to enter an integer between 1 and 10. Continue to prompt the user while the value entered does not fall within this range. When the user is successful, display a congratulatory message as many times as is the value of the successful number the user entered.

11. Create a PhoneCall class with one public field that contains the number of minutes in a call. Write a main() function that instantiates one PhoneCall object, such as myCallToGrandmaOnSunday. Assign a value to the minutes field of this object. Print the value of the minutes field. Calculate the cost of the call at 10 cents per minute, and display the results.

12. Create a Cake class. Include two public fields that contain the price of the Cake and the calorie count of the Cake. Write a main() function that declares a Cake object. Prompt the user for field values. Echo the values, and then display the cost per calorie.

13. Create a Desk class. Include three public fields: length and width of the desktop in inches, and number of drawers. Write a main() function that instantiates a Desk object. Prompt a user for the desk dimensions and number of drawers in a Desk the user is ordering. Calculate the final Desk price as follows: Any Desk with a surface under 750 square inches costs $400, otherwise the cost is $550; then add $50 for each drawer requested.

14. Create an Investment class. Include public fields for the term of the Investment in years, the beginning dollar amount of the Investment, and the final value of the Investment. Write a main() function in which you declare an Investment object. Prompt the user for the term and the initial Investment amount for this object. Print the value of the Investment after each year of the term, using a simple compound interest rate of 8%. For example, using a $1000 investment for 3 years, the output looks like Figure 2-31.

```
s Investment
Enter initial investment 1000
Enter term in years 3
after year 1, the investment is worth 1080
after year 2, the investment is worth 1166.4
after year 3, the investment is worth 1259.71
```

Figure 2-31   Output of Investment program

15. Each of the following files in the Chapter02 folder contains syntax and/or logical errors. Determine the problem in each case, and fix the program.

    a. DEBUG2-1

    b. DEBUG2-2

    c. DEBUG2-3

    d. DEBUG2-4

CASE PROJECT

In Chapter 1 you developed a Fraction class for Teacher's Pet Software. The class contains two public data fields for numerator and denominator. Using the same class, write a main() function that instantiates two Fraction objects, and prompt the user for values for each field of each Fraction. Do not allow the user to enter a value of 0 for the denominator of any Fraction; continue to prompt the user for a denominator value until a non-zero value is entered. Add statements to the main() function to display the floating-point equivalent of each Fraction object. For example, the floating point equivalent of 1/4 is 0.25. Add a message that indicates whether the fraction value is greater than the value 1.

3

UNDERSTANDING ARRAYS AND POINTERS

In this chapter, you will learn:

♦ How to use the address operator
♦ About arrays
♦ How to store values in an array
♦ How to access and use array values
♦ The value of using a constant to refer to an array's size
♦ Techniques to access some of the values in an array
♦ How to use parallel arrays
♦ How to use strings
♦ About special string-handling problems
♦ About pointers
♦ How to use a pointer in place of an array name

C++ is a powerful programming language for many reasons. C++ lets you examine and manipulate the memory addresses of variables. C++ also allows you to create arrays, or lists, of variables that you can use to efficiently store related values. Once you understand arrays, you can manipulate character strings of data. In this chapter, you will learn to use memory addresses and arrays, and learn about their relationship to each other.

USING THE ADDRESS OPERATOR

When you declare a variable with a statement such as `int myAge;`, the compiler chooses an available memory location in which to store your integer, and then associates the name myAge with that location. All modern programming languages allow you to use easy-to-remember variable identifiers like myAge so that you do not have to remember actual memory addresses.

A variable's memory address is a fixed location; a variable's address is a constant. Although you cannot choose a variable's actual memory address, you can examine it. To do so, you use the **address operator** (**&**). For example, the program in Figure 3-1 shows both the value and the address of a variable. The output is shown in Figure 3-2. The memory address appears as a **hexadecimal**, or base 16, number. The value of the actual memory address is of no use to you at this point; you use the address operator merely as a curiosity.

```
#include<iostream.h>
#include<conio.h>
void main()
  {
    int myAge = 21;
    cout<<"The value of myAge is "<<myAge<<endl;
    cout<<"The value of &myAge is "<<&myAge<<endl;
    getch();
  }
```

Figure 3-1   Program that displays the value and address of a variable

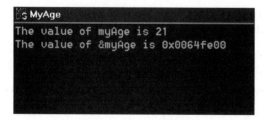

Figure 3-2   Output of program from Figure 3-1

 The hexadecimal numbering system uses the values 0 through 9, and the letters a through f to represent the decimal values 0 through 15. You indicate a hexadecimal value in C++ by beginning the number with 0x. Each column or place in a hexadecimal number is 16 times the value of the column to its right. For example, the hexadecimal number 0x10 represents 16, the hexadecimal number 0x11 represents 17, and the hexadecimal number 0x1a represents 26.

 If your system does not include "0x" in front of the hexadecimal address, your output still reflects a memory address.

3

In the following steps, you experiment with memory addresses in your computer system.

1. Open a new file in your C++ editor. Type any comments you want at the top of the file.

2. Enter the program shown in Figure 3-1. Save it as **MyAge.cpp** in the Chapter03 folder of your Student Data Disk or of the Student Data folder on your hard drive. Then compile and run it. Your second line of output might be different from that shown in Figure 3-2 if your compiler placed the myAge variable in a different memory location.

3. Place the insertion point after the last cout statement in the program, and press **Enter** to begin a new line.

4. Add statements to increase the value of myAge and to redisplay the values of myAge and its address.

++myAge;
cout<<"The value of myAge is "<<myAge<<endl;
cout<<"The value of &myAge is "<<&myAge<<endl;

You can type the two cout statements shown in Step 4, or you can copy the identical statements shown earlier in the program and paste them here.

5. Save the program as **MyAge2.cpp**, and then compile and run it. Although the address shown on your screen might differ, your results should look similar to Figure 3-3. The value of myAge has increased, but the memory address of the variable remains the same.

Figure 3-3   Output of MyAge2.cpp

6. Place the insertion point after the last cout statement in the program, and press **Enter** to begin a new line.

7. Add statements to add a new variable, yourAge, and to display its value and its address:

```
int yourAge = 35;
cout<<"The value of yourAge is "<<yourAge<<endl;
cout<<"The value of &yourAge is "<<&yourAge<<endl;
```

8. Save the file as **MyAge3.cpp**. Compile and run it. The output should look similar to Figure 3-4. Notice that the memory addresses of yourAge and myAge are different.

```
MyAge3
The value of myAge is 21
The value of &myAge is 0x0064fe00
The value of myAge is 22
The value of &myAge is 0x0064fe00
The value of yourAge is 35
The value of &yourAge is 0x0064fdfc
```

Figure 3-4   Output of MyAge3.cpp

UNDERSTANDING ARRAYS

Although the primitive (or scalar) data types—int, char, double, and float—suffice to describe the data used in many programs, it is sometimes convenient to create groups of variables that you can manipulate as a unit. A list of individual items that all have the same type is called an **array**. An array holds two or more variables with the same name and type in adjacent memory positions. The variables with the same name are distinguished from one another by their subscripts; the **subscript** is a number that indicates the position of the particular array element being used.

Anytime you need many related variables, consider using an array. For example, good candidates for array storage are lists of class grades, daily high or low temperatures, and valid stock numbers. One important feature of arrays is that each array element must be the same type. That is because different data types take up different amounts of memory. Every element within an array is always the same size as all the other elements within the same array, although the size of a particular type of element, such as int, can differ from computer system to computer system.

Remember that you can determine the size of variables in your system with the sizeof() operator. For example, to find how much memory an integer uses, you can place the following statement in a program:

```
cout<<"Integer size is "<<sizeof(int)<<
    " on this computer";
```

Output might then be: Integer size is 2 on this computer.

In C++, you declare an array by using the form *type arrayName [size]*, where *type* is any simple type, *arrayName* is any legal identifier, and *size* (in the square brackets) represents the number of elements the array contains. An **element** is a single object in an array. For example, `double moneyCollected[15];` declares an array of 15 elements, each of which is type double. The first variable in the array (or element of the array) is `moneyCollected[0]`. The last element is `moneyCollected[14]`. The number in square brackets, the subscript, should be either an integer constant or variable.

Beginning C++ programmers often forget that the first element in any array is the element with the 0 subscript. If you assume that the first element is element 1, you commit the error known as the "off by one" error.

An array name actually represents a memory address. When you declare an array, you tell the compiler to use the array name to indicate the beginning address of a series of elements. For example, if you declare an array as `int someNumbers[7];`, you are telling the compiler (which is telling the operating system) to reserve memory locations for seven integers beginning at the memory address that is represented by someNumbers. If, for example, integers require two bytes of storage on your system, then the declaration `int someNumbers[7];` reserves exactly 14 bytes of memory. You cannot tell the compiler where you want an array to be stored in memory. You can tell the compiler only the name of an array and how much storage (how many elements) you want to reserve; the compiler chooses the actual memory location.

The subscript used to access an element of an array indicates how much to add to the starting address to locate a value. For example, if you declare an array as `int someNumbers[7];`, and if an int requires two bytes of storage in your system, when you access the value of someNumbers[2], you access the value of exactly two integers, or four bytes away from the beginning address of the array. Figure 3-5 illustrates how the someNumbers array looks in memory if it is stored at memory address 3000.

An array subscript must always be an integer.

int someNumbers[7];

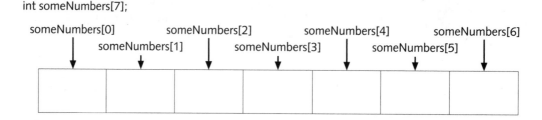

Figure 3-5   How the someNumbers array looks in memory

 Many C++ compilers do not issue warnings or errors if a subscript exceeds the size of the array. Instead, the program simply accesses memory outside the array, with unpredictable results. As the programmer, you are responsible for ensuring that the subscript remains within the intended range.

The array declaration `int someNumbers[7];` declares an array that holds seven integers. The name of the array represents the beginning address of the array. You can view the address of the array with the statement `cout<<someNumbers;`. The statement `cout<<&someNumbers[0];` produces identical output because the name of the array *is* the address of the array's first element. In the first statement, the name of the array represents the beginning address of the array. In the second statement, the address of someNumbers[0] is also the beginning address of the array.

Similarly, the statements `cout<<(someNumbers + 1);`—the address of someNumbers plus one more integer—and `cout<<&someNumbers[1]`—the address of the second element of the someNumbers array—produce identical results. These two examples produce the same output because someNumbers is the beginning address of the array. Because someNumbers is an array of type integer, someNumbers + 1 is one integer away from the beginning address of the array. That is, the address one integer away from the beginning address of the array is the address of someNumbers[1].

Storing Values in an Array

You most often create an array when you want to store a number of related variable elements. For example, assume you own an apartment building and that you charge four different monthly rents depending on whether the apartment is a studio, or has one, two, or three bedrooms. You could store the rent figures in four separately named variables such as `studioRent`, `oneRent`, `twoRent`, and `threeRent`. Alternatively, you can use an array with four elements, like the one shown below. This program segment shows the declaration of a four-element integer array named rent, and also shows how you can assign a rent value to each array element.

```
int rent[4];
rent[0] = 250;
rent[1] = 375;
rent[2] = 460;
rent[3] = 600;
```

When you declare an array like `int array[4];`, you set aside enough memory to hold four integers, but you say nothing about the values stored in those four memory locations. The values are unknown—they are whatever was stored in those memory locations before the computer reserved the locations for use by your program. Programmers often say that these memory locations are filled with **garbage**, or useless values. However, after you provide assignment statements such as `rent[0] = 250;` and `rent[1] = 375;`, the memory locations have useful values.

 You are not required to assign array values in sequential order.

Just as you can initialize a single variable when you declare it, you can provide values for an array when you declare it. The statement `int rent[4] = {250, 375, 460, 600};` provides four values for the array. The four values listed within the curly braces are assigned, in sequence, to rent[0], rent[1], rent[2], and rent[3]. It does not make any difference whether you assign values to an array upon creation, or make assignments later, as long as you assign reasonable values before you try to do anything useful with them.

If you declare an array without a size, but provide initialization values, C++ creates an array with the exact size you need. For example, the array declarations `int rent[4] = {250, 375, 460, 600};` and `int rent[] = {250, 375, 460, 600};` create identical arrays. Because you provided four values for the second declaration, C++ assumes you want an array large enough to hold four integers.

 If you do not provide enough values to fill an array, C++ fills any unassigned array elements with zeros. For example, if you declare `int rent[20] = {250, 375};`, C++ assigns 250 to rent[0], 375 to rent[1], and then fills the remaining array elements, rent[2] through rent[19], with 0. (Therefore, a convenient way to set all array elements to zero is to declare `int rent[20] = {0};`.) However, if you declare an array as `int rent[20];` and then make an assignment such as `rent[0] = 250;`, the remaining 19 array elements continue to hold garbage.

 If you try to initialize an array with too many values, as in `int array[3] = {22,33,44,55,66};`, C++ issues a syntax error message and the program does not compile.

Accessing and Using Array Values

Once an array is filled with useful values, you can access and use an individual array value in the same manner you would access and use any single variable of the same type. For example, consider the program shown in Figure 3-6, and the output shown in Figure 3-7. The program contains a single integer variable named singleInt, and an array of five integers named arrayInt. The single integer and two of the array integers have been initialized. The program demonstrates that you can use cout, the prefix increment operator, and the multiplication operator with an array element in the same manner that you use a simple, non-array variable. The same holds true for all other operations you have learned—if you can perform the operation with a single variable, then you also can perform the operation with a single array element of the same type.

```
//    Demonstrating single variables
// and array variables
#include<iostream.h>
#include<conio.h>
void main()
{
    int singleInt = 52;
    int arrayInt[5] = {12,36};
    cout<<singleInt<<endl;
    cout<<arrayInt[0]<<endl;
    ++singleInt;
    ++arrayInt[0];
    cout<<singleInt<<endl;
    cout<<arrayInt[0]<<endl;
    singleInt = singleInt * 2;
    arrayInt[0] = arrayInt[0] * 2;
    cout<<singleInt<<endl;
    cout<<arrayInt[0]<<endl;
    getch();
}
```

Figure 3-6   Program that uses single and array variables

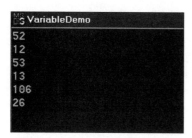

Figure 3-7   Output of program from Figure 3-6

If you need to access an element in an array, you can use the array name and a constant subscript such as 0 or 1. Alternately, you can use a variable as a subscript. For example, if you declare an integer as int sub = 0; and declare an array as int anArray[7];, you could display the value of anArray[0] with the statement cout<<anArray[sub];.

Using a variable as a subscript is particularly useful when you want to access all of the elements in an array. For example, instead of writing five cout statements to print the five elements of an array, you can place one cout statement in a loop and vary the subscript. Figure 3-8 shows how you can print five array values. The for loop prints arrayInt[0] through arrayInt[4] because x increases from 0 and remains less than 5.

3

```
int arrayInt[5] = {34, 56, 12, 3, 99};
int x;
for(x = 0; x < 5; ++x)
   cout<<arrayInt[x]<<endl;
```

Figure 3-8   Printing five array values

In a similar fashion, you can fill an array with values that the user enters from the keyboard. Figure 3-9 shows a program segment in which the user enters ten doubles that are stored in an array.

```
double prices[10];
int sub;
for(sub = 0; sub < 10; ++sub)
   {
        cout<<"Enter a price ";
        cin>>price[sub];
   }
```

Figure 3-9   Entering values into an array

When the code in Figure 3-9 executes, the user will be prompted 10 times and allowed to enter a floating point value after each prompt. The 10 values will be stored in price[0] through price[9], respectively.

Using a Constant to Refer to an Array's Size

Often, using a for loop is a convenient way to access all array elements because arrays always have a specific, known size, and for loops execute a specific, known number of times. When you want to access all array elements in sequential order, you can use a subscript that you vary from 0 to 1 less than the number of elements of the array. Therefore, it is convenient to declare a constant that is equal to the size of the array; you then can use this constant in every loop that accesses or uses all of the array elements.

Figure 3-10 shows a program that declares an array with 12 elements. Each of the three loops—data entry, arithmetic, and output—use the declared constant named arraySize. This approach has at least two advantages. First, when you use the constant to control the loop, you can be confident that you are using the same value each time. That is, you don't run the risk of typing 11 to control the input loop, but 13 to control the output loop. Second, if you ever change the size of the array, such as from 12 salespeople to 13, you change the constant in a single location. This relieves you of the task of looking through the program for every instance of 12 and replacing it with 13. You won't inadvertently miss changing one of the loop controlling values, and you won't inadvertently change a 12 value that should not be changed (such as if the commission rate had been 12 percent in the program shown in Figure 3-10).

You could use a variable named arraySize instead of a constant, and the program would work as well. However, arraySize is not meant to be changed during the execution of the program, so it makes sense to define it as a constant value.

```cpp
// Using a constant to control loops
#include<iostream.h>
#include<conio.h>
void main()
{
    const int arraySize = 12;
    double sales[arraySize];
    int a;
    // Data entry loop
    // - enter sales figure for each salesperson
    for(a = 0; a < arraySize; ++a)
        {
            cout<<"Enter sales for salesperson #"<<a<<". ";
            cin>>sales[a];
        }
    // Arithmetic loop -
    // compute 8 percent commission for each salesperson
    for(a = 0; a < arraySize; ++a)
        sales[a] = sales[a] * .08;
    // Output loop
    // - print commission for each salesperson
    for(a = 0; a < arraySize; ++a)
        cout<<"Commission for salesperson #"<<a<<" is "
            <<sales[a]<<endl;
    getch();
}
```

Figure 3-10   Using a constant to control loops

When you run the program in Figure 3-10, the statement cout<<"Enter sales for salesperson #"<<a<<". "; prints salesperson numbers 0 through 11, corresponding to the correct array subscripts. If you want the prompt to read salesperson #1 through #12, substitute a+1 for a in the cout statement.

When you access all the elements in an array, remember to access element 0 through the element with a subscript that is one less than the array size.

Accessing Elements in an Array

When you want to access a single array element, you use a subscript that indicates the position of the value you want to access. When you want to access all of the elements in an array, a for loop usually is convenient. You also might want to access several array elements, but not necessarily all of them. In such a case, a while loop provides the most convenient structure.

As an example, assume you write a program into which a teacher can enter any number of test scores, up to 30. Then the program computes the average test score. You want the program to be flexible enough so that it works whether the teacher has a class of 12, 25, or any other number of students up to 30. You want to create an array that can hold 30 test scores, but in any given execution of the program, the teacher might enter values for only some of the array elements. Figure 3-11 shows a program that allows a teacher to enter any number of test scores into an array.

```cpp
// Test average
#include<iostream.h>
#include<conio.h>
void main()
{
    int testScore[30];
    int test = 0, a;
    double total = 0;
    double average;
    cout<<"Enter first test score, or 999 to quit ";
    cin>>testScore[test];
    while(testScore[test] != 999)
        {
            total += testScore[test];
            ++test;
            cout<<"Enter next test score or 999 to quit ";
            cin>>testScore[test];
        }
    cout<<"The entered test scores are: ";
    for(a = 0; a < test; ++a)
        cout<<testScore[a]<<"   ";
    average = total/test;
    cout<<"The average test score is "<<average<<endl;
    getch();
}
```

Figure 3-11   A program that averages up to 30 test scores

The program in Figure 3-11 declares an array for 30 integer test scores, and single variables that serve as subscripts, a total, and the average. Although the test scores are integers, the average is a double so that the average can be expressed by a number, such as 82.75. Recall that when you divide an integer by an integer, the result is an integer, so for convenience this program uses type double for the total instead of type int. When you divide the double total by the integer number of tests, the resulting average is a double by default.

The program in Figure 3-11 does not use a for loop for data entry. Such a loop would require the user to enter test scores a fixed number of times. Instead, the user sees a prompt for the first test score. A while loop controls further data entry. As long as the user does not enter 999, the user's entry is added to a total, the subscript is incremented, and the user is prompted for the next test score. A value like 999 is commonly called a sentinel or a dummy value. A **sentinel** or **dummy** is any value that stops a loop's execution. Naturally, you want to choose a sentinel that cannot be a legitimate test score. The loop in Figure 3-11 ends only when the user enters 999. (If 999 is a possible test score, you want to choose a different value as the sentinel.)

Every time the user enters a test score, the subscript test is incremented. After one entry, the test variable assumes the value 1; after two entries, test has a value of 2, and so on. Each subsequent data entry value is stored as the next array element. When the user enters 999, whether 2 scores or 20 scores have been entered, the value in test is equivalent to the number of entries made. When the loop ends, the value stored in the test variable can be used for two purposes. First, it can serve as a sentinel value for the loop that displays all the entered scores. If six scores have been entered, you want to display scores 0 through 5. Second, it can be used as the divisor in the average calculation—an average can be computed by dividing the sum of all the scores by the number of test scores entered.

In the next set of steps, you enter the program from Figure 3-11 and modify the program to better understand some of its properties and discover some of its flaws.

1. Open a new file in the editor you use to write C++ programs. Copy the program from Figure 3-11, save it as **TestScores.cpp** in the Chapter03 folder of your Student Data Disk or of the Student Data folder on your hard drive. Compile it until it is error-free. Make sure you save the final, error-free version.

2. Run the program. Respond to the prompts with test scores such as **70, 80**, and **90**. Enter the sentinel value **999** to halt the data entry process and confirm that the displayed average is correct.

3. Run the program again. Respond to the prompts with test scores, such as **90, 91, 92**, and **94**, that do not produce an integer average. Enter **999** to stop the data entry, and confirm that the output average is correct.

4. Make sure to save the program. The next step can shut down your C++ compiler, and if you have not saved the program code, you will lose it. Run the program again. This time, enter more than 30 test scores before entering the 999. Nothing in the current program stops you from entering more scores than the array can hold. As the subscript increases with each pass through the loop, your next entry is stored at one location further from the beginning address of the array. Depending on the number of entries you continue to make, your system will accept the additional entries but destroy values that are in memory beyond the reserved area for your array, or the system might shut down and issue an error message. In either case, you want to correct the problem.

5. Reopen the **TestScores.cpp** file if necessary. Currently the data entry loop stops only when the user enters 999 for a test score. You want the loop to stop either

when the user enters 999, or when the number of scores exceeds 30. To make this improvement, the line that tests for the sentinel value must be changed from `while(testScore[test] != 999)`to:

while(testScore[test] != 999 && test < 30)

The test variable that keeps track of the number of the score currently being entered must be less than 30 for the loop to continue. A legitimate thirtieth test score in array position number 29 is correctly added to the total, but an illegal thirty-first test score in array position 30 is not—the loop ends before the thirty-first entry can added to the total. Save the revised program as **TestScores2.cpp**.

6. Compile and run the program. Enter 30 scores, such as **50**, thirty times. At the thirty-first prompt, enter a different value, such as **100**. The way the program works now, if you enter 30 test scores, test scores 0 through 29 are added correctly to the total before the average is computed, but the program still prompts you for a thirty-first test score that is never used and does not become part of the total or average. In the while loop, immediately after the thirtieth score (score 29) is added to the total, test is increased to 30, a prompt is issued, and the thirty-first test score is read in with the cin statement. Once again, you have entered data one element beyond the reserved memory for the array.

7. To remedy this problem, you insert an if statement to control data entry. Position the insertion point at the beginning of the statement that prompts for each score after the first score, and press the **Enter** key. Type the if statement that prevents the prompt and data entry statement from executing when test reaches a value of 30. Insert an opening curly brace on the next line, and insert a closing curly brace after the cin statement. The if block appears as follows:

if(test <ƒ30)
    {
    cout<<"Enter next test score or 999 to quit ";
    cin>>testScore[test];
    }

8. Save the file as **TestScores3.cpp**. Compile and run the program several times, and confirm that when you enter two scores, 20 scores, or 30 scores, you get the correct results. Also confirm that when you enter 30 scores you don't receive an erroneous thirty-first prompt.

9. As a final improvement to the program, insert a constant to use for the array size. Insert a new line in the program just before `int testScore[30];` and type **const int arraySize = 30;**. Then replace the three constant 30s that appear later in the program with the newly named constant, arraySize:

int testScore[arraySize];
while(testScore[test] != 999 && test < arraySize)
and
if(test < arraySize)

10. Save the program as **TestScores3.cpp**. Compile and run it, and confirm that the results are accurate.

Using Parallel Arrays

When you want to access an array element, you use the appropriate subscript. If each array element's position has a logical connection to the array value's purpose, accessing an array value is a straightforward process.

For example, consider a program that determines the health insurance premiums for employees who have 0, 1, 2, or 3 dependents. If you store the four premium amounts in an array, you can access the correct premium by using the dependent number. Of course, you should ensure that any subscript you use does not attempt to access values beyond the end of the array. Figure 3-12 shows a program that stores four premium amounts in an array, prompts the user for a number, ensures the number is no larger than 3, and displays the appropriate premium. Figure 3-13 shows the output of a typical run of the program. The program is simple because dependent numbers are small whole numbers that conveniently correspond to subscripts that arrays use.

```cpp
// Determines premiums based on dependents
#include<iostream.h>
#include<conio.h>
void main()
{
    double premium[4] = {49.95, 76.25, 93.55, 102.95};
    int dependents;
    cout<<"How many dependents do you have? ";
    cin>>dependents;
    if (dependents > 3)
        dependents = 3;
    cout<<"Your premium is $"<<premium[dependents]<<endl;
    getch();
}
```

Figure 3-12   A program that determines insurance premiums

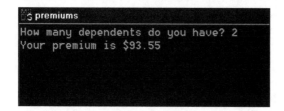

Figure 3-13   Output of program from Figure 3-12

Unfortunately, sometimes the numbers you need to access appropriate array values are not small whole numbers. Consider a company that manufactures parts that have different part numbers and prices, shown in Table 3-1. If you write a program in which you ask the user for a part number so that you can display the price, you cannot use the part number as a subscript to a price array unless you create a price array with at least 456 elements. Creating an array with 456 elements that need to store four prices is cumbersome and inefficient. A better solution is to create two arrays of just four elements each—one to hold the four part numbers, and one to hold the four prices that correspond to those part numbers. Such corresponding arrays are called **parallel arrays**.

Table 3-1 Part numbers and prices for a manufacturing company

Part number	Price
210	1.29
312	2.45
367	5.99
456	1.42

Figure 3-14 shows a program that declares two arrays. One stores the four integer part numbers; the other stores the four double prices that correspond to those part numbers. After the user enters a needed part, the program loops four times. If the needed part number is equivalent to partNum[0], then partPrice[0] is displayed. Alternately, if the needed part number is equivalent to partNum[1], then partPrice[1] is displayed.

```cpp
// Part prices
#include<iostream.h>
#include<conio.h>
void main()
{
   const int arraySize = 4;
   int partNum[arraySize] = {210, 312, 367, 456};
   double partPrice[arraySize] = {1.29, 2.45, 5.99, 1.42};

   int neededPart;
   int x;
   cout<<"Enter the part number you want ";
   cin>>neededPart;
   for(x = 0; x< arraySize; ++x)
   if (neededPart == partNum[x])
        cout<<"The price is "<<partPrice[x]<<endl;
   getch();
}
```

Figure 3-14 Program that determines part prices

In the next set of steps, you create the program that determines the correct price number for a part, and then improve the program.

1. Open a new file in your C++ editor, and type the program shown in Figure 3-14. Compile the program and correct any errors. When you have corrected all the syntax errors, save the program as **PartPrices.cpp** in the Chapter03 folder of your Student Data Disk or of the Student Data folder on your hard drive.

2. Run the program. At the prompt, enter a part number such as **367**, and confirm that the correct part price is shown.

3. Improve the program by listing the available part numbers. Place the insertion point at the beginning of the statement that prompts the user for the part number, and press the **Enter** key to start a new line. Then enter the following code that displays the available part numbers:

```
cout<<"Part number list"<<endl;
for(x = 0; x< arraySize; ++x)
    cout<<"#"<<partNum[x]<<endl;
```

4. Save the file as **PartPrices2.cpp**, then compile and run the program. The output of a typical run looks like Figure 3-15.

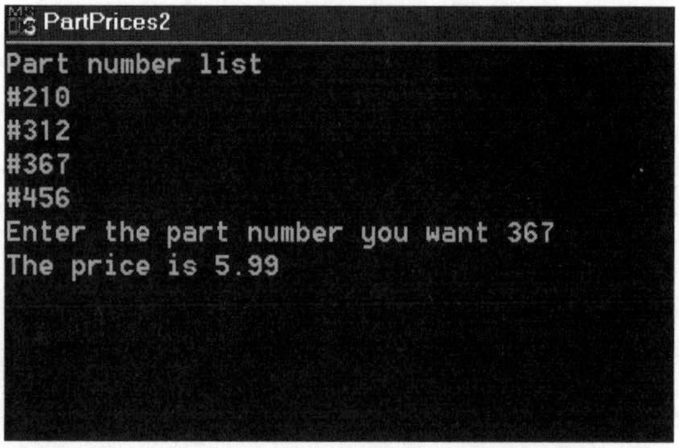

```
PartPrices2
Part number list
#210
#312
#367
#456
Enter the part number you want 367
The price is 5.99
```

Figure 3-15   Output of PartPrices2.cpp

5. The program works correctly as long as the user enters an existing part number. Run the program again and, at the prompt, enter an invalid part number such as **111**. Nothing happens. You can argue that nothing *should* happen, because there is no valid price for part 111. However, a user who thinks there is a part number 111 will be frustrated by the lack of response from the program. To make the program more user-friendly, you can add a flag variable that you initialize to 0, and turn to 1 when a price is found. At the conclusion of the program, you can check this flag variable's value and determine whether you want to display a message for the user. To add the flag variable, insert a new line among the other variable declaration lines near the top of the program, and type the following statement that declares a flag named found and initialize it to 0:

int found = 0;

6. Currently, only one statement executes when the neededPart equals a partNum—the appropriate price prints. In addition to executing the cout statement, if the comparison is true, you want to set the found flag to 1. The resulting code follows (the new code that you type is in boldface):

if(neededPart == partNum[x])
{
    cout<<"The price is "<<partPrice[x]<<endl;
    found = 1;
}

7. On the line following the if block, add a new if statement that displays an error message when the found flag has not been set to 1:

if(found ==0)
    cout<<"You entered an invalid part number!"<<endl;

8. Save the file as **PartPrices3.cpp**. Compile and run the program several times. At the prompt, enter both valid and invalid part numbers until you are assured that the program executes correctly.

An alternative to creating parallel arrays for the part numbers and their prices is to create a single array of part objects, and allow each part object to hold fields for part number and price. In the next section, you learn to create arrays of class objects.

Creating Arrays of Class Objects

Just as you can create arrays of simple types such as int and double, you can create arrays of class objects. For example, consider the Automobile class shown in the program in Figure 3-16. Each Automobile object you create has two public fields: year and milesPerGallon. You create an array of Automobiles the same way you create any other array: you use the type name, the array name, and square brackets in which you place an integer value that indicates the number of memory locations to reserve. The program in Figure 3-16 creates an array of four Automobile objects.

To access any individual class object field, you use the object's individual name, including its subscript, followed by a dot and the field name. For example, the year of the first Automobile in the fleet array is fleet[0].year. Examine the program in Figure 3-16 to see how all the fields of each Automobile object are accessed and used.

```
#include<iostream.h>
#include<conio.h>
class Automobile
{
  public:
    int year;
    double milesPerGallon;
};
void main()
{
  const int fleetSize = 4;
  Automobile fleet[fleetSize];
  int x;
  double total = 0, avg;
  for(x=0; x<fleetSize; ++x)
    {
       cout<<"Enter car year ";
       cin>>fleet[x].year;
       cout<<"Enter miles per gallon ";
       cin>>fleet[x].milesPerGallon;
       total += fleet[x].milesPerGallon;
    }
  avg = total / fleetSize;
  for(x=0; x<fleetSize; ++x)
    {
       cout<<"The "<<fleet[x].year<<" car gets "
       <<fleet[x].milesPerGallon<<endl;
    }
  cout<<"The fleet average is "<<avg<<" miles per gallon."<<endl;
  getch();
}
```

Figure 3-16   Creating an array of class objects

```
arraysofobjects
Enter car year 2001
Enter miles per gallon 12.6
Enter car year 2003
Enter miles per gallon 24.5
Enter car year 1998
Enter miles per gallon 16.7
Enter car year 2001
Enter miles per gallon 32.4
The 2001 car gets 12.6
The 2003 car gets 24.5
The 1998 car gets 16.7
The 2001 car gets 32.4
The fleet average is 21.55 miles per gallon.
```

Figure 3-17   Output of program from Figure 3-16

3

USING STRINGS

In C++ a character variable can hold a single character value, such as 'A' or '$'. Single character values are always expressed within single quotation marks. In C++, if you want to express multiple character values, such as a first name or a book title, you use double quotation marks. A C++ value expressed within double quotation marks is commonly called a **string**.

You can type two characters within single quotation marks, but only when they represent a single character. For example, '\n' represents the newline character. (Remember, the newline character contains the code that moves subsequent output to the next line.) You actually type a slash and an n within the single quotation marks, but you can do so only because the combination represents one character stored in computer memory.

You already have used strings with cout statements, as in `cout<<"Hello";`. Just as a value such as 14 is a numeric constant, a value such as "Hello" is referred to as a **string constant**. When you want to store a value such as 14 in a variable, you declare a numeric variable by giving it a type and a name. When you want to store a value such as "Hello", you must create a string variable, which is actually an array of characters.

In C++ an array of characters and a string are declared in the same way. You might create an array of characters if you need to store six one-letter department codes, or five one-letter grades that can be assigned on a test. These examples are called character arrays. When you want to store related characters, such as someone's name, you also store the individual characters in an array. However, C++ programmers do not refer to an array of characters as a string unless the last usable character in the string is the null character. The **null character** is represented by the combination '\0' (backslash and zero), or by using the constant NULL that is available if you use the statement `#include<iostream.h>` at the top of any file you compile.

The constant NULL is defined in several other include files in addition to iostream.h. However, if you are including iostream.h because you want to use cin and cout, then you automatically have access to the NULL constant.

If you want to declare a string named firstName and initialize it to "Mary", each of the following statements provides the same result. Each statement reserves five character positions, and stores an 'M' at firstName[0], an 'a' at firstName[1], an 'r' at firstName[2], a 'y' at firstName[3], and a '\0' at firstName[4].

```
char firstName[] = {"Mary"};
char firstName[5] = {"Mary");
char firstName[5] = {'M', 'a', 'r', 'y', '\0'};
```

Assuming the compiler assigns the firstName array to memory address 2000, and assuming that character variables occupy one byte of storage in your computer system, Figure 3-18 shows how firstName looks in memory.

char firstName = {"Mary"}

firstName[0]	firstName[1]	firstName[2]	firstName[3]	firstName[4]
M	a	r	y	\0

| address | 2000 | 2001 | 2002 | 2003 | 2004 |

Figure 3-18   A string in memory

When you use cout to display a string, as in the statement `cout<<firstName;`, cout begins to display characters at the memory address firstName, and continues to display characters until it encounters a NULL. Whether you write `cout<<firstName;` (output starting at firstName) or `cout<<&firstName[0];` (output starting at the address of the first character of firstName), the output is the same. Output for each statement starts at the beginning address of the array named firstName, and prints characters until the NULL is encountered. If you destroy the NULL at the end of firstName, perhaps by making the statement `firstName[4]= 'X';`, then the results of `cout<<firstName;` are unpredictable. The next NULL might be stored at the next byte of memory, or it might be hundreds or thousands of bytes away. C++ prints every character, starting at the beginning address, until it encounters the NULL.

If you create a firstName string and initialize it to "Mary", and then use the C++ statement `cout<<&firstName[1];`, the output is *ary*. Output begins at the address of firstName[1] (the 'a'), and continues until the NULL (the next character after the 'y').

You can easily provide additional space for a string. For example, the statement `char firstName[15] = {"Mary"}` assigns 'M' to firstName[0], and so on, just as in the string declared with five characters. The difference is that with this string, positions 5 through 14 are unused. The statement `cout<<firstName;` still displays the four letters of "Mary" and stops at the NULL.

Special String Handling Problems

Strings present some special handling problems. When you use the cin statement with a string, cin stops adding characters to the string when it encounters white space. Often, this means that cin stops when the user presses the Enter key. But cin also stops when the user presses the spacebar or the Tab key. Consider the short program in Figure 3-19 that prompts a user for a name. After the user enters a name, the program echoes it. If the user types *Mary* and then presses the Enter key, the output is *You entered Mary*. However, if the user types *Mary Ann* and then presses the Enter key, the output also is *You entered Mary*, as shown in Figure 3-20.

```
// Demonstrating string data entry
#include<iostream.h>
#include<conio.h>
void main()
 {
   char name[10];
   cout<<"Enter a name ";
   cin>>name;
   cout<<"You entered "<<name;
   getch();
 }
```

Figure 3-19   A program that reads a name

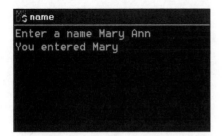

Figure 3-20   Sample run of the program from Figure 3-19

When the user types Mary Ann in the program in Figure 3-19, the cin statement accepts Mary into the string and leaves Ann waiting in an area called the **input buffer**. If the program contains a subsequent cin statement, then Ann is accepted and assigned to the string named in the second cin statement. For example, the program shown in Figure 3-21 produces the output in Figure 3-22. Even though the user types Mary Ann all at once, the first cin accepts only Mary, which is shown. The second cin accepts Ann without the user typing anything new—the Ann was in the input buffer waiting for another cin to execute.

As you continue your study of C++, you will learn how to use cin functions such as `cin.get()` to accommodate multiple word string entries.

```
#include<iostream.h>
#include<conio.h>
void main()
 {
   char firstName[12];
   cout<<"Enter a name ";
   cin>>firstName;
   cout<<"First name is "<<firstName<<endl;
   cin>>firstName;
   cout<<"First name is "<<firstName<<endl;
   getch();
 }
```

Figure 3-21   Using two cin statements

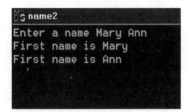

Figure 3-22   Output of program from Figure 3-21

Another string handling problem occurs when you attempt to assign one string to another. For example, suppose you have a string defined as `char clubPresident[10] = {"Eric"};` and another string defined as `char clubVicePresident[10] = {"Danielle"};`. If you want to assign the `clubVicePresident` name to the `clubPresident` name, you might suppose a statement like `clubPresident = clubVicePresident;` would be appropriate. The problem is that clubPresident and clubVicePresident are not simple variables. They are arrays, and array names are addresses. The C++ compiler, not the programmer, decides where program components are located. You cannot change the address of an array, which is what you are attempting to do by assigning a value to clubPresident.

To assign the name of the clubPresident to the same name as the clubVicePresident, you must assign each character value in the clubVicePresident name to the corresponding character location in the clubPresident name. You can take three approaches to accomplish this. One is to assign each character, one by one, as in:

```
clubPresident[0] = clubVicePresident[0];
clubPresident[1] = clubVicePresident[1];
clubPresident[2] = clubVicePresident[2];
```

… and so on.

A more elegant approach is to provide a loop to assign the characters:

```
for(x = 0; x<10; ++x)
   clubPresident[x] = clubVicePresident[x];
```

Although the looping solution moves each character from the clubVicePresident string to the clubPresident string, you can use a built-in C++ function instead. You have written main() functions to run a program, and you have used the C++ getch() function to get a character from the keyboard. Because programmers often want to store the contents of one string in another string, C++ designers provide a function that copies one string to another, relieving you of the responsibility of writing character-by-character loops each time you want to store one string in another. The function name is strcpy(). It takes the form *strcpy(destinationString, sourceString);*. For example, `strcpy(clubPresident, clubVicePresident);` results in the vice president's name being copied to the clubPresident string.

Depending on your compiler, you might have to use the statement `#include<string.h>` at the top of your file to use the strcpy() function.

A related string-handling problem occurs when you try to compare two strings. For example, if you want to determine whether clubPresident and clubVicePresident have the same name, it might seem natural to write a statement such as:

```
if(clubPresident == clubVicePresident)
    cout<<"They are the same"<<endl;
```

However, if you remember that clubPresident and clubVicePresident are array names, and therefore addresses, then you realize that the if statement is comparing only their memory addresses. Because clubPresident and clubVicePresident are two separate arrays, their addresses are never equal even though their contents can be.

You could write instructions to compare two strings by comparing each character of one string to the corresponding character in the other string, such as in the following:

```
if(clubPresident[0]==clubVicePresident[0] &&
clubPresident[1]==clubVicePresident[1]. . .
```

You also can replace this tedious method with the built-in function strcmp(). The string compare function strcmp() takes the form strcmp(firstString, secondString). If two strings are equal, then the value of the strcmp function is 0. The program in Figure 3-23 illustrates how to use the strcmp function. When firstName and secName each contain the string "Mary", then the result of strcmp(firstName,secName) is 0, indicating no difference in the names. When you replace the contents of one string with "Danielle", the result of strcmp(firstName,secName) is not 0, indicating a difference.

Depending on your compiler, you might have to add the preprocessor directive `#include<string.h>` to the program shown in Figure 3-23 in order to use the strcmp() function. If you do, you can omit it from the actual program or insert it after #include<conio.h>.

```
#include<iostream.h>
#include<conio.h>
#include<string.h>void main()
{
   char firstName[10] = {"Mary"};
   char secName[10] = {"Mary"};
   if(strcmp(firstName,secName)==0)
      cout<<firstName<<" and "<<secName<<" are the same"<<endl;
   else
      cout<<firstName<<" and "<<secName<<" are different"<<endl;
   strcpy(firstName, "Danielle");
   if(strcmp(firstName,secName)==0)
      cout<<firstName<<" and "<<secName<<" are the same"<<endl;
   else
      cout<<firstName<<" and "<<secName<<" are different"<<endl;
   getch();
}
```

Figure 3-23   Using the strcmp() function

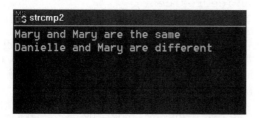

Figure 3-24   Output of program from Figure 3-23

 If the first string used in the strcmp function is alphabetically greater than the second string, as in strcmp("Zack", "Alice"), then the value of strcmp is a positive number. If the value of the first string is alphabetically less than the second string, then the value of the strcmp function is a negative number.

Declaring an array of strings poses a few special problems. To solve them, you must learn to use a two-dimensional array. For example, to declare an array of 5 names that can hold up to 10 characters each (counting the NULL), you declare char name[5][10];. The first subscript, 5, indicates that you are reserving five separate memory locations that are each ten characters long. You access each name with a single subscript. For example, to print the first name, you type cout<<name[0];. You access each character with two subscripts. For example, to print the first letter of the first name, you type cout<<name[0][0];.

Newer compilers contain a class named string. If your compiler allows, you can use #include<string> and the statement using namespace std; at the top of your file. Then you can declare a string object as string name;. To give the string an initial value, you can use string name = "Amy"; or string name("Amy");. You will learn more about classes such as string, and the meaning of namespace as you continue to study C++.

3

USING POINTERS

You can access the value of any variable by using the variable's name. In contrast, inserting an ampersand in front of the variable's name allows you to access its address.

You also can declare variables that can hold memory addresses. These variables are called pointer variables, or simply **pointers**. You declare a pointer with a type, just like other variables. The type indicates the type of variable that has an address held by the pointer. To indicate that a variable is a pointer, begin the variable's name with an asterisk. For example, int *aPointer; declares an integer pointer variable named aPointer. The aPointer variable can hold the address of any integer. For example, if you declare int myValue;, then you can make the assignment, aPointer = &myValue;. You then can output the contents of myValue in one of two ways:

        cout<<myValue;

or

        cout<<*aPointer;

The statement cout<<myValue; tells the program to display the value stored at the memory location myValue. The statement cout<<*aPointer; tells the program to display the value stored at the address held in aPointer. Because the address held in aPointer is the address of myValue, the output from both statements is the same. You interpret *aPointer as "the contents at the address pointed to by aPointer," or, more simply, as "the contents at aPointer."

You can output the address of myValue in one of two ways:

        cout<<&myValue;

or

        cout<<aPointer;

You read the first statement above as "Output the address of the variable myValue"; you read the second as "Output the value of aPointer, which currently is the address of the myValue variable."

The major difference between using a pointer name and the address operator with a variable name is that a pointer is a variable. That is, once you create a pointer, you can assign the address of any variable of the same type to the pointer, and you also can change the address stored in the pointer as many times as you want. For example, if you declare three integers named x, y, and z, and an integer pointer named aPointer, then you can make any or all of the statements aPointer = &x;, aPointer = &y;, and aPointer = &z. However, the address of a variable, such as &myValue, is a constant. You cannot assign any other value to the address of the myValue variable; its address is fixed and unalterable at the time you compile the program.

Using a Pointer Instead of an Array Name

Advanced C++ programmers use pointers for many purposes. Sometimes they use a pointer as an alternative to an array name. Remember that any array name is actually a memory address, and that pointers hold memory addresses. Therefore, a pointer also can hold an array name, as long as the pointer type and array type are the same.

The program illustrated in Figure 3-25 shows four different ways to access the same seven values. The program declares an integer array with sales figures for seven days for a small business. The program also declares an integer pointer and assigns the address of the first sales figure to that pointer. Then the program displays the same sales figures using four different methods. The four lines of output, all identical, are shown in Figure 3-26.

```
#include<iostream.h>
#include<conio.h>
void main()
{
  int sales[7] = {500, 300, 450, 200, 525, 800, 1000};
  int *p = &sales[0];
  int x;
  for(x = 0; x < 7; ++x)
     cout<<"$"<<sales[x]<<"   ";
  cout<<endl;
  for(x = 0; x < 7; ++x)
     cout<<"$"<<p[x]<<"   ";
  cout<<endl;
  for(x = 0; x < 7; ++x)
     cout<<"$"<<*(sales + x)<<"   ";
  cout<<endl;
  for(x = 0; x < 7; ++x)
     cout<<"$"<<*(p + x)<<"   ";
  cout<<endl;
  getch();
}
```

Figure 3-25   A program that uses array and pointer notation

Figure 3-26 Output of program from Figure 3-25

The first loop shown in Figure 3-25:

```
for(x = 0; x < 7; ++x)
    cout<<"$"<<sales[x]<<"   ";
cout<<endl;
```

shows traditional array and subscript notation. The array name is used with a subscript, x, that takes on the sequence of values from 0 through 6. Each of the seven sales figures is output, preceded by a dollar sign and followed by two spaces.

The second loop in the program:

```
for(x = 0; x<7; ++x)
    cout<<"$"<<p[x]<<"   ";
cout<<endl;
```

shows that the pointer variable p can be used in exactly the same manner as the array name sales. The array name sales is a memory address, or constant pointer, and p is a variable pointer that has been initialized to the beginning of the sales array. Both sales and p hold the same memory address, and either can be used with a subscript that indicates which value following the beginning address should be accessed. In other words, the subscript simply indicates how far away a value is from the starting address of the array.

The third loop shown in the program in Figure 3-25 is written using more complicated syntax:

```
for(x = 0; x < 7; ++x)
    cout<<"$"<<*(sales + x)<<"   ";
cout<<endl;
```

Although subscript notation is generally easier to understand, the third loop illustrates that if you access the contents (represented by the asterisk) of the address at sales (the beginning address of the array) plus x more integers (either 0, 1, 2, or so on), the result is that you access each succeeding value in the array.

The last loop:

```
for(x = 0; x<7; ++x)
    cout<<"$"<<*(p + x)<<"   ";
  cout<<endl;
```

is similar to the third one. The fourth loop displays the contents at the memory address p + 0, then the contents at the memory address p + 1, and so on. The address p + 0 is the same as the beginning address of the array. The address p + 1 is the same as the address one integer away from the beginning of the array, also known as &p[1], and in this case, also known as &sales[1].

As you continue to study C++, you will find many uses for pointers. For example, if you use character pointers to store constant string values, you avoid some of the problems you encountered when you used character arrays to hold constant string values. The program in Figure 3-27 declares two character pointers: firstName and secName. These pointer variables hold the address of the constants "Mary" and "Danielle". Assigning one pointer to another is much simpler than copying one string to another. Note the output shown in Figure 3-28. The result of the assignment firstName = secName; is that both pointers hold the address of the string that originally held the secName, "Danielle".

```
#include<iostream.h>
#include<conio.h>
void main()
{
  char *firstName = "Mary";
  char *secName = "Danielle";
  cout<<"First name is "<<firstName<<
    " and second name is "<<secName<<endl;
  firstName = secName;
  cout<<"First name is "<<firstName<<
    " and second name is "<<secName<<endl;
  getch();
}
```

Figure 3-27   Using pointers to hold strings

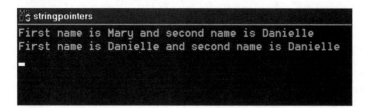

Figure 3-28   Output of program from Figure 3-27

Because pointers access computer memory locations, using pointers can be dangerous because you might point to and alter memory locations that you had no intention of altering. When you assign one variable to another, as in the statement x = y;, a copy of the value stored in y is assigned to the variable x; each variable holds its own copy of the same value. In the program in Figure 3-26, when you assign secName to firstName, you are not making a copy of the data; instead you are setting two pointers to point to the same memory location. Later, if you delete the value pointed to by one of the pointers, the other pointer is left without a value. This condition is known as creating a **dangling reference**. As you gain experience in C++, you will learn how to avoid this dangerous situation.

CHAPTER SUMMARY

❏ You can examine a variable's address by using the address operator (&).

❏ An array is a list of individual items that all have the same name and type and are located in adjacent memory positions. Array elements are distinguished from one another by their subscripts. An array name actually represents a memory address.

❏ You can assign values to array elements individually, using the assignment operator, or at initialization.

❏ You can access and use an individual array value the same way you would access and use any single variable of the same type. You can use either a constant or variable as a subscript when you access an array element.

❏ It is often convenient to declare a constant that is equal to the size of the array; this constant then can be used in every loop that accesses or uses all of the array elements.

❏ You can use a for loop to access all of the elements in an array; it is usually more convenient to use a while loop and a sentinel value to access some of the elements in an array.

❏ Programmers often use parallel arrays when they need one array to store values that correspond to values in another list of values.

❏ When you create arrays of class objects, you access the object's public fields by the object's individual name, including its subscript, followed by a dot and the field name.

❏ A C++ multiple-character value expressed within double quotation marks is commonly called a string. A value such as "Hello" is referred to as a string constant. A string variable is actually an array of characters, the last of which is the null character.

❏ Strings present some special handling problems. When you use the cin statement with a string, cin stops adding characters to the string when it encounters whitespace. You use the strcpy() function to assign one string to another, and the strcmp() function to compare the contents of one string to another.

❏ You can declare pointer variables that hold memory addresses.

❏ You can use a pointer as an alternative to using an array name.

REVIEW QUESTIONS

1. C++ uses the _____ as the address operator.

   a. ampersand

   b. dot

   c. asterisk

   d. percent sign

2. If you declare a variable as `int var = 5;` and the compiler stores var at memory address 3000, then the value of &var is _____.

   a. 5

   b. 3000

   c. 0

   d. unknown

3. A list of individual items that all have the same type is called a(n)_____.

   a. class

   b. structure

   c. array

   d. constant

4. You use a subscript to _____.

   a. indicate a position within an array

   b. identify empty classes

   c. define classes

   d. locate a variable at a specific, desired memory address

5. If you declare an array as `int numbers[10];`, then `number[1]` represents _____.

   a. the first element in the array

   b. the second element in the array

   c. the address of the array

   d. a new array with one element

6. If you declare an array as `double money[4];`, then `&money[2]` represents _____.

   a. the second element in the array

   b. the third element in the array

   c. the address of the array

   d. the address of the third element in the array

7. If you declare an array as `int scores[100];`, then the highest subscript you should use is _____.

   a. 0

   b. 99

   c. 100

   d. 101

8. If integers take two bytes of storage, then `int days[31];` reserves
   _____ bytes of memory.

   a. 30

   b. 31

   c. 60

   d. 62

9. If you want to store an integer array named list at memory location 2000, you make
   the statement _____.

   a. int list[] = 2000;

   b. &list[] = 2000;

   c. 2000 = &int list[0];

   d. You cannot locate an array at a specific address like 2000.

10. If you declare an array as `double prices[10];`, then the expression `&prices[2]`
    has the same meaning as the expression _____.

    a. prices + 2

    b. double prices[2];

    c. prices[2]

    d. &prices + &prices

11. If you declare an array as `int homeRuns[7];`, then the value of `homeRuns[0]`
    is _____.

    a. 0

    b. 7

    c. unknown

    d. illegal—you cannot access the value homeRuns[0]

12. If you declare an array as `int baskets[10] = {2,4,6};`, then the value of
    `baskets[0]` is _____.

    a. 0

    b. 2

    c. 4

    d. unknown

13. If you declare an array as `int vals[5];`, then you can double the value stored in
    vals[2] with the statement _____.

    a. vals[5] = vals[5] * 2;

    b. vals = vals * 2;

    c. vals[2] *= vals[2];

    d. vals[2] *= 2;

14. When you write a program in C++, an advantage of defining a constant to hold an array size is that _____.

    a. if you ever change the size of the array, you change the constant in a single location

    b. you are prevented from ever changing the program to accommodate a larger array size

    c. you can easily access only part of an array, if necessary

    d. you are not required to provide initial values for the array

15. A value that you use as input to stop a loop from continuing to execute is commonly called a(n) _____ value.

    a. guard

    b. sentinel

    c. initializer

    d. default

16. If you create a class named Dalmatian that has a public integer field named numSpots, then you can create an array of 101 Dalmatian objects with the statement:

    a. Dalmatian [101];

    b. Dalmatian [101].numSpots;

    c. Dalmatian litter[101];

    d. Dalmatian [101] litter;

17. If you create a class named Dalmatian that has a public integer field named numSpots, and you create an array of 101 Dalmatians named litter, then you can print the number of spots belonging to the first Dalmatian with the statement _____.

    a. cout<<Dalmatian[0].numSpots;

    b. cout<<litter[0].numSpots;

    c. c. cout<<Dalmatian.numSpots[0];

    d. cout<<litter.numSpots[0];

18. A C++ value expressed within double quotation marks is commonly called a _____.

    a. clone

    b. structure

    c. rope

    d. string

19. All C++ strings end with a(n) _____.

    a. null character

    b. period

    c. blank character

    d. exclamation point

20. If you declare an integer pointer as `int *pt;` and you declare an integer variable as `int num;`, then which of the following is legal?

   a. num = &pt;

   b. pt = #

   c. *num = *pt;

   d. &num = pt;

3

EXERCISES

1. Riley Residence Hall charges different rates for semester room and board based on the number of meals per day the student wants. The semester rate with no meals is $300. With one meal per day, the rate is $450. With two meals per day, the rate is $520, and with three meals per day, the rate is $590. Store these rates in an array. Write a program that allows a student to enter the number of meals desired per day. Output the semester room and board rate.

2. Write a program that allows the user to enter seven double values representing store sales for each day of one week. After all seven values are entered, display the value of the largest sale day.

3. Write a program that allows the user to enter 12 double values representing store sales for each month of one year. After all 12 values are entered, display the array position of the smallest value.

4. Write a program that allows the user to enter eight integer values. Display the values in the reverse order of the order they were entered.

5. Audubon High School is holding a fund-raiser. Declare an array that can hold contribution amounts for each of the four classes: freshman, sophomore, junior, and senior. Prompt the user for the four total contribution amounts. Display the four amounts and their average.

6. Addison High School is holding a fund-raiser. The freshmen, sophomores, juniors, and seniors hold a competition to see which class contributes the most money. Write a program that allows you to enter two numbers for each contribution as it comes in— the class of the contributor (1, 2, 3, or 4), and the amount contributed in dollars. For example, perhaps a junior contributes $20. The user would enter a 3 and a 20. The program continues to accept data until the user types 999 for the contributor's class. At that point, data entry is completed, so display the four class totals as well as the number of the class (1, 2, 3, or 4) that contributed the most.

7. Lucy Landlord owns five houses. She refers to these houses by the number of their street address. For example, when referring to "601 Pine", she simply says "601." The houses and their monthly rents are:

128	$500
204	$750
601	$495
609	$800
612	$940

Write a program into which Lucy can type the address number and then have the program display the appropriate rent.

8. Speedy Overnight Shipping uses four shipping methods: air, truck, rail, and hand delivery. Write a program that allows the user to type in a code, 'a', 't', 'r', or 'h'. Have the program display the shipping rate according to the following table:

Method	Rate
a	14.95
t	10.25
r	8.75
h	25.99

9. Norm's Custom Furniture Shop takes customer requests for dining room tables in oak, cherry, pine, and mahogany. Write a program that lets the user continue to enter the initial letter of a table order (for example, 'o' for oak). The user continues to enter letters, using 'z' as a sentinel. When the user has finished entering data, display a count of each code ordered.

10. Carthage Catering charges different meal prices, based on the total number of meals ordered, as follows:

Meals	Price each
1–10	14.99
11–20	12.50
21–39	10.75
40 or more	9.45

Write a program in which the user can enter the number of meals desired. Output is the price per meal and the total bill (meals ordered times price per meal).

11. Write a program that accepts your first name into a string variable. Display your name with an asterisk between each letter. For example, if your name is Lisa, display L*i*s*a.

12. Write a program that accepts your first name into a string variable. Print your name backward, for example, if your name is Lisa, display asiL.

3

13. Write a program that accepts a word into a string variable. Display a count of the number of letters in the word.

14. Write a program that accepts a word into a string variable. Display a count of the number of vowels and the number of consonants in the word.

15. Write a program that declares an array of ten integers. Write a loop that accepts ten values from the keyboard, and write another loop that displays the ten values. Do not use any subscripts within the two loops; use pointers only.

16. Each of the following files in the Chapter03 folder contains syntax and/or logical errors. Determine the problem in each case, and fix the program.

    a. DEBUG3-1

    b. DEBUG3-2

    c. DEBUG3-3

    d. DEBUG3-4

CASE PROJECT

You are developing a Fraction class for Teacher's Pet Software. The class contains two public data fields for numerator and denominator. Using the same class, write a main() function that declares an array of 5 Fraction objects. Prompt the user for values for each field of each Fraction. Do not allow the user to enter a value of 0 for the denominator of any Fraction; for each Fraction, continue to prompt the user for a denominator value until a non-zero value is entered. Display the numerator and denominator for each of the five Fraction objects. Then display the value of and array position of the highest numerator, and the value of and array position of the highest denominator.

4

USING C++ FUNCTIONS

In this chapter, you will learn:

◆ About using functions
◆ How to use procedural abstraction
◆ About scope rules
◆ How to construct function headers and prototypes
◆ How to return values from, and pass values to, functions
◆ How to use classes and objects as arguments to functions and as return types of functions
◆ How to pass addresses to functions
◆ How to use reference variables
◆ How to pass arrays to functions
◆ How to use inline functions
◆ How to use default arguments
◆ How to overload functions

No matter which computer programming language you use, large programs are usually broken down into modules. This strategy allows you to think of the programming task more abstractly—that is, you establish an overview of the major procedures before you determine the detailed steps within them. Creating modules makes it easier to work with programs, allows several programmers to write or modify modules in the same program, and enables you to create reusable program pieces. In C++, modules are known as functions. In this chapter, you learn to write functions, return values from functions, and pass values into functions. Additionally, you learn many of the finer points of using C++ functions, including using inline functions, default function arguments, and overloading.

USING FUNCTIONS AND INCLUDE FILES

Functions are modules that perform a task or group of tasks. (In other programming languages, the counterpart to a function is known as a **subroutine**, **procedure**, or **method**.) Each function can include its own variables and statements. You can write new C++ functions, and you can use functions that other programmers have written. You already have done both: you have written your own C++ main() functions, and you have used the prewritten function getch() to get a character at the end of a program. In C++, all function names are followed by a set of parentheses.

Any statement allowed in the main() function of a C++ program can be used in any other function. When you write a main() function, you can write other functions as part of the same file; alternately, you can store functions in their own files and then include them in other C++ programs with an #include statement.

Although the program in Figure 4-1 is simple, it demonstrates how a function is used within a program that displays a company logo on the monitor. Imagine that a co-worker creates a function called displayLogo() and stores it in a file called Logo.cpp. If you want to use the displayLogo() function to display your company logo and then display "Hello" on the screen, you would write the program shown in Figure 4-1.

```
#include<iostream.h>
#include<conio.h>
#include"Logo.cpp"
void main()
  {
    displayLogo();
    cout<<"Hello"<<endl;
  }
```

Figure 4-1   A main() function that uses the displayLogo() function

 Some programmers use the statement `return;` as the last line of code before the final curly brace in a void function. This statement signals that the program control returns to the calling function. However, when the void function ends, control returns to the calling program, whether or not the `return;` statement is included, so most C++ programmers don't bother typing it.

Figure 4-1 shows all that you need to use displayLogo(). You don't need to know what lines of code have been written within the displayLogo() function, nor how the function works. The function might contain one or 100 lines of code. To use this function, you need to know only the function's name and the name of the file in which it is stored (so you can use `#include` to include the file in your program).

With more complicated functions you also must know the function's argument types. You learn about function arguments later in this chapter.

If you write a program with a main() function, you cannot use `#include` to include yet another file that contains a main() function. Of all the functions included in the execution of a program, only one can be called main().

4

Notice that the #include statements used in the program in Figure 4-1 have different formats. When you use the standard files that come with the C++ compiler, angle brackets should surround the header filename. This format tells the compiler to search for the file in the standard folder that holds include files, such as iostream.h. When working with your own include files, use quotation marks. The compiler then searches in the active folder first. You also can give a full pathname such as: `#include "c:\mitchell\projects\myfile.cpp"`.

Instead of angle brackets, you can use quotation marks surrounding the standard include filenames, just as you can with your own filenames. Using quotation marks causes the compiler to look for the file in the active folder first, however, and it takes longer to locate the appropriate file. As a result, programmers generally use angle brackets for standard files, and quotation marks for their own files.

In Figure 4-1, the statement displayLogo(); is known as the **call to the function**. When the call is made, control of the program is transferred to displayLogo() and statements written in displayLogo() execute. When displayLogo() is completed, control of the program returns to main(), which then proceeds to the next instruction. When you write the main() function, you need not worry about whether displayLogo() is a function you write as part of the new program file, or whether it is stored in a separate file, requiring the #include statement.

When you write C++ programs that employ the input and output objects, cin and cout, you must use include files because cout and cin cannot be used without iostream.h. However, you can create your own include files. These files can contain functions or predefined constants. For example, if displaying your company logo simply means printing the name and address, you can write the displayLogo() function, as shown in Figure 4-2.

```
void displayLogo()
  {
    cout<<"Oriented Objects Inc."<<endl;
    cout<<"100 Division Street"<<endl;
  }
```

Figure 4-2   The displayLogo() function

The function header **void displayLogo( )** takes the same format as the **void main( )** function headers you have written. Notice in particular that a semicolon never follows any function header. Also, like the main() function, the displayLogo() function body appears within curly braces.

When you write a function like the one shown in Figure 4-2, you can compile it, but you receive error messages regarding **cout** and **endl**. They are undefined, because the iostream.h file is not included in this file. You do not need to include iostream.h in this function's file as long as the function is always used within another program that does include iostream.h (such as the program shown in Figure 4-1). However, you can add the statement **#include<iostream>** as the first statement in the function shown in Figure 4-2 so you can compile this file without error messages.

Although you can compile the file shown in Figure 4-2, you cannot execute it; it does not have a main() function. The file you can execute is the one shown in Figure 4-1; this file contains the main() function that calls the displayLogo() function. The output is shown in Figure 4-3—the company logo appears, followed by the "Hello" message.

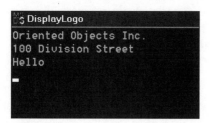

```
DisplayLogo
Oriented Objects Inc.
100 Division Street
Hello
```

Figure 4-3   Output of the program that calls the displayLogo() function

You are never required to place functions in their own files. The program file shown in Figure 4-4 compiles and executes in the same manner as the one shown in Figure 4-1. In Figure 4-4, the displayLogo() function and the main()) function coexist within the same file. No include statements are needed except those required by **cout**, **endl**, and **getch( )**. In the program shown in Figure 4-4, the displayLogo() function must be defined prior to the function that uses it. You can **define a function** by writing it above the function that uses it, or by including the function's filename at the top of the file that uses it. Programmers choose to organize a program's functions either in the same or separate files, or as they see fit.

If you want to write a function and physically place it in a file *below* the function that calls it, then you must declare the called function within the calling function. You learn how to declare functions, a process called prototyping, later in this chapter.

```
#include<iostream.h>
#include<conio.h>
void displayLogo()
  {
    cout<<"Oriented Objects Inc."<<endl;
    cout<<"100 Division Street"<<endl;
  }
void main()
  {
      displayLogo();
      cout<<"Hello"<<endl;
      getch();
  }
```

Figure 4-4   Alternative program file that uses displayLogo( )

> You cannot include a file that contains a function and then use the name of that function for another function within the file with your main() program. If you do, the compiler issues an error message saying that you have two different bodies for the same function.

In the next set of steps you write three functions—two functions that cannot execute alone, and the main() function that calls them.

1. Open a new file in your C++ editor. Write a function named myInfo() that displays at least three statements about you. For example, type the following text:

   void myInfo()
   {
   cout<<"My name is Sandy Madison."<<endl;
   cout<<"I am a full-time student."<<endl;
   cout<<"I am enrolled in a programming class."<<endl;
   }

2. Save the file as **MyInfo.cpp** in the Chapter04 folder of either your Student Data Disk or the Student Data folder on your hard drive.

3. Open a new file in your text editor, and write a function named courseInfo() that contains statements with information about the course you are taking. For example, type the following text:

   void courseInfo()
   {
   cout<<"This course teaches object-oriented programming."<<endl;
   cout<<"C++ is the programming language used."<<endl;
   }

4. Save the file as **CourseInfo.cpp** in the Chapter04 folder of either your Student Data Disk or the Student Data folder on your hard drive.

5. Open another new file, and write a program that includes the two files you just created. Within the program, call the two functions.

```
#include<iostream.h>
#include<conio.h>
#include"MyInfo.cpp"
#include"CourseInfo.cpp"
void main()
  {
    myInfo();
    courseInfo();
    getch();
  }
```

6. Save this program as **DemoFunctions.cpp** in the Chapter04 folder of either your Student Data Disk or the Student Data folder on your hard drive. Compile and run the program. Depending on the content of the statements you included within your functions, the output should look similar to Figure 4-5.

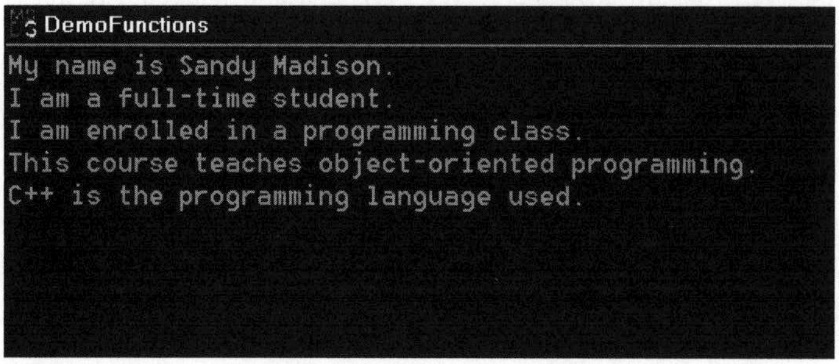

Figure 4-5   Output of DemoFunctions.cpp

USING PROCEDURAL ABSTRACTION

When you write functions that you include in other programs, you gain several benefits:

- The functions can be written once and subsequently included in any number of programs. For example, a well-written displayLogo() function might be used in dozens of programs within an organization.

- When you need to change the contents of the functions you write, you make the change in one location, and all the programs that use the function automatically receive the change. For example, if the company moves to a new location, you change the company address within the displayLogo() function. Then the change is automatically executed in every program that uses the function.

- When you write a main() program, you can condense many related actions into a single function call, making the main() program easier to write and simpler to read.

- When you use functions that already have been written for you, you gain an additional benefit: you do not need to worry about how the function works; you simply call it and let it work for you.

Writing a main() program that consists of a series of functional calls is called procedural abstraction. **Abstraction** is the process of extracting the relevant attributes of a process or object. It simplifies your concept of the process or object, allowing you to ignore inessential details.

To some extent, life would be impossible without abstraction. You use all sorts of objects— pencils, keys, forks, and so on—every day, without knowing their molecular structure. You use your telephone, although you might not understand the transmission of voice signals. As a programmer, you already have used objects such as cin and cout without knowing how each bit of the entered data is stored or displayed.

Using functions is one way to employ procedural abstraction in C++. Writing a to-do list is one way you employ procedural abstraction in everyday life. When you construct a to-do list, you note the main tasks to be accomplished. Figure 4-6 shows a to-do list you might create to remind you of tasks to accomplish during the day.

```
Write letter to Better Business Bureau
Annual review with Harrison
Gift for Mom
Lunch with Ralph
```

Figure 4-6   To-do list

You don't decide until later whether you'll print the letter on office letterhead or plain paper, or whether you'll meet with Harrison in your office or in a conference room. You don't even think about what you'll order for lunch, let alone how the digestion process works. If you got bogged down in such details, it would take too long to create the list or ever accomplish any of the tasks.

When you write a main() function, you can use the names of other functions that perform a variety of tasks. You don't need to worry about the details of the other functions, so the main program is easier to write, and easier for others to understand. Anyone reading a payroll program that uses the functions in Figure 4-7 can see the overall purpose of the program. Figure 4-7 shows a main() function that does nothing but call other functions. Even without being able to see the implementation of those functions, you can tell what the purpose of the program is.

```
void main()
  {
    computeGross();
    deductFederalTaxes();
    deductLocalTaxes();
    deductInsurance();
    printPaycheck();
  }
```

Figure 4-7   main() function employing procedural abstraction

Additionally, you can easily use any of these functions within any other program. By planning your programs with code reusability in mind, you train yourself to think in an object-oriented fashion. Reusing software components is an effective way to facilitate maintenance programming—a hallmark of object-oriented programming.

Whenever possible, you should strive to use functions that already have been written. If a colleague has written, tested, and used the displayLogo() function, it is a waste of time for you to reinvent it. If a programmer at another company has written a good deductFederalTaxes() module, it is probably less expensive to purchase and use it than to develop your own function. Similarly, when you design your own functions, keep the notion of reusability in mind. Future projects will go more smoothly if the functions you write and test now can be reused later.

In the next set of steps, you alter the myInfo() function you wrote in the last set of steps so that it includes additional information. Then you will rerun the DemoFunctions program without altering it to show how the function modification takes effect.

1. Open the **MyInfo.cpp** file that you created in the last set of steps. As the second output line, add a new statement about your birthplace. For example, type the following:

   cout<<"I was born in Dayton, Ohio."<<endl;

2. Save the file as **MyInfo.cpp** in the Chapter04 folder of either your Student Data Disk or the Student Data folder on your hard drive. Open the **DemoFunctions.cpp** file, and compile and run the program. The output should be similar to Figure 4-8. Even though you have not altered the DemoFunctions program, the output has been updated because the myInfo() function it calls has been updated.

```
DemoFunctions
My name is Sandy Madison.
I was born in Dayton, Ohio.
I am a full-time student.
I am enrolled in a programming class.
This course teaches object-oriented programming.
C++ is the programming language used.
```

Figure 4-8   Output of DemoFunctions with new myInfo() function

4

UNDERSTANDING SCOPE

Some variables can be accessed throughout an entire program, while others can be accessed only in a limited part of the program. The **scope** of a variable defines where it can be accessed in a program. To adequately understand scope, you must be able to distinguish between local and global variables. To avoid conflicts between local and global variables with the same name, you use the scope resolution operator.

Distinguishing Between Local and Global Variables

Some named objects in your life are global. At the office, if the conversation turns to Roseanne, Madonna, or Cher, you probably assume that your co-workers are talking about the same celebrities that people elsewhere talk about when they use those names. The names are **global** because they are known to people everywhere and always refer to those same celebrities. Similarly, global variables are those that are known to all functions in a program.

Some named objects in your life are **local**. When a co-worker speaks of "Jim in accounting" or "the taskmaster," you and others in your office understand the reference (and perhaps nod knowingly). People in the company across the street do not recognize these names, however. The references are local, just as some variables are local to a function.

You might have a local co-worker whose name takes precedence over, or **overrides**, a global one. If the sales manager in your company is named Roseanne, then co-workers are referring to her, and not the famous actress, when they use the name. Variables work the same way. A variable with a given name inside any function or block overrides any global variable with the same name, unless you take special action to specify use of the global variable.

Variables that are declared in a block (that is, between curly braces) are local to that block. They have the following characteristics:

- Local variables are created when they are declared within a block.
- Local variables are known only to that block.
- Local variables cease to exist when their block ends.

You can place pairs of curly braces anywhere within a C++ program and you always place curly braces at the beginning and end of every function, including main().

Therefore, variables declared within a function remain local to that function. In contrast, variables declared within curly braces within any function are local to that block.

In the program in Figure 4-9, note that the variable b comes into existence when it is declared, but ceases to exist when the program ends. The variable c has a much shorter life; it is only "alive" between the interior, nested braces. In other words, it is **in scope** between the brackets. Programmers also would say that c is **accessible** only within the braces.

```cpp
#include<iostream.h>
void main()
  {
    int b = 2;  // b comes into existence
    cout<<b;
     {
         int c = 3; // c comes into existence
         cout<<c;
     } // c dies — you can't use c anymore
    cout<<b;
  } // b dies — you can't use b anymore
```

Figure 4-9   Demonstrating scope

No variable can be accessed outside its scope, that is, beyond the block in which it is declared. You wouldn't try to use a variable before it is declared; similarly, you can't use it after it goes out of scope. Figure 4-10 shows a program that does not compile because it contains several attempts to access a variable outside its scope. Figure 4-10 also shows the use of a global variable named a. Because a is declared outside the main() function, a is accessible anywhere in the file.

The program shown in Figure 4-10 demonstrates that you can declare variables prior to or anywhere within a function, but the program does not demonstrate good technique for declaring variables. C++ programmers usually declare most of their variables inside and at the beginning of the function that uses the variables. That way, anyone reading the program sees all the variables and their types at the beginning of the function's code. A program will compile and run if the variable declarations are scattered throughout the functions, but if the variables are declared in the same place, it is easier to find them and to change their initial values later, if necessary. In addition, when you place the variables together, you can more easily see whether you are inadvertently giving two variables the same name.

C++ programmers often postpone declaring a variable at the beginning of a function when they use a loop control variable in a for statement:

```cpp
for(int x=0;x<10;++x)
    {
        cout<<x<<endl;
    }
```

Depending on your compiler, x exists only for the duration of the for loop, or until the end of the block in which the for loop resides.

```
#include<iostream.h>
int a = 1;              // declare a — it is global
void main()
   {
     int b = 2;         // declare b
     cout<<b;           // this is OK
     cout<<a;           // so is this
     {
       cout<<c;         // this won't work; c hasn't been declared yet
       int c = 3;       // declare c
       cout<<c;         // this statement is fine
       cout<<b;         // this is fine, too — still inside b's set
                        // of braces
       cout<<a;         // this is fine, too — a is global
     }                  // c goes out of scope here
     cout<<b;           // this statement is still fine
                        //    — still within b's braces
     cout<<c;           // this won't work; c is out of scope
     cout<<a;           // this is still fine
   }                    // b goes out of scope here
     cout<<b;           // won't work — program is over;
                        // b is out of scope
cout<<a;                // won't work — even though a is global
                        // all C++ statements must be in a function
                        // but if you start another function here,
                        // a is still accessible
void anotherFunction()
   {
     cout<<a;   // this is OK — a is global to this file
     cout<<b;   // won't work — b does not exist here
   }
```

Figure 4-10   An attempted misuse of variables outside their scope

 Even though you most often declare all variables at the beginning of a function, you must remember that every function body is a block. Therefore, all variables that you declare within a function are local to that function. Consider the program in Figure 4-11. The sayHello() function declares a variable named x. Because x is local to sayHello(), the main() function cannot use it. Similarly, the main() function declares a local variable named y and the sayHello() function cannot use it.

```
#include<iostream.h>
void sayHello()
  {
    int x = 12;     // x comes into existence within sayHello()
    cout<<"Hello";
    cout<<x; // 12 will display
    cout<<y;    // illegal — no y variable in this function
  }  // sayHello()'s x dies
void main()
  {
    int y = 13;
    sayHello();
    cout<<y;   // statement OK — y is local to main()
    cout<<x;   // this is not OK; x doesn't exist here
  }
```

Figure 4-11   Local variables

Figure 4-12 shows two functions, sayHello() and main(). Each x is local to the function in which it is declared; each x holds its own value. Even though they are declared within the same file, the two x's are completely different variables stored at separate memory addresses because they are declared locally within separate functions.

```
#include<iostream.h>
void sayHello ()
  {
    int x = 12;     // x comes into existence within sayHello()
    cout<<"Hello";
    cout<<x; // 12 will display
  }  // sayHello()'s x dies
void main()
  {
    int x = 13;   // x comes into existence within main()
    sayHello();
    cout<<x; // 13 will display
  } // main()'s x dies
```

Figure 4-12   More local variables

Using the Scope Resolution Operator

If the sayHello() and main() functions are written by different programmers, no conflict arises. Each programmer can use x as a variable name without destroying any values in the other's function. Just as two people can have the same name, so can two variables at different memory addresses have different names. But just as you develop different names for two Sue's who work in your office (maybe calling one Susie), you must not use the same name for two variables if they reside within the same function. A major advantage of using local variables is that many programmers can work on a large program, each writing separate functions, and they can use any variable names inside their own functions. These variables do not affect data stored in variables with the same names in other functions.

If you choose to create a global variable, you can use it even when a local variable with the same name exists. To do so, you use the **scope resolution operator**. Place this operator (the symbol ::) directly before the variable name. The :: causes the program to access the global variable, rather than the local variable. Figure 4-13 shows an example of how you can use the scope resolution operator to access a global variable that has the same name as a local variable. Within main( ), val refers to the local value, 315. When you use the scope resolution operator, you access ::val, which is 42. This situation is analogous to referring to two Sue's in your company as "Sue" and "Sue from marketing". The scope resolution operator serves to add information to and qualify a global name when the shorter version of that name conflicts with a local name.

4

```
#include<iostream.h>
int val = 42;   // global val
void main()
   {
   int val = 315;   // local val
   cout<<val;        //315 displays
   cout<<::val;      // 42 displays
   {
```

Figure 4-13   The scope resolution operator

Although you can declare global variables in any file, it is almost always considered better style to use local variables rather than global ones. This strategy represents a preliminary example of **encapsulation**, or data hiding. Think of local variables as being in a capsule, separated from all other functions which then cannot harm the values stored in the local variables. Beginning programmers often think it is easier to use global variables rather than local ones, because global variables are known to all functions. However, using global variables, rather than creating local variables in functions, is actually disadvantageous for the following reasons:

- If variables are global in a file and you reuse any functions in a new program, the variables must be redeclared in the new program. They no longer "come along with" the function.

- Global variables can be affected by any function, leading to errors. In a program with many functions, finding the function that caused an error can prove difficult.

CONSTRUCTING FUNCTION HEADERS AND PROTOTYPES

The header of a function consists of three parts:

- The type of object or variable that the function returns to the function that calls it (also known as the function's type)

- The name of the function

- In parentheses, the types and names of any variables that are passed to the function

For example, the main() functions you previously used have the header `void main()`. The displayLogo() function shown in Figure 4-2 has the header `void displayLogo()`. Each of these functions has the return type void because neither returns any value to the function that calls it. Each function name is followed by an empty pair of parentheses because neither function requires any value to be passed into them from any function that calls them.

You already know that you can write, or define, a function by placing it above and in the same file that has a calling program. You also know that you can define a function by placing it in its own file and using an include statement at the top of a calling program. You also can place a function in a file below the function that calls it. If you do so, you must declare or proto-type the function. To **prototype**, you create either a sample function outline or a description of how the actual function will look. When you declare a variable, you give it a type and a name. When you prototype a function, you declare it, so you give it a type and a name as well. A prototype contains four features:

- The type of object or variable that the function returns to the function that calls it (also known as the function's type)

- The name of the function

- In parentheses, the types of any variables that are passed to the function (the names of the variables are not required, but as a rule programmers frequently include the names)

- A semicolon. A prototype, unlike a function header, is a statement; therefore it ends with a semicolon.

You can see that the list of items required in a prototype is very similar to the list of items found in a function header. In fact, with minor differences, a function prototype must match very closely the function header to which it refers. For example, the function that displays a company logo named displayLogo() is written so that the function neither needs informa-tion from the function that calls it, nor sends any information back to the calling function. The displayLogo() function's header is `void displayLogo()`, and its prototype is `void displayLogo();`. The function header does not end in a semicolon; the prototype does. Figure 4-14 shows a complete main program that uses the displayLogo() function.

You also can write the prototype `void displayLogo();` as `void displayLogo(void);`. Because void means "nothing," these two prototypes have the same meaning. However, the pro-totype `void displayLogo()` does not mean the same thing as `displayLogo();`. You must include the keyword `void` in front of the function name to prototype a function that returns nothing. If you write a function and omit the return type, C++ assumes the function returns an integer. If you ever have written a main() function and used the header `main()` instead of `void main()`, you have received the compiler error message "Function must return a value." That is because the compiler expected main() to return an integer instead of nothing.

When programmers place auxiliary function bodies in the same file as their main() function, some prefer to store main() at the top of the file because it is most important. Others prefer to store main() at the bottom after the definitions of all the functions it uses. If, within main(), you prototype all the functions that main() uses, your program runs correctly either way.

4

```
#include<iostream.h>
#include"Logo.cpp"
void main()
  {
    void displayLogo();   // prototype of function
    displayLogo();        // call to function
  }
```

Figure 4-14   Program that prototypes displayLogo()

The statement `void displayLogo();` notifies the main program that the called function needs nothing and returns nothing. The statement `displayLogo();` actually calls the function. Although the program shown in Figure 4-14 runs without the prototype (because the include statement at the top of the file defines the displayLogo() function prior to main()), including a prototype for each function used within a C++ program is considered good style. Anyone reading the program is notified of what the function requires, and of what the function returns when it is used later in the program. Additionally, if you include a function's prototype within a program that uses the function, when you compile the program, the compiler checks to ensure you are calling the function correctly. If you are not calling the function correctly, you receive an error message from the compiler, and you can correct the error. If you do not prototype a function, the compiler does not detect any error you commit in the way you call the function. You might assume the program is correct, but when you try to run the program (or worse, someone else tries to run it), a fatal error occurs at execution time.

Some programmers write a function such as displayLogo() and save it in a file with a .cpp extension. Then they write the prototype and save it in a file with an .h extension, in which the h stands for "header." Finally, they include the .h file in the main() program file. This serves to include both the prototype and the function. Because some compiler problems can result when you compile your own files with an .h extension, this book uses .cpp as the extension for all programmer-created files.

Depending on your compiler, you can choose to or are required to use the .h extension for files you create and want to include in other programs. Some programmers prefer using a .h extension for any files that are meant to be included in other programs—in other words, for any files that do not have a main() method.

RETURNING VALUES FROM FUNCTIONS

The type of value that a function returns is also known as the **function's type** (or the function's return type). The functions you have used so far have been type void. That is, functions such as the displayLogo() function and main() do not return anything to the program that calls them. Sometimes, however, a function should send a value back to the calling program.

If you write a function that asks users to input their middle initial from the keyboard, you might prototype the function as char askUserForInitial();. This prototype indicates that the function returns a character value to the program that calls it. A programmer would say that askUserForInitial() is a function of type char, or more simply that it is a char function. Similarly, a function that computes a tax amount might return a double. Its prototype is double figureTaxes(); and it is a function of type double.

Functions used for data entry almost always return the entered data to a main() program or other calling function. For example, the purpose of the function askUserForInitial() is to prompt a user for a character entry. The main() program shown in Figure 4-15 uses the askUserForInitial() function, which is written below the main() function.

```
#include<iostream.h>
#include<conio.h>
// main program
void main()
  {
    char usersInitial;       // declare character variable
    char askUserForInitial(); // prototype function
    usersInitial = askUserForInitial(); // call function
                 // and assign return value to variable
    cout<<"Your initial is "<<usersInitial<<endl;
                 // display returned value
  }
// function
char askUserForInitial()
   {
     char letter;
     cout<<"Please type your initial and press Enter "<<endl;
     cin>>letter;
     return letter;
   }
```

Figure 4-15   Program that calls askUserForInitial()

In Figure 4-15, the main program holds two declarations: one for the character variable, usersInitial, and one for the character function, askUserForInitial(). Next, the program calls the askUserForInitial() function. The value that is returned from the function is assigned to the usersInitial variable. The screen then displays this variable.

The function askUserForInitial() declares a local variable named letter. At the prompt, the user types a character, which is stored in letter. The variable letter is local to the function. It goes out of existence when the function ends. Before the function ends, however, a copy of the contents of letter is returned to the main() program, where it is assigned to another variable, usersInitial.

 The statement `return letter;` in Figure 4-15 alternately can be written as `return(letter);`. Both statements work identically.

Figure 4-16 shows an alternate way to use the askUserForInitial() function. In this program, the value returned from askUserForInitial() is not assigned to any variable. Instead, the return value is used directly in the cout statement. This example works because askUserForInitial() acts just like a character, and is why programmers say this function is of type character or that it is a character function.

```
// main program
void main()
  {
    char askUserForInitial();// prototype function
    cout<<"Your initial is "<<askUserForInitial()<<endl;
    // display value returned from function
  }
// You can insert the askUserForInitial() function here
```

Figure 4-16   Alternate program that calls askUserForInitial()

It is perfectly legal to call a function that returns a value and then not use the value. For example, the main() program in Figure 4-17 calls askUserForInitial(), but neither displays its return value nor assigns it to any variable. When the program calls askUserForInitial(), the prompt appears and the user can enter a character. However, when the program displays its output, usersInitial does not contain the character input by the user; instead, usersInitial contains whatever values were stored in that location by chance when the variable was declared. The programmer surely meant to, but did not assign the return value of askUserForInitial() to the usersInitial variable prior to printing.

```
#include<iostream.h>
#include<conio.h>
// main program
void main()
 {
    char usersInitial;         // declare variable
    char askUserForInitial(); // prototype function
    askUserForInitial();       // call function
    cout<<"Your initial is "<<usersInitial<<endl;
          // displays garbage
 }
```

Figure 4-17   A legal but pointless use of askUserForInitial( )

In the next set of steps, you write a program that uses two functions to retrieve from the keyboard a worker's hourly rate and hours worked. The program uses the returned values to calculate and display weekly pay.

1. Open a new file in your C++ editor. Type comments indicating the purpose of this program, which is to demonstrate using functions that return values. Then type the include statements you need:

   #include<iostream.h>
   #include<conio.h>

2. Begin a main() function that declares a double variable for rate, and an integer variable for hours. The weekly pay is stored in a double variable.

   void main()
   {
       double rate;
       int hours;
       double weekly;

3. Add a statement to declare a getRate() function that returns a rate, and a getHours() function that returns hours worked:

   double getRate();
   int getHours();

4. The next statements call the functions and store their returned values in variables.

   rate = getRate();
   hours = getHours();

5. Finish the main() function by computing the weekly pay and printing it. Use the getch() function if necessary to hold the output on the screen, and include a closing curly brace to end main().

   weekly = rate * hours;
   cout<<"Weekly pay is "<<weekly<<endl;
   getch();
   }

You use the prewritten getch() function without seeing the code written for its implementation. The getch() function actually returns a character value (the character the user enters at the keyboard), so you could write a statement like `char keyboardValue = getch();`. However, because you don't care which character the user types, you have no reason to store the value in a variable.

6. After the closing curly brace of main(), you can write the getRate() function. This function prompts the user for a rate and returns the value to main(). Notice that the function uses a local variable named rate, the same name as the variable in the main() program. These are separate variables that reside at different memory addresses. Each is local to its own function.

```
double getRate()
   {
      double rate;
      cout<<"Enter your hourly rate in dollars and cents ";
      cin>>rate;
      return rate;
   }
```

7. Next, you write the getHours() function. This function prompts the user for a number of hours and returns that value to main(). Notice that the hours value is stored in a variable named time, but when it is returned to main(), the same figure will be stored in a variable named hours. Just as it was acceptable for the rate variable name to have the same name in two functions, the hours variable name can have different names in two functions. When time is returned from getHours(), its value will be assigned to rate in main(); the variable names make no difference at all.

```
int getHours()
   {
      int time;
      cout<<"Please enter the hours you worked"<<endl;
      cout<<"You must enter a whole number ";
      cin>>time;
      return time;
   }
```

8. Save the file as **HoursAndRate.cpp** in the Chapter04 folder of either your Student Data Disk or the Student Data folder on your hard drive, and then compile the program. After you correct any syntax errors, run the program. Depending on the values you supply at the input prompts, the output appears as in Figure 4-18.

```
 HoursAndRate
Enter your hourly rate in dollars and cents 12.55
Please enter the hours you worked
You must enter a whole number 40
Weekly pay is 502
```

Figure 4-18   Output of HoursAndRate.cpp

9. You also can use the return values of the getRate() and getHours() functions without storing them in any variable. If you don't declare variables to store the return values of these functions, you save the memory that would have been allocated for those variables; this is an option only if you do not need to access these the values again later in the program. In the main() function, delete the two lines that declare the rate and hours variables. Then, delete the two lines that call getRate() and getHours(), and assign their values to variables. Finally, change the line that multiplies rate by hours so that it multiplies the function return values directly: **weekly = getRate( ) * getHours( );**.

The new main() function looks like Figure 4-19.

```cpp
void main()
   {
      double weekly;
      double getRate();
      int getHours();
      weekly = getHours() * getRate();
      cout<<"Weekly pay is "<<weekly<<endl;
      getch();
   }
```

Figure 4-19   New main() function that does not store function return values

10. Save this version of the program as **HoursAndRate2.cpp** in the Chapter04 folder of either your Student Data Disk or the Student Data folder on your hard drive, and then compile and run the program. The output should be identical to that shown in Figure 4-18.

Each function in a C++ program can have only a single return type, and each time a function executes, it can return only one object or variable. A function can contain more than one return statement, but when that statement executes, it can return only one value. At that point the function ends, and the function cannot return any additional values. For example, each of the two functions shown in Figure 4-18 returns an integer. The purpose of each function is to return the larger of two values passed to the function (or the second value if the two parameters are equal).

The first version of the function contains two return statements. If the first return statement executes, control returns to the calling program immediately and the second return never executes. The first version of the function in Figure 4-20 works correctly, but the second version demonstrates superior style. The second version contains a local variable named larger. The variable is assigned the larger of x and y (or the value of y if the two variables are equal), and this value is returned to the calling function via a single return statement. The two versions of the function operate identically, but for clarity, many programmers prefer to see a single return statement as the last statement in a function body.

```
int findLarger(int x, int y)
 {
   if(x > y)
      return x;
   else
      return y;
 }

int findLarger(int x, int y)
 {
    int larger;
    if(x > y)
       larger = x;
    else
       larger = y;
    return larger;
 }
```

Figure 4-20   Two versions of findLarger()

PASSING VALUES TO FUNCTIONS

Many real-world functions you perform require that you provide information. A particular task might always be carried out in the same way, but with specific data. For example, all phone calls are placed in the same manner, but you supply a phone number to the process. All doctor's appointments are made in the same way, but you supply a date and time. Similarly, many functions need specific information from the main() or other functions that call them.

Consider a program that computes the amount of sales tax due on an item. After you prompt the user for a price, you want a function named computeTax() to calculate and print the tax amount that is due. You can create the computeTax() function as a type **void** function, as it does not need to return anything to the main() program. It does, however, need to obtain an item's price from the main() program. If the price is a double, then the computeTax()

function requires an *argument* or a *parameter* of type double. You can write the prototype for computeTax() in one of two ways:

```
void computeTax(int);
```

or

```
void computeTax(int price);
```

The prototype parentheses enclose a list of the variable types that are passed to the function; in this case the computeTax() function receives just one type of variable, an integer. You can choose to list just the type, or you can give the variable a descriptive name, such as price. If you use a name such as price, you do so to provide **documentation**; you help someone reading the function prototype to understand the function's purpose. The name price is simply descriptive; it does not have to match any variable name used anywhere else in the program. In a prototype, variable names actually play the same role as comments.

If more than one argument is passed into a function, you provide a list of arguments and separate them with commas. A type must be listed for each variable that is passed, even if two or more variables have the same type. For example, a function that computes the sum of four integers can have the prototype:

```
void funcToAddFourIntegers(int, int, int, int);
```

or

```
void funcToAddFourIntegers(int firstVal, int secondVal,
    int thirdVal, int lastVal);
```

 The variable names used in a prototype are immaterial because a function should be reusable. That is, a function that adds two integers should work for any two integers. Thus, `void sumFunction(int a, int b);` can be used with the variables c and d, with the variables score1 and score2, or with the variables januaryTotal and februaryTotal.

Figure 4-21 shows a complete program that uses the computeTax() function, and Figure 4-22 shows the results of a typical execution of the program. After the user enters the price in main(), the price is passed to the computeTax() function. You pass a value to a function when you place the value within the parentheses in the function call. Within the computeTax() function, price is known as amount. (It also would be fine if the name price were used within computeTax(), as long as every instance of amount is changed to price, including the declaration within the parentheses in the function header.) After being declared within the computeTax() function header, the variable named amount is used twice—within a multiplication calculation, and again as part of the output statement.

```
#include<iostream.h>
#include<conio.h>
void main()
  {
     double price;
     void computeTax(double price);
     cout<<"Enter an item's price ";
     cin>>price;
     computeTax(price);
     getch();
  }
void computeTax(double amount)
  {
     double tax;
     tax = amount * .07;
     cout<<"The tax on "<<amount<<" is "<<tax<<endl;
  }
```

Figure 4-21   Program using the computeTax() function

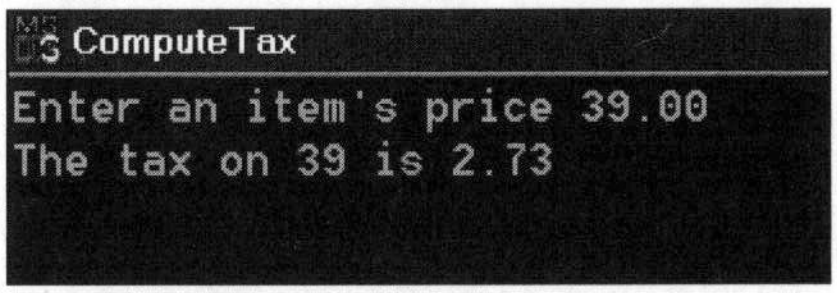

Figure 4-22   Output of the ComputeTax program

When price is passed to computeTax(), price is called an argument to the function, or an **actual parameter**, because price holds the value that will actually be used by the function computeTax(). When you use computeTax(), you do not have to pass a variable. Instead, you could pass a constant, as in the statement **computeTax(22.55);**. The computeTax() function must receive a double, but it does not matter whether the double is a variable or a constant.

When you call the computeTax() function, you cannot indicate the type for the price parameter. In other words, **computeTax(int price);** is an illegal function call. The function prototype indicates the type expected, and the function header specifies which, if any, types are accepted. Only the variable names or constant values that actually represent data to be sent to the function are needed in the function call.

The header of the computeTax() function indicates that it returns nothing to the program that calls it, but that it does accept an integer. The integer accepted from main() is a new variable declared locally within the parentheses of the computeTax() function header. Consequently, the passed variable can have either a different or the same name as the corresponding variables in the calling program. The local variable named in the function header receives a copy of the data stored in the variable in the actual parameters when this function was called. Any variable listed in a function header is known as a **formal parameter**. Such parameters serve as local variables for the function. They cease to exist when the function ends. During the life of the function, however, the formal parameter holds a copy of the value that is stored in the actual parameter in the main program, as shown in Figure 4-23.

```
void main()
  {
    .                  actual parameter price is passed to computeTax()
    .
    .
    computeTax(price);
    .
    .
  }
                       copy of actual parameter arrives and is stored in
                       formal parameter amt
void computeTax(double amt)
  {
    .
    .
    .
  }
```

Figure 4-23 The relationship between actual and formal parameters

You can pass any number of arguments to a function, as long as the function is prepared to receive them. You must make sure to use the correct order when you pass arguments to a function. For example, if you rewrite the computeTax() function so that it accepts a price and the tax rate, then one way you can write the function prototype is:

```
void computeTax(double amount, double taxRate);
```

When you call the new computeTax() function, you must make sure you pass an amount first, and then a rate. For example, to compute a 5% tax on $100.00, you write `computeTax(100.00, .05);`. It is legal to call the new computeTax() function with any two double arguments, so `computeTax(.05, 100.00);` executes, but you are calculating a 10,000% tax on five cents.

In addition to passing arguments in the correct order, make sure that the arguments you pass to a function are the correct type. If you write a function with the prototype `void determineFinalGrade(int quizScore, char termPaperGrade, double examPoints);`, and you call it with arguments that are not the right type in the right order, for example `determineFinalGrade(94.5, 35, 'A');`, then your program will not execute correctly.

In C++, a value you pass to a function will be cast to the correct type if possible. For example, you can pass an integer to a function that expects a double argument, because C++ automatically promotes integers to doubles. However, if you send a variable to a function and that variable cannot be automatically cast to the expected argument, data may be lost, incorrect results may be produced, or the program may refuse to run.

In the next set of steps, you modify the HoursAndRate program you wrote earlier so that results now print from within a function.

4

1. Open the HoursAndRate.cpp program you wrote earlier in this chapter. Immediately save it as **HoursAndRate3.cpp** in the Chapter04 folder of either your Student Data Disk or the Student Data folder on your hard drive.

2. Within the main() function, delete the line that declares the weekly variable. You no longer need this variable because the weekly pay will be calculated in a function.

3. Place the insertion point at the end of the line that declares the getHours() function (int getHours();) and press the **Enter** key to start a new line. Then, type the declaration for the function that accepts the rate and hours and calculates the weekly pay: **void printWeekly(double rate, int hours);**.

4. Place the insertion point after the statement that assigns a value to the hour variable (hours = getHours();), and press the **Enter** key to start a new line. Then, type the call to the printWeekly() function: **printWeekly(rate, hours);**.

5. At the bottom of the file, add the printWeekly() function definition. The function takes two arguments representing the rate and the hours, multiplies the arguments, stores the result in a local variable, and then prints the resulting pay value:

```
void printWeekly(double hourlyWage, int hrs)
  {
    double weekPay;
    weekPay = hourlyWage * hrs;
    cout<<"Weekly pay is "<<weekPay<<endl;
  }
```

Also delete the following text:

```
weekly = rate*hours;
cout<<"weekly pay is"<<weekly<<endl;
```

6. Save the file again, compile, and run the program. The results are the same as when you ran the original HoursAndRate program, but now all the action takes place in functions, and the main() program itself is very concise. Figure 4-24 shows the entire program listing.

```cpp
#include<iostream.h>
#include<conio.h>
void main()
    {
        double rate;
        int hours;
        double getRate();
        int getHours();
        void printWeekly(double rate, int hours);
        rate = getRate();
        hours = getHours();
        printWeekly(rate, hours);
        getch();
    }

double getRate()
    {
        double rate;
        cout<<"Enter your hourly rate in dollars and cents ";
        cin>>rate;
        return rate;
    }
int getHours()
    {
       int time;
       cout<<"Please enter the hours you worked"<<endl;
       cout<<"You must enter a whole number ";
       cin>>time;
       return time;
    }
void printWeekly(double hourlyWage, int hrs)
    {
       double weekPay;
       weekPay = hourlyWage * hrs;
       cout<<"Weekly pay is "<<weekPay<<endl;
    }
```

Figure 4-24   Program listing for HoursAndRate3.cpp

USING CLASSES AND OBJECTS AS ARGUMENTS TO FUNCTIONS AND AS RETURN TYPES OF FUNCTIONS

A function can contain a variety of combinations of actions. Some functions contain local variables declared within the function body. Some functions return and receive nothing. Others return values, receive values, or both. Functions may receive any number of variables as parameters, but may return, at most, only one variable of one type.

4

Any action you can perform with a simple, scalar variable within a function, such as declaring the variable locally, using it as an argument, or returning it, you can also perform with a class object. The program shown in Figure 4-25 shows a Customer class with two public fields, custId and custName. A main() program declares a Customer object and two functions. One function takes no arguments, but gets data for a Customer, returning a filled Customer object to the main() program, and one function takes a Customer argument and displays its values. The main() program itself is very short; after listing the declarations, it simply calls each function once. Figure 4-26 shows a typical execution.

```cpp
#include<iostream.h>
#include<conio.h>
class Customer
   {
    public:
      int custId;
      char custName[15];
   };
void main()
   {
       Customer oneCustomer;
       Customer getCustomerData();
       void printCustomerData(Customer oneCustomer);

       oneCustomer = getCustomerData();
       printCustomerData(oneCustomer);
       getch();
   }
Customer getCustomerData()
   {
       Customer cust;
       cout<<"Enter customer ID number ";
       cin>>cust.custId;
       cout<<"Enter customer's last name ";
       cin>>cust.custName;
       return cust;
   }
void printCustomerData(Customer c)
   {
     cout<<"ID is #"<<c.custId<<" and name is "<<c.custName<<endl;
   }
```

Figure 4-25   Using the Customer class with functions

Figure 4-26   Typical output of the Customer program

In the getCustomerData() function shown in Figure 4-25, a local Customer object is created just for purposes of data entry. After the user fills the custId and custName fields of the local Customer object, a copy of the object is returned to main() where it is stored in main()'s oneCustomer object. This object can then be passed to the printCustomerData() function. This function receives a copy of the oneCustomer object and refers to it by the local name c. Within the printCustomerData() function, the fields of the c object are used to display the data.

Any class field can be passed to or returned from a function just like its scalar counterpart. For example, a function that accepts an integer argument will accept an integer declared as `int x;` as well as a class object field like oneCustomer.custId.

PASSING ADDRESSES TO FUNCTIONS

Just as variable values may be passed to and returned from functions, so may variable addresses. Passing an address to a function avoids having the function copy the passed object, a process that takes time and memory. You also can pass addresses to a function if you want a function to change multiple values. (Recall that a function can return only one value — and that value must be the function's type.) If you pass addresses to a function, however, the function can change the contents at those actual memory addresses, eliminating the need to return any values at all.

Recall that you can access any variable's value by using the variable's name. In contrast, inserting an ampersand in front of its name allows you to access a variable's address. You also can create a pointer to hold a memory address.

Consider a function that determines the result of an integer division, as well as its remainder. You can write two functions to perform the two tasks, making two separate function calls, as shown in Figure 4-27.

As an alternative to the program shown in Figure 4-27, you can pass two memory addresses to one function, making a single function call, as shown in Figure 4-28.

```
#include<iostream.h>
#include<conio.h>
void main()
  {
    int a = 19, b = 7, dividend, modulus;
    int resultDiv(int num1, int num2); // prototype of the
      // function that divides a and b
    int remainder(int num1, int num2); // prototype of the
      // function that determines the remainder
    dividend = resultDiv(a, b); // call resultDiv function
    modulus = remainder(a, b); // call remainder function
    cout<<"Dividend is "<<dividend<<" and modulus is "
        <<modulus;
  }
int resultDiv(int num1, int num2)
  {
    int result;
    result = num1 / num2;
    return result; // function returns one thing —
    // the result of the division operation
  }
int remainder(int num1, int num2)
  {
    int result;
    result = num1 % num2;
    return result; // function returns one thing —
    // the result of the modulus operation
  {
```

Figure 4-27   A program that calls two functions to get two results

```
#include<iostream.h>
#include<conio.h>
void main()
  {
    int a = 19, b = 7, dividend, modulus;
    void results(int num1, int num2, int *div, int *mod);
            // prototype of the function that both
            // divides and determines the remainder
    results(a, b, &dividend, &modulus);
    cout<<"Dividend is "<<dividend<<" and modulus is "<<modulus;
  }
void results(int num1, int num2, int *oneAddress,
  int *anotherAddress)
  {
    *oneAddress = num1 / num2;
      // change the contents at oneAddress
    *anotherAddress = num1 % num2;
      // change the contents at anotherAddress
  }
```

Figure 4-28   A program that calls one function to get two results

In the program shown in Figure 4-28, four items are passed to the results() function: the value of a, the value of b, the address of dividend, and the address of modulus. In turn, the results() function receives four items:

- num1, which holds the value of a
- num2, which holds the value of b
- oneAddress, a pointer that holds the address of dividend
- anotherAddress, a pointer that holds the address of modulus

When values are stored in oneAddress and in anotherAddress, the values of dividend and modulus also are changed because they have the same address. Within the results() function, the contents pointed to by the oneAddress pointer are changed to hold the results of the division operation. Similarly, the contents at the address pointed to by the anotherAddress pointer are changed to hold the results of the modulus operation. The results() function does not need to pass any values back to the main() function, because the contents of the variables stored at the dividend and modulus addresses have been altered directly by the results() function.

Passing an address of a variable to a function has a number of advantages:

- If the function is intended to alter the variable, it alters the actual variable, not a copy of it. You do not need to return any values.
- You can write the function to alter multiple values. Functions can return only a single value, but they can alter many values that you send to passed addresses.
- When you send the address of a variable to a function, the function does not need to make a copy of the variable, a process that takes time (albeit a short time for a single variable).

The disadvantages of passing an address of a variable to a function include:

- The syntax of using the & and * is awkward and more difficult to understand than using plain variable names.
- Even if a function is not intended to alter a variable, it may do so when it has access to a variable's address.

To take advantage of the benefits of passing addresses to functions, storing them in pointer variables, and likewise eliminating the disadvantages, you can use reference variables and constant arguments.

USING REFERENCE VARIABLES WITH FUNCTIONS

A criminal who uses two names is said to have an alias. To create a second name for a variable in a program, you also can generate an **alias**, or an alternate name. In C++ a variable that acts as an alias for another variable is called a **reference variable**, or simply a reference.

Declaring Reference Variables

4

You declare a reference variable by placing a type and an ampersand in front of a variable name, as in `double &cash;`, and assigning another variable of the same type to the reference variable. For example, suppose you declare a double named someMoney and a reference named cash. When you write the statements:

```
double someMoney;
double &cash = someMoney;
```

the variables someMoney and cash both now refer to the same variable. Any change to cash modifies someMoney, and any change to someMoney alters cash. If you assign a value to either cash or someMoney, both hold the same value. The code in Figure 4-29 illustrates this technique.

 You also can declare a reference variable by inserting a space between the ampersand and the reference: `double& dough;`. This format makes sense if you think of dough as "type double reference" or "type double address."

```
double someMoney;
double &cash = someMoney;
cash = 6.78;
cout<<cash<<endl;           // displays 6.78
cout<<someMoney;            // displays 6.78
someMoney = 111.33;
cout<<cash<<endl;           // displays 111.33
cout<<someMoney;            // displays 111.33
```

Figure 4-29   Using a reference variable

A reference variable refers to the same memory address as does a variable, and a pointer holds the memory address of a variable. There are two differences between reference variables and pointers:

- Pointers are more flexible.

- Reference variables are easier to use.

Pointers are more flexible because they can store the address of any variable of the correct type. You declare a pointer to a variable by placing an asterisk in front of the pointer's name.

You assign a value to a pointer by inserting an ampersand in front of the name of the variable whose address you want to store in the pointer. If you declare an integer pointer named pnt, and then declare three integers named x, y, and z, you can assign the address of any of the three integers to pnt. For example, each statement in Figure 4-30 is a legal statement.

```
int *pnt;
int x = 4, y = 12, z = 35;
pnt = &x;
cout<<*pnt<<endl;      // output is 4
pnt = &y;
cout<<*pnt<<endl;      // output is 12
pnt = &z;
cout<<*pnt<<endl;      // output is 35
```

Figure 4-30   Using a pointer to hold different values

Figure 4-30 shows that when you want to use the value stored in the pointer, you must use the asterisk to **dereference** the pointer, or use the value to which it points, instead of the address it holds.

Passing Variable Addresses to Reference Variables

Reference variables are easier to use because you don't need any extra punctuation to output their values. You declare a reference variable by placing an ampersand in front of the variable's name. You assign a value to a reference variable by using another variable's name. The value in the reference is then output by using the variable's name. It can be easier to use a reference variable than a pointer when you want to pass the address of a variable to a function, thus allowing the function to alter the variable's memory location or to save the overhead incurred in making a copy. To work with the stored value in a reference variable, you don't need the asterisk. If you require another name for a variable, a reference is preferable. If you must hold the addresses of several different memory locations, then a pointer is required.

 You must assign a value to a reference variable when you declare it. The following is illegal:
```
int &badReference; // no assignment – illegal
```

The advantage to using reference variables lies in creating them in function headers. Figure 4-31 shows two functions. The first function is a copy of the results() function from Figure 4-28, and uses two pointer variables in its argument list. The second function shows results() rewritten to accept two references in place of the two pointers.

```
// function version that uses pointers
void results(int num1, int num2, int *oneAddress,
     int *anotherAddress)
  {
    *oneAddress = num1 / num2;
    *anotherAddress = num1 % num2;
  }
// function version that uses references
void results(int num1, int num2, int &oneRef, int &anotherRef)
  {
    oneRef = num1 / num2;
    anotherRef = num1 % num2;
  }
```

Figure 4-31   Comparing pointers and references in a function header

The same basic results() function can use two reference variables as arguments instead of using two pointers. Then you can avoid having to use the dereferencing asterisks required to access the values pointed to by oneAddress and anotherAddress.

When you pass a variable's address to a function, whether with a pointer or with a reference, any changes to the variable made by the function also alter the actual variable. In addition, the function no longer needs to make a copy of the variable.

Passing an address is a double-edged sword, however. A function that receives an address may change the variable—but sometimes you might not want the variable changed. To pass an address (thus eliminating the copy of a variable) and still protect the variable from change, you may pass a reference as a constant. Figure 4-32 shows a complete program that prototypes and calls a function with a constant reference. The function computes a 20% discount on prices over $100, and a 10% discount on prices that are $100 or less. When the main() program passes the price variable to the computeDiscount() function, the address of price is passed to a local reference that also is named price. Passing price's address eliminates the necessity of making a copy of the variable, but the function's price is unchangeable, eliminating possible error. Figure 4-33 shows the execution of the program.

```
#include<iostream.h>
#include<conio.h>
void main()
  {
      double price, priceAfterDiscount;
      double computeDiscountedPrice(const double &price);
      cout<<"Enter the price of the item ";
      cin>>price;
      priceAfterDiscount = computeDiscountedPrice(price);
      cout<<"The original price is $"<<price<<endl;
      cout<<"Your final price after discount is $"<<
        priceAfterDiscount;
      getch();
  }
double computeDiscountedPrice(const double &price)
  {
      double newPrice;
      // price = 3.33;
      //This would be illegal — price can't change
      if(price > 100.00)
         newPrice = price * .80;
      else
         newPrice = price * .90;
      return newPrice;
  }
```

Figure 4-32   Using a constant reference

```
┌─────────────────────────────────────────────┐
│ Discount                                      │
│ Enter the price of the item 12.99             │
│ The original price is $12.99                  │
│ Your final price after discount is $11.691_   │
│                                               │
└─────────────────────────────────────────────┘
```

Figure 4-33   Output of the Discount program

> The time and memory saved by passing a reference to a single variable a single time are minimal. However, if you apply the same techniques when passing many large objects that contain many fields, the time and memory savings are substantial.

Use the const modifier for all variables passed to functions when the variable should not change within the function. This practice is safe because the compiler checks to ensure that the variable is not changed inadvertently. In addition, this tactic makes your intentions clear to anyone reading your program.

If a function receives a variable as a constant, but then passes the variable to another function that does not receive the variable as a constant, most compilers will not issue an error message. You may inadvertently change a variable that should remain constant. As a programmer, it is your responsibility to declare variables as constants explicitly within any function where you want them to remain constant.

4

PASSING ARRAYS TO FUNCTIONS

An array name actually represents a memory address. Thus, an array name is a pointer. The subscript used to access an element of an array indicates how much to add to the starting address to locate a value.

The array declaration int nums[5]; declares an array that holds five integers. You can view the address of the array with the statement cout<<nums; or with the statement cout<<&nums[0];. Each statement produces identical output. In the first statement, the name of the array represents the beginning address of the array. In the second statement, the address of nums[0] also is the beginning address of the array.

Because an array name is a memory address, when you pass an array name to a function, you are actually passing an address. Therefore, any changes made to the array within the function also affect the original array. The program shown in Figure 4-34 shows a main() function that declares an array. The program prints the values, sends the array to a function that alters the values, and then prints the values again.

In both the function prototype and the function header in Figure 4-34, the array name is written with empty brackets. When an array name is passed to a function, the function identifies the starting address of the array. Therefore, you don't need to indicate a size for the array in the function header. It doesn't matter whether nums consists of four elements or 400; the starting address is the same. When you modify the values in the values array within the function, you are actually changing nums in the main program—values is an alias for nums. Figure 4-35 shows the output from the program in Figure 4-34. Although the increaseArray() function did not return any values to main(), each value in the original array was increased when its alias was increased within the function.

```
#include<iostream.h>
#include<conio.h>
void main()
  {
      int nums[4] = {4, 21, 300, 612};
      void increaseArray(int nums[]);
      int x;
      for(x = 0; x < 4; ++x)
        cout<<nums[x]<<" ";
      cout<<endl;
      increaseArray(nums);
      for(x = 0; x < 4; ++x)
        cout<<nums[x]<<" ";
      cout<<endl;
      getch();
  }
void increaseArray(int values[])
  {
      int y;
      for(y = 0; y < 4; ++y)
          ++values[y];
  }
```

Figure 4-34   Passing an array to a function

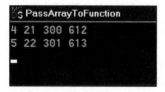

Figure 4-35   Output of the program that passes an array to a function

 The increaseArray() function in Figure 4-34 could be improved by passing the size of the array into the function. The prototype would become void increaseArray(int nums[], int elements); and the call within main() would be increaseArray(nums, 4);. Using this approach, you could control the loop within the increaseArray() function by using the variable named elements instead of using the constant 4. That way, other programs with arrays of different sizes could use the same function correctly.

Although passing an array name to a function involves passing an address, passing an array element to a function is no different than passing any single scalar variable of the same type. For example, if you declare int nums[4]; and you declare a function with the prototype void someFunction(int x);, then you can call the function with statements such as someFunction(nums[0]); or someFunction(nums[3]);. Each call simply passes one integer to the function that is declared to receive a single integer. It does not matter whether the passed integer is a single integer or a part of an array of integers.

INLINE FUNCTIONS

Each time you call a function in a C++ program, the computer must do the following:

- Remember where to return when the function eventually ends

- Provide memory for the function's variables

- Provide memory for any value returned by the function

- Pass control to the function

- Pass control back to the calling program

This extra activity constitutes the **overhead**, or cost of doing business, involved in calling a function. When a function contains many lines of code, or when a program calls a function many times, the overhead is relatively small. That's because the cost of calling the function is offset by the fact that you no longer need to write the function's lines of code many times in different locations in the program. If a group of statements is small or is not used many times, however, placing the statements in a function may be convenient but not worth the overhead.

An **inline function** is a small function with no overhead. Overhead is avoided because program control never transfers to the function. Rather, a copy of the function statements is placed directly into the compiled calling program. Figure 4-36 illustrates how to create and use an inline function. You define the function at the top of the file using the keyword inline as part of the function header. Whenever you want to use the function later in the file, you call it in the same manner you would call any other function.

```cpp
#include<iostream.h>
// note the keyword inline in the function header
inline double computeGross(double hours, double rate)
   {
       return(hours * rate);
   }
void main()
   {
     double hrsWorked=37.5, rateOfPay=12.45, gross;
     gross = computeGross(hrsWorked, rateOfPay);
           // the call to the inline function
           // looks like a regular function call
     cout<<endl<<"nGross pay is "<<gross;
   }
```

Figure 4-36   Using an inline function

The inline function appears prior to main(), which calls it. Any inline function must precede any function that calls it, which eliminates the need for prototyping in the calling function. When you compile the program, the code for the inline function is placed directly within the main() function. When you run the main() program, it executes more rapidly than a version with a non-inline function because there is less overhead. The size of the main program, however, exceeds the size of a program with a non-inline function. However, if you use the inline function many times within the same program, the program could grow dramatically because the function statements are copied at the location of each call. Therefore, you should use an inline function only in the following situations:

- When you want to group statements together so that you can use a function name
- When the number of statements is small (one or two lines in the body of the function)
- When the function is called on few occasions

 When you use an inline function, you make a request to the compiler; however, the compiler does not have to honor this request. This limitation can pose a problem if the function is included in an include or header file accessed by two different source files. If the compiler generates a message saying that an inline function has duplicate definitions, put the function in its own source file and include it just once in the compilation.

USING DEFAULT ARGUMENTS

When you don't provide enough arguments in a function call, you usually want the compiler to issue a warning message for this error. For example, the program in Figure 4-37 shows an incorrect call to a function that requires three parameters.

```
#include<iostream.h>
void main(void)
    {
        // function prototype — this function requires 3 arguments
        int compute(int length, int width, int height);
        // function call — one parameter is missing
        cout<<compute(12, 7);
    }
```

Figure 4-37   Incorrect call to a function

The code above causes the compiler to issue an error message indicating that the function call has the wrong number of parameters.

Sometimes it is useful to create a function that supplies a default value for any missing parameters. For example, you might create a function to calculate either the volume of a cube or the area of a square, such as the function shown in Figure 4-38. When you want a cube's area, you pass three parameters to the function: length, width, and height. When you want a square's area, you pass only two parameters, and a default value of 1 is used for the height. In this example, the height is a default parameter; the length and width are mandatory parameters.

```
#include<iostream.h>
void main()
   {
     double compute(int length, int width, int height = 1);
     cout<<compute(4, 4, 4); // uses three values — result is 64
     cout<<calculate(4, 4);
     //  uses two values and 1 — //result is 16
   }
int calculate(int length, int width, int height)
   {
     return(length * width * height);
   }
```

Figure 4-38   Program using a function with a default parameter

In Figure 4-38, the return statement also can be written as `return length * width * height;` without the parentheses. You can use the parentheses for clarity to show that a single computed value is the return value, but they are not required.

Two rules apply to default parameters:

- If you assign a default value to any variable in a function prototype's parameter list, then all parameters to the right of that variable also must have default values.

- If you omit any argument when you call a function that has default parameters, then you also must leave out all arguments to the right of that argument.

For example, examine the program in Figure 4-39 and notice how the default values are applied.

```
#include<iostream.h>
void main()
   {
     void badFunc(int var1 = 1, int var2);
          // illegal — if var1 has a default, then var2 must
     void functionWithDefaults(int var1,int var2=2,int var3=3);
          // legal
     functionWithDefaults();
          // illegal — a value for var1 is mandatory
     functionWithDefaults(4); // legal — output is 423
     functionWithDefaults(4, 5);  // legal — output is 453
     functionWithDefaults(4, 5, 6); // legal — output is 456
   }
   void functionWithDefaults(int one, int two, int three)
   {
     cout<<one<<two<<three;
   }
```

Figure 4-39   Examples of legal and illegal use of functions with default parameters

The function called functionWithDefaults() has one mandatory parameter and two default parameters. Therefore, you must pass at least one—but no more than three—values to the function.

 You may place default parameter values in the function header instead of the prototype if you wish. However, default values cannot appear in both places, even if you use the same value. Most C++ programmers place the default value in the prototype, because the prototype is what they usually show to other programmers who want to use their functions.

OVERLOADING FUNCTIONS

In most computer programming languages, each variable used in a function must have only one name, but C++ allows you to employ an alias. Similarly, in most computer programming languages, each function used in a program must have a unique name. For example, if you want a function to display a value's square, you could create a function that squares integers, a function that squares floats, and a function that squares doubles. Figure 4-40 shows three such functions, and each has a unique name.

```cpp
void squareInteger(int x)
   {
      cout<<"In integer function "<<x*x<<endl;
   }
void squareFloat(float x)
   {
      cout<<"In float function "<<x*x<<endl;
   }
void squareDouble(double x)
   {
      cout<<"In double function "<<x*x<<endl;
   }
```

Figure 4-40   Three non-overloaded functions that perform similar tasks

So you don't have to use three names for functions that perform basically the same task, C++ allows you to reuse, or **overload**, function names. For example, each function that squares a value can bear the name squareValue(). If you want three versions of the function, you still must write a version of squareValue() that accepts ints, doubles, and floats. C++ determines which function to call by reviewing the parameters submitted. Figure 4-41 shows three overloaded versions of squareValue(), and shows a main() program that uses them.

```
#include<iostream.h>
void squareValue(int x)
   {
     cout<<"In integer function "<<x*x<<endl;
   }
void squareValue(float x)
   {
     cout<<"In float function "<<x*x<<endl;
   }
void squareValue(double x)
   {
     cout<<"In double function "<<x*x<<endl;
   }
void main()
   {
     int i = 5;
     float f = 2.2;
     double d = 3.3;
     squareValue(i); // output is "In integer function 25"
     squareValue(f); // output is "In float function 4.84"
     squareValue(d); // output is "In double function 10.89"
   }
```

Figure 4-41   Three overloaded functions that perform similar tasks

Whether you use the functions shown in Figure 4-40 or 4-41, you still must write three versions of the function—one for each type of argument you want to support. Overloading a function's name simply allows you to use that name for more than one function. The benefit of overloading derives from your ability to use one easy-to-understand function name without regard to the data types involved. If you create and save the three overloaded functions, then whenever you write programs in which you need to square values, you must remember only the function name squareValue(). You don't have to remember three separate function names.

 C++ identifies which version of the overloaded function to call through a process known as name mangling.

When you overload a function, you must ensure that the compiler can tell which function to call. You accomplish this by making sure each overloaded function has a different argument list. For example, if you declare two functions as void someFunction(int a); and void someFunction(int b);, when you make the function call someFunction(17);, the compiler does not know which version of someFunction() to call. When the compiler cannot tell which version of a function to use, you have created **ambiguity**.

Ambiguity is particularly likely to occur by accident when you provide default values for functions. For example, consider the functions prototyped `void calculation(int a = 1);` and `void calculation(char c = 'A');`. At first glance, these functions appear to have different argument lists; one requires an integer and the other requires a character. As a matter of fact, if you make the function call `calculation(34);` or `calculation('Z');`, there is no ambiguity; the compiler knows which version you want to use. However, because both functions have default arguments, if you call `calculation();`, then ambiguity arises. The compiler does not know if you intend to call the function version with the default integer or the version with the character argument.

You will learn more about ambiguity when you learn to place functions within classes.

While functions with the same name need not perform similar tasks, your programs will be clearer if overloaded functions perform essentially the same tasks.

CHAPTER SUMMARY

- Functions are programming modules. When you call a function, you use its name to transfer control of the program to the function.

- You can define a function by writing it above the function that uses it, or by including the function's filename at the top of the file that uses it.

- When you write functions, you employ procedural abstraction—the process of extracting the relevant attributes of an object.

- Global variables are known to every function and block in a program. Local variables are accessible or in scope only within the block where they are defined. Because local variables override global variables with the same name, you must use the scope resolution operator to access such global variables.

- The header of a function consists of the return type, the name, and the argument list. A prototype, or function declaration, also contains these parts.

- A function can return a value that the calling function can use. The type of value returned is known as the function's type.

- You can pass an argument or parameter to a function. When you write a function that takes arguments, you can choose to include documenting names in the prototype. You pass a value to a function when you place the value, called the actual parameter, within the parentheses in the function call. The function makes a copy of the actual parameter and stores it in the formal parameter, which is local to the function.

❏ You can pass class objects to functions and return them from functions in the same way you work with scalar variables.

❏ Passing an address to a function allows you to avoid having the function copy the passed object and allows a function to change multiple values without returning them. However, the syntax of passing an address is awkward, and a function that receives an address can alter a variable even if that is not your intention.

❏ In C++ a variable that acts as an alias for another variable is called a reference variable. You declare a reference variable by placing a type and an ampersand in front of a variable and assigning another variable of the same type to the reference variable. You can pass a variable's address to a reference variable in a function; this makes the syntax of the function less awkward. To protect the variable from change, you may pass a reference as a constant.

❏ Because an array name is a memory address, when you pass an array name to a function, you are actually passing an address. Therefore, any changes made to the array within the function also affect the original array. The array name in a function prototype or header is written with empty brackets.

❏ An inline function is a small function with no overhead. A copy of an inline function's statements is placed directly into the compiled calling program. You should use inline functions when the number of statements is small and when the function is called infrequently.

❏ Default parameters provide values for any parameters that are missing in the function call. If you assign a default value to any variable in a function prototype's parameter list, then all parameters to the right of that variable also must have default values. If you omit any argument when you call a function that has default parameters, then you must leave out all arguments to the right of that argument.

❏ C++ allows you to reuse, or overload, function names. To prevent ambiguity, overloaded functions must have argument lists of different types.

REVIEW QUESTIONS

1. In different programming languages, program modules are known as all of the following except _____.

   a. functions

   b. procedures

   c. methods

   d. variables

2. In a C++ program, all function names are always followed by a pair of
_____.

a. parentheses

b. square brackets

c. angle brackets

d. a set of curly braces

3. When you use the name of a function where you want it to execute within a program, you are _____ the function.

a. prototyping

b. calling

c. iterating

d. defining

4. You can define a function by _____.

a. writing it below the function that uses it

b. including the function's filename at the top of the file that uses it

c. inserting a comment that describes the function's purpose

d. any of the above

5. The process of extracting the relevant attributes of an object is called
_____.

a. codification

b. object orienting

c. structuring

d. abstraction

6. A variable that is known to all functions within a file is said to be _____.

a. notorious

b. worldly

c. global

d. famous

7. Within a block or function, a local variable _____ a global one.

a. overrides

b. overloads

c. accedes to

d. replaces

8. A local variable is one that _____.

   a. is known to functions only within its own file

   b. is automatically declared for you by C++

   c. ceases to exist when its block ends

   d. has a value that does not change during its life

9. The term C++ programmers use for the extent to which a variable is known is _____.

   a. breadth

   b. scope

   c. scale

   d. reach

10. Both a function header and its prototype contain _____.

    a. the return type

    b. a coded description of what the function does

    c. actual parameters

    d. square brackets

11. Which of the following is a valid prototype for a function that accepts an integer argument and returns a double value?

    a. int function(double d);

    b. int function(double d)

    c. double function (int x);

    d. double function(int x)

12. Suppose you have a C++ program that contains an integer variable named yearOfBirth. To call a function with the prototype `void calculateAge(int yr);`, you use the statement _____.

    a. void calculateAge(yr);

    b. calculateAge(yr);

    c. calculateAge(yearOfBirth);

    d. calculateAge(int yearOfBirth);

13. Which of the following correctly calls a function that has the prototype `void computePayment(int price, double rate, int term);`?

    a. computePrice(5129.95, 8, 36);

    b. computePrice(5000, .075, 24);

    c. computePrice(10000, .10, 4.5);

    d. computePrice(2000, .09);

14. The advantages of passing an address of a variable to a function include the following, except _____.

    a. the function can alter the variable in the calling function

    b. you can write the function to alter multiple values

    c. the use of pointer notation makes passing an address easier to understand

    d. the function automatically makes a copy of the variable

15. Which of the following correctly declares a reference for `int myCreditHours;`?

    a. int &cr = myCreditHours;

    b. int *cr = myCreditHours;

    c. int cr = &myCreditHours;

    d. int *cr = &myCreditHours;

16. When you pass a reference to a function, the function can alter the variable if the reference is _____.

    a. constant

    b. not constant

    c. absolute

    d. not absolute

17. You should use an inline function when _____.

    a. it is large

    b. it has no arguments

    c. it is called infrequently

    d. it requires arguments that are addresses

18. A program contains the function prototype
`void displayData(char name[], int idNum = 0);`. Which of the following is a legal function call?

    a. displayData();

    b. displayData("Roberts");

    c. displayData("Gonzales", 345);

    d. two of the above are legal

19. Using the same function name with different argument lists is called _____ functions.

    a. overriding

    b. overloading

    c. overcompensating

    d. overreacting

20. Which of the following functions could coexist in a program with
`void function(double amount, int size);` with no ambiguity possible?
    a. void function (double amount);
    b. void function(double money, int age);
    c. void function(double a = 2.2, int b = 3.3);
    d. all of the above

4

EXERCISES

1. Write a program in which the main() function calls a MarysLamb() function. Write the MarysLamb() function, which should display the words to the song "Mary Had a Little Lamb."

2. Write a program in which the main() function uses several cout statements to print a memo to your boss. Use the company name "C++ Software Developers" at least three times in the memo. Each time you want to print the company name, instead of using a cout statement, call a function named companyName() that prints the name.

3. Write a program that asks the user to input an integer, and then calls a function named multiplicationTable(), which displays the results of multiplying the integer by each of the numbers 2 through 10.

4. Write a program that asks users for the most expensive and least expensive restaurant bills they anticipate. A function tipTable() should calculate and display 15% of each whole-dollar amount between the two entered limits.

5. Write a program that asks the user for two integers and a character, 'A', 'S', or 'M'. Call one of three functions that adds, subtracts, or multiplies the user's integers, based on the character input.

6. Write a program that includes two functions. The first function should ask a salesperson for the dollar value of daily sales, and then return this figure to the main program. The second function should calculate the salesperson's commission based on the following rates:

Sales	Commission
0 – 999	3%
1000 – 2999	3.5%
3000 – up	4.5%

The dollar value of the calculated commission should be returned to the main program, which then displays it.

7. Write a program that calculates the cost of building a desk. The main() program calls four functions. Pass all variables so that the functions make copies of any variables they receive:

◻ A function to accept as input the number of drawers in the desk. This function returns the number of drawers to the main program.

◻ A function to accept as input the type of wood—'m' for mahogany, 'o' for oak, or 'p' for pine.

◻ A function that receives the drawer number and wood type, and calculates the cost of the desk based on the following:

Pine desks are $100.
Oak desks are $140.
All other woods are $180.
A $30 surcharge is added for each drawer.
This function returns the cost to the main() program.

◻ A function to display the final price.

8. Rewrite the desk program from Exercise 7, passing all variables as reference variables and changing all the function return types to void.

9. Write a program that accepts 10 values and stores them in an array. Pass the array to a function that determines and displays the smallest and largest of the 10 values.

10. Write a program that prompts the user to enter five integers that you store in an array. Write a function called quadruple() that takes a single-integer argument and multiplies it by 4, returning the result to the calling program. Call the function once for each of the five integers, then print the quadrupled results from within the main() program.

11. Write a program that prompts the user to enter five integers that you store in an array. Write a function called quadruple() that takes the array name (or the array address) as an argument. The function multiplies each value by 4 and returns nothing to the calling program. Print the quadrupled results from within the main() program.

12. Write a program that asks students how many tests they have taken so far in a course. The program should accept any number from 1 to 5, but reprompt the user if the entry is invalid. The user can then enter the appropriate number of test scores, which you store in an array. Pass the number of tests and the array of test scores to a function that averages the student's test scores and displays the average. The function should compute a correct average whether the student has taken one, two, three, four, or five tests.

13. Write a program that allows users to enter a dollar amount for their bank account balance at the beginning of the month. Then ask the user to enter dollar amounts for any number of checks written in a month, up to 50. Store the amounts in an array and count the entries as the user makes them. Finally, ask the user to enter a monthly interest rate if the account is interest bearing, or a 0 if it is not. If the user enters 0 for the interest rate, then call a function named balanceAccount() that accepts the beginning balance, number of checks, and the array of check amounts as arguments; the function prints the final balance after all the checks have been subtracted from the

beginning balance. If the user enters a number other than 0 for the interest rate, then call an overloaded function named balanceAccount() that accepts the beginning balance, number of checks, the array of check amounts, and the interest rate as arguments. This function then computes the final balance by subtracting all the checks from the beginning balance and using the interest rate to increase the final balance before displaying it.

14. Write a function named customerCreditLimit() that accepts a double as an argument and displays the value as the amount of credit granted to a customer. Provide a default value for the function so that if a program calls the function without an argument, the credit limit displays $500. Write a main() program that proves the function works correctly, whether it is called with an argument or without.

15. Write a function that accepts two arguments, a string name of a movie and an integer running time in minutes. Provide a default value for the minutes so that if you call the function without an integer argument, the minutes default to 90. Write a main() program that proves you can call the function with a string argument alone and also with a string and an integer.

16. Create a class named Carpet that has two public data members, lengthInFeet and widthInFeet. Write a main() program that instantiates a Carpet object and assigns values to its data fields. Pass it to a function named printArea() that calculates the Carpet area in square feet and prints the results.

17. Create a class named Shirt that has the public data members collarSize and sleeveLength. Create a class named Pants that has the public data members waistSize and inSeam. Write a program that declares one object of each type Shirt and Pants and assigns values to the objects' data fields. Write two overloaded functions named printClothingFacts(). One version of the function takes a Shirt object as an argument; the other version takes a Pants object. Each version displays the facts about the piece of clothing. Your main() program should demonstrate that you can call printClothingFacts() with either type of clothing.

18. Create a class named Dog with a string field for the Dog's name. Create a class named Cat with a string field for the Cat's name. Write a program that declares one Dog and one Cat, and assign names to them. Write two overloaded methods named speak(). If you pass the Dog to speak, the speak() method should display the Dog's name and a description of how dogs speak (for example, "Spot says woof"). If you pass the Cat to the version of speak() that accepts a Cat argument, then it should display the Cat's name and a description of how cats speak (for example, "Tiger says meow").

19. Each of the following files in the Chapter04 folder contains syntax and/or logical errors. Determine the problem in each case and fix the program.

    a. DEBUG4–1

    b. DEBUG4–2

    c. DEBUG4–3

    d. DEBUG4–4

CASE PROJECT

You have been developing a Fraction class for Teacher's Pet Software. The class contains two public data fields for numerator and denominator. Using the same class, write a main() function that instantiates a Fraction object and calls each of the functions described below:

❑ An enterFractionValue() function that declares a local Fraction object, and prompts the user to enter values for the numerator and denominator. Do not allow the user to enter a value of 0 for the denominator of any Fraction. The function returns a data-filled Fraction object to the main() function.

❑ A displayFraction() function that displays any Fraction object passed to it. This function prompts the user to enter a 1 to see the Fraction in fraction format (with a slash between the numerator and denominator) or a 2 to see the Fraction in floating-point format (computed as a decimal place number).

CHAPTER
5
USING CLASSES

In this chapter, you will learn:

◆ How to include declaration and implementation sections within classes

◆ How and when to use public and private access modifiers in class definitions

◆ How to use private functions

◆ How to use the scope resolution operator with class fields and functions

◆ About the use of static variables

◆ About the this pointer

◆ About the advantages of polymorphism

Classes can contain much more than public data fields; they can contain methods that make them operate like many concrete objects in the physical world. That is, classes can *do* things as well as *contain* things, and some of their attributes and operations can be hidden from users. This chapter will show you how to add both hidden and unhidden fields and functions to your classes, and how C++ handles class functions behind the scenes.

CREATING CLASSES WITH DECLARATION AND IMPLEMENTATION SECTIONS

Classes provide a convenient way to group related data. Consider the Student class in Figure 5-1. It contains three public data fields: idNum, lastName, and gradePointAverage. C++ programmers would say that the Student class shown in Figure 5-1 is an **abstract data type (ADT)**. This term simply indicates that Student is a type you define, as opposed to types like char and int that are defined by C++. When you declare a Student object, you use the Student name just as you use scalar type names, such as `Student aSophomore;`. When you refer to aSophomore, you are including all the separate attributes that constitute aSophomore. You have already learned that you can refer to the specific attributes of aSophomore by using the object's name, a dot, and the attribute's name. For example, to display the last name of aSophomore, the correct statement is `cout<<aSophomore.lastName;`.

```
class Student
  {
      public:
         int idNum;
         char lastName[15];
         double gradePointAverage;
  };
```

Figure 5-1   A simple, but unconventional, class

Conventionally, class names begin with an uppercase letter and object names begin with a lowercase letter.

You have already created many classes that are similar to the Student class in Figure 5-1. One advantage of creating the Student class is that when you create a Student object, you automatically create all the related Student fields. Another advantage is the ability to pass a Student object into a function, or receive a Student object from a function as a returned value, and automatically pass or receive all the individual fields that each Student contains. A class like the one in Figure 5-1 provides many programming benefits, but it is not the type of class that object-oriented programmers usually create, nor does it demonstrate all the capabilities that object-oriented classes usually possess.

The first step to creating a class involves determining the attributes of an object, and subsequently dealing with the object as a whole. That's what you are doing when you decide on the field types and names for a class like the Student class. When you work with a Student object, for example, and pass it to a function, you deal with the object as a whole, and do not have to think about its internal fields. You think about the fields only when necessary, such as when you need to assign a value to a Student's idNum. A hallmark of object-oriented programming is that you think about program objects in the same way you think about their real-world counterparts. For example, when you use a real-world object like a radio, you don't think or care about how it works. Sometimes, however, you change some of the states of the radio's attributes, such as volume level or frequency selection.

Encapsulating Class Components

Just as the internal components of a radio are hidden, when you write a program and create a class name for a group of associated variables, you hide, or **encapsulate**, the individual components. Sometimes you want to change the state of some components, but often you want to think about the entity as a whole and not concern yourself with the details. Programmers sometimes refer to encapsulation as an example of using a "black box." A black box is a device that you can use, but cannot look inside to see how it works. When you use a class, you are using a group name without being concerned with the individual components; the details are hidden.

Several C++ constructs let you group variables and deal with them as a unit. If you need to create several variables of the same type, you can form an array. If you need to create variables of diverse types, you can create a class or you can create a C++ group item known as a structure. Classes and structures have similar features, but classes have advantages in what they can contain and do. C++ programmers use classes far more frequently.

When you work with concrete, real-world objects, you think about more than what components they contain or what states they possess; you also think about what the objects can do. For example, a radio's states include volume and frequency selection, but a radio also possesses a means for *changing* these states. In other words, radios have methods as well as attributes. When you change the volume or frequency, you use an **interface**, such as a dial or knob. The interface intercedes between you and the more complicated inner workings of the radio. When you design C++ classes, you should think about what the class objects will *do* and how programmers will make them do it, as well as what the class objects *contain*. Therefore your classes will contain fields, functions, and interfaces to the functions.

Designing Classes

You can think of the built-in scalar types of C++ as classes. You do not have to define those classes; the creators of C++ have already done so. For example, when the int type was first created, the programmers who designed it had to think of the following:

Q: What shall we call it?

A: int.

Q: What are its attributes?

A: An int is stored in two bytes (or four bytes, depending on your system); it holds whole–number values.

Q: What methods are needed?

A: A method to assign a value to a variable (for example, `num = 32;`).

Q: Any other methods?

A: A method to perform arithmetic with variables (for example, `num + 6;`).

Q: Any other methods?

A: Of course, there are even more attributes and methods of an int, but these are a good start.

Your job in constructing a new class is similar. If you need a class for students, you should ask:

Q: What shall we call it?

A: Student.

Q: What are its attributes?

A: It has an integer ID number, a string last name, and a double grade point average.

Q: What methods are needed?

A: A method to assign values to a member of this class (for example, one Student's ID number is 3232, her last name is "Walters", and her grade point average is 3.45).

Q: Any other methods?

A: A method to display data in a member of this class (for example, display one Student's data).

Q: Any other methods?

A: Probably, but this is enough to get started.

For most object-oriented classes, then, you declare both fields and functions. You declare a function by writing its prototype, which serves as the interface to the function. For example, you might want to create a method for a Student class that displays all the details of a Student's data. You could create a function with the prototype `void displayStudentData();` and include it in the Student class definition shown in Figure 5-2.

```
class Student
    {
        public:
            int idNum;
            char lastName[15];
            double gradePointAverage;
            void displayStudentData();
    };
```

Figure 5-2   Student class that includes one function definition

When you declare a class with a function definition such as the one shown in Figure 5-2, and you then create an object of that class, the object possesses more than access to each field—it also possesses access to the function. If you declare a Student object as `Student aSophomore;`, then you can use the displayStudentData() function by referring to `aSophomore.displayStudentData()`. Similarly, another student object, `Student aGraduate;`, could use `aGraduate.displayStudentData()`.

Implementing Class Functions

After you create a class function's prototype, you still must write the actual function. When you construct a class, you create two parts. The first part is a **declaration section**, which contains the class name, variables (attributes), and function prototypes. The second part created is an **implementation section**, which contains the functions themselves. For example, Figure 5-3 shows the Student class that includes a function implementation for displayStudentData().

```
// declaration section:
 class Student
    {
        public:
            int idNum;
            char lastName[15];
            double gradePointAverage;
            void displayStudentData();
    };
// implementation section:
void Student::displayStudentData()
{
    cout<<"Student #"<<idNum<<"'s last name is "<<lastName<<endl;
    cout<<"The grade point average for this student is "<<
        gradePointAverage<<endl;
}
```

Figure 5-3   Student class that includes one function definition and implementation

In the class definition shown in Figure 5-3, the displayStudentData() function header is preceded by the class name, Student, and the scope resolution operator (::). You must use the class name and the scope resolution operator when you implement a class function, because they tie the function to this class and allows every instantiated class object to use the function name.

 Instead of prototyping a function in the declaration section of a class and implementing that function later, you can implement it in place of the prototype. This causes the function to become an inline function. Usually, however, you should keep the function declaration and implementation separate, as in the example in Figure 5-3.

 You can refer to the scope resolution operator used in the class function header as a binary scope resolution operator, because it requires two operands: the class name to the left and the function name to the right.

Figure 5-4 shows a program that uses the Student class. Notice that each field and function can be used with the object name and the dot operator. Figure 5-5 shows the output of the program.

```
#include<iostream.h>
#include<conio.h>
void main()
  {
     Student aStudent;
     aStudent.idNum = 777;
     strcpy(aStudent.lastName, "Mercer");
     aStudent.gradePointAverage = 2.7;
     aStudent.displayStudentData();
     getch();
  }
```

Figure 5-4　Program that uses Student class from Figure 5-3

```
Student
Student #777's last name is Mercer
The grade point average for this student is 2.7
```

Figure 5-5　Output of program in Figure 5-4

In the next set of steps, you create a class that implements a function. Then you write a short demonstration program to instantiate an object of the class, and use the object's fields and function.

1. Open a new file. Type a comment identifying the program's purpose, which is to create and demonstrate a class that holds information about a college course. Then type the include statements you need:

   #include<iostream.h>
   #include<conio.h>

2. Next type the CollegeCourse class declaration section. It includes three public fields that hold the department in which the course is offered, the course number, and the number of seats available for which students can enroll. It also contains the definition for a function that shows the course data.

   ```
   class CollegeCourse
   {
     public:
       char department[4];
       int courseNum;
       int seats;
       void displayCourseData();
   };
   ```

3. Next, in the implementation section, write the displayCourseData() function that is a member of the CollegeCourse class. The function contains a single statement that displays the values of the College Course's data fields.

   ```
   void CollegeCourse::displayCourseData()
   {
     cout<<department<<courseNum<<" accommodates "<<
        seats<<"students"<<endl;
   }
   ```

4. Write a main() program that declares two CollegeCourse objects and assigns values to them. Then use the displayCourseData() function with each object.

   ```
   void main()
   {
     CollegeCourse myMondayClass = {"CIS", 115, 35};
     CollegeCourse myTuesThursClass = {"SOC", 151, 200};
     myMondayClass.displayCourseData();
     myTuesThursClass.displayCourseData();
     getch();
   }
   ```

5. Save the file as **CollegeCourse.cpp**, and store it in the Chapter05 folder on your Student Data Disk or in the Student Data folder on your hard drive. Compile and run the program. The output should look like Figure 5-6. Notice that although two different objects use the same function, each version displays data appropriate to that object.

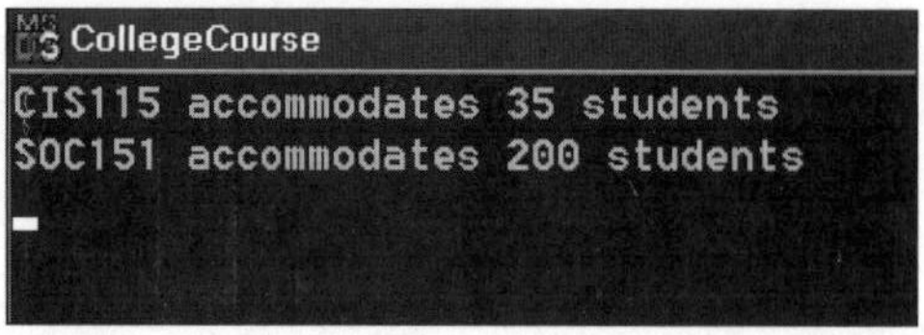

Figure 5-6   Output of college course program

DATA HIDING AND ENCAPSULATION

The Student class shown in Figure 5-3 still is not a typical object-oriented class. Object-oriented programmers strive to make their classes similar to real-world objects, which usually do not provide access to their inner workings; access is available only to the interface. For example, the internal mechanisms of a radio are encapsulated. You do not need to know how a radio picks up a specific broadcasting station; you need only know how to turn the dial to a specific station number. One technique programmers use to provide more complete object encapsulation is to make objects' data **private**.

One major asset of object-oriented programming is that the information hiding can be accomplished more completely than it is with the procedures used in procedural programs. Traditional procedural languages do not allow data to be declared as private; object-oriented languages do. You employ a primitive form of information hiding when you write a program and you use functions to which you know only the interface, yet you don't know the details of how the function works. C++ classes allow you to take data hiding a step further.

In C++, data hiding means that you can make data members of a class inaccessible to functions that are not part of that class; that is, you can make them private. In the Student class, for example, you can prevent idNum, lastName, and gradePointAverage from being displayed by any function except displayStudentData(). You can make it illegal in any main() function, or any other function in which a Student named aStudent is instantiated, to write the statement `cout<<aStudent.idNum;`. Instead, you can require programmers to use the statement `aStudent.displayStudentData();`. In other words, you can require that any programmer who uses aStudent display the Student idNumber preceded by a pound sign, and followed by the Student lastName and gradePointAverage.

Within a C++ class, you accomplish data encapsulation by making the data private instead of public. Then no program that uses the Student class and instantiates Student objects can access a Student's data fields directly. By making the displayStudentData() function *public* instead of private, you do allow programmers to use the function directly. Figure 5-7 shows the Student class with private data and a public method. You use the **access specifier** private, followed by a colon, followed by the list of class members that you want to be private. You use the access specifier public, followed by a colon, prior to the class members that you want to be public.

In addition to private data, there can be private functions, as you will see later in this chapter.

You don't actually need to tell the compiler which data members are private, because private is the default access specifier. That is, if you do nothing (write neither public nor private), all data and functions in a class are private, or inaccessible.

5

```
// declaration section:
class Student
    {
        private:
            int idNum;
            char lastName[15];
            double gradePointAverage;
        public:
            void displayStudentData();
    };
// implementation section:
void Student::displayStudentData()
{
  cout<<"Student #"<<idNum<<"'s last name is "<<lastName<<endl;
  cout<<"The grade point average for this student is "<<
        gradePointAverage<<endl;
}
```

Figure 5-7   Student class with private data

A problem arises if you try to run the program shown in Figure 5-4 and you use the new Student class shown in Figure 5-7. When you compile the program, you receive error messages indicating that the fields idNum, lastName, and gradePointAverage are **inaccessible**. This means that the main() program can't use these fields, as in the statement aStudent.idNum = 777;, because idNum is a private data field. You do not get an error message when you use aStudent.displayStudentData();, because the displayStudentData() function is public, not private.

Using Public Functions to Alter Private Data

You gain a major advantage when you make a data field private. Once you create a class, including writing and debugging all of its member functions, outside functions over which you have no control can never modify or erroneously use the private member data of any object in the class. When you create and test a class, and store its definition in a file, programs that use the definition can be prevented from using member data incorrectly. If a private member of your Student class, such as idNum, must be a four-digit number, or if you require that the idNumber always be preceded by a pound sign, functions that are not a member of your class can never change those rules (either intentionally or by accident).

However, if a program can't assign a value to a field because it is private, then the field is not of much use. You keep data private, yet gain the ability to alter it, by creating additional public functions that *can* assign values to a class's private fields. For example, if the offices at your firm are all private and you cannot communicate with the executives in them, the company won't function for long. Usually, at least receptionists are public, and you can use them to communicate with the private executives. Similarly, you communicate with the private members of a class by sending messages to the public member functions. Figure 5-8 shows the declaration for a Student class that contains three additional functions programs used to assign values to a Student's data fields. These functions are named setIdNum(), setLastName(), and setGradePointAverage(). Each is used to set the value of one of the fields within the Student class.

 Classes can contain many functions with many purposes. Usually the first functions you create for a class are those that provide a means for input and output of the class data fields.

```
class Student
{
   private:
      int idNum;
      char lastName[15];
      double gradePointAverage;
   public:
         void displayStudentData();
         void setIdNum(int num);
         void setLastName(char name[]);
         void setGradePointAverage(double gpa);
};
```

Figure 5-8   Student class with set functions for private data

You can place any lines of code you want within these functions. If you want the setLastName() function to assign a string to the Student's lastName, then you can implement the function as shown in Figure 5-9.

```
void Student::setLastName(char name[])
  {
    strcpy(lastName, name);
  }
```

Figure 5-9   The setLastName() function

The setLastName() function shown in Figure 5-9 is a member of the Student class. You can determine this because the class header contains the Student class name and the scope resolution operator. The setLastName() function takes a string argument that has the local name name. The function uses the strcpy() function to assign the passed name value to the lastName field of Student class. When you write a program in which you instantiate a Student object named aJunior, you can assign a last name to the aJunior object with a statement such as **aJunior.setLastName("Farnsworth");**. The string "Farnsworth" is passed into the aJunior's setLastName() function, where it is copied to the aJunior's lastName field.

If lastName were a public field within the Student class, then you could assign "Farnsworth" to lastName with the statement **strcpy(aJunior.lastName, "Farnsworth");**. That is, you would not have to use the setLastName() method. However, making the lastName field public would violate one of the canons of object-oriented programming: whenever possible, data should be kept private, and access to data should be controlled by public functions.

Assume that a student ID number should not be more than four digits in length. When you implement the setIdNum() function of the Student class, you can assign the ID number argument to the class idNum field only if it is a valid ID; otherwise you can **force** the idNum field to 9999. Figure 5-10 shows a setIdNum() function that operates in this way.

```
void Student::setIdNum(int num)
{
  if(num <= 9999)
    idNum = num;
  else
    idNum = 9999;
}
```

Figure 5-10   The setIdNum() function

When you use the setIdNum() function with an object like aJunior, you are assured that aJunior receives a valid idNum. If the idNum field were public, you could write a program and include the statement **aJunior.idNum = 123456;**. However, when the idNum is private, you must use the setIdNum() function. The statement **aJunior.setIdNum(123456);** results in the aJunior's idNum being set to 9999, not 123456.

The setIdNum() function in Figure 5-10 allows a negative ID number. If you use the if statement if(num >= 0 && num <=9999), then you can further limit the allowed idNum values.

Figure 5-11 shows how the setGradePointAverage() function can be written to accept a double argument and assure that the argument is no more than 4.0 before assigning it to any Student's gradePointAverage field. And grade point average above 4.0 is invalid and set to 0.

```
void Student::setGradePointAverage(double gpa)
   {
      if(gpa <= 4.0)
         gradePointAverage = gpa;
      else
         gradePointAverage = 0;
   }
```

Figure 5-11   The setGradePointAverage() function

Using a Complete Class in a Program

Figure 5-12 shows the entire Student class, all its member functions, and a short program that uses the class. Figure 5-13 shows the output. Notice in particular how the Student's grade point average is set to 0 because the program attempts to assign an invalid grade point average to the field. The public method setGradePointAverage() has exercised control over how the private data field is assigned.

Because the program shown in Figure 5-12 uses the strcpy() function, your compiler might require an additional preprocessor directive to include string.h.

```
#include<iostream.h>
#include<conio.h>
// declaration section:
class Student
 {
    private:
        int idNum;
        char lastName[15];
        double gradePointAverage;
    public:
        void displayStudentData();
        void setIdNum(int num);
        void setLastName(char name[]);
        void setGradePointAverage(double gpa);
 };
// implementation section:
void Student::displayStudentData()
{
  cout<<"Student #"<<idNum<<"'s last name is "<<lastName<<endl;
  cout<<"The grade point average for this student is "<<
     gradePointAverage<<endl;
}
void Student::setIdNum(int num)
{
   if(num < 10000)
    idNum = num;
   else
    idNum = 9999;
}
void Student::setLastName(char name[])
  {
    strcpy(lastName, name);
  }
void Student::setGradePointAverage(double gpa)
  {
    if(gpa <= 4.0)
       gradePointAverage = gpa;
    else
       gradePointAverage = 0;
  }
void main()
 {
    Student aStudent;
    aStudent.setIdNum(777);
    aStudent.setLastName("Gibson");
    aStudent.setGradePointAverage(4.7);
    aStudent.displayStudentData();
    getch();
 }
```

Figure 5-12   The fully implemented Student class, and a demonstration program

```
MH
OS  Student2

Student #777's last name is Gibson
The grade point average for this student is 0
```

Figure 5-13   Output of program that uses the fully implemented Student class

 You can use the access specifiers public and private as many times as you want in a class definition—for example, two private members, followed by one public member, followed by two more private members. It's better style, however, to group the private and public members together.

 Many C++ programmers prefer to place the public section before the private section in a class definition. The reasoning is that other programmers then see and use the public interfaces. Use the style you prefer.

In the next set of steps you modify the CollegeCourse class you created earlier so that it more closely adheres to good object-oriented programming principles.

1. If it is not still open on your screen, open the **CollegeCourse.cpp** file you created earlier in this chapter.

2. The access specifier on the first line within the class, just before the declaration of the character string for department, currently is public. Change it to **private**.

3. Place the insertion point at the end of the line that declares the seats field, and press **Enter** to start a new line. Add the access specifier **public:** (include the colon) so that the displayCourseData() function definition is public.

4. Add three new public function definitions below the displayCourseData() definition. The Student class shown in this chapter uses arguments in its set functions. In the CollegeCourse class, you write the functions so they accept data from the keyboard interactively. Therefore, they require no arguments.

   void setDepartment();
   void setCourseNum();
   void setSeats();

5. Position the insertion point after the closing curly braces for the displayCourseData() function, and press the **Enter** key to start a new line. Insert the setDepartment() function so that it accepts the user's response to a prompt for a department name.

   void CollegeCourse::setDepartment()
   {
   ** cout<<"Enter the three-letter department code for the course ";**
   ** cin>>department;**
   }

6. Add the setCourseNum() function.

```
void CollegeCourse::setCourseNum()
{
  cout<<"Enter the three-digit course number ";
  cin>>courseNum;
}
```

7. Add the setSeats() function. Do not allow any courses to have an enrollment over 300.

```
void CollegeCourse::setSeats()
{
  cout<<"Enter the number of seats for which students can enroll ";
  cin>>seats;
  while(seats>300)
    {
     cout<<"There are no classes with more than 300 students"<<endl;
     cout<<"Please enter a new number ";
     cin>>seats;
    }
}
```

8. Remove the main() function from the current file. Add a new main() function that declares a CollegeCourse named myFavoriteClass and allows the user to enter data about the course.

```
void main()
  {
  CollegeCourse myFavoriteClass;
  myFavoriteClass.setDepartment();
  myFavoriteClass.setCourseNum();
  myFavoriteClass.setSeats();
  myFavoriteClass.displayCourseData();
  getch();
  }
```

9. Save the file as **CollegeCourse2.cpp**, and store it in the Chapter05 folder on your Student Data Disk or in the Student Data folder on your hard drive. Compile and run the program. A typical run is shown in Figure 5-14.

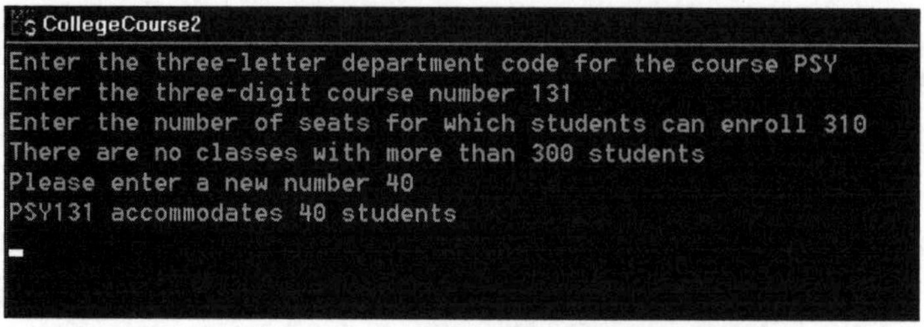

Figure 5-14   Output of the CollegeCourse2 program

USING PRIVATE FUNCTIONS

Not all functions are public. When you think of real-world objects, such as kitchen appliances, there are many public functions you control through an interface: adjusting the temperature on a refrigerator or oven, setting a cycle on a dishwasher, and so on. However, there are other functions that appliances encapsulate: a freezer might defrost itself without your help, and a dishwasher switches from the wash to the rinse cycle. With objects you create, functions also can be private if you choose.

For example, Figure 5-15 shows a revised Student class in which the functions that set the Student ID, name, and grade point average have been reclassified as private, and a new public function named setStudentData() has been added. The purpose of the new function is to call the other three functions. Figure 5-16 shows a main() function that can use this revised Student class, and Figure 5-17 shows the output of the program in Figure 5-16. With this new version of the Student class, the only way in which a main() program can set Student data is by calling the setStudentData() function. In turn, the setStudentData() function calls three other functions, passing on the appropriate parameter to each. If you choose, you can make all the functions public; then the program that uses your Student class, sometimes called the **client**, could use either the setStudentData() function or any of the individual set functions deemed appropriate at the time. You can organize your classes in the way that seems most suitable to you.

```
class Student
 {
    private:
       int idNum;
       char lastName[15];
       double gradePointAverage;
       void setIdNum(int num);
       void setLastName(char name[]);
       void setGradePointAverage(double gpa);
    public:
       void displayStudentData();
       void setStudentData(int id, char last[], double avg);
 };
void Student::displayStudentData()
{
  cout<<"Student #"<<idNum<<"'s last name is "<<lastName<<endl;
  cout<<"The grade point average for this student is "<<
     gradePointAverage<<endl;
}
void Student::setIdNum(int num)
{
   if(num < 10000)
    idNum = num;
   else
    idNum = 9999;
 }
void Student::setLastName(char name[])
 {
    strcpy(lastName, name);
 }
void Student::setGradePointAverage(double gpa)
 {
    if(gpa <= 4.0)
       gradePointAverage = gpa;
    else
       gradePointAverage = 0;
 }
void Student::setStudentData(int id, char last[], double avg)
 {
    setIdNum(id);
    setLastName(last);
    setGradePointAverage(avg);
 }
```

Figure 5-15   Student class containing private functions

```
void main()
  {
    Student aStudent;
    aStudent.setStudentData(3861, "Kryca", 3.6);
    aStudent.displayStudentData();
    getch();
}
```

Figure 5-16   A main() function that uses the Student class in Figure 5-15

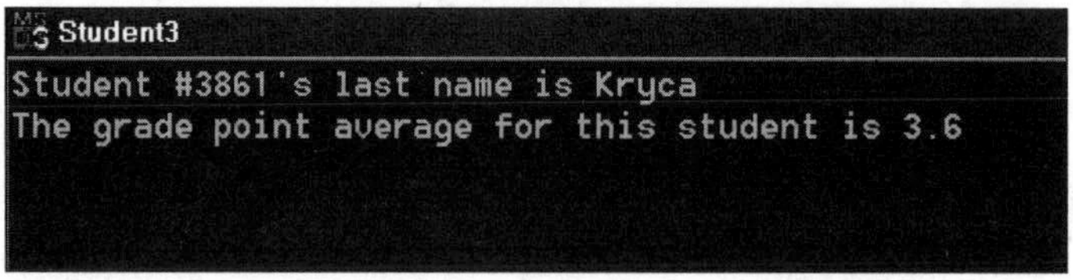

Figure 5-17   Output of the program shown in Figure 5-16

In the main() function shown in Figure 5-15, it would be incorrect to make a statement such as `aStudent.setLastName("Kryca");`. The setLastName() function is private and inaccessible to main(). The setStudentData() function can use the setLastName() function, however. Every class function always has access to its own functions and data fields, whether they are private or not.

CONSIDERING SCOPE WHEN DEFINING MEMBER FUNCTIONS

You already know about scope; a local variable is in scope only within the function in which it is declared. The scope resolution operator is a C++ operator that identifies a member function as being in scope within a class. It consists of two colons (::). Within the Student class in Figure 5-15, one public member function is displayStudentData(). The header for the function signals that setStudentData() is a member of Student: `void Student::displayStudentData()`. The header indicates that nothing is returned, Student is the class, displayStudentData() is the name of the function, and that the function requires no arguments.

Within the displayStudentData() function, the fields idNum, lastName, and gradePointAverage are shown. When you access a field such as idNum within a Student member function, you can use just the field name, but you also can use the class name and scope resolution operator with the field name. Figure 5-18 shows a displayStudentData() function that works exactly like the one in Figure 5-15. The difference is that the class for each field name has been specified.

```
void Student::displayStudentData()
{
   cout<<"Student #"<<Student::idNum<<"'s last name is "
   <<Student::lastName<<endl;
   cout<<"The grade point average for this student is "<<
   Student::gradePointAverage<<endl;
}
```

Figure 5-18   Class function that uses scope resolution with data fields

The Student class name and scope resolution operators used within the displayStudentData()
function in Figure 5-18 are completely optional; the function operates correctly without
them because the fields are part of the same class as the function itself. However, the scope
resolution operator does no harm, and leaves no doubt as to the origin of the field names; it
is equivalent to using your full formal name instead of your nickname. Just as a mother seldom uses the name Catherine Marie, opting instead for Cathy, C++ programmers usually
do not bother using the class name and scope resolution operator.

However, there are circumstances when the scope resolution operator is required with a class
field name. Whenever there is a conflict between local and class variable names, you must use
the scope resolution operator to achieve the results you want. Consider the two versions of
the Student class setIdNum() function shown in Figure 5-19. In the first version, the argument that is passed to the function is known locally as num. Within the function, idNum
refers to the Student class field, and num refers to the passed argument. In the second version of the function, the programmer called the function argument idNum. Within this second version of the function, idNum refers to the passed argument. To distinguish between
the local variable and the class field, the scope resolution operator is used with the class field
name. In the first version of the function, the class name and scope resolution operator could
have been used with the class field, but it isn't required to do so. However, the scope resolution operator must be used with the class field in the second version.

```
void Student::setIdNum(int num)
{
   if(num < 10000)
     idNum = num;
   else
     idNum = 9999;
 }
void Student::setIdNum(int idNum)
{
   if(idNum < 10000)
     Student::idNum = idNum;
   else
     Student::idNum = 9999;
 }
```

Figure 5-19   Two versions of setIdNum()

In the second function in Figure 5-19, idNum refers to only the function's local variable named idNum. The class variable with the same name is **hidden** unless you use the scope resolution operator.

USING STATIC CLASS MEMBERS

A C++ object is an instantiation of a class that can contain both data members and methods. When you create an object, a block of memory is set aside for the data members. Just as the declaration `int x;` reserves enough space in your system to hold an integer, the declaration `Student oneStudent;` reserves enough storage in your system to hold a Student object. When it is created, each class object gets its own block of memory for its data members. If you create two students, you reserve two blocks of memory; if you create an array of 100 objects, 100 blocks of memory are set aside.

Sometimes every instantiation of a class requires the same value. For example, you might want every Student object to contain a data member that holds the student athletic fee—a value that is the same for all Students. If you declare 100 Student objects, all Students need their own ID, name, and grade point average, but not all students need their own athletic fee figure. If each Student object contains a copy of the athletic fee, you repeat the same information 100 times, wasting memory. To avoid such a waste, you declare the athletic fee variable as **static**, meaning that it remains unchanged. A class variable that you declare to be static is the same (doesn't change) for all objects that are instantiations of the class. All members of the class share a single storage location for a static data member of that same class. Each instantiation of the class *appears* to be storing its own copy of the same value, but each actually just has access to the same memory location.

Static variables are sometimes called class variables because they don't belong to a specific object; they belong to the class.

When you create a non-static variable within a function, a new variable is created every time you call that function. The variable might have a different address and different initial value from the previous time you called the function. When you create a static variable, the variable maintains its memory address and previous value for the life of the program.

Defining Static Data Members

Because it uses only one memory location, a static data member is defined (given a value) in a single statement outside the class definition. Most often this statement appears just before the class implementation section. Consider the class and program in Figure 5-20. Note that the small Student class contains just two fields. In this program, every class object that you ever instantiate receives its own copy of the non-static idNum field, but the same static athleticFee value applies to every class member that is ever instantiated. When the main() function declares two Student objects, aFreshman and aSophomore, they each possess their own idNum value, but they share the athleticFee value. The output is shown in Figure 5-21.

5

```
#include<iostream.h>
#include<conio.h>
// declaration section:
class Student
  {
    private:
        int idNum;
    public:
        static double athleticFee;
        void setIdNum(int num);
        void displayStudentData();
  };
// implementation section:
double Student::athleticFee = 45.25;
void Student::displayStudentData()
{
  cout<<"Student #"<<idNum<<"'s athletic fee is $"
    <<athleticFee<<endl;
}
void Student::setIdNum(int num)
{
   if(num < 10000)
    idNum = num;
   else
    idNum = 9999;
}
void main()
{
    Student aFreshman, aSophomore;
    aFreshman.setIdNum(1234);
    aSophomore.setIdNum(2345);
    aFreshman.displayStudentData();
    aSophomore.displayStudentData();
    getch();
}
```

Figure 5-20   A class that contains a static athleticFee field

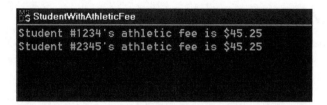

Figure 5-21   Output of program that uses two Students with a static athletic fee value

Even though each Student declared in the program shown in Figure 5-20 has a unique ID number, all Student objects share the athletic fee, which was assigned a value just once. Notice that the keyword static is used when the symbol athleticFee is declared. The keyword static is not used in the assignment statement in which it is assigned a value.

The field athleticFee is not a constant field. You could make it one in the same way you make other fields constant—by inserting the word **const** in front of its name when you declare it. Static does not mean the same thing as constant. Constant fields are never changeable; static fields are changeable, but hold the same value for every object. Constant static fields hold the same unchangeable value for every object. Because the athleticFee field in the Student class in Figure 5-20 was not declared constant, you could insert a statement like `aFreshman.athleticFee = 139.95;` into the main() function. From that point on, every Student object (the aFreshman and the aSophomore) would have an athleticFee of 139.95 instead of 45.25. Alternately, and more logically, you could just state `Student::athleticFee = 139.95;`. This also would change every Student's athleticFee field from that point on. From this example, you can see that you do not need to create any objects to use a static class variable.

Although you can use static class members with an object name or by using them with the class name, some programmers prefer to use them only with the class name. That's because they perceive static members to truly belong to the class as a whole.

A static class member exists, even when you have not instantiated any objects of the class. For example, when you use the Student class, you can access the Student::athleticFee even if you have not created any Student objects.

Using Static Functions

In the program shown in Figure 5-20, the athleticFee field is public, which is why you can access it directly, as in `Student::athleticFee = 139.95;`. If it were private, you would have to use a public function to access the value, as with any other private variable. Additionally, the function would have to be a **static function**.

As with a static data field, when you create a static member function, only one copy of the function exists for the class. You must use a static function to access a static field because static functions do not receive a pointer to the object that uses the function. You don't need to create an object in order to use a static field; therefore, you need a static function in order to access the static field. You use a static function by prefixing the function name with the class name and the scope resolution operator.

 Only one copy exists for all static and non-static member functions. The difference is that the non-static functions receive a this pointer and are associated with an object. You will learn more about the this pointer later in this chapter.

In the following set of steps, you use a private, static class variable to keep track of how many objects have been initialized. You will use a public static function to display the private static variable.

5

1. Open a new file in your C++ editor. Type the necessary include files and begin a class that holds information about business letters you write. For simplicity, this class contains just two private fields: the name of the recipient and a count of how many letters have been sent.

```
#include<iostream.h>
#include<conio.h>
#include<string.h>class Letter
   {
private:
   char recipient[20];
   static int count;
```

2. Next, add three public functions. You use one function to set a recipient's name, and add 1 to the count of Letters each time you do so. Two other functions show the recipient's name and the count value. The latter function is static because it uses the static variable. Complete the class definition with the closing curly brace and the semicolon.

```
public:
   void setRecipient(char name[]);
   void displayRecipient();
   static void displayCount();
};
```

3. Initialize the Letter count to zero.

```
int Letter::count = 0;
```

4. Write the setRecipient() function. This function uses the name passed to it as an argument in order to set the class recipient field. It also adds 1 to the count of letters assigned a recipient.

```
void Letter::setRecipient(char name[])
   {
      strcpy(recipient,name);
      ++count;
   }
```

5. Write the displayRecipient() function:

   void Letter::displayRecipient()
   ```
       {
           cout <<"Letter sent to " <<recipient <<endl;
       }
   ```

6. The displayCount() function displays the value of count.

   void Letter::displayCount()
   ```
       {
           cout<<"Current count is "<<count<<endl;
       }
   ```

7. Next, write a main() program that demonstrates how the Letter class works. Within the main() function, you declare a Letter object and initialize to 'y' a field named more. You prompt the user for a last name, assign the name to the Letter, and display the current count. (In a more complete program, you might also want to call a function that actually prints a form letter or saves the Letter objects to a file.) Then ask the user whether there are more letters. As long as the user continues to respond with any key except 'n', the process continues.

   void main()
   ```
   {
     Letter aLetter;
     char name[20];
     char more = 'y';
     while(more != 'n')
       {
       cout<< "Enter last name of recipient ";
       cin>>name;
       aLetter.setRecipient(name);
       aLetter.displayCount();
       cout<<"Do you want to send another - y or n? ";
       cin>>more;
       }
   ```

8. Add a call to the getch() function to hold the output screen, and add the closing curly brace for the main() function.

   getch();
   ```
   }
   ```

9. Save the program as **Letter.cpp**, and store it in the Chapter05 folder of your Student Data Disk or in the Student Data folder on your hard drive. Compile and run the program. A typical run is shown in Figure 5-22.

```
Letter
Enter last name of recipient Dykeman
Current count is 1
Do you want to send another - y or n? y
Enter last name of recipient Lewis
Current count is 2
Do you want to send another - y or n? y
Enter last name of recipient Evans
Current count is 3
Do you want to send another - y or n? n
```


Figure 5-22 Output of Letter program

UNDERSTANDING THE THIS POINTER

When you define a class, you include fields and functions. If the class has one non-static field and one static field such as the Employee class shown in Figure 5-23, and you then declare two Employee objects, you reserve storage for two versions of the non-static field. However, you store only one version of the static field that every object can use. It would be wasteful to store two versions of the same value. Additionally, if the static value required changing (if, for example, the company acquired a new company ID number), then each version would have to be updated.

```
class Employee
 {
    private:
       int employeeIdNum;
       const static int companyIdNum;
    public:
       void setId(const int id);
       void displayValues();
 };
const int Employee::companyIdNum = 12345;
void Employee::displayValues()
{
  cout<<"Employee #"<<employeeIdNum<<" company #"
     <<companyIdNum<<endl;
}
void Employee::setId(const int id)
{
   employeeIdNum = id;
}
```

Figure 5-23 Employee class

The program in Figure 5-24 declares two Employee objects, clerk and driver. Each needs its own employeeIdNum, but they share the companyIdNum. Figure 5-25 shows the output of the program. Just as it would be wasteful to store a shared company ID number separately for these two Employees, it also would waste space if you stored the code for the member functions setId() and displayValues() separately for each Employee. Imagine a program that stores data for 1,000 employees, or an Employee class with 20 member functions. If the same function code were stored repeatedly for every instance of a class, the storage requirements would be enormous.

```
#include<iostream.h>
#include<conio.h>
void main()
  {
    Employee clerk, driver;
    clerk.setId(345);
    driver.setId(789);
    clerk.displayValues();
    driver.displayValues();
    getch();
  }
```

Figure 5-24   Program that uses the Employee class

```
DS Employee
Employee #345 company #12345
Employee #789 company #12345
```

Figure 5-25   Output of program that instantiates two Employee objects

Luckily, C++ does not store member functions separately for each instance of a class. Instead, one copy of each member function is stored, and each instance of a class uses the same function code. Whether you make the statement `clerk.displayValues();` or `driver.displayValues();` you call the same copy of the displayValues() function. This does not mean the output results are identical, as you can see from Figure 5-25. Even though each call to the function uses the same programming instructions, each call to displayValues() uses a different memory location to access the employeeIdNum.

Because only one copy of each function exists, when you call a function, it needs to know which object to use. To ensure that the function uses the correct object, you use the object's name, such as clerk or driver, with the dot operator. The address of the correct object, clerk or driver, is then automatically passed to the displayValues() function.

Within the displayValues() function, the address of the object is stored in a special pointer called the **this pointer**. The this pointer holds the memory address of the current object that is using the function; that's why it is named this—it refers to "this object" as opposed to any other object. The this pointer is automatically supplied every time you call a non-static member function of a class. For example, when you make the function call `clerk.displayValues();`, the actual function call made by the compiler is `displayValues(&clerk);`. Similarly, when you make the function call `driver.displayValues();`, the actual function call is `displayValues(&driver);`. In other words, when you use an object, the dot operator, and a non-static function of the object's class, you actually pass the specific object's address to the function as an unseen argument. The actual argument list used by the compiler for the displayValues() function is `displayValues(Employee *this)`. The displayValues() function receives a pointer to an Employee object; the automatically supplied object address is the means by which the function knows which Employee's data to display.

Don't explicitly send the address of the object when you call a member function; if you do, the function receives two address values—the one you type and the one automatically sent.

The this pointer also is passed to member functions when they receive additional, explicitly stated arguments. Figure 5-23 shows that the Employee class setId() function receives an integer argument. In addition, it receives a pointer to the object it manipulates. When you make the statement `clerk.setId(345);`, the actual argument list used by the compiler for setId() is `setId((Employee *this, const int id);`. The actual function call used by the compiler is `setId((&clerk, 345);`. When you call a non-static member function using a class object, the first (and sometimes only) argument passed to the function is a pointer that holds the address of the object to which you are referring.

The this pointer is a constant. You cannot modify it, as in:
```
this = &someOtherObject;   // illegal!
```

Using the this Pointer Explicitly

Within any member function, you can prove that the this pointer exists and that it holds the address of the current object. You do so by using the this pointer to access the object's data fields. In Figure 5-26, displayValues() and setId() have been rewritten to explicitly refer to the this pointer. If you substitute the functions in Figure 5-26 for their counterparts in the original class definition in Figure 5-23, there is no difference in the execution of any program that uses the Employee class. The versions of the functions shown in Figure 5-26 simply illustrate that the this pointer exists, and that you can refer to the contents stored in the this pointer like you can with any other pointer—by placing an asterisk in front of the pointer's name. (The parentheses are required in `(*this).employeeIdNum` because only `this` is a pointer. Without the parentheses, the compiler would treat `this.employeeIdNum` as a pointer, which it is not—it is an integer.)

```
void Employee::displayValues()
{
   cout<<"Employee #"<<(*this).employeeIdNum<<" company #"
       <<(*this).companyIdNum<<endl;
}
void Employee::setId(const int id)
{
   (*this).employeeIdNum = id;
}
```

Figure 5-26   Member functions explicitly using the this pointer

Using the Pointer-to-Member Operator

Figure 5-27 shows yet another way to use the this pointer. The functions operate like those in Figure 5-26, but they use the C++ **pointer-to-member operator**, which looks like an arrow and is constructed by a programmer by using a dash followed by a right angle bracket (or greater-than sign). Any pointer variable that is declared to point to a class object can be used to access individual fields or functions of that class by using the parentheses and the asterisk shown in Figure 5-26. Or, the pointer-to-member operator shown in Figure 5-27 can be used.

```
void Employee::displayValues()
{
   cout<<"Employee #"<<this->employeeIdNum<<" company #"
       <<this->companyIdNum<<endl;
}
void Employee::setId(const int id)
{
   this->employeeIdNum = id;
}
```

Figure 5-27   Explicitly using the this pointer with the pointer-to-member operator

Programmers usually do not code their class member functions as shown in Figure 5-26 or Figure 5-27. The functions work fine without typing the this references. Most often, you do not have to be concerned with the this pointer. Although it's helpful to understand how the function knows which object to use, the reference is made automatically, and you don't have to think about it. There are, however, a few occasions when you might want to use the this pointer explicitly within member functions. The most common occurrence is when you want to return the pointer that was sent to a function (for example, `return(*this);`).

One type of member function does not have a this pointer: the static member function. You make a class member function static when you want to call it from outside the source file in which it is defined, or when you want to call it even if no instances of a class exist.

In the next set of steps, you explicitly add some references to the this pointer to the Letter class you wrote earlier. You are adding the reference to illustrate how the this pointer works.

1. Open the **Letter.cpp** file you created earlier in this chapter, if it is not still open on your screen.

2. Within the Letter::displayRecipient() function, change the reference to the variable recipient to **this->recipient**. The function becomes:

```
void Letter::displayRecipient()
{
    cout<< "Letter sent to "<<this->recipient<<endl;
}
```

3. Within the Letter::setRecipient() function, change the reference to recipient to **this-> recipient**, and the reference to count to **this->count**. The function becomes:

```
void Letter::setRecipient(char name[])
{
  strcpy(this->recipient,name);
  ++this->count;
}
```

You cannot change the reference to count in the displayCount() function to this->count because displayCount() is a static function, so it does not receive a this pointer.

4. Save the file as **LetterWithThis.cpp** in the Chapter05 folder on your Student Data Disk or in the Student Data folder on your hard drive. Compile and run the program. It executes just as it did before you explicitly added the reference to the this pointer.

UNDERSTANDING POLYMORPHISM

Polymorphism is the object-oriented program feature that allows the same operation to be carried out differently depending on the object. When you speak English, you use the same instructions with different objects all the time. For example, you interpret a verb differently depending on the object to which it is applied. You catch a ball, but you also catch a cold. You run a computer, a business, a race, or a stocking. The meanings of "catch" and "run" are different in each case, but you can understand each operation because the combination of the verb and the object makes the command clear.

When you write C++ (and other object-oriented) programs, you can send the same message to different objects and different types of objects. Suppose you have two members of the Employee class, clerk and driver. You can display the data of each member with the following statements: `clerk.displayValues();` and `driver.displayValues();`. No confusion arises as to which member's values should be displayed, because the correct pointer is passed as a this pointer each time you call the displayValues() function.

Similarly, suppose you have three different objects that are members of different classes: a clerk who is a member of the Employee class, a shirt that is a member of the Inventory class, and XYZCompany, a member of the Supplier class. Each object can certainly have different numbers and types of data members. The clerk has an employee idNumber and a salary. The shirt has a sleeveLength, neckSize, and price. The XYZCompany has a president, phoneNumber, dateOfLastOrder, and annualSalesFigure. Even though these objects are very different, occasionally you might need to display each of their data members. In such a case, it seems appropriate to call each function displayValues().

C++ allows you to create three very different member functions, one for each of the classes in question. For example, within an Employee class, an Inventory class, and a Supplier class, you might create the functions shown in Figure 5-28.

```
// Within the Employee class
void Employee::displayValues()
  {
    cout<<"Employee ID is "<<idNumber;
  }
// Within the Inventory class
void Inventory::displayValues()
  {
    cout<<"This shirt has a sleeve of "<<sleeveLength;
    cout<<" and a neck size "<<neckSize<<endl;
    cout<<"It sells for $"<<price<<endl;
  }
// Within the Supplier class
void Supplier::displayValues()
  {
   cout<<"President: "<<president<<" at phone"
       <<phoneNumber<<endl;
   cout<<"Last order "<<dateOfLastOrder;
   cout<<" Annual sales "<<annualSalesFigure<<endl;
  }
```

Figure 5-28 Three displayValues() functions from three separate classes

The three functions in Figure 5-28 contain statements with different content, but they all have the name displayValues(). Assuming you have declared objects of the appropriate class types, you might make three function calls as follows:

```
clerk.displayValues();
shirt.displayValues();
XYZCompany.displayValues();
```

Each of the preceding functions displays the intended object in a unique, appropriate format. The this pointer sends the appropriate address so the function uses the correct object. Because of the object's type (Employee, Inventory, or Supplier), you call the displayValues() function that is a member of the appropriate class.

The concept of polymorphism includes far more than using the same function name for different function bodies. As you continue to study C++, you will learn about the role polymorphism plays in inheritance.

When you can apply the same function name to different objects, your programs become easier to read and make more sense. It takes less time to develop a project; you also can make later changes more rapidly. C++ programmers often can write programs faster than programmers who use non-object-oriented programming languages, and polymorphism is one of the reasons why.

CHAPTER SUMMARY

- ❐ Each class you define is an abstract data type, or a group type with its own fields and functions. Each class requires a declaration section that contains field definitions and function prototypes. Each class also requires an implementation section that contains the functions themselves.

- ❐ A technique programmers use to provide more complete object encapsulation is to make most objects' data private. This allows you to control how the data fields are used. So that other programmers can use the data, most class functions are public.

- ❐ You can make functions private when you want to hide their use from client programs.

- ❐ You can use the scope resolution operator with class fields and functions. Whenever there is a conflict between local and class variable names, you must use the scope resolution operator with the class fields.

- ❐ When you declare a class variable to be static, only one copy of the variable is stored, no matter how many class objects you instantiate. You must use a static function to access a static variable.

- ❐ When you create a class, one copy of each member function is stored. Each non-static function automatically is passed a this pointer when you use the function with an object.

❑ Polymorphism is the object-oriented program feature that allows the same operation to be carried out differently, depending on the object. When you can apply the same function name to different objects, your programs can be developed more quickly and are easier to read.

REVIEW QUESTIONS

1. C++ programmers refer to a type you define as an ADT, or an _____.

   a. abstract data type

   b. alternative data theory

   c. adaptable data type

   d. anonymous default test

2. You have defined a class named Invoice that contains two public fields, invoiceNumber and amount. When you write a main() function and declare one Invoice object named anInvoice, you can display the object's amount field with the statement _____.

   a. cout<<anInvoice(amount);

   b. cout<<Invoice.amount;

   c. cout<<anInvoice.amount;

   d. None of the above

3. You have defined a class named Invoice that contains two private fields, invoiceNumber and amount. When you write a main() function and declare one Invoice object named anInvoice, you can display the object's amount field with the statement _____.

   a. cout<<anInvoice(amount);

   b. cout<<Invoice.amount;

   c. cout<<anInvoice.amount;

   d. None of the above

4. When you encapsulate class components, you _____ them.

   a. destroy

   b. hide

   c. display

   d. format

5. The word interface is most closely associated with _____.

   a. functions

   b. variables

   c. prototypes

   d. implementations

6. You create a class in two sections called _____.

 a. declaration and implementation

 b. typical and atypical

 c. common and protected

 d. abstract and concrete

7. A class named Apartment contains a function named showRent() that neither takes nor receives arguments. The correct function header for the showRent() function is _____.

 a. showRent()

 b. Apartment::showRent()

 c. void Apartment::showRent()

 d. void Apartment.showRent()

8. The operator that ties a function name to a class is the _____ operator.

 a. pointer to member

 b. this

 c. scope resolution

 d. binary

9. A technique that programmers use to provide object encapsulation is to usually make objects' data _____.

 a. private

 b. polymorphic

 c. accessible

 d. static

10. The most common arrangement for a class is _____.

 a. data members are static; functions are not

 b. data members are not static; functions are

 c. data members are public; functions are not

 d. data members are not public; functions are

11. You control how data is stored in classes by using _____.

 a. polymorphism

 b. well-written public functions

 c. anonymous classes

 d. private methods that clients cannot access

5

12. Which is true for most classes?

    a. All class functions are private.

    b. Most class functions are private.

    c. Most class functions are public.

    d. Most classes contain no functions.

13. A program that uses a class is known as the class's _____.

    a. patient

    b. superclass

    c. consumer

    d. client

14. You create a class named Car with data fields named year, make, and price. The car Class contains a non-static function named setYear() whose prototype is **void setYear(int year);**. Within this function, which statement correctly sets the class field to the value of the argument?

    a. year = year;

    b. Car::year = year;

    c. year = Car::year;

    d. Two of the above are correct.

15. You create a class named Car with data fields named year, make, and price. The car Class contains a non-static function named setMake() whose prototype is **void setMake(String carMake);**. Within this function, which statement correctly sets the class field to the value of the argument?

    a. strcpy(make,carMake);

    b. strcpy(Car::make, carMake);

    c. strcpy(Car::make, Car::carMake);

    d. Two of the above are correct.

16. You create a class named Car with data fields named year, make, and price. The car Class contains a non-static function named setPrice() whose prototype is **void setPrice(double price);**. Within this function, which statement correctly sets the class field to the value of the argument?

    a. price = price;

    b. this->price = price;

    c. price = this->price;

    d. Two of the above are correct.

17. To create just one memory location for a field no matter how many objects you instantiate, you should declare the field to be _____.

   a. private

   b. anonymous

   c. static

   d. stagnant

18. A function that you use to display a static variable must be _____.

   a. private

   b. anonymous

   c. static

   d. stagnant

19. The pointer that is automatically supplied when you call a non-static class member function is the _____ pointer.

   a. public

   b. this

   c. implicit

   d. reference

20. _____ is the feature in object-oriented programs that allows the same operation to be carried out differently, depending on the object.

   a. Encapsulation

   b. Inheritance

   c. Pointer creation

   d. Polymorphism

EXERCISES

1. Define a class named Movie. Include private fields for the title, year, and name of the director. Include three public functions with the prototypes `void setTitle(char movieTitle[]);`, `void setYear(int year);`, and `void setDirector(char dir[]);`. Include another function that displays information about a movie. Write a main() function that declares a movie object named myFavoriteMovie. Set and display the object's fields.

2. Complete the following tasks:

   a. Define a class named Customer that holds private fields for a customer ID number, last name, first name, and credit limit. Include four public functions that each set one of the four fields. Do not allow any credit limit over $10,000. Include a public function that displays a Customer's data. Write a main() program in which you declare a Customer, set the Customer's fields, and display the results.

b. Write a main() program that declares an array of five Customers. Set all the fields for each Customer, and display values for all five Customer objects.

3. Complete the following tasks:

a. Define a class named GroceryItem. Include private fields that hold an item's stock number, price, quantity in stock, and total value. Write three public functions that each set one of the three fields, based on user keyboard input. The function that sets the stock number requires the user to enter exactly four digits; continue to prompt the user until a valid stock number is entered. Include a private function that calculates the GroceryItem's total value field (price times quantity in stock) within the same function that accepts the quantity in stock input. Write a function that displays a GroceryItem's values. Finally, write a main() function that declares a GroceryItem object, assigns values to its fields, and uses the display function.

b. Write a main() function that declares an array of 10 GroceryItem objects. Assign values to all 10 items and display them.

4. Complete the following tasks:

a. Write the class definition for a Date class that contains three private integer data members: month, day, and year. Create a static member to hold a slash. Create two public member functions, setDate() and showDate(). The setDate() function accepts three integer arguments and passes them on to three private functions, setMonth(), setDay(), and setYear(). If a month is greater than 12, then set it to 12. If a day is greater than 31, then set it to 31. Write a main() program that instantiates several objects of the Date class and tests the functions.

b. Add a public function named increaseDay() to the Date class. Its purpose is to add 1 to the day field of a Date object. Write a main() function that declares a Date object. Set the Date to 10/15/2003 and display the object. In a loop, call the increaseDay() function five times, displaying each version of the Date as soon as it is increased.

c. Add instructions to the increaseDay() function so that when the day is more than 31, the month increases by 1 and the day is set to 1. Write a main() function that declares a Date object. Set the Date to 10/29/2003 and display the object. In a loop, call the increaseDay() function five times, displaying each version of the Date as soon as it is increased.

d. Add instructions to the increaseDay() function so that when the month becomes more than 12, the year increases by 1, and the month is set to 1. Write a main() function that declares a Date object. Set the Date to 12/29/2003 and display the object. In a loop, call the increaseDay() function five times, displaying each version of the Date as soon as it is increased.

5. Write the class definition for a Dog. Private data fields include name, breed, and age, and a static field for the license fee, which is $12.25. Create public member functions to set and display the data. Write a main() program that demonstrates the class operates correctly.

6. Complete the following tasks:

   a. Write a class definition for an Order class for a nightclub that contains a table number, a server's name, and the number of patrons at the table. Include a private static data member for the table minimum charge, which is $4.75. Write a main() function that declares no Order objects, but that uses a static member function to display the table minimum charge.

   b. Using the same Order class, write a main() function that declares an Order object, assigns appropriate values, and displays the Order data, including the minimum charge for the table—the minimum charge times the number of patrons at the table.

7. Define a class named CoffeeOrder. Include private integer fields that you set to a flag value of 1 or 0 to indicate whether the order should have any of the following: cream, milk, sugar, or artificial sweetener. Include a public function that takes a user's order from the keyboard and sets the values of the four fields in response to four prompts. If the user indicates both milk and cream, turn off the milk flag to allow only cream. If the user indicates both sugar and artificial sweetener, turn off the artificial sweetener flag, allowing only sugar. Include another function that displays the user's completed order. Write a main() function that declares a CoffeeOrder object and calls the data entry and display methods.

8. Each of the following files in the Chapter05 folder on your Student Data Disk or in the Student Data folder on your hard drive contains syntax and/or logical errors. Determine the problem in each case, and fix the program.

   a. DEBUG5-1

   b. DEBUG5-2

   c. DEBUG5-3

   d. DEBUG5-4

CASE PROJECT

You have been developing a Fraction class for Teacher's Pet Software. The class contains two public data fields: one for numerator and one for denominator. In keeping with the object-oriented concept of encapsulation, you make the Fraction's data private. Client programs access the Fraction's data through public functions you create.

Declare the Fraction's numerator and denominator to be private. Add two more private fields: a double that can hold the Fraction's decimal value, and a static character field that holds the slash all Fractions use when displaying their values.

In the public portion of the Fraction's declaration section, prototype an enterFractionValue() function that allows you to enter values for a Fraction's numerator and denominator. Do not allow the user to enter a value of 0 for the denominator of any Fraction.

Within the enterFractionValue() function, after the two data fields have received valid values, call a private calculateDecimalValue() function that computes the floating-point decimal equivalent of the Fraction.

In the public portion of the Fraction's declaration section, also prototype a displayFraction() function that displays a Fraction. This function prompts the user to enter a 1 to see the Fraction in fraction format (with the slash between the numerator and denominator), or a 2 to see the Fraction in floating-point format.

Write a main() program that declares a Fraction object and confirm that the class works correctly.

6

CLASS FEATURES AND DESIGN ISSUES

In this chapter, you will learn:

♦ How to classify the roles of member functions

♦ How to create constructors

♦ How to override constructor default values

♦ How to overload constructors

♦ How to create destructors

♦ How to use a class within another class

♦ How, why, and when to use the preprocessor directives #ifndef, #define, and #endif

♦ Techniques for managing attributes and functions of classes

♦ About coupling, and how to achieve loose coupling

♦ About cohesion, and how to achieve high cohesion

The ability to create classes provides a major advantage to object-oriented programming. Classes let you encapsulate data and functions, and therefore allow you to think of programming objects as you do their real-world counterparts. You have started to learn about classes; this chapter provides information about useful class features and capabilities, and offers advice on creating easy-to-use and reusable classes.

INTRODUCING MEMBER FUNCTIONS

You can create an infinite number of classes and write an infinite number of functions. You use the data members of a class to describe the state of an object, and you use the member functions to work with those data members. So far, you have learned about functions that assign values to data and then display those values. Eventually, you want to add many other specialized functions to your classes. You can classify the roles of member functions into four basic groups:

- **Inspector functions**, also called **access functions**. These functions return information about an object's state, or display some or all of an object's attributes. An inspector function typically has a name such as displayValues().

- **Mutator functions**, also known as **implementors**. These functions change an object's state or attributes. A mutator function often has a name such as setData(), which obtains values from an input device and assigns those values to an object's data members, or a name such as computeValue(), which calculates a data member based on values in other data members.

- **Auxiliary functions**, also known as **facilitators**. These functions perform some action or service, such as sorting data or searching for data. A typical name for an auxiliary function is sortAscending() or findLowestValue().

- **Manager functions**. These functions create and destroy objects for you. They perform initialization and cleanup. Called constructors and destructors, these functions have special properties that you need to understand to have full command of class capabilities.

UNDERSTANDING CONSTRUCTORS

A **constructor** is a function that is called automatically each time an object is created. You have been using constructors all along in your programs, even if you haven't realized it. When you declare a simple scalar variable, such as `int number;`, C++ calls an internal constructor function that reserves a memory location of the correct size for an integer, and attaches the name "number" to that location. The value at the number location might be anything; C++ does not automatically initialize the variable.

The definition `int number = 23;` calls a constructor that reserves memory, attaches a name, and assigns a value. This definition sends the constant value 23 to the constructor function. Although this definition does not look like a function call, the following one does: `int number(23);`. This definition does exactly the same things as the first one: it allocates memory, attaches a name, and assigns a value. You can use these two statements interchangeably.

In the same way, if you have defined a class named Employee, then `Employee clerk;` reserves memory and assigns a name, but does not initialize the values of any data members of clerk. With some Employee classes you define, you also may be able to make the statement `Employee clerk(23);`. This statement reserves memory, attaches a name, and passes a value, 23, to the clerk Employee. Possibly, the 23 is used as an Employee ID number or salary. You can't tell what the 23 is used for by looking at the statement `Employee clerk(23);`. However, assuming the statement compiles, you do know that an Employee can be constructed with an initial value in the same way that an integer can.

Because an integer is a scalar variable, only one memory location in the variable number can have a value. When you write `int number(23);`, you know where the integer constructor is assigning the 23—to the number variable. In contrast, because Employee is a class, it may have many data members. When you write `Employee clerk(23);`, you don't know which data member will receive the 23 unless you can look at the code for the constructor.

6

Until now, when you created class objects, you let C++ provide its own constructor for the objects. When an object is created, its data fields store whatever values (often called garbage values) happen to be in those positions in computer memory. After you instantiated objects in your programs, you used a mutator function with a name such as setValues() to assign useful values to data members. That process is similar to declaring a variable and assigning a value to it later. Sometimes, however, you might want to **initialize** one or more of an object's data members immediately upon creation. When you want to initialize an object, or perform other tasks when the object is created, then you must write your own constructor for the class.

Programmers often erroneously refer to the automatically supplied constructor that you get with a class as *the* default constructor, implying that this is the *only* default constructor. Actually, any constructor that requires no arguments is a default constructor, so the automatically supplied constructor is simply *an example of* a default constructor.

Writing Your Own Constructors

Write your own constructors any time you want tasks performed when an object is instantiated. Often, you want to properly define or initialize all data members in an object. Constructor functions differ from other member functions in two ways:

- You must give a constructor function the same name as the class for which it is a constructor.

- You cannot give a constructor function a return type (it's not necessary because constructors always return an object of the class to which they belong).

A constructor must have the same name as its class because the constructor is called automatically when an object is created. If you named a constructor something other than its class name, C++ would not know it was a constructor. In other words, C++ would not know the constructor was the correct function to call when an object was created.

Constructor functions are not coded with a return type. This format doesn't mean the return type is void. Because it is a type, you should not use the term void when you code a constructor. Because constructors always return one object of their class type, they are always written without a return type.

Consider the Employee class in Figure 6-1. The Employee class contains two private data fields and three public functions. Two of the functions, setValues() and displayValues(), are similar to functions you have seen many times before. The highlighted function, however, is a prototype of a new type: a constructor function. You can place the constructor prototype at any position within the list of public class members; many programmers place it first because it is the first function used by the class.

```
class Employee
  {
     private:
        int idNum;
        double hourlyRate;
     public:
        Employee();
        void setValues(const int id, const double hourly);
        void displayValues();
  };
```

Figure 6-1   Definition of an Employee class with a constructor

Rather than define objects of class Employee to have meaningless values, you can assign the default values 9999 to idNum, and 5.65 to hourlyRate. You make these assignments by writing the constructor function shown in Figure 6-2. You place this function in the implementation section of the class file, along with the other functions the class defines. You must remember to include the class name and the scope resolution operator in the constructor header—for example, Employee::Employee()—to show the constructor is a member of the class just like other member functions.

```
Employee::Employee()
  {
    idNum = 9999;
    hourlyRate = 5.65;
  }
```

Figure 6-2   Implementation of Employee constructor

You usually should provide initial values for the data members in your objects. Even if you simply set all numeric attributes to zeros and all character attributes to spaces, the results are better than the random, meaningless data that happen to be held in the memory locations where your objects are instantiated.

The constructor function Employee() shown in Figure 6-2 is called a **default constructor** because it does not require any arguments. The data members in an Employee object will be set by default. Any subsequent object instantiation, such as `Employee assistant;`, results in an object with an idNum of 9999 and an hourly rate of 5.65. Of course, you can change these values later using the setValues() function. Figure 6-3 shows a main() function that uses the Employee class, and Figure 6-4 shows the output. The first line of output shows the default values set from within the constructor. The second line of output shows the values after using the setValues() function to assign 4321 and 12.75 to the assistant's data fields.

```cpp
#include<iostream.h>
#include<conio.h>
class Employee
  {
      private:
            int idNum;
            double hourlyRate;
      public:
            Employee();
            void setValues(const int id, const double hourly);
            void displayValues();
  };
Employee::Employee()
  {
      idNum = 9999;
      hourlyRate = 5.65;
  }
void Employee::displayValues()
  {
      cout<<"Employee #"<<idNum<<" rate $"<<hourlyRate<<
          " per hour"<<endl;
  }
void Employee::setValues(const int id, const double hourly)
  {
      idNum = id;
      hourlyRate = hourly;
  }
void main()
  {
      Employee assistant;
      cout<<"Before setting values with setValues()"<<endl;
      assistant.displayValues();
      assistant.setValues(4321, 12.75);
      cout<<"After setting values with setValues()"<<endl;
      assistant.displayValues();
      getch();
  }
```

Figure 6-3 Employee class and main() function that instantiates an Employee

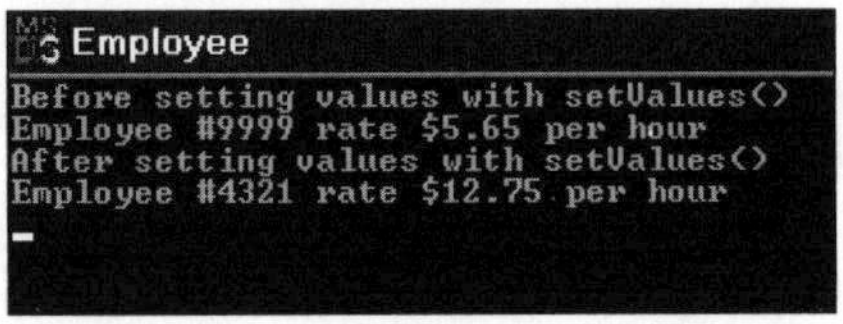

Figure 6-4 Output of program in Figure 6-3

An alternate way to create a default constructor is with the prototype `Employee(const int id=9999, const double hourly = 5.65);`. This format provides the constructor function with default values for two arguments. Figure 6-5 shows the complete class definition for the Employee class that uses this format for its constructor. If you use this Employee class with the main() function shown in Figure 6-3, the output looks just like Figure 6-4. When you create the Employee object named assistant, the default values assigned in the constructor function header are assigned to the class variables.

```cpp
class Employee
  {
    private:
     int idNum;
     double hourlyRate;
    public:
     Employee(const int id = 9999, const double hourly = 5.65);
     void setValues(const int id, const double hourly);
     void displayValues();
  };
Employee::Employee(const int id, const double hourly)
  {
    idNum = id;
    hourlyRate = hourly;
  }
void Employee::displayValues()
  {
    cout<<"Employee #"<<idNum<<" rate $"<<
        hourlyRate<<" per hour"<<endl;
  }
void Employee::setValues(const int id, const double hourly)
  {
    idNum = id;
    hourlyRate = hourly;
  }
```

Figure 6-5 Employee class with constructor that uses default arguments

A constructor in the format shown in Figure 6-5 is called a default constructor, as is the one in Figure 6-2 that takes no arguments. A constructor that requires no arguments is a default constructor, regardless of whether the constructor has an empty argument list or an argument list in which a default value is provided for each argument.

Most C++ programmers prefer providing constructor default values in the prototype. Using this style makes the programmers' intentions clear to anyone looking at the prototype. As you will learn in the next section, you can override these default values if necessary.

In the following set of steps, you create a class named Pizza. A constructor sets the default Pizza to cheese topping and a 12-inch size. The user can override these default values in response to prompts.

1. Open a new file in your C++ editor, and type the statements that include the header files you need.

   #include<iostream.h>
   #include<conio.h>

2. Define the Pizza class to contain three private fields (topping, diameter, and price), and three functions (a constructor, setValues(), and displayValues()). The constructor will contain default values for each field within its argument list.

   ```
   class Pizza
     {
       private:
          char topping[20];
          int diameter;
          double price;
       public:
          Pizza(const char top[] = "cheese",
          const int size = 12, const double pr = 8.99);
          void setValues();
          void displayValues();
     };
   ```

3. Write the Pizza constructor, which assigns each constructor argument to the appropriate class field.

   ```
   Pizza::Pizza(const char top[], const int size, const double pr)
     {
       strcpy(topping, top);
       diameter = size;
       price = pr;
     }
   ```

4. Write the displayValues () function, which produces a single line of output.

   ```
   void Pizza::displayValues()
     {
       cout<<"a "<<diameter<<" inch "<<topping<<
           " pizza. Price $"<<price<<endl;
     }
   ```

6

5. Write the setValues() function, which prompts the user for a topping and a size. Any topping other than cheese increases the Pizza price to $9.99. Any Pizza diameter greater than 12 increases the Pizza price by $1.50.

```
void Pizza::setValues()
{
  cout<<"Enter topping ";
  cin>>topping;
  if(strcmp(topping,"cheese")!=0)
       price = 9.99;
  cout<<"Enter size ";
  cin>>diameter;
  if(diameter > 12)
       price += 1.50;
}
```

6. Write a main() function that tests the Pizza class. Create a Pizza object and display it to show the default values. Then prompt the user to accept or reject these default values. If the user does not respond with 'y' for "yes", use the setValues() function to assign new values to the Pizza's data fields. Finally, use the displayValues() function to show the user the complete order, including price.

```
void main()
{
  Pizza aPizza;
  char standard;
  cout<<"The standard pizza is: ";
  aPizza.displayValues();
  cout<<"Let me take your order"<<endl;
  cout<<"Do you want the standard pizza — y or n? ";
  cin>>standard;
  if(standard != 'y')
       aPizza.setValues();
  cout<<"Your order is ";
  aPizza.displayValues();
  getch();
}
```

7. Save the file as **Pizza.cpp** in either the Chapter06 folder of your Student Data Disk, or of the Student Data folder on your hard drive. Compile and run the program. When you choose the standard Pizza, the output looks like Figure 6-6. When you choose to alter the default values, the output looks like Figure 6-7.

```
⌐ Pizza
The standard pizza is: a 12 inch cheese pizza. Price $8.99
Let me take your order
Do you want the standard pizza - y or n? y
Your order is a 12 inch cheese pizza. Price $8.99
```

Figure 6-6   Output of Pizza program using default values

```
Pizza
The standard pizza is: a 12 inch cheese pizza. Price $8.99
Let me take your order
Do you want the standard pizza - y or n? n
Enter topping onion
Enter size 18
Your order is a 18 inch onion pizza. Price $11.49
```

Figure 6-7   Output of Pizza program overriding default values

Overriding the Constructor's Default Arguments

To replace the default values assigned by a constructor, you can use a mutator function such as setValues(). As with any other function, you also can override a constructor's default values by passing arguments to the constructor when you instantiate an object.

Two rules apply to the use of default parameters with constructor functions:

- If you want to override constructor default values for an object you are instantiating, you also must override all parameters to the left of that value.

- If you omit any constructor argument when you instantiate an object, you must use default values for all parameters to the right of that argument.

The preceding rules apply when you use default arguments with any function. For example, if the prototype for an Employee class constructor is:

```
Employee(const int id = 9999, const double hourly = 5.65);
```

then the following employees all can be defined:

```
Employee assistant;              // both default values used
Employee clerk(1111);            // one default value used
Employee driver(2222,18.95);     // no default values used
```

The result of the above three instantiations is as follows:

- An assistant with the default ID of 9999, and an hourly rate of 5.65

- A clerk whose 1111 ID overrides the default idNumber, but whose hourly rate is the default 5.65

- A driver whose 2222 ID and hourly rate of 18.95 both override the default values in the constructor

> Do not make the mistake of using `Employee assistant();` to define an Employee for whom you try to accept all the default values. The C++ compiler treats this as if you are prototyping a function named assistant() that takes no arguments and returns an Employee object. Although legal, this coding doesn't define an object named assistant. The correct way to define an Employee that uses all the default values is `Employee assistant;`, with no parentheses.

In the following set of steps, you write a main() function that instantiates several objects of the Pizza class you defined earlier. You also create objects that use all, some, and none of the constructor default values.

1. Open the **Pizza.cpp** file if it is not still open. Immediately save the file as **Pizza2.cpp** in either the Chapter06 folder of your Student Data Disk, or of the Student Data folder on your hard drive.

2. Delete the **main()** function in the Pizza2 file, and replace it with the following main() function that declares four Pizza objects. Declare a standard Pizza that uses all three constructor default values. Declare three other Pizza objects that use two, one, and no default values, respectively.

```
void main()
{
  Pizza stdPizza;
  Pizza special("pineapple");
  Pizza deluxeSpecial("pepperoni", 16);
  Pizza veryDeluxeSpecial("lobster", 20, 17.99);
```

3. Add statements to display each Pizza.

```
cout<<"The standard pizza is: ";
stdPizza.displayValues();
cout<<"Today's special is ";
special.displayValues();
cout<<"The deluxe special is ";
deluxeSpecial.displayValues();
cout<<"And the very deluxe special is ";
veryDeluxeSpecial.displayValues();
```

4. Add a call to the getch() function if you need to capture a character to hold your output on the screen. Then add a closing curly brace for the main() function.

5. Save the program again. Compile and run the program. The output looks like Figure 6-8, and shows that each Pizza object uses any arguments passed to it upon construction. The output also shows that each Pizza object uses default values for any arguments not passed.

```
Pizza2
The standard pizza is: a 12 inch cheese pizza. Price $8.99
Today's special is a 12 inch pineapple pizza. Price $8.99
The deluxe special is a 16 inch pepperoni pizza. Price $8.99
And the very deluxe special is a 20 inch lobster pizza. Price $17.99
```

Figure 6-8   Output of Pizza2.cpp

Constructors are not required to have default parameters. However, you can write a constructor to require all parameters, just like any other function.

Overloading Constructors

Just like other C++ functions, constructors can be overloaded. Recall that overloading a function name allows you to use the same name for separate functions that have different argument lists. Constructor functions for a given class must all have the same name as their class. Therefore, if you provide two or more constructors for the same class, they are overloaded by definition. As with other overloaded functions, two constructor functions used in the same program must have different argument lists so that the compiler can tell them apart.

Suppose you have two kinds of employees: regular hourly employees, who get an ID number, a name, and an hourly pay rate; and contractual employees, who do not get an ID number or an hourly pay rate, but do get a name and a contractual fee. The class definition for Employee could contain two separate constructors: one that you use for Employees with ID numbers, and one for Employees without ID numbers. Figure 6-9 shows a usable Employee class definition. Notice the two constructors—one requires an argument, the other does not.

In Figure 6-9, the Employee constructor that requires an argument is implemented to use that argument as the Employee ID number. The constructor then prompts the user for the Employee's last name and hourly rate of pay. The prompts are appropriate for an hourly Employee because this constructor executes only when an Employee is instantiated with an ID number. The other constructor sets the ID number to 0 because this version executes only when the Employee is contractual; that is, when no argument is passed. The prompts within the no-argument constructor are appropriate for a contractual employee.

The program shown in Figure 6-10 uses the Employee class shown in Figure 6-9. Figure 6-11 shows the output of a typical execution.

6

```
class Employee
  {
    private:
        int idNum;
        char name[20];
        double rate;
    public:
        Employee(const int id);
        Employee();
        void displayValues();
  };
Employee::Employee(const int id)
  {
    idNum = id;
    cout<<"Enter the employee's last name ";
    cin>>name;
    cout<<"What is the hourly rate for this employee? ";
    cin>>rate;
  }
Employee::Employee()
  {
    idNum = 0;
    cout<<"Enter the last name of this contractual worker ";
    cin>>name;
    cout<<"What is the fee for this contract? ";
    cin>>rate;
  }
void Employee::displayValues()
  {
   cout<<"Employee "<<name<<" rate $"<<rate;
   if(idNum == 0)
      cout<<" for this contract"<<endl;
   else
      cout<<" per hour"<<endl;
  }
```

Figure 6-9   Employee class with overloaded constructors

```
void main()
  {
    Employee clerk(3456);
    Employee freeLanceProgrammer;
    clerk.displayValues();
    freeLanceProgrammer.displayValues();
    getch();
  }
```

Figure 6-10   main() function that uses Employee class with overloaded constructors

```
Employee3
Enter the employee's last name LaGuardia
What is the hourly rate for this employee? 14.57
Enter the last name of this contractual worker Montello
What is the fee for this contract? 2000
Employee LaGuardia rate $14.57 per hour
Employee Montello rate $2000 for this contract
```

Figure 6-11   Output of typical execution of program in Figure 6-10

6

Within the Employee class in Figure 6-9, you cannot use a default value for the idNumber to define the constructor for regular employees (for example, **Employee(const int id = 9999);**). Both constructors then would become default constructors, because neither requires arguments. With two default constructors, when you define **Employee freeLanceProgrammer;**, the compiler does not know which constructor to call. When the compiler cannot differentiate between two over-loaded constructors, they are considered ambiguous.

Although you might create several constructors for a class, most often you use only a single version of a constructor within an application. You usually create a class with several overloaded constructors so that those who use your class can choose how they instantiate objects, but your class's clients each might choose to use just one constructor version.

In the following set of steps, you create a Graduate class with three overloaded constructors—one each for a Graduate with one, two, or three college degrees. Each constructor requires the Graduate's last name and computes the Graduate's debt based on the number of degrees obtained.

1. Open a new file in your C++ text editor. Type the include statements you need as follows:

   #include<iostream.h>
   #include<conio.h>

2. Begin the Graduate class private section, which contains four string fields that hold the Graduate's last name and up to three academic degree specifications. The class also holds a double that represents the Graduate's amount of debt.

   class Graduate
   {
   ** private:**
   **   char lastName[20];**
   **   char firstDegree[5];**
   **   char secondDegree[5];**
   **   char thirdDegree[5];**
   **   double debt;**

3. Next add the public section that prototypes three overloaded constructors and a displayValues() function. Each constructor requires a last name, but differs in the number of string arguments they accept that represent academic degrees. End the class definition with a closing curly brace and a semicolon.

```
public:
    Graduate(const char last[], const char first[],
    const char second[], const char third[]);
    Graduate(const char last[], const char first[],
    const char second[]);
    Graduate(const char last[], const char first[]);
    void displayValues();
};
```

4. The first constructor implementation is for the version that requires four arguments. Each argument is assigned to the appropriate class field. If a Graduate has three degrees, the Graduate's debt is $100,000.

```
Graduate:: Graduate(const char last[], const char first[],
        const char second[], const char third[])
{
 strcpy(lastName, last);
 strcpy(firstDegree, first);
 strcpy(secondDegree, second);
 strcpy(thirdDegree, third);
 debt = 100000;
}
```

5. Next create the constructor for the Graduate who has two degrees. Initialize the third degree field to be empty by using empty quotation marks. The debt for a Graduate with two degrees is $75,000.

```
Graduate:: Graduate(char last[], const char first[],
        const char second[])
{
 strcpy(lastName, last);
 strcpy(firstDegree, first);
 strcpy(secondDegree, second);
 strcpy(thirdDegree,"");
 debt = 75000;
}
```

6. The constructor for a Graduate with a single degree initializes two of the degree fields to be empty and assumes a much lower debt figure:

```
Graduate:: Graduate(const char last[], const char first[])
  {
   strcpy(lastName, last);
   strcpy(firstDegree, first);
   strcpy(secondDegree,"");
   strcpy(thirdDegree,"");
```

```
    debt = 40000;
}
```

7. Create a displayValues() function that shows the contents of a Graduate object.

```
void Graduate::displayValues()
{
  cout<<lastName<<" has these degrees: "<<endl;
  cout<<firstDegree<<" "<<secondDegree<<"  "<<thirdDegree<<endl;
  cout<<lastName<<"'s debt is $"<<debt<<endl;
}
```

8. Finally, add a main() function that creates one constructor each for Graduates with one, two, or three academic degrees, and displays the value for each Graduate.

```
void main()
{
  Graduate aBachelor("Anderson","BA"),
  aMaster("Bell", "BS", "MS"),
  aDoctor("Carter","BA","MA","PhD");
  aBachelor.displayValues();
  aMaster.displayValues();
  aDoctor.displayValues();
  getch();
}
```

9. Save the file as **Graduate.cpp** in either the Chapter06 folder of your Student Data Disk, or of the Student Data folder on your hard drive. Compile and run the program. Your output should look like Figure 6-12, and demonstrate that each constructor works as it should.

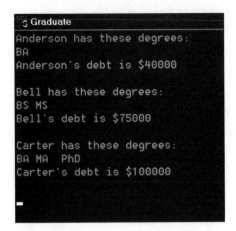

Figure 6-12 Output of Graduate.cpp

USING DESTRUCTORS

A **destructor** is a function that is called automatically each time an object is destroyed. An object is destroyed when it goes out of scope. For example, local variables are destroyed at the end of their function. Just as with constructors, you have been using destructors in your programs whether you realized it or not. When you declare a simple scalar variable, such as `int aNumber;`, the variable aNumber goes out of scope at the end of the block in which you declare it, and a destructor is called automatically. Similarly, when you declare an object such as `Employee clerk;`, the clerk object ceases to exist at the end of the block in which you declared it, and an automatically supplied destructor function executes. Just as with constructors, C++ provides a destructor if you don't declare one.

The rules for creating destructor function prototypes are similar to the rules for constructor function prototypes:

- As with constructors, you must give a destructor function the same name as its class (and therefore the same name as any constructor for that class). Unlike constructors, you must precede the destructor name with a tilde (~).

- As with constructors, you cannot give a destructor function a return type (it's not necessary because destructors never return anything).

- Unlike constructors, you *cannot* pass any values to a destructor.

A destructor must have the same name as its class (plus the tilde) because it is called automatically when an object is destroyed. If you named a destructor something other than its class name, C++ would not know that the destructor was the correct function to call.

Unlike constructors, only one destructor can exist for each class. In other words, you cannot overload destructor functions. Because destructors can neither accept nor return values, C++ would have no way to distinguish between multiple destructors.

Destructor functions have *no* return type. That doesn't mean the return type is void; void is a type.

Programmers usually do not need to perform as many tasks in destructor functions as they do in constructor functions. Typically, you need code in a destructor when an object contains a pointer to a member. You don't want to retain a pointer that holds the address of an object that has been destroyed. When your programs write data to disk files, you often want to close those files in a destructor function.

The Object class in Figure 6-13 contains one field, a constructor, and a destructor. The constructor and destructor functions have the same name as the class, but the destructor function name is preceded by the tilde (~). The program in Figure 6-14 contains a single line of code—it creates an object. When you run the program in Figure 6-14, you get the output shown in Figure 6-15. A message prints when the Object is created, and another message prints a moment later when the Object goes out of scope and is destroyed.

```
class Object
  {
    private:
      int field;
    public:
      Object();
      ~Object();
  };
Object::Object()
  {
    field = 0;
    cout<<"Object created."<<endl;
  }
Object::~Object()
  {
    cout<<"Object destroyed!"<<endl;
  }
```

Figure 6-13 The Object class

```
void main()
{
  Object obj;
}
```

Figure 6-14 A program that uses the Object class

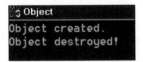
```
Object
Object created.
Object destroyed!
```

Figure 6-15 Output of program that uses the Object class

Tip If you run the program shown in Figure 6-14, the output might end before you can read the "Object destroyed!" message. However, if you add a getch(); statement to the end of the main() function while the output screen appears, the Object has not yet gone out of scope, so you still don't see the "Object destroyed!" message. The solution is to place the Object declaration within its own block in a set of curly braces within main(), and then place the getch() statement outside that block.

Figure 6-16 shows a program that creates six Objects. Figure 6-17 shows that when you create an array of objects, each is created as well as destroyed separately and automatically.

```
void main()
{
   Object obj[6];
}
```

Figure 6-16   A program that uses an array of Objects

```
Object2
Object created.
Object created.
Object created.
Object created.
Object created.
Object created.
Object destroyed!
Object destroyed!
Object destroyed!
Object destroyed!
Object destroyed!
Object destroyed!
```

Figure 6-17   Output of program that uses an array of Objects

Tip   If you want to create an array of class objects such as Object obj[6], the class must have a default constructor. If the constructors require one or more arguments (for example, `Object(int x);`), then the declaration takes the form `Object obj[3] = {Object(10), Object(20), Object(30)};` . This assigns the values 10, 20, and 30 to the first, second, and third elements of the obj array, respectively.

USING CLASSES WITHIN CLASSES

On many occasions you might want to use a class within another class. Just as you build any complex real-life item, such as an automobile, from other well-designed parts, complex classes are easier to create if you use previously written, well-designed classes as components.

Figure 6-18 shows a simple InventoryItem class that a store could use to hold stock numbers and prices of items for sale. It contains just three methods—one that sets the stock number, one that sets the price, and one that displays the item. You have written many classes like this one, and you have written many main() functions that instantiate objects such as an InventoryItem object.

Figure 6-19 shows a Salesperson class. It, too, is similar to many classes you have created and used.

```
#include<iostream.h>
class InventoryItem
  {
   private:
    int stockNum;
    double price;
   public:
    void setNum(int stkNum);
    void setPrice(double pr);
    void displayItem();
  };
void InventoryItem::setNum(int stkNum)
  {
  stockNum = stkNum;
  }
void InventoryItem::setPrice(double pr)
  {
  price = pr;
  }
void InventoryItem::displayItem()
  {
  cout<<"Item #"<<stockNum<<" costs $"<<price<<endl;
  }
```

Figure 6-18   The InventoryItem class

```
#include<string.h>
class Salesperson
  {
   private:
    int idNum;
    char name[20];
   public:
    void setId(int id);
    void setName(char lastName[]);
    void displayPerson();
  };
void Salesperson::setId(int id)
  {
      idNum = id;
  }
void Salesperson::setName(char lastName[])
  {
      strcpy(name, lastName);
  }
void Salesperson::displayPerson()
  {
      cout<<"Salesperson #"<<idNum<<" "<<name<<endl;
  }
```

Figure 6-19   The Salesperson class

Figure 6-20 shows a Transaction class. To represent a sales transaction, you want to include information about the item sold and the salesperson who sold it. You could write a transaction class that contained individual fields, such as item stock number and salesperson ID number, but it is more efficient to reuse the InventoryItem and Salesperson classes that are already created and tested. A benefit of object-oriented programming is that you can reuse well-crafted components, instead of starting from scratch each time you create a class.

When you include the InventoryItem.cpp and Salesperson.cpp files, you can use double quotation marks instead of angle brackets around the filenames. This tells the compiler that the files can be found in the same folder as the program in which they are being included.

An emerging field in the software industry is RAD—rapid application development. Its focus is on reusing well-designed components.

```cpp
#include"InventoryItem.cpp"
#include"Salesperson.cpp"
class Transaction
   {
    private:
      InventoryItem itemSold;
      Salesperson seller;
    public:
      Transaction(int item, double pr, int salesId, char name[]);
      void displayTransactionInfo();
   };
Transaction::Transaction(int item, double pr, int salesId,
    char name[])
  {
   itemSold.setNum(item);
   itemSold.setPrice(pr);
   seller.setId(salesId);
   seller.setName(name);
  }
void Transaction::displayTransactionInfo()
  {
    itemSold.displayItem();
    seller.displayPerson();
  }
```

Figure 6-20   The Transaction class

Considering Reusability and Maintenance Issues

Reusability is a major focus of thinking in an object-oriented manner. Developing a class such as InventoryItem or Salesperson and storing it in its own file for later use in other, more comprehensive, classes is a good example of planning for reuse. Additionally, creating self-contained components such as InventoryItem that you include in other classes makes **program maintenance** easier.

More than half of most programmers' time on the job (and almost all of new programmers' time) is spent maintaining or changing existing programs. For example, an administrator might decide that an InventoryItem needs a new data field or method. If the InventoryItem class file is written as part of the code of many programs, then someone must change all those programs. The more places a change must be made, the more time it takes, the more likely that an error occurs when that change is made, and the greater the chance that one of the necessary changes is overlooked. It makes sense to store a class such as InventoryItem in one location, make changes there, and use the #include statement so the new file definition is part of every program that needs it.

Figure 6-20 shows that the Transaction file uses the #include statement to include both the InventoryItem and Salesperson class definitions. The definition of a Transaction then is very simple—a Transaction consists of an item that is sold and the person who sold it. Figure 6-21 and Figure 6-22 show a short main() program that declares a Transaction, and the output produced by the program, respectively.

```
#include"Transaction.cpp"
void main()
  {
    Transaction oneSale(123, 139.95, 777, "Sherman");
    oneSale.displayTransactionInfo();
    getch();
  }
```

Figure 6-21   A main() function that uses the Transaction class

Figure 6-22   Output of program that uses the Transaction class

USING #IFNDEF, #DEFINE, AND #ENDIF

After you have created a collection of useful classes, often called a **library**, you might find that many class files contain the same #include statements. For example, the Salesperson class in Figure 6-19 is used in the Transaction class in Figure 6-20, and also might be used in classes with a name such as CustomerRelations (that includes a Salesperson object and a Customer object), or CommissionCalculation (that includes a Salesperson object and a rate variable).

Suppose you want to write a program named YearEndSalesReport in which you use a CustomerRelations object and a CommissionCalculation object. Because each of these files will contain the statement #include"Salesperson.cpp", the YearEndSalesReport will include the Salesperson.cpp class definition and implementation twice. If you compile such a program, you will receive error messages such as "Multiple declaration for Salesperson" and "Body has already been defined for…" for each of the Salesperson class functions.

To resolve this problem, you can give each class a **#define name**, which is simply an internal filename for the group of statements that make up the definition of the class. A statement that begins with a pound sign is a **preprocessor directive**, or a statement that gives instructions to the compiler. You have been using the #include preprocessor directive in every C++ program you have written.

To use #define within the Salesperson class, you can insert the directive `#define SALESPERSON_CPP` at the top of the Salesperson file. You can use any name you want, but it is conventional to use the filename with an underscore replacing the usual position of the dot in the filename. You do not have to use all uppercase letters in the name of the preprocessor #define directive, but it is conventional to do so.

Using the #define directive alone does not provide much benefit. Instead, it is usually coupled with two other directives: **#ifndef** and **#endif**. The C++ directive #ifndef allows you to test whether a class has already been defined in a project. The #ifndef directive means "if not defined." If you place an #ifndef at the beginning of a class, and the class has not been defined, then the #define directive will be implemented. If the class has already been defined, everything up to the #endif directive will be ignored. The #endif directive means that you have reached the end of the decision that caused the #define to take place.

Figure 6-23 shows how the #ifndef, #define, and #endif directives should appear within the Salesperson.cpp class file. The statement they make is "If SALESPERSON_CPP has not been defined in this project, define all the following code as SALESPERSON_CPP." When you write a program that includes the Salesperson class multiple times, the first inclusion causes the Salesperson code to be named SALESPERSON_CPP and imported into the final project. At the second inclusion, SALESPERSON_CPP already has been defined, the answer to #ifndef is false, and the code isn't included a second time.

```
#ifndef SALESPERSON_CPP
#define SALESPERSON_CPP
class Salesperson
  {
    private:
      int idNum;
      // ************* rest of class goes here
void Salesperson::displayPerson()
  {
    cout<<"Salesperson #"<<idNum<<" "<<name<<endl;
  }
#endif
```

Figure 6-23 Salesperson class definition with #ifndef, #define, and #endif directives

Even if you have more than one `#include "Salesperson.cpp"` directive in the same project, the definitions are created only once.

IMPROVING FUNCTIONS

As you write larger and more complicated programs, be sure to spend time on planning and design. Think of an application you use, such as a word processor or spreadsheet. The number and variety of user options are staggering. It is impossible for a single programmer to write such an application, so thorough planning and design are essential for the components to work together properly. Each class you design must be well thought out. A final product is great only if each component is well designed—just ask anyone with a $30,000 car that leaks oil.

The following sections describe how to improve your functions by selecting member data and meaningful function names, reducing coupling between functions, and increasing cohesion within a function.

Selecting Member Data and Function Names

Usually, it is easier to select the data members you want in a class than it is to select the member functions. When you define an Employee class, for example, you realize that the Employee has a first name, last name, Social Security number, and so on. You might not predict all the different tasks you want to perform, though. Are any special functions required when the Employee is hired? Do you need a method to decide on raises or promotions? Are there complicated insurance or tax calculations to be performed? Must any special procedures be completed when the Employee is terminated? When you begin to design a class and select its member functions, you need to consider the following questions:

- Will special initialization tasks be necessary? Must you guarantee that class data members begin with specific values? If so, you should explicitly declare a constructor function.

- Will any special clean-up tasks be carried out when a class object goes out of scope? Must you ensure that a pointer is not left pointing to nothing? Must you free any memory that has been explicitly allocated during the life of the class object? If clean-up tasks are needed, you should explicitly declare a destructor function.

- Will class data members be assigned values after their construction? Will class data values need to be displayed? Will class data members need operations (such as arithmetic, sorting, or capitalization) performed on them? These tasks are performed by your other member functions.

When you know what data members and functions you need, you can give them legal C++ identifiers. An often-overlooked element in class design is the selection of good data member and function names. Of course, C++ identifiers must not include spaces and cannot begin with a number, but you also must apply other general guidelines:

- **Use meaningful names.** A data member named someData or a function named firstFunction() makes a program cryptic. You will forget the purpose of these identifiers, even in your own programs. All programmers occasionally use short, nondescriptive names, such as x or val, in a short program written to test a function. In a professional class design, however, names should be meaningful.

- **Use pronounceable names.** A data name like zbq is neither pronounceable nor meaningful. Sometimes, a name looks meaningful when you write it, but goout() might mean "go out" to you, and mean "goot" to others. However, standard abbreviations do not always have to be pronounceable. For example, anyone in business interprets ssn as a Social Security number.

- **Be judicious in your use of abbreviations.** You might save a few keystrokes if you create a class function called getStat(), but is its purpose to output static variables, determine the status of flags, or print statistics?

- **Avoid using digits in a name.** Zero (0) can be confused with the letter "O" and "1" (one) can be misread as a lowercase L ("l"). In a short test program, it is sometimes convenient to name variables var1 and var2, but a final professional class design should use clearer names. The name budgetFor2001, however, probably will not be misinterpreted and is therefore acceptable.

- **Use capitalization freely in multiword names.** The goout() function is better written as goOut(). A function name such as initializeintegervalues() is far more readable when it is changed to initializeIntegerValues(). Some C++ programmers prefer to use underscores to separate words, as in initialize_integer_values().

- **Include a form of "to be," such as "is" or "are," in names for variables that hold a status**. For example, whether the isOverdrawn variable is of type integer or boolean (a C++ type that holds true or false), the intent is clearer than if the variable is simply called Overdrawn. Using "is" or "are" also can help avoid confusion between data member names and function names. For example, isDone is probably a data member that indicates whether a procedure has finished; Done alone is ambiguous.

- **Often a verb–noun provides a good combination for a function.** Names such as computeBalance() or printTotal() are descriptive.

The C++ type that holds a value that is either true or false is named bool. Older compilers do not support the bool type, but use numeric values to indicate true and false. Any expression that evaluates as 0 is false; all other expressions are true.

Some unprofessional programmers name functions or data members after their dogs or favorite vacation spots. Not only does this approach make their programs more difficult to understand, but it also marks them as amateurs.

When you begin to design a class, the process of determining which data members and functions you need and what names they should receive can seem overwhelming. The design process is crucial, however. When you are given your first programming assignment, the design process might very well have been completed already. Most likely, your first assignment will be to write or modify one small member function in a much larger class. The better the original design, the easier your job will be.

When you design your own classes as a professional, you should make all identifiers as clear as possible so that you can assign the individual functions to other programmers for writing and, eventually, for maintenance. When you design your own classes as a student, you still need to make all identifiers as clear as possible so that you can keep track of your work. You want to identify what needs to be done, choose names for those processes, and then write the code that makes up those processes.

Luckily, you do not have to write a C++ class or program completely before you can see whether the overall plan works. Most programmers use stubs during the initial phases of a project. **Stubs** are simple routines that do nothing (or very little); you incorporate them into a program as placeholders. For example, if you need to write a calculateInsurancePremium() function that consists of many decisions and numeric calculations, you might write an empty version such as the following:

```
double calculateInsurancePremium()
   {
      return(0.0);
   }
```

Once you have written this stub function, you can call it from the appropriate places within a program you are creating. This allows you to test the order of operations in the main() program. After the main() program works correctly, you can return to the stub function and begin to code the complicated logic that belongs in it.

Reducing Coupling Between Functions

Coupling is a measure of the strength of the connection between two functions; it expresses the extent to which information is exchanged by functions. Coupling is either **tight coupling** or **loose coupling**, depending on how much one function depends on information from another. Tight coupling, which features much dependence between functions, makes programs more prone to errors; there are many data paths to manage, many chances for bad data to pass from one function to another, and many chances for one function to alter information needed by another. Loose coupling occurs when functions do not depend on others. In general, you want to reduce coupling as much as possible because connections between functions make them more difficult to write, maintain, and reuse.

You can evaluate whether coupling between functions is loose or tight by looking at several characteristics:

- The intimacy between functions. The least intimate situation is one in which functions have access to the same global structures or variables; these functions have tight coupling. The most intimate way to share data is by passing parameters by value—that is, passing a copy of the variable from one function to another.

- The number of parameters that are passed between functions. The loosest (best) functions pass single parameters rather than entire structures, if possible.

- The visibility of accessed data in a function prototype. When you define a function, if you can state how it receives and returns values, it is highly visible and, therefore, loosely coupled. If a function alters global values, you do not see those values in a prototype, and the function is not loosely coupled.

Usually, you can determine that coupling is occurring at one of several levels. **Data coupling** is the loosest type of coupling and, therefore, the most desirable. This type of connection is also known as simple data coupling or normal coupling. Data coupling occurs when functions share a data item by passing parameters. For example, a class named Student, such as the one shown in Figure 6-24, might include a member function to determine eligibility for the dean's list.

```
class Student
  {
    private:
        int studentID;
        double gpa;
    public:
        void deansList(const double gpa);
  };
void Student::deansList(const double gpa)
  {
    if(gpa>=3.0)
        cout<<"Dean's List!"<<endl;
  }
```

Figure 6-24   A Student class with a function that uses data coupling

The deansList() function receives a single data member, which it receives as a constant, so the member's value cannot be altered by mistake. This approach represents data coupling, and is good programming practice. Many of the functions you have written so far in this text have used data coupling.

Data-structured coupling is similar to data coupling, but an entire data structure is passed from one function to another. For example, a function that receives a Student object as an argument (as opposed to a single field) provides an example of data-structured coupling.

Control coupling occurs when one function passes a parameter to another, controlling the other function or telling it what to do. For example, control coupling occurs when a function takes one of several actions based on the value of a parameter. Of course, this kind of coupling is appropriate at certain times, but it implies that any function that calls the decision-making function is aware of how the function works, because an appropriate choice had to be made.

The control coupling illustrated in Figure 6-25 is relatively tight. It can present a problem, because if you change the whatToDo() function, all functions that use whatToDo() must know about the change or they won't send the appropriate choice. Whenever you must keep track of all functions that might call a second function, the opportunity for errors in a system increases dramatically.

```
void whatToDo(int choice)
  {
     if(choice == 1)
        doFirstThing();
     else if(choice == 2)
        doSecondThing();
     else
        doLastThing();
  }
```

Figure 6-25   A function that demonstrates control coupling

You easily can reduce the coupling demonstrated in the whatToDo() function in Figure 6-25 in one of two ways. Each involves keeping the choice variable and the three possible function calls together in the same function.

- Eliminate the whatToDo() function, and let the functions that call whatToDo() call doFirstThing(), doSecondThing(), or doLastThing() on their own.

- Do not pass the choice variable to the whatToDo() function, but place the prompt and data entry for choice within the whatToDo() function where it is directly connected to the three possible outcomes.

External coupling and **common coupling** occur when two or more functions access the same global variable or global data structure, respectively. In either case, data can be modified by more than one function, which makes a program harder to write, read, and modify.

Pathological coupling occurs when two or more functions change each other's data. An especially confusing situation arises when functionOne() changes data in functionTwo(), functionTwo() changes data in functionThree(), and functionThree() changes data in functionOne(). Pathological coupling makes programs extremely difficult to follow and should be avoided at all costs.

Increasing Cohesion Within a Function

Analyzing coupling allows you to see how functions connect externally with other functions. You also want to analyze how well the internal statements of a function accomplish the purposes of the function. **Cohesion** refers to how well the operations in a function relate to one another. In highly cohesive functions, all operations are related. Such functions are usually more reliable than those with low cohesion. Highly cohesive functions are considered stronger, and make programs easier to write, read, and maintain.

Functional cohesion occurs when all of the function operations contribute to the performance of only one task. It is the highest level of cohesion; you should strive for functional cohesion in all functions you write. For example, consider the square() function definition in Figure 6-26.

```
double square(double number)
  {
       return(number*number);
  }
```

Figure 6-26   A functionally cohesive function

 If you can write a sentence describing what a function does and use only two words, such as "Cube value" or "Print answer," the function is probably functionally cohesive.

The function square() is highly cohesive; it performs one simple task, squaring a number. It is easiest to imagine mathematical functions as functionally cohesive because they often perform one simple task, such as adding two values or finding a square root. However, a function also would have high functional cohesion if the task was initializing the data members of a class or displaying a message. Because functionally cohesive functions perform a single task, they tend to be short. The issue is not size, however. If it takes 20 statements to perform one task in a function, then the function is still cohesive.

You might work in a programming environment with rules such as "No function will be longer than can be printed on one page" or "No function will have more than 30 lines of code." The rule-maker is trying to achieve more cohesion, but such rules represent an arbitrary way of doing so. It's possible for a two-line function to have low cohesion, and, although less likely, a 40-line function might also possess high cohesion.

Sequential cohesion arises when a function performs operations that must be carried out in a specific order, on the same data. It is a slightly weaker type of cohesion than functional cohesion because the function might perform a variety of tasks. The tasks are linked together because they use the same data, often transforming it in a series of steps. For example, Figure 6-27 shows a function that takes a ticket order. The takeOrder() function prompts for a quantity, and continues to prompt until the number entered is 12 or less. It then computes the price of the order at 12.50 per ticket, and applies a 10% discount if the customer has ordered 10 or more tickets.

The steps in the function in Figure 6-27 are sequentially cohesive because they operate in a specific order on the same data. Note that you must enter the quantity correctly before the orderAmount can be calculated or the discount taken. Often you can break down a sequentially cohesive function into more functionally cohesive units. For practical purposes, however, a sequentially cohesive function is an acceptable programming form.

```
double takeOrder(void)
  {
   int quantity;
   double ticketPrice = 12.50,orderAmount;
   cout<<"Enter quantity you are ordering "<<endl;
   cin>>quantity;
   while(quantity>12)
   {
        cout<<"Invalid! No orders over a dozen!"<<endl;
        cin>>quantity;
   }
   orderAmount = ticketPrice * quantity;
   if (quantity > 9)
     orderAmount = orderAmount * .90;
   return(orderAmount);
  }
```

Figure 6-27   A sequentially cohesive function

 If you write a sentence describing what a function does and use words such as "first," "next," or "finally," the function probably is not functionally cohesive, but is sequentially cohesive. Beware, though; it might be only temporally cohesive.

Communicational cohesion occurs when functions contain statements that perform tasks that share data. The tasks are not related—just the data. Communicational is considered a weaker form of cohesion than is functional or sequential cohesion. For example, consider a determineScore() method that calculates a prospectScore. The prospectScore is a value that increases with the likelihood that a customer will buy your product; you increase this score based on knowledge you gain through market research. Figure 6-28 shows the determineScore() function.

```
int determineScore(Customer cust)
{
    int score = 0;
    if(cust.income > 40000)
        ++score;
    if(cust.maritalStatus == 1)
        ++score;
    if(cust.age > 35)
        ++score;
    if(strcmp(cust.area, "urban"))
        ++score;
    return(score);
}
```

Figure 6-28   A communicationally cohesive function

The determineScore() function is communicationally cohesive because its steps share data; the value prospectScore is adjusted repeatedly throughout the function. Other examples of communicational cohesion are functions that validate a value by performing several tests (Is the value positive? Is it less than 100? Is it a perfect square?), and functions that perform several different operations on the same data, based on an input value.

If you write a sentence describing what a function does and you repeatedly use the same noun, the function probably is communicationally cohesive. A typical sentence is "Input the year, make sure it is a valid year, determine if it is a leap year, and print the year."

Temporal cohesion arises when the tasks in a function are related by time. The prime examples of temporally cohesive functions in C++ classes are constructors and destructors. These functions might contain a variety of tasks that are unrelated to one another in any functional sense, but that must be performed upon the creation or destruction of an object—that is, at the same time.

If you can write a sentence describing what a function does, and you use words such as "initialize" or "free memory," the function likely has temporal cohesion.

Procedural cohesion arises when, as with sequential cohesion, the tasks of a function are performed in sequence. Unlike sequential cohesion, however, with procedural cohesion, the tasks do not share data. For example, main() functions are often procedurally cohesive. They consist of a list of tasks that must be performed in sequence, but are very different. For example:

```
void main()
    {
    getInput();
    validateData();
    computeResults();
    printResults();
    }
```

It is acceptable to use procedural cohesion in main() functions. The main() function in the above example also can be called a **dispatcher function**, because it sends messages to a sequence of (supposedly) more cohesive functions. If you sense that a class member function has only procedural cohesion, you probably want to turn it into a dispatcher function.

Logical cohesion arises when a member function performs one or many tasks depending on a decision, whether the decision takes the form of a switch statement or a series of if statements. The actions performed might go together logically—that is, they might perform the same type of action—but they don't work on the same data. For example, one of three different error messages might print depending on an error code, or one of four different mathematical calculations might be carried out based on an operation symbol entered via the keyboard. Like a function that has procedural cohesion, a function that has only logical cohesion probably should be turned into a dispatcher function.

Coincidental cohesion, as the name implies, is based on coincidence. The operations in a function just happen to be placed together. Obviously, this type of connection is the weakest form of cohesion and is considered undesirable. If you modify others' programs, you might see examples of coincidental cohesion. Perhaps the program designer did not plan well, or perhaps an originally well-designed program was modified to reduce the number of modules in a program, leaving unrelated statements grouped in a single function.

There is a time and a place for shortcuts. If you need a result from spreadsheet data in a hurry, you can type in two values and take a sum rather than creating a formula with proper cell references. If a memo must go out in five minutes, you don't have time to change fonts or add clipart with your word processor. If you need a quick programming result, you might use cryptic variable names, tight coupling, and coincidental cohesion. When you create a professional application, however, you should keep professional guidelines in mind.

Which is more important, loose coupling or high cohesion? Unfortunately, the only good answer is, "it depends on the situation." Unlike many other aspects of programming, these issues do not provide hard and fast rules. However, if you remain aware of coupling and cohesion issues as you design your programs and classes, your work will be superior and your code will be easier to maintain.

Chapter Summary

- You can classify the roles of member functions into four basic groups: inspector, mutator, auxiliary, and manager functions.

- A constructor is a function that is called automatically each time an object is created. Constructors have the same name as their class, and often are used to initialize an object's data fields. A default constructor requires no arguments, either because it has an empty argument list, or because all arguments in the list have default values.

- If you want to override constructor default values for an object you are instantiating, you also must override all parameters to the left of that value. If you omit any constructor argument when you instantiate an object, you must use default values for all parameters to the right of that argument.

- If you provide two or more constructors for the same class, they are overloaded by definition. As with other overloaded functions, two constructor functions used in the same program must have different argument lists so that the compiler can tell them apart.

- A destructor is a function that is called automatically each time an object is destroyed. It has the same name as its class, preceded with a tilde.

- You can use a class within another class, which gives you the ability to reuse well-crafted components instead of starting from scratch each time you create a class.

- You can't compile a program that includes the same file multiple times. You must use the preprocessor directives #ifndef, #define, and #endif to solve this problem.

❑ When you create classes, you must decide on attributes and functions. The fields and functions should have meaningful, pronounceable names. Writing stubs is a useful technique for managing the large number of functions some classes require.

❑ Coupling is a measure of the strength of the connection between two functions. Tight coupling, which features dependence between functions, makes programs more prone to errors; loose coupling occurs when functions do not depend on others.

❑ Cohesion refers to how well the operations in a function relate to one another. Highly cohesive functions are usually more reliable than those with low cohesion.

REVIEW QUESTIONS

1. Which of the following is not a classification of class member functions?

   a. inspector functions

   b. detective functions

   c. mutator functions

   d. auxiliary function

2. The function that is called automatically each time an object is created is a
   _____.

   a. compiler

   b. builder

   c. constructor

   d. destructor

3. Which of the following is equivalent to `double money = 4.56;`?

   a. `double 4.56 = money;`

   b. `money double = 4.56;`

   c. `double money(4.56);`

   d. `float money = 4.56;`

4. A class named Carpet contains three data fields, `int length`, `int width`, and `double price`. A program declares `Carpet myRug(129.95);`. You know that
   _____.

   a. the length is 129.95

   b. the width is 129.95

   c. the price is 129.95

   d. You do not know any of the above.

5. The most common use of constructors is to _____.

   a. initialize data fields

   b. perform mathematical calculations

   c. call mutator functions

   d. deallocate memory

6. Which of the following is a legal constructor definition for a class named Table?

   a. Table();

   b. void Table();

   c. TableConstructor();

   d. All of the above are legal constructor definitions.

7. A constructor that requires no arguments is an example of a _____ constructor.

   a. no fault

   b. default

   c. faultless

   d. static

8. A constructor is defined as `LightBulb(int watts = 60);`. When you define an object as `LightBulb oneBulb(90);`, the watts variable will be set to _____.

   a. 0

   b. 60

   c. 90

   d. 150

9. A constructor is defined as `Computer(int ramSize = 512, int diskDrives = 2, double price = 1000);`. Which of the following is a legal statement that uses the constructor?

   a. `Computer myMachine(128);`

   b. `Computer myMachine(1234.56);`

   c. `Computer myMachine(256, 899.99);`

   d. All of the above are legal.

10. When you want to override one of four constructor default values for an object you are instantiating, you also must _____.

   a. override all parameters to the right of the one you want to override

   b. override all parameters to the left of the one you want to override

   c. override all parameters in the constructor

   d. not override any other parameters in the constructor

11. A constructor has been defined as `Picture(char medium[] = "oil",
    int value = 0);`. Which of the following can you use to declare an oil Picture
    valued at $2000?

    a. `Picture myArtWork(2000);`

    b. `Picture myArtWork("oil", 2000);`

    c. `Picture myArtwork;`

    d. Two of the above

12. A constructor has been defined as `Picture(char medium[] = "oil",
    int value = 0);`. Which of the following can you use to declare an oil Picture
    valued at $0?

    a. `Picture myArtWork;`

    b. `Picture myArtWork();`

    c. `Picture myArtwork(0, "oil");`

    d. Two of the above

13. Whenever a class contains two constructors, the constructors are _____.

    a. default constructors

    b. destructors

    c. overloaded

    d. static

14. A constructor has been defined as `FlowerSeed(int daysToGerminate = 7);`.
    Which of the following constructors could coexist with the defined constructor with-
    out ambiguity?

    a. `FlowerSeed(int daysToGerminate);`

    b. `FlowerSeed();`

    c. `FlowerSeed(int daysToGerminate = 10,
       int heightWhenGrown = 18);`

    d. `FlowerSeed(int daysToGerminate, double heightWhenGrown);`

15. When an object goes out of scope, a(n) _____ is called automatically.

    a. destructor

    b. constructor

    c. overloaded function

    d. operating system error message

16. Which is a legal destructor for the Game class?

    a. `Game();`

    b. `~Game();`

    c. `void ~Game();`

    d. Two of the above are legal destructors for the Game class.

17. The primary reason you want to use `#define`, `#ifndef`, and `#endif` is to
_____.

    a. provide names for class constructors and destructors

    b. save memory

    c. avoid declaring a class twice

    d. ensure a class has been declared before using it

18. A function must calculate federal withholding tax for each employee's paycheck. The best function name is _____.

    a. fwt() for Federal Withholding Tax, because it is short

    b. governmentTakesTooMuch() because it makes a political statement and amuses your co-workers

    c. calculatefederalwithholdingforeachemployee() because it is very descriptive

    d. calculateWithholdingTax() because it is descriptive and capitalizes each new word

19. The measure of the strength of the connection between two functions is called
_____.

    a. coupling

    b. cohesion

    c. pathological

    d. blending

20. The best functions have _____.

    a. low cohesion and loose coupling

    b. low cohesion and tight coupling

    c. high cohesion and loose coupling

    d. high cohesion and tight coupling

EXERCISES

1. Perform the following tasks:

    a. Create a class named TestClass that holds a single private integer field and a public constructor. The only statement in the constructor is one that displays the message "Constructing". Write a main() function that instantiates one object of the TestClass. Run the program and observe the results.

    b. In a separate file, write another main() function that instantiates an array of ten TestClass objects. Run this program and observe the results.

2. Write the class definition for a Date class that contains three integer data members: month, day, and year. Include a constructor that assigns the date 1/1/2000 to any new object that does not receive arguments. Also include a function that displays the Date

object. Write a main() program in which you instantiate two Date objects—one that you create using the default constructor values, and one that you create using three arguments—and display its values.

3. Create a Person class that includes fields for last name, first name, and zip code. Include a default constructor that initializes last name, first name, and zip code to "X" if no arguments are supplied. Also include a display function. Write a main() program that instantiates and displays two Person objects: one that uses the default values, and one for which you supply your own values.

4. Create a class named MagazineSubscription. Include fields for the subscriber (use the Person class you created in Exercise 3) and the subscription's expiration date (use the Date class you created in Exercise 2). Include a constructor that takes two arguments—a Person and a Date. Also include a display function that displays MagazineSubscription fields by calling the Person and Date display functions. Write a main() program in which you instantiate a Person object and a Date object. Use these as arguments to the constructor that instantiates a MagazineSubscription object. Display the MagazineSubscription object.

5. Create a class named SavingsAccount. Provide fields for the account number, balance, and interest rate. Provide two constructors. One sets each field to 0; the other takes an account number argument and sets the account's opening balance to $100 at 3% interest. Include a function that displays an account's data fields. Write a main() program that instantiates one SavingsAccount object of each type and displays their values.

6. Create a class named RealtorCommission. Fields include the sale price of a house, the sales commission rate, and the commission. Create two constructors. Each constructor requires the sales price (expressed as a double) and the commission rate. One constructor requires the commission rate to be a double, such as .06. The other requires the sale price and the commission rate expressed as a whole number, such as 6. Each constructor calculates the commission value based on the price of the house multiplied by the commission rate. The difference is that the constructor that accepts the whole number must convert it to a percentage by dividing by 100. Also include a display function for the fields contained in the RealtorCommission class. Write a main() program that instantiates at least two RealtorCommission objects—one that uses a decimal and one that uses a whole number as the commission rate. Display the RealtorCommission object values.

7. Create a class named StudentGrade. Include fields for a student ID number, last name, numeric test score, possible points, and letter grade. Create a constructor that requires the student ID, name, and test score, and allows a fourth parameter that holds possible test points. If a value for possible points is not passed to the constructor, the possible points value defaults to 100. (If a 0 value is passed for possible points, force possible points to 1 so that you do not divide by 0 when calculating a grade.) The constructor calculates the student's percentage (divides score by possible points) and assigns a letter grade based on: 90% and above (A), 80% (B), 70% (C), and 60% (D). Create a main() program that instantiates and displays enough StudentGrade objects to test a variety of scores and possible point values.

8. Create a class named Car. The Car class contains a static integer field named count. Create a constructor that adds 1 to the count and displays the count each time a Car is created. Create a destructor that subtracts 1 from the count and displays the count each time a Car goes out of scope. Write a main() program that declares an array of five Cars. Output consists of five constructor messages and five destructor messages, each displaying the current count, similar to the output in Figure 6-29.

Figure 6-29   Output of program using Car array

9. a. Create a class named Date that contains fields for a month, day, and year, and two functions—one that sets the three field values and one that displays them. Create a class named Time that contains fields for hours and minutes, and two functions—one that sets the two field values and one that displays them.

   b. Create a class named DentalAppointment. Include fields for the patient's last name, the date, the time, and the duration of the appointment in minutes. Use the Date and Time classes for the date and time. Allow a DentalAppointment to be constructed with or without an argument for appointment duration, and force the duration to 30 minutes when no argument is supplied. The constructor prompts the user for the patient's name, and the month, day, year, hour, and time of the appointment, and then sets all the class fields accordingly. Write a main() program that instantiates at least two DentalAppointment objects—one that uses an appointment duration argument and one that does not. Demonstrate that all the methods work correctly.

10. Create a class named IceCreamCone with fields for flavor, number of scoops, type of cone, and price. Unless arguments are supplied, flavor defaults to "Vanilla", number of scoops defaults to 1, and cone type defaults to "Sugar". The constructor calculates the price based on 75 cents per scoop, with an additional 40 cents for a waffle cone. Write a main() program demonstrating that the class works correctly.

11. Create a class named Family. The class contains a string field for a surname and an array of six integers that hold up to six family member ages. Create six constructors that will accept as arguments a name and any number of ages of family members from 1 to 6. Each constructor should assign the name and as many ages as appropriate. Assign 0 to any unused ages for a Family object. Each constructor should display a unique message, for example: "The Douglass family is a medium-sized family consisting of 3 people who are 30, 28, and 2 years old." Write a main() program demonstrating that each version of the constructor works correctly.

12. Each of the following files in the Chapter06 folder contains syntax and/or logical errors. Determine the problem in each case, and fix the program.

a. DEBUG6-1

b. DEBUG6-2

c. DEBUG6-3

d. DEBUG6-4

CASE PROJECT

You have been developing a Fraction class for Teacher's Pet Software that contains several fields and functions. Add another private field that stores any whole number portion of a Fraction object.

Add two constructors to the class. The first accepts two integer values representing the numerator and denominator. If a single integer is passed to the constructor, use it as the numerator, and use a default value of 1 for the denominator. If no values are passed to the constructor, use a value of 0 for the numerator and 1 for the denominator. When any Fraction is constructed with a 0 argument for the denominator, force the denominator value to 1.

The second constructor requires three arguments: a whole number portion for a fraction, a numerator, and a denominator. This constructor executes when any fraction abject is instantiated using three arguments.

Each constructor determines whether the Fraction value is greater than 1. If it is, compute the whole number value and store it in the whole number field, and reduce the numerator of the Fraction accordingly. For example, a Fraction created as Fraction(2/7) stores 0 in the whole number field, 2 in the numerator, and 7 in the denominator. A Fraction created as Fraction(7/2) stores 3 in the whole number field, 1 in the numerator, and 2 in the denominator.

Add two new member functions to the Fraction class. The first function, called greatestCommonDenominator(), finds the largest number that can divide evenly into both the numerator and denominator. For example, the greatest common denominator of 8 and 12 is 4. The second function, named reduceFraction(), reduces a Fraction to its proper format. For example, the fraction 8/12 should be reduced to 2/3. To reduce a fraction, you find the greatest common denominator of both the numerator and denominator, then divide both by that number. Whenever a Fraction object is constructed, automatically reduce the Fraction to the proper format.

Include a Fraction function that displays a Fraction's value as a floating point number, and then displays the value as a fraction. Include the whole number portion, a space, the numerator, a slash, and the denominator (for example, 4 1/2). If the whole number is 0, do not display the whole number portion of the Fraction (for example, 5/7, not 0 5/7); if the numerator is 0, do not display the fraction portion of the Fraction. If the whole number is 0 and the numerator is 0, then simply display 0.

Write a main() program that declares several Fraction objects, and confirm that the class works correctly.

7

UNDERSTANDING FRIENDS

Encapsulation and data hiding are two primary features of object-oriented programs. You use encapsulation when you place data and functions together in a capsule as objects. You use data hiding when you create private class members; they remain inaccessible to functions that are not part of the class. In the classes you have written, you took advantage of data hiding: once you create a class, including writing and debugging all of its member functions, no outside function can ever modify or use the private member data in your class. Only the functions that are part of your class can access the class's private data. This approach ensures you that all data members are used correctly and appropriately.

Sometimes, however, it is convenient to allow an outside, nonmember function to have access to a private data member. For example, you might have two objects that belong to different classes, and you want a single function to use data members from each object. If the function is a member of the first class, it doesn't have access to the data in the second class; if the function is a member of the second class, it doesn't have access to the data in the first. One solution to this dilemma is to create special functions called friend functions.

WHAT ARE FRIENDS?

A **friend function** is a function that can access private data members of a class, even though the function itself is not a member of the class. A **friend class** is a class whose functions can all access private data members of another class. When you bestow friendship on someone, you give your friend access to private information you don't want the outside world to know. For example, you might tell a friend your salary, or provide your friend with embarrassing details of your high school days. In a similar way, a C++ function or class that is a friend has access to the private information in a class.

A friend function can access private data from a class of which it is not a member, but a friend function cannot be a friend on its own. That is, when you create a function, you cannot simply call it a friend function and declare it to be the friend of a class, thus allowing access to the private data in the class. Instead, when you create a class, you must declare the names of the functions you will allow to be friends of your class; you must specifically name all functions that will have access to a class's private data.

The friend relationship is always one-sided. A class declaration must state which functions will be its friends; functions cannot declare that they are friends of a class. You can think of a class as *bestowing* friendship on a function. When you think about the principles of data hiding and encapsulation, this idea makes sense. You use data hiding to make data members in a class private so that you can control access to them. Making data members private would be futile if any function could declare itself to be a friend of your class and then alter its private data. When creating a class, you must consciously decide whether any outside functions will have access to your private data, and you must explicitly bestow friendship on those functions.

Because friend functions can access private data, and the data members are private for a reason, friend functions should be used only when absolutely necessary. Use friend functions only when it makes sense that a nonmember function should be able to use a private piece of data. Don't write friend functions simply to overcome data encapsulation—that approach violates the spirit of object-oriented programming.

HOW TO DECLARE A FUNCTION AS A FRIEND

Figure 7-1 shows a class named Customer. The class contains data fields for a customer number and balance. The class contains three functions; two are members of the class. The default constructor for the Customer class supplies values for the data fields if none are provided when a Customer object is instantiated. The displayCustomer() function displays the values stored in a Customer object. The third function (whose prototype and implementation are highlighted in Figure 7-1) is not a member of the Customer class; instead it is a friend.

```
class Customer
{
 friend void displayAsAFriend(Customer cust);
 private:
    int custNum;
    double balanceDue;
 public:
    Customer(const int num = 0, const double balance = 0.0);
    void displayCustomer();
 };
Customer::Customer(const int num, const double balance)
 {
   custNum = num;
   balanceDue = balance;
 }
void Customer::displayCustomer()
 {
    cout<<"In the member function"<<endl;
    cout<<"Customer #"<<custNum<<" has a balance of $"
        <<balanceDue<<endl;
 }
void displayAsAFriend(Customer cust)
 {
    cout<<"In the friend function:"<<endl;
    cout<<"Customer #"<<cust.custNum<<" has a balance of $"<<
        cust.balanceDue<<endl;
 }
```

Figure 7-1   The Customer class

As shown in the Customer class in Figure 7-1, the member function displayCustomer() is similar to many functions you have seen. As a member of the Customer class, the displayCustomer() function meets the following conditions:

- Requires the class name Customer and the scope resolution operator in the function header

- Must have access to the private fields custNum and balanceDue

- Must be declared in the public section of the class definition, so that a main() program (or any other client function) can use it

The function displayAsAFriend() is not a Customer member function. It must meet the following conditions:

- Cannot use the class name Customer and the scope resolution operator in the function header

- Need not be declared in the public section of the class definition

- Must use the C++ keyword friend in its declaration

As a nonmember function, displayAsAFriend() can be declared in the public section, the private section, or first in the class as it is here (which is actually a private section by default). Because the displayAsAFriend() function is neither public nor private, you can prototype it in any portion of the class declaration you want. Some programmers place friend function prototypes first in a class declaration, to separate them from member functions. Other programmers place friend function prototypes wherever most of the other function prototypes are stored, which is usually the public section. (Also, because a friend function is simply a nonmember function, it acts more like a public member than a private one, so placing the friend function's declaration within the public section might make sense to you.)

A function that displays private data from a single class should be a member function of that class. The displayAsAFriend() function only displays data from the Customer class, so there really is no need for it to be a friend function. It is created as a friend in Figure 7-1 for discussion purposes, and to contrast the syntax of friends with that of member functions.

You are not required to use the word friend within the function name of a friend function. The name displayAsAFriend() is used here to remind you that the function is a friend. A more typical name for this function would be display() or displayValues().

The prototypes of displayCustomer() and displayAsAFriend() exhibit the differences between class functions and friend functions. The prototype `void displayCustomer();` shows that the displayCustomer() function takes no arguments. In reality, the function does take one argument—the this pointer. All member functions receive a this pointer that contains a reference to the object using the function. The function can display the Customer idNum and balanceDue because the function is a member of the Customer class, and receives a this pointer to a Customer object that contains those fields.

On the other hand, the void `displayAsAFriend(Customer cust);` prototype shows that displayAsAFriend receives a Customer object as an argument. Because displayAsAFriend() does not receive a this pointer, it must receive a copy of the object whose idNum and balanceDue it will use. Ordinarily, a function could not use a statement like `cout<<cust.idNum;` because idNum is a private field. Instead, an ordinary function has to use a public Customer function to access the private data. However, displayAsAFriend() is allowed to use cust.idNum and cust.balanceDue directly, because it is a friend to the Customer class.

When any function tries to access an object's private data member, the compiler examines the list of function prototypes in the class declaration, and one of three things happens:

- The function is found to be a member function, and access is approved.
- The function is found to be a friend function, and access is approved.
- The function is not found to be a member or a friend, and access is denied; you receive an error message.

Figure 7-2 shows a short demonstration program that uses both the member and friend display functions within the Customer class. The program declares a Customer named onePatron. You can access the member function by using the object name, the dot operator, and the member function's name. You access the friend function by using the function's name and passing onePatron to the function as an argument. You can't use an object and dot in front of the friend function name because the friend function is not a Customer class member. You must pass the Customer object to the friend function because it does not receive a this pointer.

```
void main()
  {
    Customer onePatron(3815, 259.25);
    onePatron.displayCustomer();
    displayAsAFriend(onePatron);
    getch();
}
```

Figure 7-2   A main() program using the Customer class

A class can have any number of friend functions; you simply list the friend function prototypes as you do the member function prototypes. The only difference is that the friend function prototypes are preceded by the keyword friend.

USING A FRIEND FUNCTION TO ACCESS DATA FROM TWO CLASSES

Figure 7-3 shows the definition section of a CustTransaction class. You might create a CustTransaction object for each customer transaction, such as a purchase of an item, payment on an account, or return of an item. The transaction has an identification number, and contains a field that identifies the customer who made the payment, purchase, or return. A field also holds the amount of the transaction. Periodically, you might want to update a customer's record (a Customer class object) with transaction information. For example, a customer might start the month with a $200 balance and make a payment of $150. After updating, the customer's record should show a $50 balance.

```
class CustTransaction
  {
    private:
     int transactionNum;
     int custNum;
     double paymentAmount;
    public:
     CustTransaction(const int transNum = 0,
     const int num = 0, const double amt = 0.0);
  };
```

Figure 7-3   Definition section of the CustTransaction class

In a program that updates customer accounts, you typically match transactions to the appropriate customer, and then subtract transaction payments from the customer's balance owed. In other words, a paymentAmount from the CustTransaction class is applied to the balanceDue from the Customer class by subtracting the values.

 You might design a full-blown CustTransaction class so that purchases and returns are stored as positive numbers, and payments are stored as negative numbers. Alternatively, each transaction can be stored with a code that indicates the type of transaction it is. For this example, assume all transactions are payments (stored in the paymentAmount field), and are stored as positive numbers.

If you create a function that performs the payment application operation, you have at least five choices (although four of these are inferior choices):

- You can make the balanceDue field in the Customer class public, and the paymentAmount field in the CustTransaction class public. Then any function can use and modify them. However, this violates a basic principle of object-oriented programming.

- If you create a payment application function that is not a member of either the Customer or the CustTransaction class, the function will not have access to the private data fields of either class.

- If you make the payment application function a member of the Customer class, the function has access to balanceDue, but not to paymentAmount, which is private within the CustTransaction class.

- If you make the payment application function a member of the CustTransaction class, the function has access to paymentAmount, but not to balanceDue, which is private within the Customer class.

- You can make the payment application function a friend of both classes.

Figure 7-4 shows a function named applyTransaction() that you can use as a friend function. It takes two arguments, a Customer and a CustTransaction. The friend function also displays data from the Customer object, subtracts the payment amount of the CustTransaction object from the balance due of the Customer object, and displays CustTransaction data. If applyTransaction() was a Customer member function, it would not have access to CustTransaction data, and vice versa. As a friend, the applyTransaction() function has access to all the data it needs.

```
void applyTransaction(Customer cust, CustTransaction trans)
{
  cout<<"Customer #"<<cust.custNum<<
    " original balance of $"<< cust.balanceDue<<endl;
  cust.balanceDue -= trans.paymentAmount;
  cout<<"After transaction #"<<trans.transactionNum<<
    " for $"<<trans.paymentAmount<<
    " the new balance is "<<cust.balanceDue<<endl;
}
```

Figure 7-4   The applyTransaction() function

Using a Forward Reference

To use the applyTransaction() function as a friend to both the Customer and the CustTransaction class, you must declare the function as a friend within each class. Then you can place the Customer and CustTransaction classes and the applyTransaction() function in the same file with a main() program that uses them, or you can place each in its own file and use #include statements in the file with the main() function. Whichever approach you choose, however, when you try to compile a main() function that uses both classes, error messages indicate that some data members are inaccessible.

The declaration of the applyTransaction() function is:

```
friend void applyTransaction(Customer cust, CustTransaction trans);
```

The declaration refers to both the Customer and the CustTransaction class as arguments. If you place the Customer class definition first, and then declare the applyTransaction() friend function within the Customer class definition, the class CustTransaction has not yet been defined. If you place the CustTransaction definition first, and then declare the applyTransaction() friend function within the CustTransaction definition, the class Customer has not yet been defined. Either way, one of the class definitions makes reference to an undefined class.

You already know you must declare a variable before using it. You also must declare, or prototype, a function before you use it. Similarly, a class must be declared before you use it. The most common solution to this dilemma is to make a forward reference to one of the classes. A **forward reference** lets the compiler know that the class exists, and that the details will come later. You make a forward reference by using the keyword class, naming the class, and ending the statement with a semicolon. Figure 7-5 shows a forward reference that allows the applyTransaction() function to be a friend to both Customer and CustTransaction. The forward declaration of CustTransaction allows the Customer class to refer to the CustTransaction class without causing a compiler error. Alternatively, you could use a forward reference to declare the Customer class, and then define the CustTransaction class and the Customer class. Figure 7-6 shows a fully developed program including a forward class declaration, two class definitions, a friend function, and a main() function. The output from the program is shown in Figure 7-7.

```
class CustTransaction;    // a forward reference
class Customer
  {
      // declarations go here — including
      // friend applyTransaction() declaration
  };
class CustTransaction
  {
      // declarations go here — including
      // friend applyTransaction() declaration
  };
```

Figure 7-5   Forward declaration of CustTransaction class

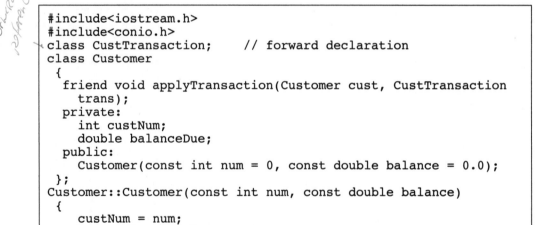

```
#include<iostream.h>
#include<conio.h>
class CustTransaction;    // forward declaration
class Customer
  {
    friend void applyTransaction(Customer cust, CustTransaction
      trans);
    private:
      int custNum;
      double balanceDue;
    public:
      Customer(const int num = 0, const double balance = 0.0);
  };
Customer::Customer(const int num, const double balance)
  {
      custNum = num;
      balanceDue = balance;
  }
```

Figure 7-6   Using a friend function with two classes

```
class CustTransaction
 {
 friend void applyTransaction(Customer cust,
    CustTransaction trans);
 private:
   int transactionNum;
   int custNum;
   double paymentAmount;
 public:
   CustTransaction(const int transNum = 0, const int num = 0,
     const double amt = 0.0);
 };
CustTransaction::CustTransaction(const int transNum,
     const int num, const double amt)
 {
    transactionNum = transNum;
    custNum = num;
    paymentAmount = amt;
 }
void applyTransaction(Customer cust, CustTransaction trans)
 {
    cout<<"Customer #"<<cust.custNum<<" original balance of $"
    <<cust.balanceDue<<endl;
    cust.balanceDue -= trans.paymentAmount;
    cout<<"After transaction #"<<trans.transactionNum<<
        " for $"<<trans.paymentAmount<<
        " the new balance is "<<cust.balanceDue<<endl;
 }
void main()
 {
    Customer onePatron(3815, 259.25);
    CustTransaction onePayment(101, 3815, 52.23);
    applyTransaction(onePatron, onePayment);
    getch();
 }
```

Figure 7-6   Using a friend function with two classes (continued)

```
 ⊊ applyTransaction
Customer #3815 original balance of $259.25
After transaction #101 for $52.23 the new balance is 207.02
```

Figure 7-7   Output of program that applies CustTransaction to Customer

When two classes refer to each other, you can choose to forward declare either one, and then define the other class first. The same principle holds true if three, four, or more classes share a friend function that makes reference to all the classes. In this case you:

- Forward declare all the classes except one.
- Define the class you did not forward declare, and include the friend function prototype in the class definition.

- Define all classes that you did forward declare. The forward declared classes will contain the same friend function prototype as the first class you defined.

- Define the friend function itself.

In the next set of steps you define two classes that will be used by a computer repair company. Each repair technician receives one-half of the fee that the computer repair company charges for each job the technician completes. One class stores data about each technician—an ID number and a payment amount due to the technician. Another class stores data about each job—a job number, technician ID number, and fee. You use two friend classes—to compare and associate technicians with their jobs, and to update a technician's pay based on 50% of each job fee.

1. Open a new file in your C++ editor and type the include statements you need.

```
#include<iostream.h>
#include<conio.h>
```

2. The two classes you define are named Technician and Job. Because the classes share friend functions that use both classes, make a forward reference to Job before you define the Technician class.

```
class Job;
```

3. The Technician class contains two friend functions. The first, computePay(), takes a Technician and a Job as arguments. The Technician's pay is increased by half the Job fee, so the Technician is passed by reference. That is, the address of the Technician object is used by computePay() to alter the value in the Technician's pay field. The second friend function, compareWorkerToJobs(), checks whether a Technician's number is associated with specific jobs. This function receives a Technician, an array of Jobs, and an integer indicating the number of Jobs in the array. The function compares the Technician to each Job in the array, and adds to the Technician's pay if the Job belongs to the Technician.

```
class Technician
{
    friend void computePay(Technician &tech, Job job);
    friend void compareWorkerToJobs(Technician tech, Job jobs[],
        int numJobs);
```

4. Add the private fields, a constructor definition, and a setTechnicianData() function to the class. Finish the class definition with a closing curly brace and a semicolon.

```
private:
    int techNum;
    double pay;
public:
    Technician(const int num = 0);
    void setTechnicianData();
};
```

5. Create a default constructor for the Technician class. You can instantiate a Technician object with or without an ID number. The Technician's pay is always initialized to 0.

```
Technician::Technician(const int num)
{
  techNum = num;
  pay = 0;
}
```

6. Create a setTechnicianData() function that both prompts the user for, and assigns an ID number to, a Technician.

```
void Technician::setTechnicianData()
{
  cout<<"Enter technician ID number ";
  cin>>techNum;
}
```

7. The Job class definition includes the same friend functions as the Technician class—three private data fields representing the job number, technician number, and fee. The Job class definition also includes a public function that sets a Job's data fields.

```
class Job
{
  friend void computePay(Technician &tech, Job job);
  friend void compareWorkerToJobs(Technician tech, Job jobs[],
    int numJobs);
  private:
    int jobNum;
    int techNum;
    double fee;
  public:
    void setJobData();
};
```

8. The setJobData() function prompts for values for, and assigns the values to, the Job's data fields.

```
void Job::setJobData()
{
  cout<<"Enter job number ";
  cin>>jobNum;
  cout<<"Enter technician number assigned to job #"<<
    jobNum<<" ";
  cin>>techNum;
  cout<<"Enter fee for this job ";
  cin>>fee;
}
```

7

9. The friend function, computePay(), receives a reference to a Technician and a copy of a Job. The function then increases the Technician's pay by half of the Job fee, and the details of the computation are shown.

```
void computePay(Technician &tech, Job job)
{
    tech.pay += job.fee * .50;
    cout<<"After job #"<<job.jobNum<<" for $"<<job.fee<<
    " the new total due technician #"<<tech.techNum<<
    " is "<<tech.pay<<endl;
}
```

10. The compareWorkerToJobs() friend function receives a Technician, an array of Jobs, and the number of Jobs in the array. You use a for loop to compare the Technician's ID number to the Technician number stored with each Job in the array. When the ID numbers are equivalent, the Technician's pay is increased by one-half of the fee charged for the Job.

```
void compareWorkerToJobs(Technician tech, Job jobs[], int numJobs)
{
    int x;
    for(x = 0; x < numJobs; ++x)
    {
        if( tech.techNum == jobs[x].techNum)
            computePay(tech, jobs[x]);
    }
}
```

11. Save the file as **TechnicianJobs.cpp** in the Chapter07 folder of either your Student Data Disk or the Student Data folder on your hard drive, and compile the file, correcting any errors. You cannot execute the file because you have not yet included a main() program.

Each class created in the steps above contains the same two friend functions. Each function must be declared as a friend because each function will access private data from each class. In the next set of steps you add a main() function to the file. The main() function declares five Jobs (which could just as easily be 50) and one Technician. After the user supplies data for the Jobs and Technician, the program accumulates the fees owed the Technician for jobs the Technician performed.

1. At the bottom of the TechnicianJobs.cpp file, add a main() function that declares an array of five jobs for a day. Also declare one Technician.

```
void main()
{
    Job todaysJobs[5];
    Technician worker;
```

2. Declare an integer that you can use as a subscript to the array, then loop five times so the user can enter data for five Job objects.

```
int x;
for(x=0; x<5; ++x)
    todaysJobs[x].setJobData();
```

3. Add a statement to display the program's purpose for the user, then call the setTechnicianData() function to get an ID number for the Technician.

```
cout<<"Compute pay for one technician "<<endl;
worker.setTechnicianData();
```

4. Call the compareWorkerToJobs() function, passing the Technician, the list of Jobs, and the number of Jobs. This function determines which Jobs in the array apply to the Technician, and accumulates a total pay amount due for this Technician.

```
compareWorkerToJobs(worker, todaysJobs, 5);
```

5. Add a **getch();** statement to hold the screen output if necessary, and add a closing curly brace for the main() function.

6. Save the program as **TechnicianJobs.cpp** and compile it. Enter data as you are prompted. Your results should be similar to those shown in Figure 7-8. Notice that the first, third, and last jobs are correctly identified as belonging to Technician #24.

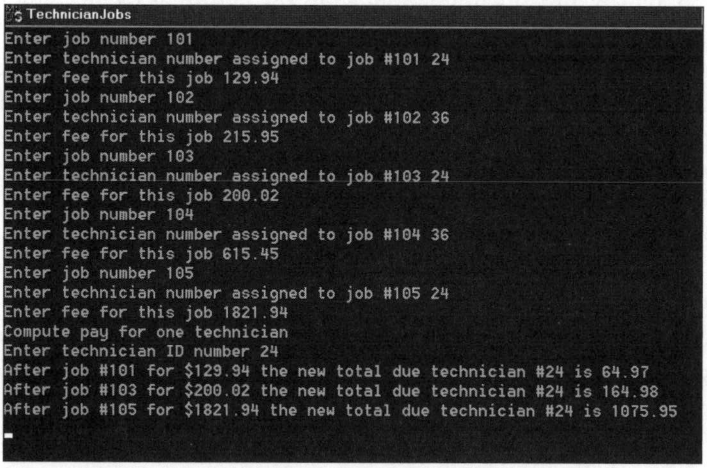

7

Figure 7-8   Output of TechnicianJobs program

TWO INSTANCES OF A CLASS USING A FRIEND

You can use a friend function to access private data members from objects that belong to two different classes. If you want a function to have access to two or more instances of the *same* class, you can use either a class member function or a friend function.

For example, suppose you create a customer transaction class similar to the CustTransaction you used earlier in this chapter. (Figure 7-9 shows a definition section you can use in a CustTransaction class.) The CustTransaction class contains information about a Transaction—a transaction number, customer number, and payment amount. For simplicity, the class contains a single member function—a constructor.

```
class CustTransaction
  {
  private:
    int transactionNum;
    int custNum;
    double paymentAmount;
  public:
      CustTransaction(int tNum = 0, int cNum = 0,
        double amt = 0.0);
};
```

Figure 7-9   Definition section of a CustTransaction class

Often a customer has several transactions in a billing period, and you might choose to sum all of them before applying the total to the customer balance. In other words, you want to add two (or more) individual transactions to create an object that holds the billing period's summary transaction, which subsequently is applied to the customer record. The new summary transaction object belongs to the same class as an individual transaction; it holds the numeric sum from more than one transaction. To distinguish a summary object from a regular transaction, you use a predetermined transaction number, such as 999, to signal the presence of a summary record.

 As an alternative to creating a friend function to add class objects, you might consider overloading an operator. (You learn how to do this in the next chapter.)

You can sum two CustTransaction objects without creating a friend function. You simply create a member function for the CustTransaction class. The prototype is:

`CustTransaction addTransactions(const CustTransaction aPayment);`

The return type of the addTransactions() function is CustTransaction, because it returns a new object that holds the special transaction number 999 and a total of transaction amounts for the billing period. The function addTransactions() receives one argument, a copy of a CustTransaction. When you instantiate two CustTransaction objects, you use one object's members-only access privilege to the addTransactions() function, receive a copy of the other object as an argument, then produce a total that is stored in a third object.

You can instantiate three members of the CustTransaction class as follows:

```
CustTransaction firstTrans(101, 888, 12.99),
        secondTrans(102, 888, 7.00), totalTrans;
```

After you instantiate the three members, you then can sum the firstTrans and secondTrans into a totalTrans in two ways:

```
totalTrans = firstTrans.addTransactions(secondTrans);
```

or

```
totalTrans = secondTrans.addTransactions(firstTrans);
```

In other words, you can pass a copy of the second transaction to the first transaction's call to its member function named addTransactions(), or you can just as easily pass a copy of the first transaction to the second's call to its member function addTransactions(). Figure 7-10 shows a complete copy of the CustTransaction class, including the addTransactions() member function.

```
class CustTransaction
{
   private:
      int transactionNum;
      int custNum;
      double paymentAmount;
   public:
      CustTransaction(int transNum = 0, int num = 0,
      double amt = 0.0);
      CustTransaction addTransactions(const
         CustTransaction aPayment);
};
CustTransaction::CustTransaction(const int transNum,
   const int num, const double amt)
{
   transactionNum = transNum;
   custNum = num;
   paymentAmount = amt;
}
CustTransaction CustTransaction::
   addTransactions(const CustTransaction aPayment)
{
   CustTransaction billingSummary; // local, temporary object
   billingSummary.transactionNum = 999;
   billingSummary.custNum = custNum;
   billingSummary.paymentAmount = paymentAmount +
         aPayment.paymentAmount;
   return(billingSummary);
}
```

Figure 7-10   CustTransaction class with addTransactions() member function

As shown in Figure 7-10, the addTransactions( ) function is a member of the CustTransaction class, and receives a copy of another transaction—called aPayment—from the same class. The function creates a local temporary instantiation of CustTransaction called billingSummary. The billingSummary.transactionNum is set to 999, which is the code for summary records. The billingSummary.custNum is set to the custNum of the object that called or invoked the addTransactions() function—in other words, the custNum pointed to by the this pointer:

```
billingSummary.custNum = custNum;
```

The assignment of the custNum can alternatively be written as:

```
billingSummary.custNum = this->custNum;
```

Another option is to assign the custNum as:

```
billingSummary.custNum = aPayment.custNum;
```

because you can assume you wouldn't call this function to add two transactions unless they were for the same customer. You therefore assume (or add an if statement to double-check) that the this.custNum (custNum of calling object) is the same as the aPayment.custNum (that is, the custNum of the passed object).

Finally, within addTransactions( ), the billingSummary.paymentAmount is set equal to the sum of the invoking object's (firstTrans) paymentAmount and the passed object's (secondTrans) payment amount. A copy of the entire, newly constructed and defined billingSummary is returned to the calling function, where totalTrans receives it.

Making addTransactions( ) become a member function of the CustTransaction class works perfectly well. If you think on a higher level, however, you usually do not add transactions in this way. Making addTransactions( ) into a member function requires that one instance of the class (firstTrans) invoke the function, and that the other instance of the class (secondTrans) serve as an argument to the function. The second transaction seems to have a subsidiary role. Perhaps it should play such a role if it alters the first transaction, but it does not. In simple arithmetic, two numbers added to produce a total are treated equally; it doesn't matter which one comes first. In business, two handwritten transactions added to produce a summary record are treated equally; it doesn't matter which one precedes the other. Because a major principle of object-oriented programming is to more closely model real-world objects, making one transaction subsidiary to another violates the spirit of objects.

One way to avoid a subsidiary transaction is to create a friend function to the CustTransaction class. Each added object must be passed to the function, but the two objects will appear to be treated more equally. As the new function is a friend function, it does not have a this pointer. Thus, both transaction objects are passed, and neither transaction appears to have priority. (You can say that neither object owns the function.) Figure 7-11 shows complete class declarations and a short demonstration program using a friend function to add transactions. The output appears in Figure 7-12.

```
#include<iostream.h>
#include<conio.h>
class CustTransaction
  {
    friend CustTransaction addTransactions(CustTransaction
      firstTrans, CustTransaction secondTrans);
    private:
      int transactionNum;
      int custNum;
      double paymentAmount;
    public:
      CustTransaction(int transNum = 0, int num = 0,
          double amt = 0.0);
      void displayTransaction();
};
CustTransaction::CustTransaction(const int transNum,
  const int num, const double amt)
  {
    transactionNum = transNum;
    custNum = num;
    paymentAmount = amt;
  }
void CustTransaction::displayTransaction()
  {
    cout<<"Transaction number #"<<transactionNum<<
      " for customer #"<<custNum<<": $"<<paymentAmount<<endl;
  }
CustTransaction addTransactions(CustTransaction firstTrans,
    CustTransaction secondTrans)
  {
    CustTransaction billingSummary; // local, temporary object
    billingSummary.transactionNum = 999;
    billingSummary.custNum = firstTrans.custNum;
    billingSummary.paymentAmount = firstTrans.paymentAmount +
        secondTrans.paymentAmount;
    return(billingSummary);
  }
void main()
{
    CustTransaction first(101, 2345, 139.95),
                    second(102, 2345, 40.02),
                    total;
    total = addTransactions(first,second);
    first.displayTransaction();
    second.displayTransaction();
    total.displayTransaction();
    getch();
}
```

Figure 7-11   CustTransaction class with addTransactions() friend function

7

```
AddTransactionsFriendFunction
Transaction number #101 for customer #2345: $139.95
Transaction number #102 for customer #2345: $40.02
Transaction number #999 for customer #2345: $179.97
```

Figure 7-12   Output of program using a friend function to add transactions

You are not required to write the addTransactions() function in Figure 7-11 to return a CustTransaction object. If you want to write a version of addTransactions that returns a double or a void, you certainly can do so. In Figure 7-11, CustTransaction was chosen as the return type for the addTransactions() function because it seems natural that when you add two class objects, the result is another object of the same type.

You create a friend function to add two transactions for the same reason you keep some class data members private. Although your programs would run if the transactions were added with a member function instead of a friend function, or if the data members were public instead of private, the design of the class would no longer be object-oriented. When you think of two real-life objects as being equals in a task, such as when you add two transactions together, then their programming language counterparts also should be equal when you manipulate them in an object-oriented program function.

In the following set of steps, you create a friend function to compare two Loan objects and determine whether they are equal. You consider two loans equal if they are for the same amount at the same interest rate.

You could write a comparison function that is a member of the Loan class, but by creating a friend function that takes two Loan arguments, you treat the Loans as equals in the comparison. The comparison function, which you name areLoansEqual(), returns an integer—a 1 if the Loans are equal, and a 0 if they are not.

1. Open a new file in your C++ editor. Include the files you need, and begin the Loan class by defining a friend function that returns an integer and takes two Loan objects as arguments.

```
#include<iostream.h>
#include<conio.h>
class Loan
  {
    friend int areLoansEqual(Loan firstLoan, Loan secondLoan);
```

2. Finish the class definition by providing private data members for a loan number, amount, and rate, and by providing public functions that set and display the Loan values.

```cpp
private:
    int loanNum;
    double loanAmount;
    double rate;
public:
    void setLoan();
    void displayLoan();
};
```

3. The setLoan() member function prompts the user for values for each of the three data fields.

```cpp
void Loan::setLoan()
{
    cout<<"Enter loan number ";
    cin>>loanNum;
    cout<<"Enter amount of loan ";
    cin>>loanAmount;
    cout<<"Enter interest rate ";
    cin>>rate;
}
```

In a professional program, you add statements to the setLoan() function that ensure the user enters an interest rate in the correct format. For example, 5 percent is represented as .05 rather than 5. One approach is to follow the statement `cin>>rate;` with a loop: `while(rate<1.00) { cout<<"Express rate as a decimal number "; cin>>rate}`.

4. The displayLoan() function lists the Loan details. You can express the decimal loan rate as a percentage by multiplying by 100. For example, .05 is equivalent to 5%.

```cpp
void Loan::displayLoan()
{
    cout<<"Loan number #"<<loanNum<<" for $"<<
        loanAmount<<" Rate: "<<(rate*100)<<"%"<<endl;
}
```

5. The friend function, areLoansEqual(), takes two Loan arguments. Initialize an integer variable, named trueOrFalse, to 0. Then, if both Loan amounts and both Loan rates are equal, change the trueOrFalse variable to 1. If the Loan amounts

are not the same, or the Loan rates are not the same, the trueOrFalse variable retains a 0 value. Return the trueOrFalse value to the calling function.

```
int areLoansEqual(Loan firstLoan, Loan secondLoan)
   {
     int trueOrFalse = 0;
     if(firstLoan.loanAmount == secondLoan.loanAmount &&
       firstLoan.rate == secondLoan.rate)
     trueOrFalse = 1;
     return(trueOrFalse);
   }
```

6. Include a main() function that demonstrates the use of the friend comparison function. Begin by creating an array of Loans named portfolio. Supply values for each Loan in the array, then display the Loan objects.

```
void main()
   {
     Loan portfolio[5];
     int x;
     for(x = 0; x < 5; ++x)
       portfolio[x].setLoan();
     cout<<endl<<"The loans are:"<<endl;
     for(x = 0; x<5; ++x)
       portfolio[x].displayLoan();
```

7. Finally, write a loop that compares the first Loan object to each of the others in the array. Write a loop that compares the first Loan (element 0) with each of the others, beginning with the second Loan object (element 1). Any time the areLoansEqual() function returns a 1, the if statement is evaluated as true, and you can display a message indicating that the Loans are equivalent.

```
for(x = 1; x < 5; ++x)
   if(areLoansEqual(portfolio[0], portfolio[x]))
     {
       cout<<endl<<"The first loan has the same amount and rate as "
         <<endl;
       portfolio[x].displayLoan();
     }
```

8. Add a **getch();** statement and closing curly brace, and save the file as **Loan.cpp** in the Chapter07 folder of either your Student Data Disk or the Student Data folder of your hard drive.

9. Compile and run the program. A typical program execution is shown in Figure 7-13.

```
MS Loan
Enter loan number 1001
Enter amount of loan 2000
Enter interest rate .06
Enter loan number 1002
Enter amount of loan 2000
Enter interest rate .07
Enter loan number 1003
Enter amount of loan 5000
Enter interest rate .06
Enter loan number 1004
Enter amount of loan 2000
Enter interest rate .06
Enter loan number 1005
Enter amount of loan 50
Enter interest rate .10

The loans are:
Loan number #1001 for $2000 Rate: 6%
Loan number #1002 for $2000 Rate: 7%
Loan number #1003 for $5000 Rate: 6%
Loan number #1004 for $2000 Rate: 6%
Loan number #1005 for $50 Rate: 10%

The first loan has the same amount and rate as
Loan number #1004 for $2000 Rate: 6%
```

Figure 7-13   Output of Loan program

MAKING A FRIEND OF A MEMBER OF ANOTHER CLASS

Classes can bestow friendship on nonmember functions; they also can bestow friendship on functions that are members of other classes.

Consider two classes developed for a college registration system. One class is named StudentRequest; it holds a student idNum and a course section in which the student requests enrollment. The other class, named CourseRec, holds information about one section of a course, including a section number, enrollment limit, and current enrollment.

When a student requests enrollment in a specific section, you want to access the current enrollment figure for the section and determine whether there is room for the student, based on the class size limit. In other words, a StudentRequest function needs access to a CourseRec private data member.

 The student enrollment request example shows a class granting friendship to a single function that is a member of another class. You may, however, grant friendship to as many member functions of other classes as is appropriate.

A possible solution that allows a StudentRequest to access private CourseRec data is to create a function named grantEnrollment() that belongs to the StudentRequest class; the CourseRec class may then bestow friend status on the grantEnrollment function. The grantEnrollment() function can be used to compare the current enrollment and the enrollment limit, and thereby determine whether the class has space for the student making the request.

Creating the class definitions for the preceding example requires three operations:

- Forward declare the class that is granting friendship, because the class that holds the friend will use this class name.

- Declare the class containing the function that will be a friend.

- Define the class that is granting friendship. When you name the function that is a friend, you must use the name of the class where the function is a member, and you also must use the scope resolution operator.

The class definitions for CourseRec and StudentRequest are shown in Figure 7-14. Notice the sequence of the forward declaration of CourseRec, the declaration of StudentRequest with the grantEnrollment() prototype, and the CourseRec declaration, which makes a friend of grantEnrollment().

```
class CourseRec;      // forward declaration of CourseRec so
                      //StudentRequest can refer to it
class StudentRequest
  {
    private:
      int idNum;
      int secRequest;
    public:
      StudentRequest(const int id, const int req);
      void grantEnrollment(CourseRec &oneClass);
          // member function to grant enrollment in class
  };
StudentRequest::StudentRequest(const int id,const int req)
  {
    idNum = id;
    secRequest = req;
  }
```

Figure 7-14   Definitions of CourseRec and StudentRequest

```
class CourseRec
  {
    private:
      int sectionNum;
      int enrollLimit;
      int enrollCurrent;
    public:
    CourseRec(const int sec, const int lim, const int curr);
        // constructor
    friend void StudentRequest::grantEnrollment
      (CourseRec &oneClass);
          // grantEnrollment is a friend
  };
CourseRec::CourseRec(const int sec, const int lim, const int curr)
  {
    sectionNum = sec;
    enrollLimit = lim;
    enrollCurrent = curr;
  }
void StudentRequest::grantEnrollment(CourseRec &oneClass)
  {
      if(oneClass.enrollCurrent >= oneClass.enrollLimit)
        cout<<idNum<<" Enrollment denied - class full"<<endl;
      else
        {
         cout<<idNum<<" Enrollment accepted"<<endl;
         ++oneClass.enrollCurrent;
        }
  }
```

Figure 7-14   Definitions of CourseRec and StudentRequest (continued)

If you don't place the functions in the correct order, you will have trouble compiling a program with a friend function that is a member of another class. As shown in Figure 7-14, you should implement a class member friend function after the classes involved are defined.

The constructors for the two classes in Figure 7-14 contain nothing unusual; they simply assign values to the private data fields. The grantEnrollment() function is a public member of the StudentRequest class. When grantEnrollment() is called, it receives a reference variable containing the course section requested by the student. The body of the function compares current enrollment with the section enrollment limit. If there's no room, the student ID is shown, along with the message: "Enrollment denied—class full". If there is enough room for the student, not only are the student ID and an "Enrollment accepted" message shown, but the class section's current enrollment also is increased.

Notice the use of the StudentRequest class name and the scope resolution operator when grantEnrollment() is declared as a friend within the CourseRec class. The class name is necessary because grantEnrollment() is defined within the StudentRequest class. The grantEnrollment() function can access and even alter a private member of the CourseRec class, because the CourseRec class has granted friendship to StudentRequest's grantEnrollment() function.

Figure 7-15 shows a program that uses the CourseRec and StudentRequest classes. Three StudentRequest objects are instantiated; each requests class section 101. One CourseRec is instantiated for Psych section 101, which has a current enrollment of 28 and a limit of 30—that is, room for two more students. Figure 7-16 shows the output of the program.

```
void main()
  {
      StudentRequest Molly(334, 101),
          Alfonso(488,101),
              Eric(599, 101);        // three students
      CourseRec Psych(101, 30, 28); // one course
      Molly.grantEnrollment(Psych);
      Alfonso.grantEnrollment(Psych);
      Eric.grantEnrollment(Psych);
      getch();
  }
```

Figure 7-15   Program that makes three StudentRequests

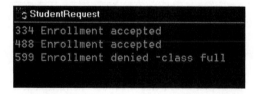

Figure 7-16   Output of StudentRequest program

 Usually, you begin object names with a lowercase letter. Because these object names in the preceding example are also human names, Molly, Alfonso, and Eric are capitalized.

Figure 7-16 shows that the enrollment requests by Molly (student #334) and Alfonso (student #488) are accepted. The section size limit is then reached. When Eric (student #599) makes a request, his enrollment is denied.

 You usually would not name objects Molly, Alfonso, or Eric. Human names are used here to make it easier for you to follow the logic in the program.

In the next set of steps you write a program that can be used for classroom scheduling. Two classes of objects are needed: Courses and Rooms. When a Course section is scheduled, a search is made for a Room that holds the number of students that might enroll. You can create a room assignment function that is not only a member of the class that holds class sections, but also a friend of the Room class. Because it is a friend of the Room class, the room assignment function can access seat limit data that are private to the Room class.

 For these classroom-scheduling steps, assume that once a room is scheduled for a section, no other sections may be held in that room at any other time during the week. A more complicated scheduling program also would account for the day of the week and the time of day.

1. Open a new file and enter the include statements you need, followed by a forward declaration of the Room class.

   #include<iostream.h>
   #include<conio.h>
   class Room;

2. Next, enter the code for a class similar to the CourseRec class used in Figure 7-15. This class is named Course, and contains only a section number, an enrollment limit, and a room number as private data members. The class has a constructor with mandatory parameters for section number and enrollment limit, but the room number is set to 0 (zero) until a room assignment is made. The Course class also includes a display function, and a function that assigns a Room number for the course.

   ```
   class Course
      {
          private:
                  int sectionNum;
                  int enrollLimit;
                  int roomNum;
          public:
              Course(const int sec, const int lim);  // constructor
              void showClassRoom(void);
                  // function to display class and room data
              void roomAssign(Room &aRoom);
                  // function to assign a Room for a Course
      };
   ```

3. The Course constructor assigns a section number and maximum class size, and initializes the assigned room number to 0.

   ```
   Course::Course(const int sec, const int lim)
      {
          sectionNum = sec;
          enrollLimit = lim;
          roomNum = 0;
      }
   ```

7

4. The showClassRoom function displays the course section and room number with an additional message if no room assignment has been made for the Course.

```
void Course:: showClassRoom()
    {
    cout<<"Section #"<<sectionNum<<" is assigned to "
        <<roomNum<<endl;
    if(roomNum == 0)
      cout<<"No assignment made for section  "
          <<sectionNum<<endl;
    }
```

5. Add a Room class that includes data fields for the room number, the number of student seats available in the room, and a field that is set to 1 or 0 to indicate whether a Course has already been assigned to the room. The Room class includes a constructor. It also makes a friend of the Course class roomAssign() function. That way, a Course object can access a Room's private data in order to determine how many students a Room can hold, and whether the Room is already occupied by another Course.

```
class Room
    {
        friend void Course::roomAssign(Room &aRoom);
        private:
            int roomNum;
            int seatLimit;
            int roomIsOccupied;
        public:
            void setRoomData(const int rm, const int seats, const int occ);
    };
```

6. The setRoomData() function assigns three arguments to the appropriate fields.

```
void Room::setRoomData(const int rm, const int seats, const int occ)
    {
        roomNum = rm;
        seatLimit = seats;
        roomIsOccupied = occ;
    }
```

7. The roomAssign() function is a member of the Course class. It takes a Room argument. If a Course does not have a room assignment, that is, if the roomNum for a Course is still 0, then the roomAssign() function checks two fields belonging to the Room argument. If the Room is not occupied (that is, if the value of roomIsOccupied is 0), and the Room can hold the Course (that is, if the seatLimit for the Room is greater than or equal to the number of potential students in the Course), the Room is then marked as occupied and the Room's number is assigned to the Course.

```
void Course::roomAssign(Room &aRoom)
    {
    if (roomNum == 0)
```

```
        if(!aRoom.roomIsOccupied && aRoom.seatLimit >= enrollLimit)
          {
           aRoom.roomIsOccupied = 1;
           roomNum = aRoom.roomNum;
          }
    }
```

8. Write a main() function that demonstrates how the classes work. First, create a few class objects and give them section numbers and enrollment limits as follows:

```
void main()
  {
      Course English(801,25);      // English section 801 has 25 students
      Course Accounting(802,15);
         // Accounting section 802 has 15 students
      Course Biology(803,40);   //Biology section 803 has 40 students
```

9. Create an array of Rooms where Courses can meet, and a variable to use as a subscript with the array. Give each Room a room number, student capacity, and a value representing occupied or unoccupied.

```
Room rm[5];
int x;
// Some typical room data
rm[0].setRoomData(101,20,1); // room holds 20; occupied
rm[1].setRoomData(102,20,0); // room holds 20; available
rm[2].setRoomData(103,30,0); // room holds 30; available
rm[3].setRoomData(104,30,1); // room holds 30; occupied
rm[4].setRoomData(105,20,0); // room holds 20; available
```

10. Use a for loop to cycle through all the Rooms and determine whether each can accommodate the English, Accounting, or Biology Course.

```
for(x=0;x<5;++x)
  {
     English.roomAssign(rm[x]);
     Accounting.roomAssign(rm[x]);
     Biology.roomAssign(rm[x]);
  }
```

11. Finally, display each Course so that you can see which Room, if any, was assigned to the Course. Add a call to the getch() function and a closing curly brace for the main() function.

```
English.showClassRoom();
Accounting.showClassRoom();
Biology.showClassRoom();
getch();
}
```

12. Save the file as **RoomAssign.cpp** in the Chapter07 folder of either your Student Data Disk or the Student Data folder of your hard drive. Compile and run the program. Your output should look like Figure 7-17. When you run the program, the first Room, 101, is passed to each Course's roomAssign() function. Room 101 is unsuitable for any class, because it is occupied. Then Room 102 is passed to each class's roomAssign() function. Room 102 can't be used for the English class, section 801, because there aren't enough seats in the Room. However, the Accounting class, section 802, can use Room 102, and the assignment is made. Room 103 is then passed to each class; it is suitable for the English class, and the assignment is made. The Biology class, section 803, does not fit into any of the Rooms, and so does not get a Room assignment.

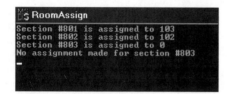

Figure 7-17   Output of Room Assignment program

13. Change the values for the Rooms and Courses in your program and run it again. Confirm that the appropriate Room assignments are made.

MAKING A FRIEND OF ANOTHER CLASS

You can bestow friendship on a function that is a member of another class, or on several functions that are members of another class. In addition, you can bestow friendship on all functions that are members of another class, either by making each function a friend, or by making a friend of the entire class.

To grant friendship to an entire class, construct the class definition simply by writing the keyword `friend` followed by `class` and the name of the class. Figure 7-18 shows the definition of a CourseRec class that grants friendship to a StudentRequest class.

```
class CourseRec
   {
      friend class StudentRequest;
      private:
        int sectionNum;
        int enrollLimit;
        int enrollCurrent;
      public:
        CourseRec(const int sec, const int lim, const int curr);
        void displayCourseData();
   };
```

Figure 7-18   Granting friendship to a class

 When you grant friendship to another class, the word class is optional. In other words, `friend class StudentRequest;` and `friend StudentRequest;` both grant friendship to the entire StudentRequest class.

When you grant friendship to a class, every function that is a member of the class becomes a friend of the granting class. When you make a class such as StudentRequest become a friend of CourseRec, it does not mean CourseRec is a friend of StudentRequest. CourseRec can be a friend of StudentRequest, but only if you declare it to be so within the StudentRequest definition. In other words, if ClassOne bestows friendship on ClassTwo, then ClassTwo does not automatically bestow friendship on ClassOne. Additionally, if ClassOne bestows friendship on ClassTwo, and ClassTwo bestows friendship on ClassThree, it does not mean ClassThree is a friend of ClassOne. Each friendship must be explicitly declared.

CHAPTER SUMMARY

❑ A friend function is a function that can access private data members of a class, even though the function itself is not a member of the class. Only a class may bestow friendship on its friends.

❑ A friend function does not use the class name and the scope resolution operator in the function header. A friend function can be declared in either the private or public section of the class definition, and must use the C++ keyword friend in its friend declaration. A class may have any number of friend functions.

❑ You can create a function that is a friend to multiple classes. When you do, you must make a forward reference to all the classes except one, define the class you did not forward declare, define all the classes that you did forward declare, and finally, define the friend function itself.

❑ If you want a function to have access to two or more instances of the *same* class, you can use either a class member function or a friend function. If you use a member function, you violate the object-oriented programming principle of modeling real-world objects. By using a friend function, you treat the class objects equally.

❑ Classes can bestow friendship on functions that are members of other classes. When you name the function that is a friend, you must use the name of the class where the function is a member, as well as use the scope resolution operator.

❑ You can bestow friendship on an entire class. When you grant friendship to a class, every function that is a member of the class becomes a friend of the granting class.

REVIEW QUESTIONS

1. A friend function is a function that can access private data members of _____.

   a. any class

   b. the classes that have granted it friendship

   c. the classes it has granted friendship to

   d. no classes except the class of which it is a member

2. Which of the following statements is true?

   a. A friend function can declare itself to be a friend of a class.

   b. A friend function can declare itself to be a friend of another function.

   c. Both of the above are true.

   d. None of the above are true.

3. A function that has been declared to be a friend of a class has access to the _____ data in the class.

   a. public

   b. private

   c. both of the above

   d. none of the above

4. Which of the following statements is true?

   a. A class bestows friendship on a friend function.

   b. A friend function bestows friendship on a class.

   c. A function bestows friendship on a friend class.

   d. A friend class bestows friendship on a function.

5. A member function _____.

   a. requires the class name and the scope resolution operator in the function header

   b. has access to the class's private fields

   c. Both of the above are true.

   d. None of the above are true.

6. A friend function _____.

   a. requires the class name and the scope resolution operator in the function header

   b. has access to the class's private fields

   c. Both of the above are true.

   d. None of the above are true.

7. A friend function must be declared in the _____ section of a class declaration.

   a. private

   b. public

   c. either private or public

   d. None of the above. You do not declare friend functions within a class definition.

8. Unlike friend functions, member functions _____.

   a. require arguments

   b. require prototypes

   c. must be public

   d. receive a this pointer

9. When any function tries to access an object's private data member, if the function is a member function of the same class as the object, access is _____.

   a. approved

   b. approved only if the function is public

   c. approved only if the function is private

   d. denied

10. When any function tries to access an object's private data member, if the function is a friend function of the class of the object, access is _____.

    a. approved

    b. approved only if the function is public

    c. approved only if the function is private

    d. denied

11. A class may have _____ friend function(s) at most.

    a. one

    b. two

    c. twelve

    d. an unlimited number

7

12. To use a function as a friend to two classes, you must _____.

    a. declare the function as a friend within each class

    b. declare each class as a friend of the function

    c. declare the function as a friend of one class, and as a member of the other

    d. declare one class as a friend to the other class

13. Declaring a class name before defining the class is making a _____.

    a. prototype

    b. formal declaration

    c. forward reference

    d. premature definition

14. When two classes refer to each other, you can choose to _____.

    a. forward declare either one, then define that class first

    b. forward declare either one, then define the other class first

    c. forward declare the larger class, then define the larger class first

    d. forward declare the smaller class, then define the smaller class first

15. When three classes share the same friend, you must forward declare _____ class(es).

    a. zero

    b. one

    c. two

    d. three

16. If you want a function to have access to two or more instances of the same class, you can use _____ function.

    a. a friend

    b. a member

    c. either a class member function or a friend function

    d. a nonmember, non-friend

17. A Lamp class and a Bulb class each have a private field defined as `int wattage;`. The Lamp and Bulb classes have granted friendship to a function with the prototype `void changeBulb(Lamp aLamp, Bulb aBulb);`. Within the changeBulb() function, which statement is legal?

    a. this.wattage = aBulb.wattage;

    b. aLamp.wattage = this.wattage;

    c. aLamp.wattage = aBulb.wattage;

    d. All of the above statements are legal.

18. A Lamp class and a Bulb class each have a private field defined as int wattage;.
The Bulb class has granted friendship to a function with the prototype
void Lamp::changeBulb(Bulb aBulb);. Within the changeBulb() function,
which statement is correct?

   a. this.wattage = aBulb.wattage;

   b. wattage = aBulb.wattage;

   c. aBulb.wattage = wattage;

   d. All of the above statements are legal.

19. When you declare a function to be a friend of a class, and the function is a member of
another class, you must use the name of the class where the function is a member, and
use the _____ operator.

   a. class containment

   b. binary resolution

   c. scope resolution

   d. scope containment

20. Within class A, to grant friendship to class B, you write _____.

   a. friend B;

   b. friend class B;

   c. either of the above

   d. none of the above

7

EXERCISES

1. Create two classes. The first holds sales transactions. Its private data members include
the date, amount of sale, and salesperson's ID number. The second class holds salespeople, and its private data members include each salesperson's ID number and
name. Each class includes a constructor with which you can set the field values.
Create a friend function that is a friend of both classes and displays the date of sale,
amount, and salesperson name for each sale. Write a short main() demonstration
program to test your classes and friend function.

2. Create two classes. The first holds customer data—specifically, a customer number and
zip code. The second, a class for cities, holds the city name, state, and zip code.
Additionally, each class contains a constructor that takes arguments to set the field values. Create a friend function that displays a customer number and the customer's city
name. Write a brief main() program to test the classes and friend function.

3. Create a class to hold a daily weather report with data members such as dayOfMonth,
highTemp, lowTemp, amountRain, and amountSnow. The constructor initializes the
fields with default values: 99 for dayOfMonth, -9999 for highTemp, 9999 for
lowTemp, and 0 for amountRain and amountSnow. Include a function that prompts

the user and sets values for each field so that you can override the default values. Instantiate 30 WeatherReport objects and initialize them with sample data.

At the end of the month, a month-end object is created. Initialize the object with default values; then use a friend function to store the high temperature, low temperature, and rain and snow totals for the month in the object. The friend function takes two WeatherReport objects—the summary object and one day's object—and it returns an updated summary object. If the day's high temperature is higher than the summary object's high, then replace the summary high. If the day's low temperature is lower than the summary object's low, then replace the summary low. Accumulate rain and snow in the summary object. Write a program to create a month-end weather report from the 30 daily reports.

4. Create a class, such as apartment number and monthly rent, to hold data for apartments you rent. Create a second class for tenants. Include data members such as name, phone number, and apartment number. Include any appropriate functions you think these classes should contain. Create a member function for the tenant class that can access and display the tenant's apartment number, name, and monthly rent amount. ~~Make the Tenant class a friend of the Apartment class.~~ Write a demonstration program for your classes.

5. Create a Book class that contains fields for title, author's name, and price of the Book. Create an Author class with fields for name, street address, and royalty rate as a percentage. Each class contains a function to set the field values. Use a friend function to display a Book's title, author, author's address, price of the Book, and royalty amount per book. Write a demonstration program that shows that the classes and functions work correctly.

6. Create a Movie class with fields for title, year, and rating (G, PG, PG–13, or R). Create a Family class with fields for the family's surname and the age of the youngest family member. Include any appropriate functions you think these classes should contain. Create a friend function that compares a Family to a Movie, returning a 1 if the Family can watch the Movie as a family, or a 0 if it cannot. Write a main() program that contains an array of 10 Movies. Create a Family. List all the titles of Movies the Family can watch, based on the following criteria:

Youngest Family Member	Movies the Family Can Watch
17	G, PG, PG–13, or R
13	G, PG, or PG–13
10	G or PG
under 10	G

7. Create a class named Veterinarian. Include the doctor's name, address, and phone number. Create a class named Pet with the Pet's name, owner's name, age of Pet, breed of Pet, and veterinarian's name. Both classes contains set and display functions. Create a Pet class member function that displays the Pet's name, owner's name, and Veterinarian's name when the doctors' names within the Pet and Veterinarian's class are the same. The Veterinarian class should bestow friendship on this function. Write a

main() function that contains a Veterinarian object and an array of 10 Pets, some of which use the Veterinarian object. Use the Pet class member function to display data about every Pet that is seen by the Veterinarian.

8. Create a class named Appointment for use by a doctor's office. The class includes a patient's name and number of minutes scheduled. Include functions to set and display an Appointment's values. A constructor should initialize the patient name to "Total" and the minutes to 0 (zero). Create a friend function that can add the minutes for two Appointments, thus creating an Appointment with the word "Total" in the patient name field, and a sum of the minutes in the minutes field. Write a main() program that declares an array of 12 Appointments for a day and sums their minutes, producing a total Appointment object for the day. Display the values of each of the 12 Appointments and the total Appointment object.

9. Each of the following files in the Chapter07 folder contains syntax and/or logical errors. Determine the problem in each case, and fix the program.

   a. DEBUG7-1

   b. DEBUG7-2

   c. DEBUG7-3

   d. DEBUG7-4

7

CASE PROJECT

You have been developing a Fraction class for Teacher's Pet Software. Create two functions that will be friends to the Fraction class.

The first friend function takes two Fraction arguments and sums them, creating a third Fraction. Make sure that the sum Fraction is in proper format. For example, when you add 1/4 and 1/4, the sum should be 1/2, not 2/4.

The second friend function takes two Fraction arguments and compares them, returning a 1 if the Fractions are equal, and 0 if they are not. Fractions are equal when their reduced values are equal. Thus 1/2 and 3/6 should be considered equal.

Write a main() program in which you declare several Fraction objects and demonstrate that your friend functions work as expected.

8

OVERLOADING OPERATORS

> ## In this chapter, you will learn:
>
> - ♦ About the benefits of overloading
> - ♦ About the rules that apply to operator overloading
> - ♦ How to overload math operators
> - ♦ How to overload operators to work with a class object and a primitive object
> - ♦ How to chain multiple mathematical operations in a statement
> - ♦ How to overload the insertion (<<) operator for output
> - ♦ How to overload the extraction operator (>>) for input
> - ♦ How to overload the prefix and postfix ++ and -- operators
> - ♦ How to overload the == operator
> - ♦ How to overload the = operator
> - ♦ How to overload the subscript and parentheses operators

You are already familiar with overloading:

- You overload your vocabulary when you distinguish between opening a door, opening a bank account, opening your eyes, and opening a computer file.

- You overload ordinary C++ functions when you give two functions the same name, but different argument lists.

- You overload C++ constructor functions by creating two constructors for the same class. Constructors, by definition, must have the same name. Therefore, when a class contains multiple constructors, they are overloaded.

C++ operators are the symbols you use to perform operations on objects. You have used many operators, including arithmetic operators, logical operators, and the insertion and extraction operators. In this chapter, you will learn to overload these C++ operators so they work with any classes you create.

UNDERSTANDING THE BENEFITS OF OVERLOADING

Having more than one function with the same name is beneficial because you can use one easy-to-understand function name without paying attention to the data types involved. You already are familiar with the concept of polymorphism, meaning "many forms." Polymorphism allows the same operation to be carried out differently, depending on the object. When you overload a verb such as open, the verb is said to be polymorphic; when you overload a function, the function name is polymorphic.

Purists find a subtle difference between overloading and polymorphism. Some reserve the term polymorphism (or pure polymorphism) for situations in which one function body is used with a variety of arguments. For example, a single function that can accept either a Student or a Worker object is polymorphic. (You create such functions in the next chapters as you learn about inheritance and templates.) The term "overloading" is applied to situations where you define multiple functions with a single name (for example, three functions all named square() that square integers, floats, and doubles). Certainly, the two terms are related; both refer to the ability to use a single name to communicate multiple meanings. For now, think of overloading as a primitive type of polymorphism. You will be able to distinguish between overloading and polymorphism more precisely after completing this book.

 The use of functions that are distinguished by their number or types of arguments is sometimes called parametric overloading.

Using the + Operator Polymorphically

Separate actions can result from what seems to be the same operation or command. This occurs frequently in all computer programming languages, not just object-oriented languages. For example, in most programming languages, and applications such as spreadsheets and databases, the + operator has a variety of meanings. A few of them include:

- Alone before a value (called unary form), + indicates a positive value, as in the expression +7.

- Between two integers (called binary form), + indicates integer addition, as in the expression 5 + 9.

- Between two floating-point numbers (also called binary form), + indicates floating-point addition, as in the expression 6.4 + 2.1.

Expressing a value as positive is different from using the + operator to perform arithmetic, so the + is polymorphic in that it can take one or two arguments and have a different meaning in each case. This reflects how people are used to thinking about the + sign. The code generated by the computer differs when you use the + in its unary form, rather than binary form. In addition, although most people don't realize it, the code generated by the compiler for integer addition often differs dramatically from the code created for floating-point addition, so the + is overloaded; that is, distinct procedures are carried out, based on the arguments. Even though the two types of addition force the computer to perform two separate procedures, spreadsheet and database users (as well as programmers) do not concern themselves with the multiple-object code routines. They think of the binary + operation as a single operation—addition. The creators of C++, and most other programming languages and applications, have encapsulated the precise + operations so the programmers or users can concentrate on the higher-level processes of their jobs.

> In addition to overloading, compilers often need to perform coercion or casting when the + symbol is used with mixed arithmetic. In C++, when an integer and floating-point number are added, the integer is coerced into a floating-point number before the appropriate addition code executes.

Although it is convenient that the + symbol between two numbers means addition whether the two numbers are integers, doubles, or floats, the creators of C++ (and other programming languages) were not *required* to overload the + symbol. Overloading the + would be unnecessary if separate symbols—perhaps I+ and F+—were used for integer addition and floating-point addition. However, if programmers had to use separate symbols for integer and floating-point addition, their written expressions would look confusing and unnatural, and it would take longer to learn a programming language. Separate symbols also would be needed for integer and floating-point subtraction, multiplication, and division, not to mention many other operations, such as using the comparisons greater than and less than. Just as other people can understand "open" correctly when you provide the context of "door" or "eyes," the + sign is understood in context by the compiler. Of course, overhead (time and memory) is involved when the compiler must determine which type of action to initiate when it encounters a +. Nevertheless, using the computer's time and memory to perform this task is preferable to using the programmer's time and memory to keep track of unnatural symbols.

OVERLOADING OPERATORS—THE RULES

Operator overloading is the process by which you apply operators to your own abstract data types. The +, -, *, and / symbols make it easy to work with built-in data types such as int and double. Because programmers already understand how these symbols operate with simple data types, it is convenient to use the same symbols with your classes. For example, if you create a Student class and instantiate two objects, firstStudent and secondStudent, then adding the Students with the expression `firstStudent + secondStudent` is natural.

When you add two integer values, as in `6 + 3`, it is clear what should be added. Classes, however, contain a variety of data members. As a result, if you want the compiler to perform arithmetic with two class objects, you must tell the compiler what you mean. When you add two Students using the + operator, you might intend to add their tuition bills, their credit hours, or their library fines. You might intend that when you add two Students, you add each of the preceding fields. Whatever your intention is regarding the Students, you can invoke the appropriate operations only when you properly overload the + operator within the Student class.

Although you can overload the + operator to have any meaning, good programming style dictates that you endow the operator with a reasonable meaning. For example, an Employee class might contain a name, department number, and salary. You would never need to add two employees' names or department numbers, but you might want to add their salaries. Similarly, if you have 100 instances of Employee, you might want to obtain a total salary figure.

Besides overloading an operator to add two Students or two Employees, you also can overload an operator to work with diverse types. You might have a Salesperson class that contains a data member for annual sales, and a Client class that contains a data member for annual revenue. You might want to perform division with these two dissimilar classes to determine a particular Client's percentage contribution to a particular Salesperson's annual sales total. Overloading the / operator would be a good choice for such an operation.

You overload an operator by making it a function; subsequently, you can use it just like any other function. However, in the same way that the modulus operator, %, is not defined for use with floating-point values, you don't overload every available operator for each defined class. Rather, you choose the operators that you need and that make sense for your class.

C++ operators are classified as unary or binary, depending on whether they take one or two arguments, respectively. Table 8-1 lists the unary C++ operators you can overload; Table 8-2 lists the binary operators that you can overload. If an operator is normally defined to be unary only, then you cannot overload it to be binary, and vice versa. If an operator, such as + is either binary or unary, you can overload it in either one or both contexts.

If a unary operator can be placed only in front of objects with built-in C++ types, then the same holds true for your classes when you overload the operator. In other words, the expression !Employee is allowed; the expression Employee! is not.

Table 8-1   Unary operators that can be overloaded

Operator	Usual use	Associativity
->	member	left to right
->*	indirect pointer to member	left to right
!	not	right to left
&	address of	right to left
*	indirection (dereference)	right to left
+	positive value	right to left
-	negative value	right to left
++	increment	right to left
--	decrement	right to left
~	complement	right to left

Table 8-2   Binary operators that can be overloaded

Operator	Usual use	Associativity
*	multiplication	left to right
/	division	left to right
%	remainder (modulus)	left to right
+	addition	left to right
-	subtraction	left to right
<<	shift bits to left	left to right
>>	shift bits to right	left to right
>	greater than	left to right
<	less than	left to right
>=	greater than or equal to	left to right
<=	less than or equal to	left to right
==	equal to	left to right
!=	not equal to	left to right
&&	logical AND	left to right
||	logical OR	left to right
&	bitwise AND	left to right
|	bitwise inclusive OR	left to right
^	bitwise exclusive OR	left to right
=	assignment	right to left
+=	add and assign	right to left
-+	subtract and assign	right to left
*=	multiply and assign	right to left
/=	divide and assign	right to left
%=	modulus and assign	right to left
&=	bitwise AND and assign	right to left
|=	bitwise OR and assign	right to left
^=	bitwise OR and assign	right to left
<<=	shift left and assign	right to left
>>=	shift right and assign	right to left
()	function call	left to right
[]	array element subscript	left to right
->	member pointer	left to right
new	allocate memory	right to left
delete	deallocate memory	right to left
,	comma	left to right

8

Tables 8-1 and 8-2 list the normal use for each operator that can be overloaded. When you overload any of these operators to use with your classes, C++ does not require that you use the operator for its usual purpose. For example, you can legally overload the + symbol to mean subtraction, although it obviously would be poor programming practice.

In addition, Tables 8-1 and 8-2 list the normal associativity for each operator. **Associativity** refers to the order in which actions within an expression are carried out. You cannot change associativity when you overload operators. For example, the assignment operation takes place from right to left, as in the statement `int x = 8;`. You cannot change assignment for your classes so that it takes place from left to right. For example, if you overload the = operator to work with an Employee class, you can never use the statement `2376 = Employee;`.

You also cannot change the normal precedence of any operator. Table 8-3 lists operators in order of precedence. Those at the top of the list have the highest precedence; that means they execute first. (Operators in the same cell of the table have equal precedence.) For example, you cannot cause addition to occur before multiplication in an expression that uses simple variables such as `x + y * z;`. If you overload the addition and multiplication operators for a class and create three objects, the same rules apply—multiplication occurs before addition.

Table 8-3   Precedence of operators

Operator	Description
::	scope resolution
. (dot operator) -> [ ] ( ) ++ --	member member pointer array element subscript function call postfix increment postfix decrement
++ -- ! + - * & new delete	prefix increment prefix decrement not positive value negative value dereference address allocate memory deallocate memory
* / %	multiply divide modulus
+ -	addition subtraction
<< >>	insertion extraction

Table 8-3   Precedence of operators (continued)

Operator	Description
< > <= >=	less than greater than less than or equal greater than or equal
== !=	equal to not equal to
&&	logical AND
||	logical OR
= += -= *= /= %=	assignment add and assign subtract and assign multiply and assign divide and assign modulus and assign

Five operators cannot be overloaded; they are listed in Table 8-4. In addition to the prohibited operators, you cannot overload operators that you invent. For example, because C++ does not include a $ operator, you may not define this symbol as an overloaded operator.

Table 8-4   Operators that cannot be overloaded

Operator	Usual use
. (dot operator)	member
*	pointer to member
::	scope resolution
?:	conditional
sizeof	size of

Operators cannot be overloaded for the C++ built-in types; these types can be overloaded only for classes. For example, you cannot change the meaning of the binary + operator to mean anything other than addition when you use it with two integers.

OVERLOADING MATH OPERATORS

When you code an expression such as 4 + 7, C++ understands that you intend to carry out binary integer addition because of the context of the + symbol. When you code an expression such as regularSal + bonus, if C++ can recognize regularSal and bonus as declared double variables, then floating-point addition takes place. Similarly, when you code aClerk + aSecretary, if C++ can recognize aClerk and aSecretary as two instances of a class, then C++ tries to find an overloaded operator function you have written for the + symbol for that class. The name of the operator function that overloads the + symbol is **operator+( )**.

Assume that you have an Employee class with two data members—idNum and salary—and three member functions—a constructor, a member function that adds two Employees' salaries, and an overloaded + operator that sums two Employees' salaries. The class definition is shown in Figure 8-1. The syntax of the addTwo() function contains nothing new; this member function takes a constant Employee object argument and returns a double. Within the function, the salary for the this. Employee and the salary for the argument Employee are summed, and the result is returned to the calling function. If you write a main() function that declares a double named sum and two objects of Employee type—clerk and driver, for example—you could use either of the following statements to sum the salaries of the two Employee objects:

```
sum = clerk.addTwo(driver);
sum = driver.addTwo(clerk);
```

```
class Employee
  {
      private:
          int idNum;
          double salary;
      public:
          Employee(const int id, const double sal);
          double addTwo(const Employee &emp);
          double operator+(const Employee &emp);
  };
Employee::Employee(const int id, const double sal)
  {
      idNum = id;
      salary = sal;
  }
double Employee::addTwo(const Employee &emp)
  {
      double total;
      total  = salary + emp.salary;
      return (total);
  }
double Employee::operator+(const Employee &emp)
  {
      double total;
      total  = salary + emp.salary;
      return (total);
  }
```

Figure 8-1   Defining an Employee class with an addTwo() function and an overloaded + operator

It's also a logical choice for you to create each of the summing functions in the Employee class to return an Employee summary object instead of a double. You can design your class functions in any way that makes sense to you; a double is used here for simplicity.

In other words, you could use the clerk's addTwo() function and pass the driver to it, or use the driver's addTwo() function and pass the clerk to it. Either way, the result is the sum of the two salaries.

The operator+() function in Figure 8-1 can work like any other member function. When you examine the code for the addTwo() and operator+() functions in Figure 8-1, you see that the only difference is the function name. As with the addTwo() function, you can use any Employee object to control the function, and any Employee object as an argument. Thus, the following two statements produce identical results:

```
sum = clerk.operator+(driver);
sum = driver.operator+(clerk);
```

If the operator+() function works exactly like the addTwo() function, why not just use the addTwo() function? The answer is that, instead of the awkward `sum = clerk.operator+(driver);`, the operator+() function allows you to leave off the word operator in the function name and add either of the following statements:

```
sum = clerk + driver;
sum = driver + clerk;
```

The syntax involved in using the + operator alone is intuitively understood by anyone who has added simple numeric variables: you use an operand, an operator, and another operand. Figure 8-2 shows a main() function that uses each of the Employee class member functions, and Figure 8-3 shows the output. The results are the same when you use the addTwo() function, the operator+() function using its full name, or the operator+() function using just the +. However, the syntax used with the standalone + is simpler, more natural, and easier to remember.

8

```
void main()
{
 Employee aClerk(222,415.75);
 Employee aDriver(333,612.44);
 double sum;
 sum = aClerk.addTwo(aDriver);
 cout<<"Using addTwo(): "<<sum<<endl;
 sum = aClerk.operator+(aDriver);
 cout<<"Using operator+(): "<<sum<<endl;
 sum = aClerk + aDriver;
 cout<<"Using +: "<<sum<<endl;
 getch();
}
```

Figure 8-2   A program that uses the Employee class

```
Employee
Using addTwo(): 1028.19
Using operator+(): 1028.19
Using +: 1028.19
```

Figure 8-3   Output of Employee program

Paying Attention to the Order of the Operands

You can choose to overload any of the arithmetic operators for any classes you develop. Then you can use the corresponding operator symbol in a natural way with class objects. For example, Figure 8-4 shows how you might overload the − operator to subtract two Employee objects from each other, thus subtracting their salaries.

```
double Employee::operator-(const Employee &emp)
  {
     double difference;
     difference = salary - emp.salary;
     return (difference);
  }
```

Figure 8-4   The operator-() function for the Employee class

When you use the operator-() function in Figure 8-4, you must use the two Employee objects in the correct order. Just as integer subtraction produces different results when you reverse the operands (8 − 2 is different from 2 − 8), so does overloaded operator subtraction. When you use a subtraction statement such as `diff = clerk − driver;` in a C++ program, the clerk object is the object that calls the operator-() function. Within the function in Figure 8-4, the reference to salary is a reference to this.salary, or the clerk's salary. The second operand in the expression `clerk — driver` is the driver; it is the driver who becomes the passed argument emp in the function header, and who requires the object name and dot operator within the function body. Because of the way the Employee::operator-() is written, subtraction takes place in the usual and expected order.

In the following set of steps you create a class for a SalesOffice. The class will include an overloaded division operator (operator/) so you can divide one office's sales by anothers to determine the ratio of their sales.

1. Open a new file in your C++ editor and type the include statements you need.

```
#include<iostream.h>
#include<conio.h>
#include<string.h>
```

2. Create the SalesOffice class definition. Each SalesOffice will have a name and a sales figure. You provide a constructor that initializes the SalesOffice data fields with supplied arguments. You also overload the division operator so you can divide one SalesOffice's sales figure by another's to determine the ratio of their sales.

```
class SalesOffice
   {
      private:
        char officeName[20];
        double sales;
      public:
        SalesOffice(const char office[], const double salesAmt);
          //constructor
        double operator/(const SalesOffice &office);
          //overloaded operator /
   };
```

3. The constructor simply assigns provided values to the SalesOffice's fields.

```
SalesOffice::SalesOffice(const char office[], const double salesAmt)
   {
      strcpy(officeName, office);
      sales = salesAmt;
   }
```

4. The operator/() function divides the sales figure from one SalesOffice by the sales figure from another SalesOffice. The ratio is a double, so the return type for operator/() is a double. It is important that the sales figure for the this object is divided by the sales figure for the argument object so division works as expected.

```
double SalesOffice::operator/(const SalesOffice &office)
   {
      double ratio;
      ratio  = sales / office.sales;
      return (ratio);
   }
```

As you improve the SalesOffice class, you might add code that ensures that office.sales is not 0 (zero) before attempting to divide the sales figure by it.

5. Add a main() function that declares two SalesOffice objects—north and south—and compares their sales. The main() function will display the ratio times 100, and express the percentage as a whole number.

```
void main()
{
    SalesOffice north("North", 2454.88);
    SalesOffice south("South", 2830.92);
    double ratio;
    ratio = north / south;
    cout<<"The North Office has "<<(ratio * 100)<<
        "% of the sales of South Office"<<endl;
    getch();
}
```

6. Save the program as **SalesOffice.cpp** in the Chapter08 folder of either your Student Data Disk or the Student Data folder on your hard drive. Then compile and run the program. The output looks like Figure 8-5; the ratio of the sales of the two SalesOffices is expressed as a percentage.

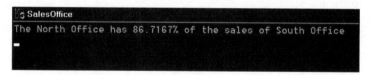

SalesOffice

The North Office has 86.7167% of the sales of South Office

Figure 8-5   Output of SalesOffice program

7. Next, you create a more practical program. Delete the SalesOffice constructor prototype, and replace it with the following:

SalesOffice();

8. Save the file as **SalesOffice2.cpp**.

9. Replace the existing constructor with an interactive one:

```
SalesOffice::SalesOffice()
{
    cout<<"Enter office name ";
    cin>>officeName;
    cout<<"Enter sales figure ";
    cin>>sales;
}
```

10. In the public section of the class definition, add a new function prototype:

double getSales();

In the implementation section, add the getSales() function that returns the sales amount:

```
double SalesOffice::getSales()
{
    return sales;
}
```

11. Replace the existing main() function with a more complicated one that declares an array of six SalesOffice objects. When the objects are constructed, the user is prompted for data. The main() function searches for the SalesOffice with the highest sales figure, then uses the overloaded operator/() function to find the ratio of each office's sales to the sales of the office with the biggest figure.

```
void main()
{
    const int numOffices = 6;
    int x;
    int positionOfBiggest;
    SalesOffice office[numOffices];
    double ratio;
    double biggest;
    biggest = office[0].getSales();
    for(x = 1; x< numOffices; ++x)
      if( office[x].getSales() > biggest)
        {
          biggest = office[x].getSales();
          positionOfBiggest = x;
        }
    for(x = 0; x< numOffices; ++x)
        {
          ratio = office[x] / office[positionOfBiggest];
          cout<<"The ratio of office "<<(x + 1)<<" to the biggest is "
            <<(ratio * 100)<<"%"<<endl;
        }
    getch();
}
```

12. Save the program again (as **SalesOffice2.cpp**). Compile and run the program. Figure 8-6 shows a typical execution.

8

```
SalesOffice2
Enter office name North
Enter sales figure 50.00
Enter office name East
Enter sales figure 100.00
Enter office name Southwest
Enter sales figure 200.00
Enter office name Central
Enter sales figure 145.67
Enter office name West
Enter sales figure 195.00
Enter office name South
Enter sales figure 125.00
The ratio of office 1 to the biggest is 25%
The ratio of office 2 to the biggest is 50%
The ratio of office 3 to the biggest is 100%
The ratio of office 4 to the biggest is 72.835%
The ratio of office 5 to the biggest is 97.5%
The ratio of office 6 to the biggest is 62.5%
```

Figure 8-6 Output of SalesOffice2.cpp

OVERLOADING AN OPERATOR TO WORK WITH A CLASS OBJECT AND A PRIMITIVE TYPE

When you add two objects using the + operator, the objects do not have to be the same type. For example, you can add an integer and a double with an expression such as `5 + 7.84`. If you want to add a class object and a primitive object, you can, but you must overload the + operator appropriately. Figure 8-7 shows an overloaded + operator Employee class function that adds a double to an Employee's salary. The function takes a double argument, and declares a temporary Employee object. The this pointer within the function contains the object that called the function; that object contains an idNum and a salary. You use the existing idNum for the temporary object, but use a salary that is increased by the value of raise.

```
Employee Employee::operator+(const double raise)
 {
      Employee temp;
      temp.idNum = idNum;
      temp.salary = salary + raise;
      return (temp);
 }
```

Figure 8-7 The operator+() function that adds an Employee and a double

When you add the operator+() function from Figure 8-7 to the Employee class and declare an Employee object named aClerk, then you can write a statement such as `aClerk = aClerk + 50.00;`. This statement increases the aClerk's salary by $50. Alternatively, the statement `anotherClerk = aClerk + 50.00;` retains the aClerk salary at its original value. Within the operator+() function, the temporary Employee object is assigned the aClerk's idNum and Salary plus $50.00. The temporary object is returned to the calling function where it is assigned to another Clerk. In other words, the addition statement sets anotherClerk's idNum to aClerk's idNum, and anotherClerk's salary to $50.00 more than aClerk's salary. The aClerk object on the left side of the + in each expression is the this object within the operator+() function. You can think of the aClerk object to the left of the + as "driving" the function. When the function returns the temp Employee object, then an Employee with an increased salary is returned to the calling function.

You cannot overload operators that work with C++'s built-in data types. For example, you cannot overload the + that works with two doubles to make it do anything but add two doubles. Similarly, you can't overload operators whose first operand is an object that is a built-in type, even if the second operand is a class object. For example, you cannot write a function that allows you to code `aClerk = 50.00 + aClerk;`, where the double is the driving operand in front of the + operator. When the compiler encounters a double (or any other built-in data type) as the first operand in a mathematical operation, the + that follows works only with other built-in type objects.

USING MULTIPLE OPERATIONS IN A STATEMENT

Most modern programming languages allow several operators to be used in the same statement. For example, to add three values in C++, you write a statement like `total = a + b + c;`. Because one purpose of operator overloading is to create class operators that work "naturally" like built-in operators, your class operators should have the same capability.

 If you want to sum three values in an older programming language such as assembler or RPG, you first must add two values, producing a temporary total. Then, in a separate statement, you add the third value to that total.

Figure 8-8 shows a Sale class that includes an overloaded operator+() function. When a store makes a Sale, a Sale object is created, storing the receipt number and the amount of the Sale. The overloaded operator+() function is written to allow the addition of multiple Sale objects in sequence, for example: `aShirt + aTie + pants`. The function assigns 999 as a dummy receipt number to any summed object, to distinguish it from a regular receipt.

```
class Sale
  {
    private:
     int receiptNum;
     double saleAmount;
    public:
     Sale(const int id, const double sale);   //constructor
     Sale operator+(const Sale transaction);
     void showSale();
  };
Sale::Sale(const int num, const double sale)
  {
    receiptNum = num;
    saleAmount = sale;
  }
Sale Sale::operator+(const Sale transaction)
  {
    Sale temp(999,0);
    temp.saleAmount = saleAmount + transaction.saleAmount;
    return (temp);
  }
void Sale::showSale()
  {
    cout<<"Sale #"<<receiptNum<<" for $"<<saleAmount<<endl;
  }
```

Figure 8-8 The Sale class

The operator+() function should return a Sale object, rather than a reference to a Sale object. If operator+() returns a pointer to temp, the returned pointer is meaningless because when the operator+() function ends, the local variable temp goes out of scope.

If you write the overloaded operator+() function in the Sale class in Figure 8-8 to return a double instead of a Sale, then you cannot use a statement that adds multiple Sale objects in sequence, such as the one highlighted in the main() program in Figure 8-9. If the operator+() function returns a double, then you receive an error message similar to "Illegal structure operation." Because the associativity of addition occurs from left to right, the attempt to execute the addition highlighted in Figure 8-9 follows this sequence:

1. The left-most + operator is encountered, and C++ recognizes a Sale on each side of the + symbol. The overloaded operator+() function is called, and saleAmounts for aShirt and aTie are added. A double is returned.

2. The next + operator is encountered. A Sale object is found as the operand to the right of the +, but a double value is used as the operand to the left. You have not created a function that can handle this situation (your function adds Sale + Sale), nor is there a built-in + operation that can handle it (although there is one for double + double), so an error message appears.

```
void main()
{
  Sale aShirt(222,29.95);
  Sale aTie(223, 40.00);
  Sale pants(224, 49.20);
  Sale total(0,0);
  total = aShirt + aTie + pants;
  total.showSale();
  getch();
}
```

Figure 8-9   Program that adds three Sale objects

When the Sale class operator+() function does not return a double, but instead returns an object of Sale type (as shown in Figure 8-8), the multiple addition works correctly. The sequence of events now occurs as follows:

8

1. The left-most + operator is encountered, and C++ recognizes a Sale object on each side of the + symbol. The overloaded operator+() function is called, and saleAmounts for aShirt and aTie are added. A temporary Sale object with the total sale ($69.95) is returned.

2. The next + operator is encountered. A Sale object now is found on each side of the +—the temporary object returned by the first addition, and the pants object. The overloaded operator+() function is called again. The saleAmounts for the temporary object and the pants are added, and a new temporary Sale object with the total sale ($119.15) is returned.

3. The temporary object is assigned to the total Sale object.

The results of the execution of the program in Figure 8-9 are shown in Figure 8-10.

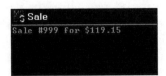

Figure 8-10   Output of Sale program

 C++ forces you to use the built-in precedence rules for your class operators. Therefore, if you define both operator*() and operator+(), and then code a statement such as `aShirt + aTie * pants`, then the usual precedence rules are followed. That is, the multiplication takes place before the addition.

 If you want to be able to add either a double or a Sale object to a Sale object, then simply write both versions of the overloaded operator for the class.

OVERLOADING OUTPUT

You already know that C++ automatically overloads several of its operators. The + operator is understood differently when used in unary context from how it's understood in binary context. The << operator also is overloaded by C++. It is both a bitwise left-shift operator and an output operator; it is called the insertion operator when used for output. The << operator acts as an output operator only when cout (or another output stream object) appears on the left side. Therefore, you can see that cout becomes the this object in the overloaded operator<<() function.

You do not need to understand the use of << as a bitwise left-shift operator to understand that it is overloaded, or understand how to use it with cout. If you're curious, however, bitwise left-shift simply means that each bit in a given byte takes the value of the bit to the right. Thus, 00010100 becomes 00101000. The left-most bit is lost, and the new right-most bit becomes a 0. Incidentally, the binary number 00010100 is 20, and 00101000 is 40; left-shifting is actually just a tricky way of multiplying by 2 (as long as the left-most bit, which represents the sign, doesn't change).

When you use cout in a program, you must include #include<iostream.h>. The iostream.h file defines the cout object, which is actually a member of a class named ostream. The iostream.h file overloads << with functions that output each of C++'s built-in data types. For example, the following overloaded operator<<() function prototype can be used to output an integer:

```
ostream& operator<<(ostream &out, int n);
```

The preceding function, called operator<<(), returns a reference to ostream. It accepts two arguments: a reference to ostream (locally named out in this example) and an integer (locally named n in this example). In other words, the function receives both an address where output will go and a value to output; the function returns the address where the next output will go. Recall how the overloaded + operator in the Sale class in Figure 8-8 returns a Sale object so that more than one addition operation can be carried out within the same statement. Similarly, cout's operator<<() function returns the next address for output, ensuring that a statement with multiple outputs like cout<<22<<33; will work. The statement cout<<22 returns a reference to an object that 33 can use.

Programmers sometimes refer to the use of multiple calls to the same operator function (for example, cout<<22<<33;) as stacking or chaining.

The reason that the cout overloaded << operator needs to receive a reference to ostream is because << is a friend function, which you will recall, has no this pointer (unlike a member function).

C++ overloads the << operator to work with the built-in data types; you also may overload the << operator to work with your own classes. Instead of a showSale() function for a Sale object that requires the statement `total.showSale();` (as in Figure 8-9), you might prefer a more natural form:

```
cout<<total;
```

To overload the << operator so it can work with a Sale object, you must add the overloaded operator<<() function to the Sale class. The prototype is:

```
friend ostream& operator<<(ostream &out, const Sale &aSale);
```

 The "out" in the operator<<() definition is not a keyword. It is a programmer-chosen local name for the reference to ostream. You can use any legal C++ variable name you choose.

The operator<<() function is a friend to the ostream class. It receives a reference to an ostream object, called out within the function, and a reference to a Sale, called aSale within the function. The Sale reference is const because the output should not alter the Sale's data. The contents of the function body can display a Sale with any desired text and in any format you want. For example, Figure 8-11 shows a usable operator<<() function for the Sale class.

```
ostream& operator<<(ostream &out, const Sale &aSale)
   {
       out<<"Sale #"<<aSale.receiptNum
           <<" for $"<<aSale.saleAmount<<endl;
       return (out);
   }
```

Figure 8-11   Overloaded operator<<() function for the Sale class

In Figure 8-11, the function name is not `Sale::operator<<()`. The operator<<() function is not a member of the Sale class; it is a friend. It is a friend function instead of a member function so that the operator can access the private members of the ostream class and the Sale class, and then operate like the built-in versions of << . Because operator<<() is not a member of the Sale class, you cannot output the values receiptNum and saleAmount without using a Sale object and a dot operator. The operator<<() function does not receive a this pointer. Therefore, it cannot directly refer to any objects' data. The data that prints is the data that belongs to the argument named aSale.

After you include the overloaded operator<<() function in the Sale class, any program that includes a Sale declaration such as `Sale aShirt;` can subsequently use a statement such as `cout<<aShirt;` to display the aShirt's data. The statement that uses cout is only a few characters shorter than `aShirt.showSale();`, but the statement makes Sale appear to be a built-in data type. Using the overloaded << operator allows the use of simpler program statements; the class takes care of all the details.

In the following set of steps, you overload the insertion operator to work with the SalesOffice class you created earlier in this chapter.

1. Open the **SalesOffice.cpp** file (not SalesOffice2.cpp) you created earlier in this chapter.

2. Just after the opening curly brace of the SalesOffice class, insert the following prototype for the overloaded operator<<() function:

   friend ostream& operator<<(ostream& out,
   **   const SalesOffice &anOffice);**

3. After the complete operator/() function and just before the main() function, insert the implementation of the operator<<() function:

   ostream& operator<<(ostream& out, const SalesOffice &anOffice)
   {
   ** out<<"The "<<anOffice.officeName<<**
   **   " Office sold $"<<anOffice.sales<<endl;**
   ** return(out);**
   }

4. Within the main() function, just after the statement that computes the ratio between north and south, and just before the statement that begins: `cout<<"The North Office has"`, insert two cout statements that display the details of the north and south SalesOffices, respectively:

   cout<<north;
   cout<<south;

5. Save the modified program as **SalesOffice3.cpp**. Compile and run the program. Your output should look like Figure 8-12.

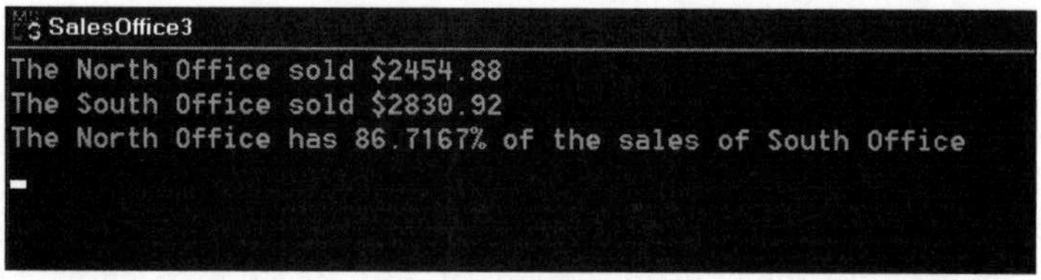

Figure 8-12   Output of SalesOffice3.cpp

OVERLOADING INPUT

If the << operator can be overloaded for output, it makes sense that the >> operator also can be overloaded for input. The advantage of overloading operators such as >> is that the resulting programs look cleaner and are easier to read.

Consider a Sale class like the one in Figure 8-8 that contains a receiptNum and a saleAmount. You can create an extraction operator, or operator>>() function, that uses istream (which is defined in iostream.h, along with ostream) by using a prototype as follows:

```
friend istream& operator>>(istream &in, Sale &aSale);
```

Within the preceding function you can code data entry statements that allow a user to enter values for any or all of a Sale's data fields. Within the operator>>() function, the name in is used to hold an istream object, and aSale is used to hold a Sale object; you can substitute any legal C++ names you choose. Unlike the operator<<() function, the Sale object that receives data values cannot be passed to this function as a constant. That's because this function needs to change Sale's data values through keyboard data entry. Figure 8-13 shows the implementation of the operator>>() function for the Sale class.

```
istream& operator>>(istream &in, Sale &aSale)
  {
    cout<<endl;    // to clear the buffer
    cout<<"Enter receipt number ";
    in>>aSale.receiptNum;
    cout<<"Enter the amount of the sale ";
    in>>aSale.saleAmount;
    cout<<endl<<"      Thank you!"<<endl;
    return(in);
  }
```

Figure 8-13   Overloaded operator>>() function for the Sale class

You could improve the operator>>() function shown in Figure 8-13 by adding code that verifies valid receipt numbers and sale amounts. No matter how many instructions you place within the operator>>() function, however, when you write a program that uses a Sale class member such as aShirt, you need only the following code: `cin>>aShirt;`. That simple input statement generates all the prompts and verifications you need to fill a Sale object with appropriate data.

In the following steps, you add an overloaded operator>>() function for the SalesOffice class.

1. Open the **SalesOffice3.cpp** file if necessary.

2. Just after the opening curly brace of the SalesOffice class, insert the following prototype for the overloaded operator>>() function:

   friend istream& operator>>(istream& in, SalesOffice &anOffice);

8

3. After the complete operator<<() function and just before the main() function, insert the implementation of the operator>>() function:

```
istream& operator>>(istream& in,  SalesOffice &anOffice)
   {
    cout<<"Enter the name of the office ";
    in>>anOffice.officeName;
    cout<<"Enter the sales figure ";
    in>>anOffice.sales;
    return(in);
   }
```

4. Delete the existing main() function, and replace it with the simpler main() function that: declares two SalesOffice objects, allows the user to enter data for the two objects, and displays the two objects. Notice that arguments are required when you construct the two SalesOffice objects because the only existing SalesOffice constructor function requires arguments.

```
void main()
{
    SalesOffice officeA("",0);
    SalesOffice officeB("",0);
    cin>>officeA;
    cin>>officeB;
    cout<<officeA;
    cout<<officeB;
    getch();
}
```

5. Save the revised file as **SalesOffice4.cpp**. Compile and run the program. Figure 8-14 shows a typical program execution.

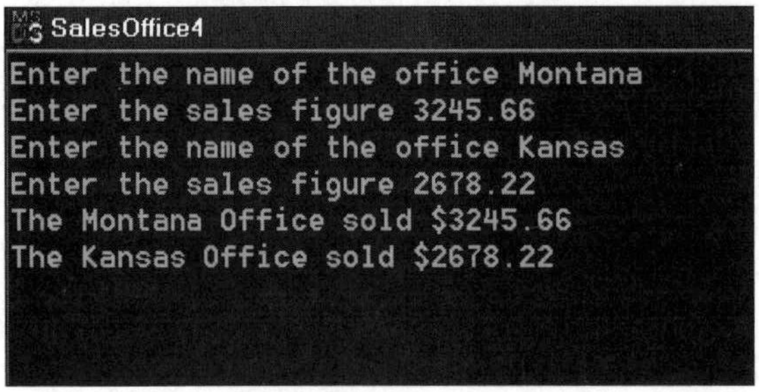

Figure 8-14   Output of SalesOffice4.cpp

OVERLOADING ++ AND – –

With C++, you use ++ to increment variables, and -- to decrement variables. It's important to notice the difference in how expressions are evaluated when the ++ or -- is placed before a variable, rather than after it.

When a prefix operator such as ++ is used in an expression, the mathematical operation takes place before the expression is evaluated. When the postfix operator is used, the expression is evaluated before the mathematical operation takes place. Figure 8-15 illustrates the difference in how the prefix and postfix ++ operators work.

```
int num;
num = 3;
result = ++num;
cout<<result;      // displays 4
cout<<num;         // displays 4
// reinitialize num
num = 3;
result = num++;
cout<<result;      // displays 3
cout<<num;         // displays 4
```

Figure 8-15   Using the prefix and postfix ++ operators with an integer

Figure 8-15 shows that when you use the prefix ++ operator on the num variable, first the variable increases, then it is evaluated and assigned to the result. In other words, num increases to 4, then result takes on the value 4. When num is reset to 3 and then assigned to result using the postfix ++ operator, however, the num variable evaluates as a 3, then is assigned to result, and finally num increases. So, result holds the original value of num—3—even though at the end of the operation, num itself holds the value 4. You can overload the prefix ++ or -- operators to use with your own class objects, just like you can overload other operators. When you use ++ or -- with class objects, the same prefix/postfix rules apply as they do with simple built-in types.

Consider an Inventory class definition with data members for a stock number and a quantity sold. Its three functions are a constructor, an overloaded operator<<() function for output, and an overloaded operator++() function for incrementing the quantity sold each time a sale occurs. Figure 8-16 shows the class.

```
class Inventory
  {
    friend ostream& operator<<(ostream& out, const Inventory
      &item);
    private:
      int stockNum;
      int numSold;
    public:
      Inventory(const int stknum, const int sold);
      Inventory& operator++();
  };
Inventory::Inventory(const int stknum, const int sold)
  {
    stockNum = stknum;
    numSold = sold;
  }
ostream& operator<<(ostream &out, const Inventory &item)
  {
    out<<"Item #"<<item.stockNum<<" Quantity: "<<
      item.numSold<<endl;
    return(out);
  }
Inventory& Inventory::operator++()
  {
    ++numSold;
    return(*this);
  }
```

Figure 8-16   The Inventory class

Within the operator++() function in the Inventory class, you can write the statement that increases numSold in several different ways. The statements `numSold++;`, `numSold = numSold + 1;`, and `numSold += 1;` all would work.

You might choose to have the ++ operator increase the stockNum rather than increase the numSold. When you overload any operator, you decide how it works for its class.

Within the operator++() function in the Inventory class in Figure 8-16, the numSold variable is increased. When you write a program that instantiates an Inventory object, the object's numSold increases when you place ++ in front of the object's name. Figure 8-17 illustrates a main() function that declares an Inventory object that is initialized with 475 items sold. The main() function increments the object twice, and displays the result after each operation. The results of the program are shown in Figure 8-18.

```
void main()
{
  Inventory anItem(101, 475);
  cout<<anItem;
  ++anItem;
  cout<<anItem;
  ++anItem;
  cout<<anItem;
  getch();
}
```

Figure 8-17   A program using the Inventory class

```
Inventory
Item #101 Quantity: 475
Item #101 Quantity: 476
Item #101 Quantity: 477
```

Figure 8-18   Output of Inventory program

The operator ++() function in Figure 8-16 executes without the line `return (*this);` because the this pointer is returned automatically by the operator++() function. It's clearer to someone reading the program, however, if you explicitly return the this pointer as the last statement in the function.

It's not necessary to learn anything new to be able to overload the prefix operator ++. The operator++() function returns a reference to an Inventory object, and it takes no arguments. Because the function is a member function of the Inventory class, it receives a this pointer to the object that calls it; therefore, no information need be passed to the operator++() function. The reference to the Inventory object returned is a reference to the this object—that is, a reference to the newly incremented object that was passed to the function.

To overload a decrement operator, you simply prototype the function as `Inventory& operator−−();` and place appropriate statements within the function body.

Using Postfix Increment and Decrement Operators

A problem arises if you want to use a postfix ++ operator as well as a prefix ++ operator with a class. As with all overloaded functions, C++ needs a method to distinguish between two functions with the same name. When you overload any C++ function, you must supply different argument lists; for the postfix ++ operator, you use an integer argument. The Inventory class postfix operator++() function prototype is:

```
Inventory& operator++(int);
```

8

The int argument to the Inventory class operator++() function is a dummy argument. You do not actually pass an integer to the operator++() function when you want to use the postfix ++. The int is present only to help C++ tell the difference between the prefix and postfix operators, and subsequently distinguish the two functions. In other words, if you call the prefix ++ operator function with a statement such as **++item;**, the function *without* the dummy argument executes; if you call the postfix operator function with a statement such as **item++;**, the function *with* the dummy argument executes.

You can give the dummy integer argument a name if you want. For example, you can code the Inventory operator++() function header as:

```
Inventory& Inventory::operator++(int x)
```

If you use x within the function, you will see that it contains a 0. There is no purpose in giving the variable a name, however, and it is considered unconventional programming to do so.

OVERLOADING THE == OPERATOR

At this point, writing an operator==() function should be an easy task. You simply decide what will constitute equality in class members. When you create your own classes, you choose whether equivalency means that every data field must be equivalent, or only specific data members. The operator==() function may return either an integer or a boolean variable representing true or false. Figure 8-19 shows two versions of an overloaded operator==() function for the Inventory class. Each of these functions considers two Inventory objects to be equal if their stock numbers are equal. The first version returns a 0 when the stockNum of the this object and the argument object are different; it returns 1 if the stock numbers are the same. The second version returns a bool. A variable of type **bool** can hold one of two values: true or false. Some older C++ compilers do not support the bool type; with those compilers you would use the first version of operator==() that returns an integer. Either of the functions shown in Figure 8-19 allows Inventory objects to be compared using ==, as in the statement:

```
if(itemA == itemB)
    cout<<"The stock numbers are the same"<<endl;
```

```
// Version that returns an int
int Inventory::operator==(const Inventory& item)
  {
  int truth = 0;
  if(stockNum == item.stockNum)
    truth = 1;
  return(truth);
  }
// Alternate version that returns a bool
bool Inventory::operator==(const Inventory& item)
  {
  bool truth = false;
  if(stockNum == item.stockNum)
    truth = true;
  return(truth);
  }
```

Figure 8-19   Overloaded operator==() function for the Inventory class

8

OVERLOADING THE = OPERATOR

Like +, -, ++, --, and all the other operators, the = operator can be overloaded for use with your own classes. Unlike the other operators, if you don't define the = operator, C++ provides a definition for you. Earlier in this chapter (see Figure 8-9) you saw that when you properly overload the + operator for the Sale class, you can create four Sale objects and use the statement `total = aShirt + aTie + pants;`. The assignment operator (the equal sign) correctly assigned to the total Sale object all the values of the fields of the temporary summary object created in the addition operation. Similarly, if you write `aShirt = aTie;` you assign all the values of all the fields of aTie to the aShirt object without having to write a function to overload the = operator. If you intend to use the = operator to assign the value of every field of the class object on the right of the = operator to each corresponding field of the class object on the = operator's left, then you do not need to write an overloaded = operator.

If you want the = operator to do something other than assign each member, then you must create a custom operator=() function. In addition, if the class contains data fields that are pointers, you should create a custom function.

If a class contains a pointer and one member object is copied to another member object, then two objects will contain pointers to the same memory. This overlap might not pose a problem unless one of the objects is deleted or goes out of scope. When the destructor function is called for the first object, the memory to which that object points is released. Now the second object contains a pointer to deallocated memory.

Consider a class for the videos owned by a video rental store. Class data members for each Movie include a title and the number of copies owned. Functions include a constructor, destructor, and showMovie() function. Figure 8-20 shows the class.

```
class Movie
  {
   private:
     char *title;
     int numberOfCopies;
   public:
     Movie(const char *name = '\0', const int c = 0);
     ~Movie();
     void showMovie(void);
  };
Movie::Movie(const char *name,const int c)
  {
   title = new char[strlen(name)+1];
            // include  string.h to use strlen function
   strcpy(title,name);    // copy name to movie title
   numberOfCopies = c;
  }
Movie::~Movie()
  {
   delete title;
  }
```

Figure 8-20   The Movie class

Recall that destructor function names always begin with a tilde (~).

The movie title within the Movie class is defined as **char *title;**. The title is stored as a character pointer to save memory. If you define a Movie title as char title[10], you don't allow enough room for many long Movie titles. However, if you define the title as **char title[100];**, you waste a lot of memory when a Movie's title is short. Because the length of Movie titles varies widely, you might want to allocate memory dynamically during construction, based on the exact amount of storage needed. You can use the **new operator** to allocate exactly as much memory as you need. The new operator locates as much available memory as you ask it to, and returns the address where the memory is found. You use a pointer variable for title so it can hold the address of the newfound memory.

When you allocate memory using the new operator, it's still possible that not enough memory is available. You will learn how to handle this problem when you study C++ exception handling.

The constructor in Figure 8-20 uses the strlen() function from the string.h class to determine the exact length of the name of the Movie in the argument list. Then, to allow room for the NULL character at the end of the string, you add 1. For example, if a Movie title contains four characters, then the highlighted statement in the Movie constructor allocates five new characters whose address is stored in the title pointer.

Whenever you allocate memory with the new operator, you should delete the reserved memory when the object using it goes out of scope. Because the Movie title is allocated with the new operator, the Movie destructor function shown in Figure 8-20 uses the delete operator to free the previously allocated memory.

Figure 8-21 shows a program that declares two Movie objects. This sample program uses unconventional blocking to illustrate the potential error situation. The program instantiates a Movie named film1, then, within a new block, instantiates another Movie named film2. When the built-in = operator is used in the highlighted statement, each field of film2 is copied to film1; both Movie objects have title pointer variables that point to the characters "Wizard of Oz" in memory, and each object holds a 5 in the numberOfCopies field. The first two calls to the showMovie() function confirm that the copy is successful.

8

```
void main()
{
  Movie film1("ET",2);
    {
      Movie film2("Wizard of Oz",5);
      film1 = film2;
      film1.showMovie();
      film2.showMovie();
    } // film2 is destroyed here
  film1.showMovie();
  }
  getch();
}
```

Figure 8-21   Program that uses the Movie class

At the first closing curly brace in the program in Figure 8-21, film2 goes out of scope and the memory reserved for film2's title is released by the Movie destructor function. That means the title pointer in the film1 object is pointing to deallocated memory. When you use the showMovie() function with film1 for the second time, the title holds garbage, as shown in the output in Figure 8-22.

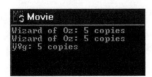

Figure 8-22   Output of Movie program without overloaded = operator

You can avoid the preceding problem by overloading the = operator so the two Movie title pointers don't point to the same memory. As shown in the function in Figure 8-23, when film2 is copied to film1 using the = operator, you deallocate the memory that holds film1's title, allocate new memory for film1's title, and copy film2's title to the film1 object. Finally, you copy the integer variable that holds the number of copies of the Movie. When you insert the overloaded operator=() function (and its prototype) into the Movie class, the output of the main() program shown in Figure 8-21 looks like Figure 8-24.

```
void Movie::operator=(Movie &otherMovie)
  {
    if (title!=NULL) // If a title for the first Movie exists
      delete(title);        // delete it
      // allocate enough new memory for the copied title
    title = new char[strlen(otherMovie.title) + 1];
      // copy the title to the new memory
    strcpy(title, otherMovie.title);
      // copy the number of copies variable
    numberOfCopies = otherMovie.numberOfCopies;
  }
```

Figure 8-23   Overloaded operator=() function for the Movie class

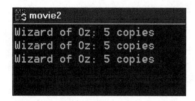

Figure 8-24   Output of Movie program with overloaded = operator

OVERLOADING [ ] AND ( )

C++ provides two special operators, the subscript operator and the parentheses operator, that can be used as adjuncts to the more conventional operators.

The **subscript operator**, operator[ ], is declared like any other function, but called in a manner similar to accessing an array element. As with every other operator, you can include any instructions you want within an operator[ ] function. Typically, you use this function to perform a task that both requires an argument and does not quite fit into another operator's usual meaning.

Consider a Book class such as the one shown in Figure 8-25. Its data members include title, author, and price. When the price changes, it might be convenient to create an overloaded operator=() function that assigns a new price. However, you can't use the operator=( ) function for this purpose, because you already have developed this function to change every data member of a Book object and to correctly copy the pointer members that hold the Book's title and author. Of course, you could create a standard member function to alter the Book's price, and give it a name such as changeBookPrice(), but you also can use an operator[ ] function.

```
class Book
  {
     friend ostream& operator<<(ostream& out, const Book &aBook);
     private:
       char *title;
       char *author;
       double price;
     public:
       Book(const char *bookTitle = '\0', const char *writer =
        '\0',const double amount = 0);
       ~Book();
       void operator=(Book &otherBook);
       void operator[](double newPrice);
  };
Book::Book(const char *bookTitle,const char *writer,
     const double amount)
  {
     title = new char[strlen(bookTitle)+1];
     strcpy(title,bookTitle);
     author = new char[strlen(writer) + 1];
     strcpy(author, writer);
     price = amount;
  }
Book::~Book()
  {
     delete title;
     delete author;
  }
void Book::operator=(Book &otherBook)
     {
     if (title!=NULL)
       delete(title);
     title = new char[strlen(otherBook.title) + 1];
     strcpy(title, otherBook.title);
     if (author!=NULL)
       delete(author);
     author = new char[strlen(otherBook.author) + 1];
     strcpy(author, otherBook.author);
     price = otherBook.price;
  }
ostream& operator<<(ostream& out, const Book &aBook)
  {
     out<<aBook.title<<" by "<<aBook.author<<"$"<<
      aBook.price<<endl;
     return(out);
  }
void Book::operator[](double newPrice)
  {
     price = newPrice;
  }
```

Figure 8-25   The Book class

8

The operator[]() function in the Book class in Figure 8-25 returns nothing and receives a double. As a Book class member function, it also receives a this pointer to the calling object. Figure 8-26 shows a simple main() program that uses a Book class object. The program instantiates a Book, displays its values, uses the overloaded subscript operator to change the price, and displays the Book object with its new price. Figure 8-27 shows the output.

```
void main()
  {
   Book aBook("Cujo","King",19.95);
   cout<<aBook;
   aBook[14.75];
   cout<<aBook;
   getch();
  }
```

Figure 8-26   Program that uses a Book object

Figure 8-27   Output of Book program

Even though the 14.75 within the brackets in Figure 8-26 looks similar to a subscript, it obviously is not. For one thing, aBook is not an array; for another, array subscripts must be integers. Instead, 14.75 simply represents a price, and the brackets provide an easy way to assign a value to one data member of the class.

Using the Parentheses Operator

Like the subscript operator, you can use the **parentheses operator** to make multiple assignments within a class. For example, to overload the parentheses operator to assign both an author and a price to a member of the Book class, you can create the function shown in Figure 8-28. The overloaded() function takes two arguments and assigns them to the appropriate data members. When you add this function and its prototype to the Book class definition, the Book class contains three ways to assign values to a Book: the = assigns three fields, the () assigns two fields, and the [ ] assigns one field.

```
void Book::operator()(char *newWriter, double newPrice)
  {
    if (author!=NULL)
        delete(author);
    author = new char[strlen(newWriter) + 1];
    strcpy(author, newWriter);
    price = newPrice;
  }
```

Figure 8-28   The operator() function for the Book class

When you run the program shown in Figure 8-29, you produce the output in Figure 8-30. At first glance, the highlighted aBook object appears to be a function, but aBook is an object, and the function is the parentheses operator function. The availability of the subscript and parentheses operator functions allows the programmer to create specialized functions in addition to, or that don't seem appropriate for, the other operator symbols.

```
void main()
  {
    Book aBook("Cujo","King",19.95);
    cout<<aBook;
    aBook("Johannsenn", 14.75);
    cout<<aBook;
    getch();
  }
```

Figure 8-29   Program that uses the overloaded parentheses operator with a
               Book object

```
 $ book2
Cujo by King $19.95
Cujo by Johannsenn $14.75
```

Figure 8-30   Output of program using parentheses operator function

CHAPTER SUMMARY

❏ The built-in + operator is polymorphic in C++; it can take one or two arguments and have a different meaning in each case. This feature allows programmers to use the + operator in a natural way.

❏ Operator overloading is the process by which you apply operators to your own abstract data types. You overload an operator by making it a function; subsequently, it may be used just like any other function. If an operator is normally defined to be only unary, then you cannot overload it to be binary, and vice versa. You cannot change normal associativity or precedence when you overload operators.

❏ The name of the operator function that overloads the + symbol is operator+(). The syntax involved in using the + operator alone is simpler, more natural, and easier to remember than using an ordinary member function. Similar advantages apply to overloading all the other C++ operators.

❏ You can overload the + operator to add two class objects, or a class object and a primitive object. You can't overload any operators whose first operand is an object that is a built-in type, even if the second operand is a class object.

❏ To enable you to chain mathematical operations, you overload the operator functions to return a class object.

❏ The << operator is overloaded by C++; it is both a bitwise left-shift operator and an output operator. You also can overload it to work with class objects. This function, called operator<<(), is a friend function; it returns a reference to ostream. It accepts two arguments: a reference to ostream and a copy of the object to output.

❏ The >> operator can be overloaded for input. The function is a friend function and typically contains prompts, data entry statements, and data verification code.

❏ When you overload the prefix and postfix ++ and -- operators to work with your classes, the same prefix/postfix rules apply as they do with simple built-in types. To distinguish between the two types, postfix operators use a dummy integer argument.

❏ You overload the operator==() function to return either an integer or a boolean variable representing true or false.

❏ If you don't define the = operator, C++ provides a definition for you. If you want the = operator to do something other than assign each member of a class, then you must create a custom operator=() function. In addition, if the class contains data fields that are pointers, you should create a custom function.

❏ You overload the subscript and parentheses operators to handle situations where no other operator is appropriate, or when the appropriate operator already is in use. The subscript operator takes a single argument; the parentheses operator can take multiple arguments.

REVIEW QUESTIONS

1. Which of the following is a legal example of the way overloading is used in C++?

    a. creating two member functions for a class

    b. creating two constructors for a class

    c. creating two destructors for a class

    d. all of the above

2. The primary advantage to overloading functions is _____.

    a. you can use one function name for every operation you want to perform with a class

    b. you can use one class name for many types of items

    c. you can use one function name for similar operations, regardless of the data types involved

    d. you do not have to write separate code for the bodies of functions that perform similar tasks

3. The built-in * operator is _____.

    a. polymorphic

    b. recursive

    c. retroactive

    d. all of the above

4. Applying operators to your own abstract data types is called _____ overloading.

    a. abstract

    b. parametric

    c. polymorphic

    d. operator

5. Which of the following is true?

    a. You overload an operator by making it an argument to a function.

    b. You should overload every C++ operator for each new class you create.

    c. To avoid confusion, you should not overload operators to carry out tasks that are similar in meaning to the built-in version of the operator.

    d. Operators that are normally defined to be only unary must remain unary when you overload them.

8

6. Which of the following operators can be overloaded to be binary?

  a. >

  b. ->

  c. ++

  d. !

7. _____ refers to the order in which actions within an expression are carried out.

  a. Overloading

  b. Associativity

  c. Communicativity

  d. Operating

8. Which of the following operators can be overloaded?

  a. .

  b. &

  c. ::

  d. ?:

9. If you have correctly overloaded the * operator to multiply two members of the Furniture class, and you have declared two Furniture objects, aDesk and aChair, then which of the following is a legal expression?

  a. `Furniture * Furniture`

  b. `aDesk * aChair`

  c. `Furniture * aChair`

  d. all of the above

10. If you have correctly overloaded the * operator to multiply two members of the Furniture class, and you have declared two Furniture objects, aDesk and aChair, then which of the following is a legal expression?

  a. `aChair.operator*(aDesk)`

  b. `aChair * aChair`

  c. `aChair * aDesk`

  d. all of the above

11. The Shipment class holds information about a shipment, including its weight. An overloaded division operator divides a Shipment's totalWeight field into the number of packages in the Shipment to determine the average package weight. The function header is `int Shipment::operator/(int packages)`. Which of the following statements is correct within the function?

  a. `int numPackages = Shipment / packages;`

  b. `int numPackages = totalWeight / packages;`

    c. `int numPackages = packages.totalWeight / packages;`

    d. `int numPackages = packages.totalWeight / totalWeight;`

12. An overloaded subtraction operator subtracts two Shipment objects from each other, returning an integer that represents the difference in their totalWeight variables. The subtraction operator works as expected, with the object to the right of the minus sign being subtracted from the object to the left, The function header is `int Shipment::operator-(Shipment ship);`. Within the function, which of the following is correct?

    a. `int difference = ship - totalWeight;`

    b. `int difference = totalWeight - ship;`

    c. `int difference = ship.totalWeight - totalWeight;`

    d. `int difference = totalWeight - ship.totalWeight;`

13. The Student class contains an overloaded addition operator which allows a number of credits to be added to a Student's totalCredits. The function header is `Student Student::operator+(int newCredits)`. The = operator has not been overloaded. Which of the following is correct in a program that declares a Student object named aStudent?

    a. `aStudent = 3 + aStudent;`

    b. `aStudent = aStudent + 3;`

    c. both of the above

    d. none of the above

14. To be able to add three or more objects in sequence, as in `x + y + z`, you must overload the + operator to _____.

    a. accept multiple arguments

    b. accept no arguments

    c. return an object of the same type as the arguments

    d. return a primitive type

15. When you overload the << operator to work with a class object, you must _____.

    a. make the operator function a friend function

    b. make the operator function a member function

    c. return an object of the same type as the class

    d. return a simple built-in type

8

16. Which of the following is the correct prototype for an overloaded insertion operator for the Shipment class?

   a. `ostream& operator<<(ostream &out, const Shipment &anOrder);`

   b. `friend ostream& operator<<(ostream &out, const Shipment &anOrder);`

   c. `friend ostream& operator<<(ostream out, const Shipment anOrder);`

   d. `friend ostream operator<<(ostream &out, const Shipment &anOrder);`

17. The primary advantage to overloading >> and << to use with class objects is _____.

   a. you write less code than with standard input and output functions

   b. the << and >> functions, being member functions of the class, have access to private class data

   c. the program code that uses the functions contains syntax that is easy to understand

   d. all of the above

18. The difference between the function prototypes for the overloaded prefix and postfix ++ for any class is the _____.

   a. return type

   b. function name

   c. argument list

   d. all of the above

19. If you do not overload an = operator for a class _____.

   a. C++ provides you with a built-in version

   b. you must write a regular member function to copy one object to another

   c. you cannot use the class objects in mathematical expressions

   d. you cannot use = with class objects

20. The overloaded operator>>() function for the Shipment class allows the user to enter a value for the shipWeight field. The function header is
   `istream operator>>(istream &input, Shipment &anOrder)`. Which of the following is the correct statement?

   a. `cin>>shipWeight;`

   b. `in>>shipWeight;`

   c. `input>>shipWeight;`

   d. `istream>>shipWeight;`

EXERCISES

1. Complete the following tasks:

   a. Design a Job class with three data fields—Job number, time in hours to complete the Job, and rate per hour charged for the Job.

   b. Include overloaded extraction and insertion operators that get and display a Job's values.

   c. Include overloaded + and − operators that return integers that indicate the total time for two Jobs, and indicate the difference in time between two Jobs, respectively.

   d. Write a main() program demonstrating that all the functions work correctly.

2. Complete the following tasks:

   a. Design a class to hold a JobBid. Each JobBid contains a bid number and a quoted price. Each JobBid also contains overloaded extraction and insertion operators.

   b. Include an overloaded operator<() function. A JobBid is considered lower than another JobBid when the quoted price is lower.

   c. Write a main() function that declares an array of four JobBid objects. Find and display the lowest JobBid.

3. Complete the following tasks:

   a. Design a PhoneCall class that holds: a phone number to which a call is placed, the length of the call in minutes, and the rate charged per minute. Overload extraction and insertion operators for the class.

   b. Overload the == operator to compare two PhoneCalls. Consider one PhoneCall to be equal to another if both calls are placed to the same number.

   c. Create a main() program that allows you to enter 10 PhoneCalls into an array. If a PhoneCall has already been placed to a number, do not allow a second PhoneCall to the same number.

4. Complete the following tasks:

   a. Design a SoccerPlayer class that includes three integer fields: a player's jersey number, goals, and assists. Overload extraction and insertion operators for the class.

   b. Include an operator>() function for the class. One SoccerPlayer is considered greater than another if the sum of goals plus assists is greater.

   c. Create an array of 11 SoccerPlayers, then use the > operator to find the player who has the greatest total of goals plus assists.

5. Complete the following tasks:

   a. Design a Dog class that includes fields for a breed (for example, "Labrador") and eye color. Include extraction and insertion operators.

   b. Overload an operator*() function for the Dog class. When you multiply two Dogs, the result is a Dog. If the two operand Dogs are the same breed, then the resulting Dog is that breed; if the two operand Dogs have different breeds, then the resulting

8

Dog is "Mixed" breed. Use an expression similar to `int eyeSelection = rand() % 2;` to assign a random number, 0 or 1, to an eyeSelection variable. (Include <stdlib.h> at the top of your file to access the rand() function.) When the random number chosen is 0, use the eye color from the first operand Dog for the resulting Dog's eyes; when the random number is 1, use the eye color of the second Dog.

c. Write a main() function. Declare four parent Dogs. Assign the same breed to two Dogs, and different breeds to each of the other two Dogs. (You will have a total of three breeds.) In a loop, multiply each pair eight times, and display the results.

6. Complete the following tasks:

a. Design a Meal class with two fields—one that holds the name of the entrée, the other that holds a calorie count integer. Include a constructor that sets a Meal's fields with arguments, or uses default values when no arguments are provided.

b. Include an overloaded insertion operator function that displays a Meal's values.

c. Include an overloaded extraction operator that prompts a user for an entrée name and calorie count for a meal.

d. Include an overloaded operator+() function that allows you to add two or more Meal objects. Adding two Meal objects means adding their calorie values and creating a summary Meal object in which you store "Daily Total" in the entrée field.

e. Write a main() program that declares four Meal objects named breakfast, lunch, dinner, and total. Provide values for the breakfast, lunch, and dinner objects. Include the statement `total = breakfast + lunch + dinner;` in your program, then display values for the four Meal objects.

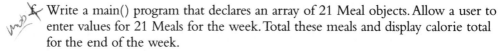 Write a main() program that declares an array of 21 Meal objects. Allow a user to enter values for 21 Meals for the week. Total these meals and display calorie total for the end of the week.

7. Complete the following tasks:

a. Create a PhoneBook class. Fields include first name, last name, area code, and phone number. The constructor prompts the user for, and assigns values to, the fields.

b. Include an insertion operator that displays the values of each field.

c. Overload the operator[]() function to change a PhoneBook object's phone number (but not area code).

d. Overload the operator()() function to change the area code and phone number.

e. Write a main() program in which you declare an array of five PhoneBook objects and assign data to each. Using a loop, display numbers 1 through 5, along with each object's data. Prompt the user to select a number 1 through 5 to modify a PhoneBook Entry. When the user has chosen an entry, ask whether the user wants to alter an entire entry, alter the entire phone number including the area code, or alter just the phone number and not the area code. Accept new data values accordingly. If the user wants to modify an entire entry, create a temporary object, assign values, and use the built-in = operator to assign the temporary object to the correct location in the array. If the user wants to change the area code and phone number, or change the phone number only, prompt for values, then use either the [] or () operator to assign the new values to the proper existing object within the array. After the update has taken effect, redisplay the five PhoneBook entries.

8. Complete the following tasks:

   a. Design a Friend class with data fields for first name, last name, and age. The constructor takes arguments for the three fields, providing default values if arguments are not provided. Allocate storage for first and last name dynamically. The destructor deletes allocated memory. Include functions to output a Friend's data.

   b. Write a main() program that declares three Friend objects to which you assign data. Declare a fourth Friend object named best that holds your best Friend. Display each Friend, and ask the user to respond whether this Friend is the user's best Friend. Assign the chosen Friend object to the best object, and display the best Friend.

9. Each of the following files in the Chapter08 folder contains syntax and/or logical errors. Determine the problem in each case, and fix the program.

   a. DEBUG8-1

   b. DEBUG8-2

   c. DEBUG8-3

   d. DEBUG8-4

8

CASE PROJECT

Running Case

You have been developing a Fraction class for Teacher's Pet Software. Each fraction contains a numerator, a denominator, a whole number portion, and a floating-point equivalent field. Each Fraction also has access to several functions you have developed.

   a. Add four arithmetic operators, +, -, *, and /. Remember that to add or subtract two Fractions, you first must convert them to Fractions with a common denominator. You multiply two Fractions by multiplying the numerators and multiplying the denominators. You divide two Fractions by inverting the second Fraction, then multiplying. After any arithmetic operation, be sure the Fraction is in proper format; for example, 1/2 * 2/3 results in 1/3, not 2/6.

   b. Add an operator==() function that compares the value of two Fractions.

   c. Add operator>() and operator<() functions that compare the values of two Fractions.

   d. Add extraction and insertion operators for the Fraction class.

e. Write a main() program that declares an array of 10 randomly generated Fraction values, for which each numerator is a random value between 1 and 5 inclusive. You can generate a random number using an expression such as `int randValue = rand() % highest;`, where highest is one value higher than the largest number you want to generate. For example, rand() % 5 returns a random number between 0 and 4 inclusive. To generate a number between 1 and 5 instead of 0 and 4, you add 1 to randValue. Include <stdlib.h> to access the rand() function. For each Fraction, generate a random number for the numerator and assign the value 10 to the denominator. Reduce each of the ten randomly generated Fractions to its proper form (for example, 2/10 is 1/5) and display them.

f. Remove the statements from main() that display the ten Fraction objects. Add statements to the main() program that prompt the user to choose between four operations for an arithmetic drill—addition, subtraction, multiplication, or division. After the user has selected an operation, generate five problems using five pairs of Fractions from the 10-element array. Display a problem (for example, if the user chooses addition, the problem might be "1/10 + 3/10") and allow the user to enter an answer from the keyboard. After each keyboard answer, notify the user whether the answer was correct.

g. Add code to the main() function that allows the user up to three attempts to correctly answer each problem.

h. Add code to the main() function that keeps score. At the end of the program, display a message similar to "You got 3 correct out of 5 problems".

i. Alter the main() program to generate random numbers between 6 and 10 inclusive for the denominators as well as the numerators.

9

UNDERSTANDING INHERITANCE

In this chapter you will learn:

- About inheritance and its benefits
- How to create a derived class
- About restrictions imposed with inheritance
- How to choose a class access specifier
- How to override and overload parent class functions within a child class
- How to use a constructor initialization list
- How to provide for a base class constructor within a derived class
- How to override the class access specifier
- How to use multiple inheritance
- About the special problems posed by multiple inheritance
- How to use virtual inheritance

Inheritance is the principle that knowledge of a general category can be applied to more specific objects. Specifically, inheritance in C++ means you can create classes that derive most of their attributes from existing classes. Inheritance saves you time because you don't have to start from scratch every time you want to create a class. Instead, when you use inheritance to create a class, you expand on an existing class.

In this chapter, you learn about various types of inheritance, and their advantages and disadvantages.

UNDERSTANDING INHERITANCE

You are familiar with the concept of inheritance from situations unrelated to programming. When you hear the term "inheritance," you probably think of genetics. You know that your hair and eye color have been inherited. You may have selected a family pet or a variety of plants for your garden on the basis of its genetic traits. With genetic inheritance, you often think about hierarchies of classifications—your Siamese is a member of the cat family, which is a mammal, which is an animal, and so on.

With any subject matter, your knowledge of existing hierarchies makes it easier to understand new information. If a friend tells you he's getting an item that belongs to the "Carmello" category, you might be uncertain what he means. If he tells you that the item is a variety of tomato, you understand many of a Carmello's traits without ever having seen one—that is, you know a Carmello tomato has the general traits of a tomato (but possibly different traits than a "Beefsteak" tomato). If you had not heard of the tomato category, your friend could explain that a tomato is a member of the fruit category, and you would at least have an idea that a Carmello must grow, have seeds, and probably be edible.

When you organize a hard disk, you use a form of inheritance. Your C drive probably contains a number of folders, each of which contains folders that contain more specific material. For example, your Schoolwork folder might contain a MathDepartment folder that contains a CollegeAlgebra folder. You can picture class inheritance as being similar.

Objects used in computer programs also are easier to understand if you can place them within a hierarchy of inheritance. Suppose you have written several programs with a class named Student. You have learned the names of the data fields, and you understand what the various member functions do. If you need to write a program using a new class named FirstYearStudent, the job is easier if FirstYearStudent is inherited from a class named Student. The FirstYearStudent class may require some additional data members and functions (perhaps an applicationFee field or an orientation() method) that other Student objects do not require, but FirstYearStudent also will have the more general Student members with which you are already familiar. You need to master only the new members.

The FirstYearStudent class inherits from the Student class, or is **derived** from it. The Student class is called a **parent class**, **base class**, **superclass**, or **ancestor**; the FirstYearStudent class is called a **child class**, **derived class**, **subclass**, or **descendant**.

In many real-life cases, a derived class might not possess all of its parents' traits. For example, you may be the only redhead in your family, and some fruits should not be eaten. Similarly, child class members might not possess all the traits of their parents' class. For example, members of the FirstYearStudent class might require a different display format than members of the Student class. Thus, a useful feature of C++ inheritance is that the descendant class can override inappropriate attributes from the parent. When you **override** a function, you substitute one version of the function for another.

UNDERSTANDING THE ADVANTAGES PROVIDED BY INHERITANCE

Inheritance is considered a basic building block of object-oriented programming. To be truly "object-oriented," a programming language must allow inheritance. One major feature of object-oriented programming is its ability to create classes from ones that already exist. Programs in which you derive new classes from existing classes offer several advantages:

- You save time because much of the code needed for your class is already written.

- You save additional time because the existing code has already been tested—that is, you know it works correctly; it is **reliable**.

- You save even more time because you already understand how the base class works, and you can concentrate on the complexity added as a result of your extensions to the class.

- In a derived class, you can extend and revise a parent class without corrupting the existing parent class features. In other words, you don't have to modify a parent class to get it to work correctly with your new category of objects; you leave the original class alone.

- If other classes have been derived from the parent class, the parent class is even more reliable—the more its code has been used, the more likely it is that logical errors have already been found and fixed.

 In some object-oriented programming languages, such as Java and SmallTalk, every new class must inherit from an existing class that is built into the language. C++ is sometimes called a hybrid object-oriented programming language because you can create original base classes without deriving them from some other class. You have been creating classes without inheritance throughout this text.

Despite its advantages, inheritance is not used as often as it could be. In many companies, a program is needed quickly to solve a particular problem. Developing good, general-purpose software from which more specific classes can be inherited is more difficult and time-consuming than writing a "quick and dirty" program to solve an immediate problem. Because the benefits of creating a good, reusable base class are usually not realized in one project, programmers often have little incentive to design software from which derived classes can be created in the future. If programmers take the time to develop reliable base classes, however, future programming projects will go much more smoothly.

 With C++, you cannot inherit regular functions and variables, only classes.

CREATING A DERIVED CLASS

Consider a class originally developed by a company to hold an individual's data, such as an ID number and name. The class, named Person, is shown in Figure 9-1. It contains three fields, and two member functions that set and display the data field values.

 A fully developed Person class most likely would contain street address information, a phone number, and other personal data. Additionally, you might include a constructor and destructor. For simplicity, this Person class is short.

```
class Person
  {
    private:
      int idNum;
      char lastName[20];
      char firstName[15];
    public:
      void setFields(int num, char last[], char first[]);
      void outputData();
  };
void Person::setFields(int num, char last[], char first[])
  {
    idNum = num;
    strcpy(lastName, last);
    strcpy(firstName,first);
  }
void Person::outputData()
  {
    cout<<"ID #"<<idNum<<" Name: "<<firstName<<" "<<
      lastName<<endl;
  }
```

Figure 9-1   The Person class

The company that uses the Person class soon realizes that the class can be used for all kinds of individuals—customers, full-time employees, part-time employees, and suppliers all have names and numbers as well. The Person class appears to be a good candidate to be inherited by new classes.

 Often, you can distinguish child and parent classes in the same way you distinguish a person's first and last names. Your last name represents a category of people (all the members of your family), while your first name is a specific "example" of the family. John Franklin is a specific Franklin, and a Customer Person is a more specific example of a Person.

To create a derived class, you include the following elements in the order listed:

- Keyword class
- Derived class name
- Colon
- Class access specifier, either public, private, or protected
- Base class name
- Opening brace
- Class definition statements
- Closing brace
- Semicolon

For example, Figure 9-2 shows the shell, or outline, of a Customer class that inherits the members of the Person class. This class uses public inheritance, which is most common.

9

```
class Customer : public Person
  {
       // other statements go here
  };
```

Figure 9-2   The Customer class shell

A common programmer error is to place two colons after the derived class name in the class header line. C++ will then issue an error message because two colons indicate class scope, and the class has yet to be completely declared. Declaring a derived class requires using a single colon after the new class name.

The Customer class shown in Figure 9-2 contains all the members of Person because it inherits them. In other words, every Customer object has an idNum, lastName, and firstName, just as a Person object does. Additionally, you can define the Customer class to include additional data member, balanceDue, and two more functions: setBalDue() and outputBalDue(). A complete Customer definition is shown in Figure 9-3.

You can say every child class object "is a" parent class object. For example, every Customer "is a" Person, not vice versa.

```
class Customer : public Person
  {
      private:
          double balanceDue;
      public:
          void setBalDue(double bal);
          void outputBalDue(void);
  };
void Customer::setBalDue(double bal)
  {
      balanceDue = bal;
  }
void Customer::outputBalDue()
  {
      cout<<"Balance due $"<<balanceDue<<endl;
  }
```

Figure 9-3   The Customer class

After you define Customer class, you can write a program such as the one in Figure 9-4; the output appears in Figure 9-5. When the Customer class is a child of the Person class, then a Customer object can use the functions that belong to its own class, as well as those of its parent.

```
void main()
  {
      Customer cust;
      // the next two functions are defined
      // in the base class Person
      cust.setFields(215,"Santini","Linda");
      cust.outputData();
      // the next two functions are defined
      // in the derived class Customer
      cust.setBalDue(147.95);
      cust.outputBalDue();
  }
```

Figure 9-4   A program that uses a Customer

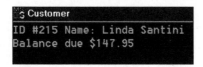

Figure 9-5   Output of program that uses a Customer

Of course, a Customer object can use its own class's member functions, setBalDue() and outputBalDue(). Additionally, it can use the Person functions, setFields() and outputData(), as if they were its own.

In the next set of steps you create two classes, Car and Convertible. The Car class serves as a base class and includes features common to all cars—an ignition that is off or on, and a current speed. The Convertible class extends the Car class so that a Convertible possesses the added feature of a top that lowers and raises.

1. Open a new file in your C++ editor, and type the include statements you need to create the Car class.

   #include<iostream.h>
   #include<conio.h>

2. The Car class contains two integer fields. One holds a flag indicating whether the ignition is on; the other holds the Car's current speed in miles per hour. There are four member functions: two functions that turn the ignition on and off, a function that sets the Car's speed, and a function that displays a Car's states. (If your compiler supports type bool, you can use it as the type for isIgnitionOn instead of int.)

   ```
   class Car
     {
           private:
                   int isIgnitionOn;
                   int speed;
           public:
                   void turnIgnitionOn();
                   void turnIgnitionOff();
                   void setSpeed(int mph);
                   void showCar();
     };
   ```

3. The function that displays the values of a Car's fields uses the value of the isIgnitionOn flag to determine whether the Car is running. It also displays the current speed of the Car.

   ```
   void Car::showCar()
     {
        if(isIgnitionOn)
           cout<<"Ignition is on. ";
        else
           cout<<"Ignition is off. ";
        cout<<"Speed is "<<speed<<endl;
     }
   ```

9

4. The two functions named turnIgnitionOn() and turnIgnitionOff() are similar; each sets the value of the isIgnitionOn flag, using 1 to represent true and 0 to represent false. (If your compiler supports type bool, you can use the C++ keywords true and false in place of 1 and 0, respectively, in the two functions.) Additionally, when you turn the ignition off, it makes sense to set the Car's speed to 0.

```
void Car::turnIgnitionOn()
{
   isIgnitionOn = 1;
}
void Car::turnIgnitionOff()
{
   speed = 0;
   isIgnitionOn = 0;
}
```

5. The setSpeed() function takes an integer argument and uses it to set the value of the speed field. However, no Car is allowed a speed greater than 65 miles per hour, and no Car is allowed any speed other than 0 if the ignition is off.

```
void Car::setSpeed(int mph)
{
   if(isIgnitionOn)
      if (mph <= 65)
            speed = mph;
      else
            speed = 65;
   else
      cout<<"Can't set speed - ignition is off!"<<endl;
}
```

6. Add a main() function that demonstrates the functions at work. The main() function declares a Car object, turns the Car on and sets a speed, shows the Car values, and so on.

```
void main()
{
      Car myCar;
      myCar.turnIgnitionOn();
      myCar.setSpeed(35);
      myCar.showCar();
      myCar.setSpeed(70);
      myCar.showCar();
      myCar.turnIgnitionOff();
      myCar.showCar();
      getch();
}
```

7. Save the file as **Car.cpp** in the Chapter09 folder of either your Student Data Disk or the Student Data folder on your hard drive. Then compile and run the program. The output appears in Figure 9-6.

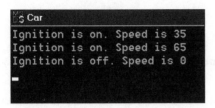

```
Car
Ignition is on. Speed is 35
Ignition is on. Speed is 65
Ignition is off. Speed is 0
```

Figure 9-6   Output of Car.cpp

The Car class doesn't contain anything unusual; you have already created many classes like it. You could create a similar class from scratch to use for a Convertible, but it is more convenient to create a child class derived from Car. You create the Convertible class and a demonstration program in the next set of steps.

1. Remove the entire main() function from the Car.cpp file, and save the abbreviated file as **Convertible.cpp**. You will create the Convertible class within this new file. (Alternatively, you could save the abbreviated Car.cpp file by itself and include it in a new Convertible.cpp file.)

2. At the bottom of the file, after the existing Car class code, define the Convertible class as an extension of the Car class. The Convertible class contains one new data member named isTopUp that holds the status of the Convertible's top. Three functions work with this data field: one puts the top up; another puts it down; and the third prints a message regarding the top's status.

```cpp
class Convertible: public Car
{
    private:
        int isTopUp;
    public:
        void putTopUp();
        void putTopDown();
        void showTopStatus();
};
```

3. The functions putTopUp() and putTopDown() set the isTopUp field to 1 and 0, respectively.

```cpp
void Convertible::putTopUp()
{
    isTopUp = 1;
}
void Convertible::putTopDown()
{
    isTopUp = 0;
}
```

9

4. The showTopStatus() function prints an appropriate message based on the status of the isTopUp field.

```
void Convertible::showTopStatus()
{
  if(isTopUp)
    cout<<"Top is up."<<endl;
  else
    cout<<"Top is down."<<endl;
}
```

5. Finally, create a main() function that declares a Convertible object and uses the functions to start the Convertible, set the speed, put the top down and up, and so on.

```
void main()
{
    Convertible myCar;
    myCar.turnIgnitionOn();
    myCar.setSpeed(35);
    myCar.putTopDown();
    myCar.showCar();
    myCar.showTopStatus();
    myCar.setSpeed(70);
    myCar.showCar();
    myCar.showTopStatus();
    myCar.putTopUp();
    myCar.turnIgnitionOff();
    myCar.showCar();
    myCar.showTopStatus();
    getch();
}
```

6. Save the file again as **Convertible.cpp**. Compile and run the program. The output looks like Figure 9-7. Notice that the Convertible object has access to all the Car functions as well as its own more specific functions.

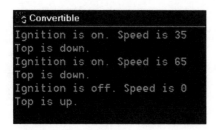

Figure 9-7 Output of Convertible.cpp

UNDERSTANDING INHERITANCE RESTRICTIONS

Figure 9-8 shows a modified version of the Customer class outputBalDue() function, originally presented in Figure 9-3. The improvement lies in the addition of the Customer ID number to the explanation of the output. It makes sense that because a Customer has an idNum (as well as a lastName and firstName) inherited from the Person class, the Customer class outputBalDue() function should be able to access it. However, if you replace the original outputBalDue() function with the one shown in Figure 9-8, programs that use the function no longer run. The error message states that idNum is **inaccessible**; that is, the Customer class function cannot use it.

```
void Customer::outputBalDue()
  {
       cout<<"ID #"<<idNum<<" Balance due $"<<balanceDue<<endl;
  }
```

Figure 9-8   The modified outputBalDue() function

9

When a class serves as a base class to other classes, all of its members can be used within the child class functions, except for private members. That's why idNum is not accessible within the Customer class member function. When you think about data hiding and encapsulation, this restriction makes sense. You make class data members private so they cannot be accessed or altered by nonmember functions. If anyone could access your private data members by simply extending your class through inheritance, then using the private keyword would be pointless. You create private data to require that users of your class access the data only through the public functions you have written. While having private members is a good idea, it often is inconvenient. There are times when you want a child class object to be able to access private data members that it owns, but that originated with the parent.

Fortunately, C++ provides an alternative to private and public specifiers. The **protected** specifier allows members to be used by class member functions and by derived classes, but not by other parts of a program. In other words, protected data and functions can be accessed only by objects that are members of their own class, or by objects that are children of their class. Thus, the rewritten Person class definition in Figure 9-9 represents a good candidate for an inheritable base class. Using the Person class as a base, and extending it with the Customer class, the Customer functions can access the protected fields idNum, firstName, and lastName as if they were their own. With the substitution of protected for private in the Person class definition, the Customer class's outputBalDue() function in Figure 9-8 works correctly.

```
class Person
    {
       protected:
           int idNum;
           char lastName[20];
           char firstName[15];
       public:
           void setFields( int num,  char last[], char first[]);
           void outputData();
    };
}
```

Figure 9-9   The Person class with protected data

You never are required to define data as protected rather than private, simply because a class is a base class. You use protected access as a convenience, so that derived classes can use the base class data fields without having to go through the base class's public functions. If you want a child class to access data only through public parent class functions, then continue to declare the parent class fields as private.

Besides being unable to directly access private members of a parent class, there are several other restrictions on derived classes. For example, a child class function cannot use its parent class's constructor. The following are never inherited:

- constructor functions

- destructor functions

- friend functions

- static data members

- static member functions

- overloaded new operators

- overloaded = operators

If a derived class requires any of the preceding items, the item must be explicitly defined within the derived class definition.

Not only are friend functions not inherited; class friendship also is not inherited.

Choosing the Class Access Specifier

When you define a derived class, you can insert one of the three class access specifiers (public, private, or protected) just prior to the base class name. For example, you can write any of the following:

```
class Customer : public Person
class Customer : protected Person
class Customer : private Person
```

C++ programmers usually use the public access specifier for inheritance. If a derived class uses the public access specifier, then the following statements are true:

- Base class members that are public remain public in the derived class.

- Base class members that are protected remain protected in the derived class.

- Base class members that are private are inaccessible in the derived class.

If a derived class uses the protected access specifier, then the following statements are true:

- Base class members that are public become protected in the derived class.

- Base class members that are protected remain protected in the derived class.

- Base class members that are private are inaccessible in the derived class.

If a derived class uses the private access specifier, then the following statements are true:

- Base class members that are public become private in the derived class.

- Base class members that are protected become private in the derived class.

- Base class members that are private are inaccessible in the derived class.

No matter which access specifier you use when creating a child class, access to parent class members never becomes more lenient than originally coded.

In other words, private base class members are always inaccessible in any classes derived from them. With private inheritance, both public and protected base class members become private. With protected inheritance, both public and protected base class members become protected. With public inheritance, both public and protected base class members retain their original access status.

If you do not use an access specifier when you create a derived class, access is private by default.

Figure 9-10 shows a class named DemoBasePerson that contains three data members. For illustration, one field is private, another is protected, and the third field is public. The setPerson() and showPerson() functions also are public.

```
class DemoBasePerson
  {
     private:
          double salary;
     protected:
          int age;
     public:
          char initial;
          void setPerson(double sal, int years, char init);
          void showPerson();
  };
void DemoBasePerson::setPerson(double sal, int years, char init)
  {
     salary = sal;
     age = years;
     initial = init;
  }
void DemoBasePerson::showPerson()
  {
     cout<<"Salary $"<<salary<<" Age: "<<age<<
        " Initial: "<<initial<<endl;
  }
```

Figure 9-10   The DemoBasePerson class

In the DemoBasePerson class in Figure 9-10, the showPerson() function can refer to salary, age, and initial. The function has access to all three data fields by virtue of being a member of the same class. Because the showPerson() function is public, a main() program (or any other nonmember function) that uses the DemoBasePerson class can use showPerson() to access any of the three data members.

Although it is unusual to make a class data member public, the field initial is public in the DemoBasePerson class. A main() program (or other nonmember function) can refer to initial directly, without using a member function. For example, if you declare a DemoBasePerson object named someBody, as shown in Figure 9-11, then the statement cout<<someBody.initial; works correctly and produces the output in Figure 9-12.

```
void main()
  {
     DemoBasePerson someBody;
     someBody.setPerson(218.75, 24, 'C');
     cout<<"Directly from the main() function, initial is "
         <<someBody.initial<<endl;
     /* cout<<"Directly from the main() function, age is "
         <<someBody.age<<endl; */
     /* cout<<"Directly from the main() function, salary is "
         <<someBody.salary<<endl; */
     getch();
  }
```

Figure 9-11   Program using the DemoBasePerson class

```
Person
Directly from the main() function, initial is C
```

Figure 9-12   Output of program that uses a public field with an object

9

The two highlighted and commented cout statements in Figure 9-11 are not correct. If you remove the comment designation from either of these statements, the program does not compile. The DemoBasePerson class fields age and salary are not accessible from within the main() program because they are not public.

Assume you create three derived classes from the DemoBasePerson class: Introvert, SomewhatShy, and Extrovert. The classes are named to reflect their degree of accessibility— Introvert inherits with private access, SomewhatShy inherits with protected access, and Extrovert inherits with public access.

The Introvert class, shown in Figure 9-13, inherits privately. The Introvert class has four data members: salary, age, initial, and idNum. The showIntrovert() function can use idNum because both the function and the field are members of the same class. This function also can access initial and age, which are public and protected, respectively, in the DemoBasePerson class, but are private in the Introvert class. The Introvert class cannot use salary; the statement that attempts to do so is commented out and highlighted in Figure 9-13. Because it was private in Person, salary remains inaccessible to the Introvert class member function showIntrovert().

```
class Introvert : private DemoBasePerson
  {
    private:
        int idNum;
    public:
        void showIntrovert();
  };
void showIntrovert()
  {
    cout<<"ID #"<<idNum<<endl;
    cout<<" Age: "<<age<<" Initial: "
        <<initial<<endl;
    // cout<<"Salary $"<<salary;
  }
```

Figure 9-13   The Introvert class

The showIntrovert() function in Figure 9-13 *could* call the showPerson() function, which is public in DemoBasePerson and private in Introvert, and the showPerson() function could then access salary. A main() program that instantiates an Introvert object cannot access any of the four data items directly; all four fields are private to the Introvert class.

If you create another class named IntrovertChild that inherits from Introvert, then IntrovertChild's functions cannot access any of the data or function members of the Person class. All were inherited privately by Introvert, so Introvert's descendants do not inherit them.

The SomewhatShy class, in Figure 9-14, inherits with protected access. Like Introvert, the SomewhatShy class also has four data members. Of course, the function showShy() can reference idNum, but it also can reference age and initial, both of which are protected in the SomewhatShy class. When a SomewhatShy object is instantiated in the main() program, that object can use the showShy() function to access idNum, initial, or age. The showShy() function, however, cannot access salary directly. The showShy() function has access to the showPerson() function, which is inherited as protected. The showShy() function can call showPerson(), which then can use salary.

There really is no difference in the way Introvert and SomewhatShy can access data members—each of these classes can access its own idNum field and the protected and public members of its parent. Neither class can access the private member of its parent. The difference between these classes is that if Introvert and SomewhatShy each became a base class to yet another derived class, then the child of SomewhatShy could access public or protected members of both SomewhatShy and DemoBasePerson. No child of Introvert could access any of the Person class members; they would all become private to Introvert.

```
class SomewhatShy : protected DemoBasePerson
  {
    private:
          int idNum;
    public:
          void showShy();
  };
SomewhatShy::showShy()
  {
    cout<<"ID #"<<idNum<<endl;
    cout<<" Age: "<<age<<" Initial: "
        <<initial<<endl;
    // cout<<"Salary $"<<salary;
  }
```

Figure 9-14   The SomewhatShy class

The Extrovert class inherits with public access, as shown in Figure 9-15. Even though Extrovert inherits with public access, the salary field still is not available—the salary field is private in DemoBasePerson, and cannot be used. If you create a descendant of Extrovert named ExtrovertChild, the ExtrovertChild can access all the public and protected members of both Extrovert and DemoBasePerson. Additionally, a main() program can access even an Extrovert's initial field directly—it is public in DemoBasePerson, and continues to be public in Extrovert.

```
class Extrovert : public DemoBasePerson
  {
    private:
      int idNum;
    public:
      void showExtrovert();
  };
void Extrovert::showExtrovert()
  {
    cout<<"ID #"<<idNum<<endl;
    cout<<" Age: "<<age<<" Initial: "
        <<initial<<endl;
    // cout<<"Salary $"<<salary;
  }
```

Figure 9-15   The Extrovert class

To summarize the use of three class access specifiers with class data members:

- If a class has private data members, they can be used only by member functions of that class.

- If a class has protected data members, they can be used by member functions of that class and by member functions of derived classes.

- If a class has public data members, they can be used by member functions of that class, by member functions of derived classes, and by any other functions' including the main() function of a program.

With one generation of inheritance, there are nine possible combinations, as shown in Table 9-1. Remember the following:

- Private data can be accessed only by a class's member functions (or friend functions), and not by any functions in derived classes.

- If a class serves as a base class, most often its data members are protected, and its member functions are public. Data members are created protected rather than public so that only member functions or child class member functions can access them.

- The access specifier in derived classes is most often public, so that the derived class can refer to all nonprivate data and functions of the base class.

- When a class is derived from another derived class, the newly derived class never has any more liberal access to a base class member than does its immediate predecessor.

Table 9-1   Summary of child class member access rules

Member access in parent class	Access specifier used in inheritance	Member's access in child class
private	private	inaccessible
private	protected	inaccessible
private	public	inaccessible
protected	private	private
protected	protected	protected
protected	public	protected
public	private	private
public	protected	protected
public	public	public

OVERRIDING AND OVERLOADING PARENT CLASS FUNCTIONS

When a new class is derived from an existing class, the derived class has access to nonprivate member functions in the base class. The new class also can have its own member functions. Those functions can have names that are identical to the function names in the base class. Any child class function with the same name and argument list as the parent overrides the parent function; any child class function with the same name as the parent, yet with an argument that differs from the parent's, overloads the parent function.

Recall the Person class from Figure 9-9. It contains three fields (idNum, lastName, and firstName) and two functions, setFields() and outputData(). The setFields() function is repeated in Figure 9-16.

```
void Person::setFields(int num, char last[], char first[])
  {
     idNum = num;
     strcpy(lastName, last);
     strcpy(firstName,first);
  }
```

Figure 9-16   The Person::setFields() function

You can create a class named Employee that derives from Person. The Employee class inherits the members of Person; additionally, it includes a department number and an hourly pay rate. The Employee class also includes a new setFields() function because it has additional data members—department and pay rate—that must be accommodated. Figure 9-17 shows the definition of the Employee class. The highlighted setFields() function has the same name as the setFields() function in the parent Person class, but has an extended argument list so that values can be assigned for department number and pay.

```
class Employee : public Person
  {
      private:
           int dept;
           double hourlyRate;
      public:
           void setFields(int num, char last[], char first[],
                int dep, double sal);
  };
```

Figure 9-17   The Employee class

The Employee setFields() function receives values for fields that are defined in the parent Person class, as well as for fields defined within the Employee class. Employee::setFields() could directly assign values to idNum, lastName, and firstName, as shown in Figure 9-18. The highlighted lines of code in Figure 9-18 are identical to lines of code in the parent class version of setFields(), so you can rewrite the Employee class setFields() function to call Person's setFields() function. This version appears in Figure 9-19. You can use either version of Employee::setFields(), the one shown in Figure 9-18 or Figure 9-19, but the one in Figure 9-19 requires less work on your part and takes advantage of code reusability.

```
void Employee::setFields( int num, char last[], char first[],
     int dep, double sal)
{
    idNum = num;
    strcpy(lastName, last);
    strcpy(firstName,first);
    dept = dep;
    hourlyRate = sal;
}
```

Figure 9-18   Employee::setFields() directly assigning field values

```
void Employee::setFields( int num, char last[],
     char first[], int dep, double sal)
{
    Person::setFields(num, last, first);
    dept = dep;
    hourlyRate = sal;
}
```

Figure 9-19   Improved Employee::setFields() that calls Person::setFields()

In the highlighted statement in the setFields() function in Figure 9-19, the values for num, last, and first are passed to the parent class function, where they are assigned to the appropriate fields. It's important to use the parent class name (Person) and the scope resolution operator. Without them, the Employee::setFields() function attempts to call itself, which is incorrect.

When you use the Employee class defined in Figure 9-17 to instantiate an Employee object with a statement such as `Employee aWorker;` , then the statement `aWorker.setFields();` uses the child class function with the name setFields(). When used with a child class object, the child class function overrides the parent class version. On the other hand, the statement `aWorker.outputData();` uses the parent class function because no child class function has the name outputData(). Figure 9-20 shows a main() function that creates two objects—a Person object and an Employee object. Each object uses a unique setFields() function, but uses the same outputData() function. The output is shown in Figure 9-21.

```
void main()
{
    Person aPerson;
    aPerson.setFields(123,"Kroening","Ginny");
    aPerson.outputData();
    cout<<endl<<endl; // double space
    Employee worker;
    worker.setFields(987,"Lewis","Kathy",6,23.55);
    worker.outputData();
}
```

Figure 9-20   Program using a Person and an Employee

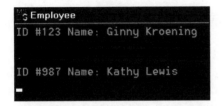

Figure 9-21   Output of Program Using Person::outputData() for a Person and an Employee

The output in Figure 9-21 shows that even though you set fields for a Person and an Employee by using separate functions that require separate argument lists, you use the same outputData() function that exists within the parent class for both a Person and an Employee. If you want the Employee class to contain its own outputData() function, you can override the parent version of that function as well. Figure 9-22 shows the Person and Employee class versions of outputData(). If you add the Employee::outputData() function to the class (and add a prototype for the function in the class definition), then when you run the same main() function shown in Figure 9-20, the new output looks like Figure 9-23.

```
void Person::outputData()
{
   cout<<"ID #"<<idNum<<" Name: "<<firstName<<" "<<
   lastName<<endl;
}
void Employee::outputData()
{
   Person::outputData();
   cout<<"Department #"<<dept<<" Pay rate $"<<hourlyRate<<endl;
}
```

Figure 9-22   Person and Employee class versions of outputData()

9

Within the Employee::outputData() function, it's important to use the class name Person and the scope resolution operator in the statement Person::outputData(). If the Person class name is not used, the Employee::outputData() function calls itself. That call results in another call to itself, and an infinite loop executes.

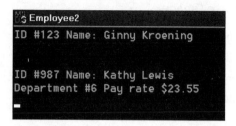

```
Employee2
ID #123 Name: Ginny Kroening


ID #987 Name: Kathy Lewis
Department #6 Pay rate $23.55
```

Figure 9-23   Output using Employee::outputData() instead of Person::outputData()

The different output formats in Figure 9-23 demonstrate that the outputData() function called using the Person object differs from the outputData() function called using the Employee object. Any Person object calls the Person functions. If a class derived from Person has functions with the same names as the Person class functions, the new class functions override the base class functions. The exception occurs when you use a class specifier with a function name, as in `worker.Person::setFields(id,last,first);` or `worker.Person::outputData();`. Using the class name Person indicates precisely which class setFields() or outputData() function should be called. Thus, a child class object can use its own functions or its parent's (as long as the parent functions are not private). The opposite is not true—a parent object cannot use its child's functions. In other words, an Employee is a Person and can do all the things a Person can do. However, every Person is not an Employee; therefore, a Person cannot use Employee functions.

 A derived class object can be assigned to a base class object, as in `aPerson = worker;`. The assignment causes each data member to be copied from worker to aPerson, and leaves off any data for which the base class doesn't have members. The reverse assignment cannot take place without writing a specialized function.

 You can create an array of parent class objects, and store either parent or child class objects in each element of the array.

The functions used by members of the Employee class remain separate from those used by members of the Person class. These functions are not overloaded. Overloaded functions, you will recall, require different parameter lists, and the outputData() functions in Person and Employee have identical parameter lists. Instead, Employee's outputData() function *overrides* the outputData() function defined in Person.

If a base class contains a function that the derived class should not have, you can create a dummy, or empty, function with the same name in the derived class. If a derived class object uses this function name, no statements are executed.

In summary, when any class member function is called, the following steps take place:

1. The compiler looks for a matching function (name and argument list) in the class of the object using the function name (also called the class of the object **invoking the method**).

2. If no match is found in this class, the compiler looks for a matching function in the parent class.

3. If no match is found in the parent class, the compiler continues up the inheritance hierarchy, looking at the parent of the parent, until the base class is reached.

4. If no match is found in any class, an error message is issued.

In the next set of steps, you create a RaceCar class as a child of the Car class you created earlier. A RaceCar has all the attributes of a Car, but its maximum allowed speed is higher.

9

1. Open the **Car.cpp** file. Remove the main() function and save the file as RaceCar.cpp.

2. Change the Car class private access specifier to protected so that when you extend the Car class, its child can use the Car data fields directly.

3. At the bottom of the file, define the RaceCar class to extend Car and include one new function—a setSpeed() function that overrides the Car class setSpeed() function.

```
class RaceCar: public Car
   {
   public:
      void setSpeed(int mph);
   };
```

4. Implement the RaceCar::setSpeed() function so that it sets the RaceCar speed to the value passed into the function, as long as the speed is not more than 145 miles per hour. Recall that the Car speed limit is only 65 miles per hour.

```
void RaceCar::setSpeed(int mph)
   {
   if(isIgnitionOn)
      if (mph <= 145)
            speed = mph;
      else
            speed = 145;
   else
         cout<<"Can't set speed - ignition is off!"<<endl;
   }
```

5. Write a main() function that instantiates a Car and a RaceCar. Use the setSpeed() function to attempt to set the speed of each object to 80, and then display the results.

```
void main()
{
    Car aCar;
    RaceCar aRaceCar;
    aCar.turnIgnitionOn();
    aCar.setSpeed(80);
    cout<<"Car at 80 mph: ";
    aCar.showCar();
    aRaceCar.turnIgnitionOn();
    aRaceCar.setSpeed(80);
    cout<<"Race car at 80 mph: ";
    aRaceCar.showCar();
    getch();
}
```

6. Save the file as **RaceCar.cpp** and compile it. Execute the program. The results appear in Figure 9-24. When you attempt to set the Car speed to 80, it is reduced to 65. However, 80 is an acceptable speed for a RaceCar. Each object uses its own class' version of the setSpeed() function.

```
 RaceCar
Car at 80 mph: Ignition is on. Speed is 65
Race car at 80 mph: Ignition is on. Speed is 80
```

Figure 9-24   Output of RaceCar.cpp

7. Change the speed values for the Car and the RaceCar, then compile and run the program again to ensure that the functions work correctly, whether the set speed is higher or lower than the cutoff values of 65 and 145.

Overriding a base class member function with a derived member function demonstrates the concept of polymorphism. Recall that polymorphism permits the same function name to take many forms. When you inherit functions and then override them with identically named functions that have identical argument lists in a subclass, the same message can be carried out appropriately by different objects. Just as the command "Play!" invokes different responses in a CD player and a baseball player, a program command with a name such as showCar()—or setValues() or giveInstructions() or any other name—can invoke different responses in different objects. This process models the way things work in the real world, and is a basic feature—and advantage—of object-oriented programming.

USING CONSTRUCTOR INITIALIZATION LISTS

Many classes use a constructor function to provide initial values for fields when a class object is created; that is, many constructor functions simply contain a series of assignment statements. For example, consider an Item class with two data members and a constructor, as shown in Figure 9-25. The constructor assigns its two arguments to the appropriate fields.

```
class Item
  {
      protected:
          int itemNum;
          double itemPrice;
      public:
          Item(int n, double p);
  };
Item::Item(int n, double p)
  {
      itemNum = n;
      itemPrice = p;
  }
```

Figure 9-25   The Item class

As an alternative to the separate prototype and implementation of the constructor shown in Figure 9-25, you can implement the constructor within the declaration section for the class as an inline function. This eliminates the need for a separate function body. Figure 9-26 demonstrates this method for defining the class; the inline function is highlighted.

```
class Item
  {
      protected:
          int itemNum;
          double itemPrice;
      public:
          Item(int n,double p){itemNum = n,itemPrice = p;};
  };
```

Figure 9-26   Alternate definition of the Item class

The curly braces and assignment statements that constitute the body of the Item constructor in Figure 9-26 can be written as separate statements. Often, because it's so short, you write an inline function body on a single line for convenience.

As another alternative, you can replace the assignment statements within a constructor body for Item with a constructor initialization list. A **constructor initialization list** provides values for class fields in the same statement that contains the constructor definition. The constructor initialization list is inserted after the argument list for the constructor function, and is preceded by a single colon. For example, the Item class can be rewritten as shown in Figure 9-27; the constructor initialization list is highlighted.

```
class Item
  {
      protected:
            int itemNum;
            double itemPrice;
      public:
            Item(int n,double p): itemNum(n),itemPrice(p){};
  };
```

Figure 9-27   Item class using constructor initialization list

The constructor initialization list shown in Figure 9-27 initializes itemNum with the value of n and itemPrice with the value of p. As a result, itemNum and itemPrice are given the correct values, just as with the original constructor. The curly braces following the list remain empty because you no longer need any assignment statements in the body of the function. (The braces could contain other statements if needed.)

Understanding the Difference between Assignment and Initialization

The difference between assignment and initialization is often very subtle, and programmers sometimes mingle the two terms rather casually. When you declare a simple scalar variable and give it a value, you can declare and assign in two separate statements, for example:

```
int z;
z = 100;
```

Alternatively, you can initialize a variable, declaring it and assigning it a value within a single statement, for example:

```
int z = 100;
```

or

```
int z(100);
```

When you declare a variable without an initial value, it holds garbage until you make an assignment. When you initialize a variable, you give it a value at its creation. This subtle difference applies to class objects just as it does to scalar variables: constructor initialization lists provide values for class members upon construction. Because assignment statements within a constructor function also provide values at construction, there also is a subtle distinction between using such statements and using a constructor initialization list. However, there are at least four reasons to understand the use of constructor initialization lists:

- Many C++ programmers prefer this method, so it is used in many programs.

- Technically, a constructor should initialize rather than assign values.

- Reference variables and constant class members cannot be assigned values; they must be initialized.

- When you create a derived class and instantiate an object, a parent class object must be constructed first. You add a constructor initialization list to a derived class constructor to construct the parent class. You learn about this feature in the next section.

PROVIDING FOR BASE CLASS CONSTRUCTION

When you instantiate an object in a C++ program, you automatically call its constructor function. This pattern holds true whether you write a custom constructor or use a default constructor. When you instantiate a derived class object, a constructor for its base class is called first, followed by the derived class constructor. This format is followed even if the base and derived classes both have only default constructors. If a base class does not contain a default constructor—that is, if the base class contains only constructors that require arguments—then you must provide a constructor for every derived class, even if the derived class does not need a constructor for any other reason.

For example, consider a class developed for all items sold by a pet store. As shown in Figure 9-28, the PetStoreItem class might contain data members for stock number and price. The constructor uses a constructor initialization list to assign values to the data fields.

```
class PetStoreItem
   {
      protected:
            int stockNum;
            double price;
      public:
            PetStoreItem(int stk, double pr) :
                  stockNum(stk), price(pr) {};
   };
```

Figure 9-28   The PetStoreItem class

The management personnel of a pet store might want to create several derived classes from PetStoreItem. For example, a specialized class would be appropriate for PetStoreAnimals sold in the store; other specialized classes might support food items, pet accessories, books, training classes, and so on. You can create a derived PetStoreAnimal class that contains all members of

PetStoreItem, plus a data field for the age of the pet and its own constructor. Figure 9-29 shows the class definition for PetStoreAnimal. (The constructor for the class is not yet complete.)

```
class PetStoreAnimal: public PetStoreItem
  {
     protected:
          int petAge;
     public:
          PetStoreAnimal(int age);
              // constructor not complete yet
  };
```

Figure 9-29 The PetStoreAnimal class with incomplete constructor

If the PetStoreAnimal class were merely a base class, its constructor could have the following format:

```
PetStoreAnimal::PetStoreAnimal(int age)
  {
     petAge = age;
  }
```

If PetStoreAnimal were a simple base class, the PetStoreAnimal class constructor would require just an integer argument that would be assigned to the petAge field. However, because PetStoreAnimal is derived from PetStoreItem, a PetStoreAnimal object is constructed, and the PetStoreItem class constructor also will be called. The PetStoreItem constructor requires arguments for stockNum and price, so those arguments have to be provided.

 If you fail to call a needed base class constructor in the initialization list for a derived class (for example, not calling the PetStoreItem constructor when constructing a PetStoreAnimal), you will receive an error message such as "Cannot find default constructor to initialize base class."

The prototype for the PetStoreAnimal class constructor must provide values for all the arguments it needs as well as all the arguments its parent needs. In other words, the PetStoreAnimal class needs values for the stock number and price (so PetStoreItem can be constructed), as well as an age (so PetStoreAnimal can be constructed). Figure 9-30 shows the complete, functional PetStoreAnimal class.

Just as a simple scalar variable may be initialized in a constructor initialization list, so may a class object. In Figure 9-30, the PetStoreItem constructor is called from the PetStoreAnimal constructor header. Three values are passed to the PetStoreAnimal constructor, and two of the three immediately are passed on to the PetStoreItem constructor. The call to the PetStoreItem constructor is placed within the PetStoreAnimal constructor initialization list because PetStoreItem must receive values for stockNum and price. The PetStoreItem constructor must be called because a PetStoreAnimal object is incomplete without PetStoreItem. In other words, a child class object cannot exist if no parent object exists first.

```
class PetStoreAnimal : public PetStoreItem
    {
       protected:
            int petAge;
       public:
            PetStoreAnimal(int stk, double price, int age);
    };
PetStoreAnimal::PetStoreAnimal(int stk, double price,
      int age) : PetStoreItem (stk, price)
    {
            PetStoreAnimal::petAge = age;

    }
```

Figure 9-30 The PetStoreAnimal class

When you construct a derived class object, the base class constructor is called first. When a derived class object is destroyed, the opposite order prevails: the child class destructor is called first and the base class destructor is called last. Although it is not required, if you list child class constructor arguments in the same order as you list the parent class constructor arguments, your programs will be easier to follow and maintain.

Figure 9-31 shows one more option for coding the PetStoreAnimal class. In this example, the constructor initialization list initializes both PetStoreItem and petAge. The advantage to using this format is that it is more concise, and it reflects the true purpose of stk, price, and age—they are initialization values.

```
class PetStoreAnimal : public PetStoreItem
    {
       protected:
            int petAge;
       public:
            PetStoreAnimal(int stk, double price, int age) :
                PetStoreItem(stk,price), petAge(age){};
    };
```

Figure 9-31 Alternate code for the PetStoreAnimal class

If a default base class constructor exists, then no compiler error arises if you omit the call to the base class constructor when deriving a class. It is perfectly okay to use the default base class constructor with a derived class if that suits your purpose.

You do not have to pass a variable to a base class constructor that requires an argument; you can pass a constant of the same type. For example, if you want all PetStoreAnimal objects to cost $99.95, then you might create a PetStoreAnimal constructor such as:

```
PetStoreAnimal(int stk, int age) :
    PetStoreItem(stk,99.95), petAge(age){};
```

OVERRIDING INHERITED ACCESS

Nine inheritance access specifier combinations are possible: base class members that are private, protected, or public can be inherited with private, protected, or public access. In addition, you can override the class access specifier for any specific class members. You override the class access specifier when it does not suit your needs for some members of a class. For example, consider the DemoBasePerson base class from Figure 9-10 (repeated as Figure 9-32 for your convenience). It contains data field members of each of the three types.

```
class DemoBasePerson
  {
      private:
          double salary;
      protected:
          int age;
      public:
          char initial;
          void setPerson(double sal, int years, char init);
          void showPerson();
  };
void DemoBasePerson::setPerson(double sal, int years, char init)
  {
    salary = sal;
    age = years;
    initial = init;
  }
void DemoBasePerson::showPerson()
  {
    cout<<"Salary $"<<salary<<" Age: "<<age<<
        " Initial: "<<initial<<endl;
  }
```

Figure 9-32   The DemoBasePerson class

If a derived class, SomewhatShy, uses the protected access specifier when inheriting from DemoBasePerson, then the following statements hold true:

- The field named salary, which is private in DemoBasePerson, is inaccessible in the derived class.

- The field named age, which is protected in the base class, remains protected in the derived class.

- The field named initial, which is public in the base class, becomes protected in the derived class.

- The functions setPerson() and showPerson(), which are public in DemoBasePerson, become protected in the derived class.

In other words, all public and protected members of the base class become protected in the child class, and all private members of the base class remain inaccessible to the child class.

Suppose you want three of the protected and public members of the base class (age, initial, and setPerson()) to remain protected in SomewhatShy, but you want the showPerson() function to become public. You still can derive SomewhatShy with protected access, but you also can override the SomewhatShy class protected access specifier for just the showPerson() function. In the SomewhatShy class definition, you write the code shown in Figure 9-33. The highlighted statement shows that access for the showPerson() function is public within SomewhatShy, even though all other public members of Person are protected within SomewhatShy. Notice that you do not use parentheses after the name of the showPerson() function in the statement that alters its access. If you do, the C++ compiler attempts to declare the same function multiple times.

```
class SomewhatShy : protected DemoBasePerson
     // inheritance is still protected
{
     public:
          DemoBasePerson::showPerson;
          // showPerson() is public in the SomewhatShy class
};
```

Figure 9-33   SomewhatShy class with one function's access overriding the class access specifier

For the showPerson() function to become public within SomewhatShy, the highlighted statement in Figure 9-33 must appear in the public section of the SomewhatShy class. Additionally, the DemoBasePerson class name and scope resolution operator must appear before the showPerson() function name. Finally, and most oddly, no parentheses appear after the showPerson() function name within the child class. The use of showPerson indicates neither a function definition nor a function call, and you must omit the parentheses to compile the program without errors.

The showPerson() function that is public within the DemoBasePerson class also is public in the SomewhatShy class, even though protected inheritance was used. The showPerson() function can be used in a main() program (or other function) with any DemoBasePerson object or any SomewhatShy object. If showPerson() remained protected, only functions that were members of Person or SomewhatShy could use it.

Within the SomewhatShy class, the protected access specifier is overridden for the showPerson() function. In this example, showPerson() is allowed more liberal access than are other inherited class members, but the function does not have more liberal access than it originally has in DemoBasePerson. You can never override a function's original access specifier in a parent class to make it more liberal in the child.

However, you can override the inherited access to make an individual member's access more conservative. For example, you can define SomewhatShy as shown in Figure 9-34. The inheritance access specifier for the class is protected, so the initial field, which is public in the base class, ordinarily would be inherited as protected. However, the definition in Figure 9-34 makes initial private. Because private access is less liberal than protected, such a designation is acceptable.

```
class SomewhatShy : protected Person
    // inheritance is still protected
{
    private:
        Person::initial;
        // initial is private
    public:
        Person::showPerson;
        // showPerson() is public in the SomewhatShy class
};
```

Figure 9-34   Providing a data member with more restricted access

For most C++ classes, data is private or protected, and most functions are public. Most inheritance is activated with public access so that child class members retain the same access that's available in the parent class. However, you can achieve a variety of effects by inheriting with any of the three access specifiers, and overriding the access specifier for particular child class members.

USING MULTIPLE INHERITANCE

A base class may have many derived classes. For example, a company might create an Employee base class, and derive SalariedEmployee, HourlyEmployee, and ContractEmployee classes from it. A college may use a base class named Student, and derive UnderGraduate and Graduate classes from it.

A child class also can derive from more than one base class; this type of inheritance is called **multiple inheritance**. For example, a company may have two classes: Product and Employee. Product contains data members such as productNumber and productPrice. Employee contains empNumber and empSalary. Perhaps when the company obtains a patent, objects of a new class, Patent, are instantiated. The company wants Patent objects to contain data about both the Product and the Employee who developed the product. The two base classes are defined in Figures 9-35 and 9-36.

```cpp
class Product
    {
        protected:
            int productNumber;
            double productPrice;
        public:
            void setData(int num, double price);
            void showData();
    };
void Product::setData(int num, double price)
    {
        productNumber = num;
        productPrice = price;
    }
void Product::showData()
    {
        cout<<"Product #"<<productNumber<<" Price $"
            <<productPrice<<endl;
    }
```

Figure 9-35   The Product class

```cpp
class Employee
    {
        protected:
            int empNumber;
            double empSalary;
        public:
            void setData(int num, double salary);
            void showData();
    };
void Employee::setData(int num, double salary)
    {
        empNumber = num;
        empSalary = salary;
    }
void Employee::showData()
    {
        cout<<"Employee #"<<empNumber<<" Salary $"
            <<empSalary<<endl;
    }
```

Figure 9-36   The Employee class

The new Patent class, shown in Figure 9-37, inherits from both Product and Employee. The Patent class includes all members of each of its parents' classes. You create a class that inherits from multiple parents by using an inheritance access specifier and class name for each parent, separating the parents with a comma. The child class can contain new members (the Patent class has a patentNum field and two functions), but it also contains all the fields and functions of each parent.

```cpp
class Patent: public Product, public Employee
  {
      private:
           int patentNum;
      public:
           void setData(int patent, int itemNum,
                double price, int empNum, double salary);
           void showAll();
  };
void Patent::setData(int patent, int itemNum, double price,
      int empNum, double salary)
  {
      patentNum = patent;
      Product::setData(itemNum, price);
      Employee::setData(empNum, salary);
  }
void Patent::showAll()
  {
      cout<<"Patent #"<<patentNum<<endl;
      Product::showData();
      Employee::showData();
  }
```

Figure 9-37   The Patent class

You can place any statement you like within the setData() and showAll() functions of the Patent class shown in Figure 9-37, including calling the parent class functions. In this case, you must use the correct parent class name and the scope resolution operator when you use setData() and showData(), because each parent class contains functions with the same name.

Figure 9-38 shows a main() function that uses a Patent object, and Figure 9-39 shows the output. Five arguments are passed to the Patent class setData() function. The first argument is used for the patent number, the next two are passed to the Product setData() function, and the last two are passed to the Employee setData() function.

```
void main()
  {
    Patent aNewInvention;
    aNewInvention.setData(1101, 222, 39.95, 444, 850.55);
    aNewInvention.showAll();
    getch();
  }
```

Figure 9-38 A main() function instantiating a Patent object

```
Patent #1101
Product #222 Price $39.95
Employee #444 Salary $850.55
```

Figure 9-39 Output of Patent program

9

You already use multiple inheritance each time you include iostream.h in a program. Each cin and cout object is derived from other classes. (Chapter 10 provides more details on multiple inheritance.)

In the next set of steps, you create two classes. The Investment class holds data about Investment objects, such as initial value and profit figures. The House class holds data about House objects, such as number of bedrooms and square footage. Both of these classes serve as parents to a third class, HouseThatIsAnInvestment.

1. Open a new file in your C++ editor. Type the include statements you will need.

    #include<iostream.h>
    #include<conio.h>
    #include<string.h>

2. Create the Investment class definition. Each Investment object will have an initial value, a current value, and a profit calculated from those two values. The class also contains setData() and showData() functions.

    class Investment
      {
        protected:
            double initialAmount;
            double currentValue;
            double profit;
        public:
            void setData(double initial, double current);
            void showData();
      };

3. The implementations of setData() and showData() are straightforward.

```
void Investment::setData(double initial, double current)
{
    initialAmount = initial;
    currentValue = current;
    profit = currentValue - initialAmount;
}
void Investment::showData()
{
    cout<<"Investment current value $"<<currentValue<<endl;
    cout<<"Investment initial value $"<<initialAmount<<endl;
    cout<<"Profit is $"<<profit<<endl;
}
```

4. The House class contains fields for the street address of a House, square feet of living area, and number of bedrooms.

```
class House
{
    protected:
        char address[30];
        int squareFeet;
        int numBedrooms;
    public:
        void setData(char add[], int sqFt, int bedrms);
        void showData();
};
```

5. Like the Investment class functions, the House class functions are ordinary.

```
void House::setData(char add[], int sqFt, int bedrms)
{
    strcpy(address,add);
    squareFeet = sqFt;
    numBedrooms = bedrms;
}
void House::showData()
{
    cout<<"The house at "<<address<<" has "<<numBedrooms<<
        " bedrooms and "<<endl" "<<squareFeet<<
        " square feet of living area"<<endl;
}
```

6. A HouseThatIsAnInvestment inherits from both Investment and House. Its constructor takes five arguments that are used to fill the five fields in this class.

```
class HouseThatIsAnInvestment : public Investment, public House
{
    public:
```

```
        HouseThatIsAnInvestment(char add[], double purchPrice,
            double currValue, int sqFt, int numBedrooms);
        void showHouse();
};
```

7. The constructor for HouseThatIsAnInvestment requires five arguments. The address, square footage, and number of bedrooms are passed to the House class setData() function; the purchase price and current value are passed to the Investment class setData() function.

```
HouseThatIsAnInvestment::HouseThatIsAnInvestment(char add[],
    double purchPrice, double currValue,
    int sqFt, int numBedrooms)
{
    Investment::setData(purchPrice, currValue);
    House::setData(add, sqFt,numBedrooms);
}
```

8. The showHouse() function employs its own specialized code and uses existing, inherited showData() functions from the Investment and House classes. The class distinguishes between a good and bad investment by the presence of a profit. The profit field is accessible within the HouseThatIsAnInvestment class, because profit is protected within the parent class, and inheritance is public.

```
void HouseThatIsAnInvestment::showHouse()
{
    cout<<"Investment data on house:"<<endl;
    Investment::showData();
    House::showData();
    if(profit > 0)
        cout<<"This house was a good investment"<<endl;
    else
        cout<<"This house was a bad investment"<<endl;
}
```

9. Add a main() function that declares a HouseThatIsAnInvestment and demonstrates that the inheritance works.

```
void main()
{
    HouseThatIsAnInvestment
        aHouse("712 First Street",160000,168000,1900,3);
    aHouse.showHouse();
    getch();
}
```

10. Save the file as **HouseThatIsAnInvestment.cpp**. Compile and run the program. The output is shown in Figure 9-40.

```
HouseThatIsAnInvestment
Investment data on house:
Investment current value $168000
Investment initial value $160000
Profit is $8000
The house at 712 First Street has 3 bedrooms and
    1900 square feet of living area
This house was a good investment
```

Figure 9-40   Output of HouseThatIsAnInvestment.cpp

11. Experiment with removing the House and Investment classes from the HouseThatIsAnInvestment file and placing the classes in their own files. Use #include statements at the top of the HouseThatIsAnInvestment file to include the two parent classes. Compile and run the program. The output is the same as in Figure 9-40.

DISADVANTAGES OF USING MULTIPLE INHERITANCE

Some programmers are vehemently opposed to using multiple inheritance. They may even insist that when multiple inheritance is needed, you should suspect a bad class design. Multiple inheritance is never required to solve a programming problem; the same results always can be achieved through single inheritance. For example, the Patent class could inherit from the Product class alone, but could contain an Employee object as a data member instead of inheriting from two classes.

You already have encountered one problem with multiple inheritance: if two parent classes contain members with the same name, then the awkward syntax of using the scope resolution operator is required when using those members. Even though the dilemma of identically named functions in two parent classes is resolved fairly easily, many programmers avoid multiple inheritance because of this type of problem. You have learned that a derived class often must call its parent class constructor with an initialization list. A derived class with more than one parent must provide for the constructors of all parents, so the syntax can become quite complicated. The definition of a class that inherits from a single parent is almost always easier to understand and less prone to error than the definition of a class that inherits from two base classes.

 As proof that multiple inheritance is never required, consider that the object-oriented languages SmallTalk and Java allow only single inheritance.

In the next set of steps you alter the House and Investment classes you created earlier so they each contain a constructor that requires arguments. You have to modify the HouseThatIsAnInvestment class to accommodate the constructor requirements of its parents.

1. If it is not still open, open the **HouseThatIsAnInvestment.cpp** file. Immediately save the file as **HouseThatIsAnInvestment2.cpp**.

2. Modify the Investment class so that an initial value for the Investment is required at construction. It makes sense that when an Investment is created, the initial value is known, the current value is the same as the initial value, and the profit is zero. Add the following constructor definition to the public section of the Investment class definition section:

   Investment(double initial);

3. It also makes sense that the setData() function should alter only the current value of an Investment (and recalculate the profit) because the initial value never changes. Change the prototype for the setData() function to:

   void setData(double current);

4. Below the class definition for Investment, add the new constructor implementation.

   ```
   Investment::Investment(double initial)
   {
      initialAmount = initial;
      currentValue = initial;
      profit = 0;
   }
   ```

5. Change the setData() function so it no longer requires an initial figure as an argument. You must change the function header and remove the assignment of the initial value. The new function appears as follows:

   ```
   void Investment::setData(double current)
   {
      currentValue = current;
      profit = currentValue - initialAmount;
   }
   ```

6. It makes sense that a House constructor should require the address. The square footage and number of bedroom values can change through remodeling, but the address remains fixed. Add a new constructor prototype, and replace the setData() function prototype to the public section of the House class declaration section as follows:

   House(char add[]);
   void setData(int sqFt, int bedrms);

7. Add a House constructor and modify the setValues() function to reflect the changes in their definitions.

```
House::House(char add[])
{
        strcpy(address,add);
}
void House::setData(int sqFt, int bedrms)
{
   squareFeet = sqFt;
   numBedrooms = bedrms;
}
```

8. Change the constructor header for the HouseThatIsAnInvestment class so that although it still takes five arguments, two are passed immediately to the parent classes, House and Investment. The other three data values are passed to the appropriate setData() function. That is, the current value of the investment is passed to the Investment setData() function, and the bedroom and square footage figures are passed to the House setData() function.

```
HouseThatIsAnInvestment::HouseThatIsAnInvestment
   (char add[], double purchPrice, double currValue,
    int sqFt, int numBedrooms) : House(add),Investment(purchPrice)
{
   Investment::setData(currValue);
   House::setData(sqFt,numBedrooms);
}
```

You can call the parent constructors in the child class constructor definition instead of calling them in the function header, as is done here. However, you also would have to include the two setData() calls within curly braces as part of the definition, and the definition would be very long. When a constructor requires its own statements as well as those that pass values to a parent class, it is better to call the parent constructors in the child class constructor header than in its prototype.

9. Save the file using its current name, **HouseThatIsAnInvestment2.cpp**. Compile and run the program. If you have not altered any of the initialization values in the main() function, then the output is still the same as in Figure 9-40. The HouseThatIsAnInvestment class has provided values for each of its parent's constructors.

USING VIRTUAL BASE CLASSES

You already know that a base class may have many descendants through single inheritance. A college might use a Person base class, for example, and create child classes Student, Employee, and Alumnus. You also know that a class may inherit from two other classes through multiple inheritance. For example, a StudentEmployee class might inherit from both Student and Employee, as StudentEmployee objects might take advantage of already-developed functions in each of its parent classes. The class definition for StudentEmployee would begin as follows:

```
class StudentEmployee: public Student, public Employee
```

StudentEmployee inherits from both Student and Employee, and both Student and Employee inherit from Person. Thus, StudentEmployee ends up with two copies of Person. To avoid this duplicate inheritance, you use the keyword virtual when you define each of the child classes. The word **virtual** indicates that the base class should be used only once. The headers of the classes become:

```
class Student : virtual public Person
```

and

```
class Employee : virtual public Person
```

Now when StudentEmployee is defined as

```
class StudentEmployee: public Student, public Employee
```

the members of Person are included just once in StudentEmployee. An additional problem arises with the constructor functions in this situation. When a StudentEmployee object is constructed, it needs to construct its base classes. If its base classes, Student and Employee, both are constructed as usual, then Person is constructed twice. Therefore, when you write the StudentEmployee class constructor, it must handle the construction needs of Student, Employee, and Person.

For example, if Person requires values for ID number and name, Student requires a grade point average, Employee requires an hourly rate, and StudentEmployee requires a limit on the number of hours allowed to work per week, then the StudentEmployee constructor might take the following form:

```
StudentEmployee (int idNum, char name[], double gradePoint,
    double hourlyRate, int workHoursLimit ):
    StudentEmployee (workHoursLimit), Person(idNum, name),
    Student(gradePoint),Employee(hourlyRate) { };
```

If the Student and Employee classes did not use the word virtual, each would construct a Person. Because the virtual keyword is used when Student and Employee inherit from Person, the construction of Student and Employee does not prompt the construction of Person. Instead, StudentEmployee must construct all of its ancestors; that is, StudentEmployee must construct Person, Student, and Employee.

9

Chapter Summary

❐ Inheritance allows you to create classes that derive most of their attributes from existing classes. The existing class is the parent class, base class, or superclass; the new class is a child class, derived class, or subclass.

❐ Programs in which you create classes that are derived from existing classes offer several advantages: you save time because much of the code needed for your class is already written and tested. Additionally, you already understand how the base class works and can concentrate on the new complexity added by your extensions to the class.

❐ To create a derived class, you include the keyword class, the derived class name, a colon, a class access specifier, and the base class name in the class header; as with other classes, definition statements within a pair of curly braces follow. The derived class contains all the members of its parent, as well as any new members you define for the child class.

❐ When a class serves as a base class to others, all of its members can be used within the child class functions, except for any private members. The protected specifier allows members to be used by class member functions and by derived classes, but not by other parts of a program. Additionally, the following are never inherited: constructor functions, destructor functions, friend functions, static data members, static member functions, overloaded new operators, and overloaded = operators.

❐ When you define a derived class, you can insert one of the three class access specifiers (public, private, or protected) just prior to the base class name. Any private base class members are always inaccessible in any classes derived from them. With private inheritance, both public and protected base class members become private. With protected inheritance, both public and protected base class members become protected. With public inheritance, both public and protected base class members retain their original access status. The access specifier in derived classes most often is public, so that the derived class can refer to all nonprivate data and functions of the base class.

❐ You can override parent class functions within a child class. You can resolve name conflicts using the scope resolution operator.

❐ As an alternative to separate prototypes and implementation of a constructor, you can use a constructor initialization list.

❐ When you declare a variable without an initial value, it holds garbage until you make an assignment. When you initialize a variable, you give it a value at its creation. Technically, a constructor should initialize rather than assign values, so many programmers prefer using a constructor initialization list, rather than coding separate assignment statements within a constructor body. Reference variables and constant class members must be initialized, and parent class objects must be constructed before their children.

❐ If a base class does not contain a default constructor, then you must provide a constructor for use by the derived class. The child class constructor must provide values for all the arguments it needs, as well as all the arguments its parent needs.

❑ You can override the class access specifier when it does not suit your needs for some of the members of a class. You can never override a function's original access specifier in a parent class to make it more liberal in the child. However, you can override the inherited access to make an individual member's access more conservative.

❑ Using multiple inheritance, a child class can derive from more than one base class. The child class can contain new members, but it also contains all the fields and functions of each parent.

❑ Multiple inheritance poses special problems, and some programmers are opposed to its use. The syntax needed to resolve name conflicts and to provide for multiple constructors can become complicated.

❑ When a base class is parent to two or more classes that in turn are co-parents to another generation, you risk duplicate inheritance. To remedy this situation, you use the keyword virtual when you define each of the child classes; this indicates that the base class should be used only once.

REVIEW QUESTIONS

1. The principle that knowledge of a general category can be applied to more specific objects is _____.

   a. inheritance

   b. polymorphism

   c. object-oriented

   d. overriding

2. A derived class also can be called a _____ class.

   a. super

   b. base

   c. child

   d. parent

3. Parent class is to child class as _____.

   a. subclass is to superclass

   b. base class is to derived class

   c. derived class is to driven class

   d. child class is to superclass

4. Which of the following is not an advantage of inheritance?

   a. You save time because much of the code needed for your class is already written.

   b. You save time because the existing code has already been tested.

   c. You save time because you already understand how the base class works.

   d. You save time because parent classes always provide more detail than child classes.

5. Which of the following pairs of class names is most likely to represent a parent/child relationship?

   a. Army/Military

   b. Dollar/Currency

   c. Song/Lullaby

   d. Cat/Dog

6. The most commonly used inheritance access specifier is _____.

   a. private

   b. protected

   c. public

   d. promoted

7. To indicate that class X is a child of class Y, and that inheritance is public, the class definition is _____.

   a. class X ::public class Y

   b. class X : public class Y

   c. class Y :: public class X

   d. class Y : public class X

8. If a field named someField is private in the parent class, and a child class inherits with public access, then within the child class someField is _____.

   a. private

   b. protected

   c. public

   d. inaccessible

9. If a field named someField is public in the parent class, and a child class inherits with public access, then within the child class someField is _____.

   a. private

   b. protected

   c. public

   d. inaccessible

10. If a field named someField is public in the parent class, and a child class inherits with protected access, then within the child class someField is _____.

   a. private

   b. protected

   c. public

   d. inaccessible

11. If a member of a base class named Base is protected, then it can be used by functions that are _____.

   a. members of Base

   b. members of children of Base

   c. both of these

   d. none of these

12. Within a class that serves as a parent class, _____.

   a. all data fields must be protected

   b. no data fields can be private

   c. all functions must be public

   d. None of the above

13. Which of the following are inherited?

   a. constructor functions

   b. void functions

   c. friend functions

   d. operator=() functions

14. Class A has a protected field named field A. When a class B is derived from class A, and C is derived from class B, then you know that class C _____.

   a. has more liberal access to fieldA than class B does

   b. does not have more liberal access to fieldA than class B does

   c. has access to fieldA

   d. does not have access to fieldA

15. Class A contains a void public function named functionA() that requires an integer argument. Class B derives from class A, and also contains a void public function named functionA() that requires an integer argument. An object of class A can use _____.

   a. the class A version of the function

   b. the class B version of the function

   c. both of the above

   d. none of the above

16. Class A contains a void public function named functionA() that requires an integer argument. Class B derives from class A, and also contains a void public function named functionA() that requires an integer argument. An object of class B can use _____ .

   a. the class A version of the function

   b. the class B version of the function

   c. both of the above

   d. none of the above

17. A constructor initialization list provides _____ .

   a. a summary of overloaded versions allowed for a constructor

   b. the types and names of arguments required by a constructor

   c. the types and names of arguments overridden by a constructor

   d. values for class fields in the same statement as the definition of the constructor

18. Class A serves as a base class to class B, and B is a parent to class C. When you instantiate a class B object, the first constructor called belongs to class _____ .

   a. A

   b. B

   c. C

   d. none of the above

19. A parent class named Parent contains a protected member named parentField. A class named Child derives from Parent with public access. Which is true?

   a. You can override the public access so parentField is private within Child.

   b. You can override the public access so parentField is public within Child.

   c. Both of the above are true.

   d. None of the above are true.

20. Which statement is true in C++?

   a. A child class can have multiple parents.

   b. A parent class can have multiple children.

   c. Both of the above are true.

   d. None of the above are true.

EXERCISES

1. Complete the following tasks:

   a. Create a base class named Rectangle that includes data members for length and width, as well as functions to assign and display those values. Derive a class named Block that contains an additional data member to store height, and contains functions to assign and display the height. Write a main() program that demonstrates the classes by instantiating and displaying the values for both a Rectangle and a Block.

   b. Add a member function to the Rectangle class that computes the area of a Rectangle (length multiplied by width). Add a member function to Block that has the same name, but overrides the computation with a volume calculation (length by width by height). Write a main() program that demonstrates the classes.

2. Create a base class named Book. Data fields include title and author; functions include those that can set and display the fields. Derive two classes from the Book class: Fiction, which also contains a numeric grade reading level, and NonFiction, which contains a variable to hold the number of pages. The functions that set and display data field values for the subclasses should call the appropriate parent class functions to set and display the common fields, and include specific code pertaining to the new subclass fields. Write a main() function that demonstrates the use of the classes and their functions.

3. Create a class named MusicalComposition that contains fields for title, composer, and year written. Include a constructor that requires all three values and an appropriate display function. The child class NationalAnthem contains an additional field that holds the name of the anthem's nation. The child class constructor requires a value for this additional field. The child class also contains a display function. Write a main() function that instantiates objects of each class and demonstrates that the functions work correctly.

4. A CollegeCourse class includes fields representing department, course number, credit hours, and tuition. Its child, LabCourse, includes one more field that holds a lab fee charged in addition to the tuition. Create appropriate functions for these classes, and write a main() function that instantiates and uses objects of each class.

5. Complete the following tasks:

   a. Create a class named Account for a bank. Data members include an account number and a balance. Functions include a constructor that requires the account number and balance parameters. A display function is also included. Derive two classes from Account: Savings, which includes an interest rate that is required by the constructor, and Checking, which includes a monthly fee that is required by the constructor. Write a main() program to demonstrate the classes.

   b. Add a default constructor to the Account class. Write a main() function that declares an array of five Account objects. In a loop, prompt the user to enter a 'c' to create a Checking object, or an 's' to create a Savings object. Whether it is Checking or Savings, begin each Account with a 0 (zero) balance, and number

9

each Account sequentially beginning with 1001. Initialize Checking Accounts with a $3.25 fee, and Savings Accounts with an interest rate of 3%. Display each Account as it is created. At the end of main(), display each of the five Accounts using the Account class display function.

c. Create a Customer class for a bank. Select appropriate data members and functions. Derive a class, CustomerAccount, that inherits from both Customer and Account. Write a main() function that instantiates a CustomerAccount object and demonstrates its functions.

6. Create a RestaurantFood class that holds the name and price of a food item served by a restaurant. Its constructor requires arguments for each field. Create a HotelService class that holds the name of the service, the service fee, and the room number to which the service was supplied. Its constructor also requires arguments for each field. Create a RoomService class that inherits from both RestaurantFood and HotelService. Whenever you create a RoomService object, the string "room service" is assigned to the name of the service field, and $4.00 is assigned to the service fee inherited from HotelService. In a main() function, instantiate a RoomService object that inherits from both classes. For example, a "steak dinner" costing $19.99 is a "room service" provided to room 1202 for a $4.00 fee.

7. Create a Painting class that holds the painting title, artist name, and value. All Paintings are valued at $400 unless they are FamousPaintings. The FamousPainting subclass overrides the Painting value and sets each Painting's value to $25,000. Write a main() function that declares an array of 10 Painting objects. Prompt the user to enter the title and artist for each of the 10 Paintings. Consider the Painting to be a FamousPainting, if the artist is one of the following: Degas, Monet, Picasso, or Rembrandt. Display the 10 Paintings.

8. Each of the following files in the Chapter09 folder contains syntax and/or logical errors. Determine the problem in each case, and fix the program.

   a. DEBUG9-1

   b. DEBUG9-2

   c. DEBUG9-3

   d. DEBUG9-4

CASE PROJECT

You have been developing a Fraction class for Teacher's Pet Software. Each fraction contains a numerator, denominator, a whole number portion, and a floating-point equivalent field. Each Fraction also has access to several functions you have developed.

a. Create a MathProblem class that holds fields for four Fraction objects: the first Fraction operand in a problem, the second Fraction operand in a problem, the user's answer to a problem, and the correct answer to a problem. The MathProblem class also contains a character field that stores an operator (such as +), and contains an integer or bool field named isAnswerCorrect, indicating whether the user correctly answered the problem. For example, a MathProblem object containing 1/2 +, and 1/4 for the operands and operators, 3/4 for the correct answer, and 3/8 for the user's answer would contain a 0 or false in the isAnswerCorrect field.

b. Include a function named setProblem() that sets a MathProblem's values with arguments that include two Fraction operands and an operation. This function calculates and stores the correct answer, assigns 0 to the user's answer, and sets isAnswerCorrect to 0 or false. Include a displayProblem() function that displays the math problem as a question, and an askUserForAnswer() function that accepts the user's answer from the keyboard and assigns an appropriate value to isAnswerCorrect.

c. Include any other MathProblem functions you feel are useful and appropriate.

d. Write a main() program that declares five MathProblem objects you can use to test a student's fraction arithmetic skills. Assign random Fraction values to the MathProblems. In a loop, display the problems and accept the answers. When the five problems are completed, display the problems, along with the student's answer, the correct answer, and a message indicating whether the student is right or wrong. Finally, show the student a score indicating the percentage of problems answered correctly.

e. Create a class named DoublingMathProblem that derives from MathProblem. The DoublingMathProblem class includes a setProblem() function that overrides its parent's setProblem() function. This version requires a single Fraction argument; this argument is used as both the first and second operand in a problem. The operator for a doubling problem is always +. In other words, each DoublingMathProblem is a problem such as 1/3 + 1/3 where a Fraction value is doubled.

f. Write a main() program that declares five DoublingMathProblem objects you can use to test a student's fraction arithmetic skills. In a loop, display the problems and accept the answers. When the five problems are completed, display the problems, along with the student's answer, the correct answer, and a message indicating whether the student is right or wrong. Finally, show the student a score indicating the percentage of problems answered correctly.

9

ADVANCED INPUT AND OUTPUT

> **In this chapter you will learn:**
> ◆ How cout and cin possess the same traits as other C++ objects
> ◆ How to use istream member functions, particularly get(), ignore(), and getline()
> ◆ How to use ostream member functions, particularly setf(), unsetf(), width(), and precision()
> ◆ How to create your own manipulator functions
> ◆ How to use built-in manipulators
> ◆ How to create a manipulator that takes an argument
> ◆ About computer files and the data hierarchy
> ◆ How to perform file output
> ◆ How to read a file from within a program
> ◆ How to write class objects to files
> ◆ How to read a data file into class objects

From the first time you wrote a line of code in C++, you used cout to display data; shortly thereafter, you used cin for input. You could use the cin and cout objects long before you knew anything about object-oriented programming, in part because cout and cin resemble real-world objects (your screen and your keyboard), and real-world objects are easy to understand. In this chapter, what you have learned about object-oriented programming in general will help you gain a deeper understanding of input and output.

Throughout your C++ programming experiences, you have written functions. Now that you understand how your own classes and member functions work, you can take advantage of one of the most powerful aspects of modern programming languages—using the classes and functions that other programmers have already created for you.

UNDERSTANDING CIN AND COUT AS CLASS OBJECTS

You can think of cout and cin as real-world objects. Like other C++ objects you have created, cout and cin are members of a class. Their class is derived from another class (which is derived from yet another class), so they use inheritance. The cout and cin objects can take advantage of overloaded operators such as << and >> which are used for shifting bits in other contexts. Shifting bits will be discussed in chapter 13. The cout and cin objects also use polymorphism—they can generate different machine instructions when placed with different types of variables (with integers rather than characters, for example). In other words, cout and cin have all the characteristics of any class objects you have created throughout this book.

You don't have to understand objects or classes to use cin or cout. That's part of the appeal of object-oriented programming. Just as you can use a microwave oven without knowing how it works, you can use well-designed C++ objects without knowledge of the implementation details.

When you include iostream.h in a program, you are including a file that contains the definition for a derived class named iostream. In C++, a **stream** is a sequence of characters used to perform input and output operations. The name iostream is short for "Input and Output" stream. The grandparent base class from which iostream is derived is named ios. The istream and ostream classes are both derived from ios. The istream class handles input, and includes a definition of the extraction operator >>. The ostream class handles output, and includes a definition of the insertion operator <<. The iostream class is derived from both istream and ostream, so iostream inherits all the properties of both parent classes, including the >> and << operators. The iostream class is a working example of multiple inheritance. Figure 10-1 illustrates the relationships among ios, istream, ostream, and iostream.

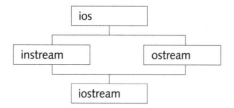

Figure 10-1   isostream's family tree

USING ISTREAM MEMBER FUNCTIONS

In C++, the easiest way to read in a character is to use cin with the extraction operator, for example, `cin>>someVariable;`. The extraction operator is actually an overloaded function named operator>>(). You can overload the >> operator to work with your own class objects. If you create a class named Person and declare a Person named someOne, >> can be overloaded, and then you can write `cin>>someOne;`. Similarly, the creators of C++ also have overloaded >> to work with all built-in data types, so you can make statements such as `cin>>someInteger;` and `cin>>someDouble;`.

Using the get() Function

Another member function of the istream class is get(). The **get() function** takes a character argument and returns a reference to the object (the istream class) that invoked the get() function. Therefore more than one get() function can be included in a statement. Its prototype has the following form:

```
istream& get(char &c);
```

The get() function takes a reference to a character as an argument, and returns a reference to the istream class. You use get() with the cin object just like you use other member functions with an object—you use the object name, the dot operator, and the function name. For example, the following code segment uses two statements to accept three characters from the keyboard.

```
char first, middle, last;
cin.get(first);
cin.get(middle).get(last);
```

The cin.get() statement can retrieve any character, including the Enter key.

Most compilers overload get() so that, in addition to taking a character reference as an argument, it also can take no argument. The following version of the get() function returns the character being read in as an integer. Its prototype is:

```
int get();
```

The preceding form of the function often is used when it doesn't matter which character is extracted, and you do not need to store the character. For example, the following statements allow a program to wait for the user to press a key; there is no need to store the value of the key.

```
cout<<"Press any key to continue";
cin.get();
```

You have also used the getch() function to accept a keyboard character.

The istream class get() function also is overloaded so that it can take two or three arguments. The prototype is as follows:

```
istream& get(char *str, int len, char c = '\n');
```

The preceding form of get() allows you to input a string of characters. The first argument is a pointer that holds the address of the string. The second argument is the number of

10

characters that will be stored. The third argument is the character that terminates the entry, often called the **delimiter character**. The default value to stop data entry, as you can see from the prototype, is the Enter key, which coded as '\n'. If you don't supply an alternative third argument, the Enter key automatically becomes the signal to end data entry.

Recall that a character pointer or the name of a character array can be used as a string address.

The second argument of the get() function—the number of characters to be stored—is very important. Without the second argument, a user could destroy memory by entering a string of characters that was longer than the area prepared to receive it. Figure 10-2 contains a program in which a 10-character array is set up for userName. Because the length of the string is limited to 10 in the cin.get() statement, if a user enters a name longer than nine characters, only the first nine characters and a string-ending null character will be stored. If no provision was made to limit the user's entry, a long entry could be stored starting at the address of the userName array, but when the entry continued past the end of the array , it would destroy other values stored in memory beyond the locations reserved for userName. Figure 10-3 shows the output of the UserName program when the entered name is short enough to fit in the allocated area. Figure 10-4 shows the output when the entered name is too long.

The output in Figures 10-3 and 10-4 illustrate one benefit of using the get() function instead of the extraction operator (>>) for keyboard data entry. Using cin with the operator>>() will bypass all whitespace characters (blanks, tabs, and newline characters) and stop accepting characters when whitespace is entered, but the get() function accepts whitespace characters into the variable arguments.

Programmers refer to the character for which each bit holds a 0 as a null character. The C++ constant that represents this value is called NULL.

```cpp
#include<iostream.h>
#include<conio.h>
void main()
  {
    const int nameSize = 10;
    char userName[nameSize];
    cout<<"Enter your name ";
    cin.get(userName,nameSize);
    cout<<"Hello, "<<userName<<endl;
    getch();
  }
```

Figure 10-2   The UserName program

Figure 10-3   Output of UserName program

Figure 10-4   Output of UserName program handling a long name

> In Figure 10-4, nine characters are shown—7 in Barbara, a space, and a J. The tenth character in the accepted string is the NULL character, which terminates all strings.

One unfortunate side effect of the get() function is that it leaves unused characters in the input stream. A subsequent call to get() retrieves the next (unused) character, whether or not that retrieval was intended. For example, when you modify the program in Figure 10-2 with the highlighted additions shown in Figure 10-5, you'll receive the output shown in Figure 10-6. You can't enter the class grade; the program seems to fly past the statement that gets the let-ter grade. The first `cin.get()` statement accepts your name from the keyboard, but leaves the newline character ('\n') in the input stream. The second `cin.get()` statement should retrieve your letter grade, but instead accepts the Enter key that you press after you enter your name. As shown in Figure 10-6, the program doesn't stop to obtain your grade, because the second call to get() already has been satisfied with the newline character.

```
#include<iostream.h>
#include<conio.h>
void main()
 {
    const int nameSize = 10;
    char userName[nameSize];
    char grade;
    cout<<"Enter your name ";
    cin.get(userName,nameSize);
    cout<<"Hello, "<<userName<<endl;
    cout<<"Enter your grade in this class ";
    cin.get(grade);
    cout<<"Your grade is "<<grade<<endl;
    getch();
 }
```

Figure 10-5   The UserNameAndGrade program

10

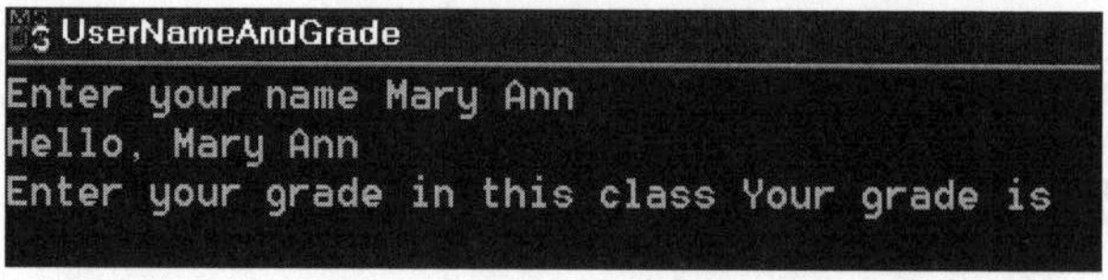

Figure 10-6 Output of UserNameAndGrade program

The program output shown in Figure 10-6 includes your first name and a newline (instead of a grade) for the letter grade. To allow the user to enter a grade, you could add a third cin.get() statement to the program, as shown in Figure 10-7. The purpose of the highlighted get() statement is to accept the Enter key that follows entry of the name. Programmers say this call to the get() function **absorbs** or **consumes** the extra character. Figure 10-8 shows the output of this program.

The program in Figure 10-7 accepts a user's name after the prompt, and then uses the separate `cin.get()` statement to read the newline character. The character is not stored because no variable name is used as an argument to get().

```
#include<iostream.h>
#include<conio.h>
void main()
 {
    const int nameSize = 10;
    char userName[nameSize];
    char grade;
    cout<<"Enter your name ";
    cin.get(userName,nameSize);
    cout<<"Hello, "<<userName<<endl;
    cin.get();           //consumes Enter key
    cout<<"Enter your grade in this class ";
    cin.get(grade);
    cout<<"Your grade is "<<grade<<endl;
    getch();
 }
```

Figure 10-7 The UserNameAndGrade program that allows the Enter key

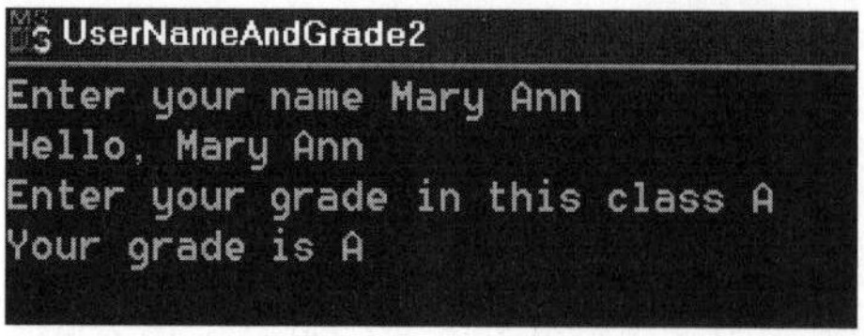

Figure 10-8 Output of UserNameAndGrade2

If you declare a character variable named holdEnter, then the statement `cin.get(holdEnter);` could be used in place of the highlighted statement in Figure 10-7. The holdEnter variable stores the Enter key that the user presses after entering a name. If the program in Figure 10-7 continued with more data entry, you also would want to add another `cin.get();` (or `cin.get(holdEnter);`) statement after the entry of the grade initial. The Enter key pressed after grade entry is consumed, and does not affect subsequent data entry.

If you run the program in Figure 10-7 and enter a name that is too long, the output looks like Figure 10-9. In this case, the `cin.get(userName, nameSize);` statement accepts the first ten characters of "Barbara Jean", but replaces the 'e' in "Jean" with the string-terminating NULL character. Then the 'a' in Jean is accepted into the grade variable. In this case, the 'n' and newline characters from "Jean" are still waiting in the input stream and could be accepted by additional cin.get() statements.

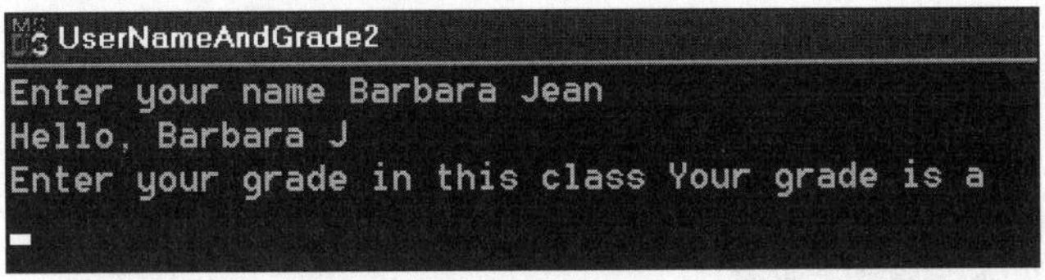

Figure 10-9   Output of UserNameAndGrade2 with a long name

Using the ignore() Function

It is impossible to guess how many cin.get() statements are needed to consume all the potential additional letters of a name if you use the UserNameAndGrade2 program—imagine the challenge of a name such as Barbara Penelope. A superior alternative is to use the **ignore() function** to ignore or skip any additional characters left in the input stream.

The prototype of the ignore() function is:

```
istream& ignore(int length = 1, char c = '\n');
```

where *length* indicates the maximum number of characters to ignore, and the character argument indicates the consumed character that stops the ignore() function. The prototype indicates that if you leave off the delimiting character argument, then the newline character is used by default. Additionally, if you leave off the length, then 1 is used by default. Typically, programmers use the ignore() function as shown in the highlighted statement in Figure 10-10. A high number (such as 100) is used for the length to ensure that even the longest name is accommodated. The output in Figures 10-11 and 10-12 show that whether the entered name is short or long, all characters that should not be part of the name are consumed, and the grade entry can proceed as intended. Unlike with the get() function, the delimiting character ('\n' in the program in Figure 10-9) is absorbed when you use ignore().

```
#include<iostream.h>
#include<conio.h>
void main()
 {
    const int nameSize = 10;
    char userName[nameSize];
    char grade;
    cout<<"Enter your name ";
    cin.get(userName,nameSize);
    cout<<"Hello, "<<userName<<endl;
    cin.ignore(100,'\n');
    cout<<"Enter your grade in this class ";
    cin.get(grade);
    cout<<"Your grade is "<<grade<<endl;
    getch();
 }
```

Figure 10-10   The UserNameAndGrade program using ignore()

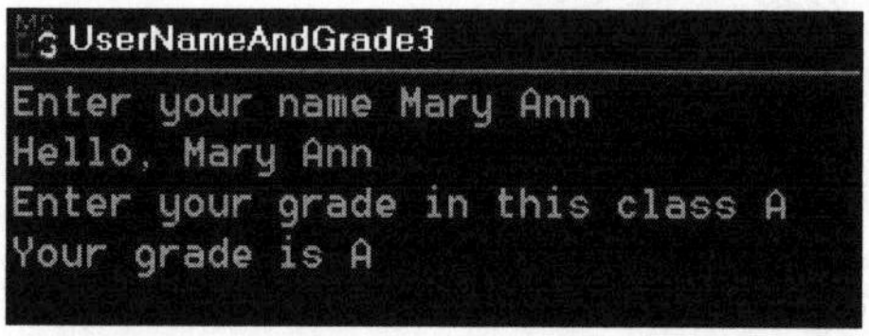

Figure 10-11   Output of UserNameAndGrade3 with short name

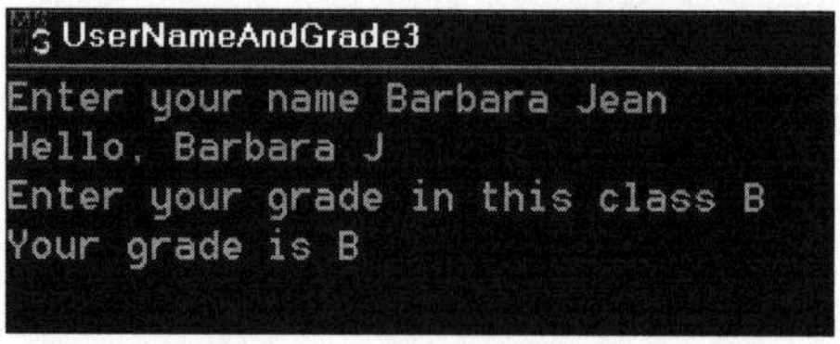

Figure 10-12   Output of UserNameAndGrade3 with long name

Using the getline() Function

As an alternative to using an extra call to get() to absorb the Enter key after character data entry, or using the ignore() function to absorb any number of characters, you can include another istream member, getline(). Its prototype is:

```
istream& getline(char *str, int len, char  c = '\n');
```

The getline() function reads a line of text at the address represented by str. It reads text until it reaches either the length used as the second argument or the character used as the third argument. (If you don't supply a third argument, the line-ending character becomes '\n' by default.) Like the ignore() function, getline() discards the newline character, so any additional data entry begins fresh. The program in Figure 10-13, and the output in Figure 10-14, show how the getline() function correctly accepts characters up to and including the default newline delimiter. The getline() function absorbs the newline character, so the subsequent prompt for and echo of the listing status character operates as intended.

```cpp
#include<iostream.h>
#include<conio.h>
void main()
  {
    const int phoneSize = 16;
    char phoneNumber[phoneSize];
    char listedStatus;
    cout<<"Enter your phone number ";
    cin.getline(phoneNumber,phoneSize);
    cout<<"Your number is "<<phoneNumber<<endl;
    cout<<"Enter an L if you are listed in the phone book,"
      << endl;
    cout<<" O if listed with the operator only, ";
      cout<<" or N if not listed ";
    cin.get(listedStatus);
    cout<<"Listed status is "<<listedStatus<<endl;
    getch();
}
```

Figure 10-13   The UserPhoneNumber program

Figure 10-14   Output of UserPhoneNumber program

When you use a delimiter other than '\n' with getline(), the getline() function consumes the delimiter but leaves the subsequent Enter key in the input stream, so you still must account for it. The program in Figure 10-15 and its output in Figure 10-16 illustrate the use of get() to consume the Enter key by getline(). When you use the program in Figure 10-15, you enter a phone number, the pound sign, and the Enter key. The getline() function consumes the pound sign, but the highlighted get() function is needed to consume the Enter key so the key is not used as the listedStatus code.

The difference between get() and getline() is the way each handles the delimiter character. The getline() function consumes the delimiter character; the get() function does not.

Some compilers contain a bug that requires you to press Enter twice after using the getline() function.

```
#include<iostream.h>
#include<conio.h>
void main()
  {
    const int phoneSize = 16;
    char phoneNumber[phoneSize];
    char listedStatus;
    cout<<"Enter your phone number";
    cout<<"followed by a pound sign (#)";
    cin.getline(phoneNumber,phoneSize, '#');
    cin.get();  // for the Enter key
    cout<<"Your number is "<<phoneNumber<<endl;
    cout<<"Enter an L if you are listed in the phone book,"
      <<endl;
    cout<<" O if listed with the operator only,";
      cout<<"or N if not listed ";
    cin.get(listedStatus);
    cout<<"Listed status is "<<listedStatus<<endl;
    getch();
}
```

Figure 10-15   The UserPhoneNumber2 program

```
UserPhoneNumber2
Enter your phone number followed by a pound sign (#) 847-322-9088#
Your number is 847-322-9088
Enter an L if you are listed in the phone book,
 O if listed with the operator only, or N if not listed N
Listed status is N
```

Figure 10-16   Output of UserPhoneNumber2

Other istream Member Functions

Most compilers support other istream member functions with names such as eof(), bad(), and good(); you will learn more about these later in this chapter. For now, the point is that the istream class is not mysterious. It is just a class, and cin is just an object that already has been instantiated for you. As an object, cin—like objects of any other class—contains member functions. You use those member functions with the dot operator and the function name.

USING OSTREAM MEMBER FUNCTIONS

The concepts you have learned while studying the cin object apply to the cout object as well. It is a member of a class (the ostream class), which supports member functions and overloaded operators just like the istream class—or any other class, for that matter. (You already know how to use one overloaded ostream class operator function—the operator<<() function.) Besides member functions, and just like other class objects, the cout object also has data members, or states.

Using Format Flags with setf() and unsetf()

Many of the states of the cout object are contained in a single long integer field, in which each bit represents some condition of the object. For example, the bit that represents "show positive sign" might be turned on. If so, any positive value subsequently sent through the output stream will be preceded by a plus sign (+) when that value is shown.

C++ actually instantiates three ostream objects. Besides cout, which is associated with the standard output device (usually a monitor), C++ includes cerr and clog, which are used for error conditions.

10

The arguments that determine the state of the cout object are called **format flags** or **state flags**. All format flags begin with `ios::`. As you know from your work with classes, :: is the scope resolution operator, and its use indicates that format flags are members of the ios base class. Some commonly used format flags are:

- `ios::left`—left-justifies output within the field size, which may be set by the width() function (described in a following section)
- `ios::right`—right-justifies output within the field size
- `ios::dec`—formats numbers in decimal (base 10)
- `ios::hex`—formats numbers in hexadecimal (base 16)
- `ios::oct`—formats numbers in octal (base 8)
- `ios::showpos`—inserts a + before positive numbers
- `ios::showpoint`—displays the decimal point and six decimal positions for all floating-point numbers

One member function of the ios class, the **setf() function**, takes arguments that set the bits of cout; that is, the arguments turn the bits in the flag on or off. Like any member function, setf() is called by using an object's name, followed by a dot, followed by the function name. The statement `cout.setf(ios::showpos);` turns on the bit that forces the display of the plus sign with positive numbers. Subsequent output will show the + with positive values. Another member function, **unsetf()**, can be used to deselect the bit: `cout.unsetf(ios::showpos);`.

You probably will prefer using manipulators rather than using ostream member functions. However, it's important that you understand how ostream member functions work so you can write your own manipulators. (Manipulators are discussed in the next section of this chapter.)

Using the setf() function, you also can combine format flags using the bitwise OR operator (|). The following statements, when placed together, produce output that is signed, in base 10 format, and with six decimal places: the output appears as +4.000000.

```
cout.setf(ios::showpos | ios::dec | ios::showpoint);
cout<<4.0;
```

Using the width() Function

You can change the output field width with the iostream member **width() function**. This function defines the size of the output field in which the passed argument will be displayed. By default, the argument will be right-aligned in this field. Of course, you can use the ios:: left format flag to change the default alignment. For example, the following pair of statements produces three blanks followed by 13, for a total output of five characters.

```
cout.width(5);
cout<<13;
```

The width() function applies only to the first subsequent field to be output. As a result, you must call it each time you want a width specification to take effect. For example, the program in Figure 10-17 produces the output shown in Figure 10-18. The width is set to 10, then the constant value 22 appears in a loop. The width setting applies only to the first instance of 22; the remaining 22s are not assigned a field width. In the second loop in the program in Figure 10-17, the width() function is recalled each time prior to displaying 33, so the 33 is right-aligned in a 10-space field each time it appears.

```
#include<iostream.h>
#include<conio.h>
void main()
  {
    int x;
    cout.width(10);
    for(x = 0; x < 3; ++x)
        cout<<22<<endl;
    for(x = 0; x < 3; ++x)
      {
        cout.width(10);
        cout<<33<<endl;
      }
    getch();
  }
```

Figure 10-17   DemoWidth program

Figure 10-18 Output of DemoWidth program

If the value you provide for the width() function is not large enough to include all of the displayed value, then the width designation is simply ignored. For example, the following statements display 5555 on the screen, not 55 as you might expect.

```
cout<<width(2);
cout<<(5555);
```

The creators of C++ assumed that seeing an actual value is more important than having the value properly aligned.

Using the precision( ) Function

You can use the **precision( ) function** to control the number of significant digits you see in the output. For example, the constant 12.5432 contains six digits. To display just four digits, giving the output as 12.54, you can use the following statements:

```
cout.precision(4);
cout<<12.5432;
```

If you want to control the number of positions shown to the right of the decimal point (instead of simply the number of significant positions visible), you must combine `cout.setf(ios::fixed);` and `cout.precision();`. When the ios::fixed flag is turned on, then the value used as the argument to the precision() function becomes the number of decimal places shown, instead of the precision.

Unlike the width() function, the precision() function applies to all subsequent output fields until the precision is reset.

 No matter how many decimal positions a number contains, C++ will print six positions if you do not explicitly set a precision for output.

In the next set of steps, you declare an array of doubles, assign values with different numbers of significant digits, and then display all the values using the same precision.

1. Open a new file in your C++ editor. Enter the statements to include the files you need, start the main() function, and declare the variables and constants you

will use. You will use a field size of 10 for display, and an array size of 5 to hold five double values.

```
#include<iostream.h>
#include<conio.h>
void main()
    {
        int x;
        const int fieldSize = 10;
        const int arraySize = 5;
        double values[arraySize];
```

2. Set the first array element to a number with three positions, one of which is to the right of the decimal point. Then, in a loop, set each subsequent array element to .10 times the previous one. This stores the values 23.4, 2.34, .234, .0234, and .00234 in the array.

```
values [0] = 23.4;
for (x = 0; x < (arraySize - 1); ++x)
        values[x+1] = values[x] * .10;
```

3. To confirm that the array values are what you expect, print each in a field of size 10. You must use the width() function to reset the field width for each output.

```
for(x = 0; x < arraySize; ++x)
    {
        cout.width(fieldSize);
        cout<<values[x]<<endl;
    }
```

4. Set the precision with a call to the precision() function, then issue a statement to that effect.

```
cout.precision(2);
cout<<"After precision(2) call"<<endl;
```

5. In a loop, display each value again.

```
for(x = 0; x < arraySize; ++x)
    {
        cout.width(fieldSize);
        cout<<values[x]<<endl;
    }
```

6. Add a call to the **getch( );** function if you need it to hold your output screen. Then add the closing curly brace for the program.

7. Save the file as **DemoPrecision.cpp** in the Student Data folder of your Student Data Disk or of your hard drive. Compile and run the program. The output appears in Figure 10-19. The top half of the output screen shows the calculated values stored in the array. The bottom half has each array element shown

with a precision of 2. In other words, each line shows the two most significant digits, 2 and 3, in their proper position relative to the decimal point.

```
MR
DS  DemoPrecision
        23.4
        2.34
        0.234
       0.0234
      0.00234
After precision(2) call
           23
          2.3
         0.23
        0.023
       0.0023

```

Figure 10-19   Output of DemoPrecision program

 You will learn how to control the number of positions that print to the right of the decimal point in the next section.

10

CREATING MANIPULATOR FUNCTIONS

The code to produce output in the desired format using the ostream member functions can become quite tedious to write. For example, if you need to display a variable named amountMoney in currency format with a dollar sign, in base 10, in a field size of eight, you might write the code shown in Figure 10-20. You need three statements before you can output the actual dollar figure you want to be shown:

```
cout<<'$';
cout.setf(ios::dec | ios::showpoint);
cout.width(8);
cout<<amountMoney<<endl; // the figure is finally output
```

Figure 10-20   Writing amountMoney in currency format

The amountMoney variable would be shown with a dollar sign in base 10 in a field of eight. If you needed to display more money values, then the first statement, cout<<'$';, and the last statement, cout.width(8);, would have to be executed again before you could display the next figure. Additionally, if you wanted to display each dollar figure with two decimal places, you might require a number of if statements to determine the proper precision()

function setting prior to each output. (Amounts under 1.00 require two precision positions, amounts under 10.00 require three precision positions, and so on.)

When you use the iostream member functions(), not only are a lot of statements needed to obtain the correct format, but nothing in the final cout statement (cout<<amountMoney<<endl;) indicates the format you are using. If the program is revised (and almost all programs are revised eventually) and new statements are added between the several cout calls, it becomes difficult for someone reading the program code to see how amountMoney will look on output.

When you create a manipulator function, the desired results become much clearer. A **manipulator function** is used to manipulate, or change, the state of the cout object. Any output manipulator function you create should take as an argument an instance of ostream as a reference. It also should return the same input argument. This approach allows manipulators to be chained or stacked with other calls to the cout insertion operator.

 You can code manipulators for cin as well as cout, but you are less likely to need to do so.

For example, you could write a manipulator to format output as currency, as shown in Figure 10-21. The function contains statements that display the dollar sign, set some ios flags, and set the width. You could incorporate the same statements into your program body and get the same effect. The difference is, when the statements are packaged as a function that receives and returns a reference to ostream, you can code cout<<currency<<amountMoney; to display the value with the proper formatting. The results are not different, but the code is clearer and concise.

```
ostream& currency(ostream &s)
  {
      cout<<'$';
      cout.setf(ios::dec | ios::showpoint);
      cout.width(8);
      return s;
  }
```

Figure 10-21   The currency manipulator function

In the function shown in Figure 10-21, a reference to ostream is passed into the function as an argument. When you write cout<<currency<<amountMoney;, the currency function receives the current ostream reference. This reference is updated within the function three times—when the '$' prints, when setf() is called, and when width() is called. The new address is returned to the calling program where amountMoney is the next value passed to ostream. As with other function you can place any C++ statements within the body of a

manipulator function you may do so. As long as you receive an ostream reference and return the reference, you can use the manipulator with the insertion operator and the cout object.

Many programmers find that it's convenient to create a library of manipulator functions they can use to create formats they frequently need.

USING BUILT-IN MANIPULATORS

Some manipulators are so useful that they are already coded and placed in libraries included with your C++ compiler. You already have used the endl manipulator to output a newline character and flush the output stream. It is easy to use endl because you can chain it with the insertion operator (<<) within the same statements as other output.

In addition to endl, C++ provides a flush operator to flush the stream without sending a newline character, and also provides an ends operator to send a null (or space) character rather than a newline.

Using the setprecision() Manipulator

10

You use the **setprecision( ) manipulator** to specify the number of decimals that will print. The setprecision() manipulator works like the precision() function—it specifies the number of significant digits to display. However, it is considered a manipulator instead of a member function because you chain a call to setprecision() along with other output and the insertion operator, rather than using an object and a dot operator, as you do with cout.precision().

Any C++ manipulator, such as setprecision(),that takes an argument requires the inclusion of the iomanip.h file in your program. Any manipulator, such as endl, that does not take an argument does not require the inclusion of iomanip.h.

The program in Figure 10-22 produces the output in Figure 10-23. The program uses the setprecision() manipulator in a loop, and increases the value of its argument from 0 through 6. When the precision is set to 0, the output still shows one decimal place, which is the minimum that can be shown while still expressing the value. When the precision is set to 1, one decimal place again is shown. The value .8888 becomes .9 when set to display a single decimal place. When the setprecision() argument is smaller than the number of digits in the output value, rounding takes place. When the argument to the setprecision() manipulator is greater than or equal to the number of digits in the value to be output, then the full value is shown.

```
#include<iostream.h>
#include<conio.h>
#include<iomanip.h>
void main()
  {
      int x;
      for(x = 0; x < 7; ++x)
            cout<<"precision "<<x<<"   "<<
                  setprecision(x)<<0.8888<<endl;
      getch();
  }
```

Figure 10-22   The DemoPrecision2 program

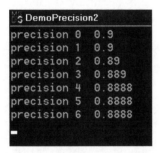

Figure 10-23   Output of DemoPrecision2.cpp

The setprecision() manipulator doesn't perform any functions that the cout.precision() member function can't accomplish, but the statement that actually outputs the data includes the precision, and the intention is clearer.

 With many compilers, if you include the iomanip.h file, you don't have to include the iostream.h file—iomanip.h also includes iostream.h.

Using the setw( ) Manipulator

The **setw( ) manipulator** allows you to set the width of a field for output. Use of the setw() manipulator requires inclusion of the iomanip.h file, because setw() requires an argument that represents the width of the output field. The setw() manipulator works like the width() member function you can use with the cout object; the advantage of using setw() is its chaining capability in a cout statement. As with the width() function, output is right-justified in the field, and if the parameter sent to setw() is too small to support the displayed value, then the width is simply ignored. Also like the width() function, you must repeat setw() for each new output, even if you write just one cout statement. For example, cout<<setw(5)<<123<<456<<endl; produces two spaces followed by 123 (because 123

is shown in a field of 5), followed immediately by 456. The 456 does not have a width of 5. The statement `cout<<setw(5)<<123<<setw(5)<<456<<endl;` produces two spaces, 123, two more spaces, and 456.

 The setw() manipulator function code actually uses the member function cout.width().

Using the setiosflags() and resetiosflags() Manipulators

Two additional manipulators, setiosflags() and resetiosflags(), each perform several manipulations, depending on the flags (such as ios::dec or ios::showpoint) they receive as arguments. The **setiosflags() manipulator** turns on bit codes for the attributes named as arguments; the **resetiosflags() manipulator** turns off those bit codes. As with other manipulators, the advantage of using setiosflags() and resetiosflags() relates to their ability to be placed in a cout statement chain, as opposed to using a cout.setf() member function call prior to actual data output. As with setf(), the bitwise OR operator (|) can be used with setiosflags() or resetiosflags(), as in the following:

`cout<<setw(7)<<setiosflags( ios::hex | ios::left)<<24;`

The preceding code displays 24 as output left-aligned in a field of size seven, in hexadecimal format.

In the next set of steps, you combine the setprecision() and setiosflags() manipulators to produce output that displays decimal values with a fixed number of decimal places in a column. You use the fixed and showpoint iosflags to display numeric output that has a fixed number of decimal places and that shows the decimal point, even with whole numbers. You use setprecision(2) to display two decimal positions with each value.

1. Open the **DemoPrecision.cpp** file you created earlier in this chapter. Immediately save it as **DemoPrecision3.cpp**.

2. Position the insertion point at the end of the `#include<conio.h>` statement, and press **Enter** to start a new line. Add a statement to include the iomanip.h file.

   #include<iomanip.h>

3. Delete the line that has the statement cout.precision(2);.

4. Change the statement `cout<<"After precision(2) call"<<endl;` to read:

   cout<<"After setprecision(2) call"<<endl;

5. Remove the statement cout<<values[x]<<endl; that appears as the second-to-last line of code in the program, and replace it with:

   cout<<setprecision(2)<< setiosflags(ios::fixed | ios::showpoint)<< values[x]<<endl;

6. Save the program as **DemoPrecision3.cpp**, then compile and run it. The output looks like Figure 10-24.

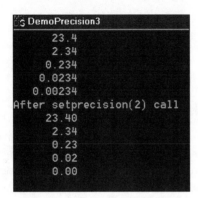

```
DemoPrecision3
      23.4
       2.34
       0.234
       0.0234
       0.00234
After setprecision(2) call
      23.40
       2.34
       0.23
       0.02
       0.00
```

Figure 10-24 Output of DemoPrecision3.cpp

CREATING MANIPULATORS THAT REQUIRE AN ARGUMENT

Users of specific compilers like Microsoft Visual C++ will have to use an alternate technique to create usable manipulators. See Appendix A for details.

To create a manipulator that does not require an argument, you must write a function that receives and returns an ostream reference argument. To use a manipulator that requires no arguments, you must use the manipulator name with the insertion operator, as in the statement `cout<<currency<<moneyAmount<<endl;`. The currency manipulator (defined in Figure 10-21) and the endl manipulator (a built-in manipulator) share a trait: when you use either one you use its name alone—no parentheses and no explicitly passed argument can be included. Some built-in manipulators such as setprecision() and setw() require arguments, and you must use a set of parentheses with them; you also can create a manipulator that requires an explicit argument.

To create a manipulator that takes an argument, you must write two functions. When you use a manipulator that requires no argument, such as endl or the currency manipulator developed above, the address of the output or input stream is passed to the function. With manipulators, such as setw(), that take an argument both the address of the stream and the argument itself must be passed to the manipulator function. This task is handled by the **omanip()** **function**, which is defined in the file iomanip.h.

Figure 10-25 shows a currency manipulator to which a user passes a value that holds the field width. The figure also shows a main() function that uses the currency manipulator. Figure 10-26 shows the output of the program from Figure 10-25.

```
#include<iostream.h>
#include<conio.h>
#include<iomanip.h>
ostream& curren(ostream &s, int fieldSize)
  {
      cout<<'$';
      cout.setf(ios::fixed | ios::showpoint);
      cout.precision(2);
      cout.width(fieldSize);
      return s;
  }
omanip<int> currency(int fieldSize)
  {
      return omanip<int>(curren, fieldSize);
  }
void main()
  {
      double someMoney = 13.5678;
      cout<<currency(7)<<someMoney<<endl;
      getch();
  }
```

Figure 10-25   The currency manipulator with an argument

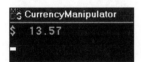

Figure 10-26   Output of CurrencyManipulator.cpp

In Figure 10-25, the main() program calls the currency function, passing a 7 as the argument that indicates field width. This function actually overloads the insertion operator (named omanip) to take both the address of the curren() function and the passed field size. The curren() function does the actual "work" of formatting the next value to be output. The resulting output is formatted with a dollar sign followed by two spaces, and the value of someMoney is formatted to two fixed decimal places. When someMoney is shown in a field of size 7, the digits and decimal point of 13.57 occupy five positions, and leave the leading two positions as spaces.

The use of the angle brackets in each reference to **omanip<int>** indicates that omanip is actually a class template function. (Template creation is covered in Chapter 11.) Like many facets of object-oriented programming, you can use the omanip function without understanding how it works internally. For now, you can use it any time you want to create a manipulator that takes an argument. If you want to write a currency manipulator that takes an argument which is not an int, you must substitute the type of the argument your manipulator takes for each highlighted occurrence of int in the currency function in Figure 10-25.

In the next set of steps, you create a manipulator that formats a part number for a manufacturing company. Part numbers that are less than 1000 are assigned to the Alpha Division for servicing; others are assigned to the Beta Division. Part numbers are correspondingly formatted with an A and a dash, or a B and a dash prior to the number. Additionally, three-digit part numbers are assigned a leading 0 to turn them into four-digit part numbers. In other words, part 123 becomes A-0123, while part 4567 becomes B-4567.

1. Open a new file in your C++ editor. Type the include statements you need as follows:

```
#include<iostream.h>
#include<conio.h>
#include<iomanip.h>
```

2. Create the function that actually does the work of creating a properly formatted part number. The function named part() takes both an ostream reference and a character that will serve as the prefix to a part number (A or B). The code and a dash are sent to the output stream; a zero is sent if the code is 'A' because code 'A' indicates a three-digit part number. The ostream reference is returned by the function.

```
ostream& part(ostream &s, char code)
{
    cout<<code<<"-";
    if(code=='A')
        cout<<"0";
    return s;
}
```

3. The partNumFormat() function overloads the insertion operator to take the address of the part() function and the character code.

```
omanip<char> partNumFormat(char code)
{
    return omanip<char>(part, code);
}
```

4. Write a main() program that prompts the user for a part number. The program continues the prompt until the user enters a part number of three or four digits, that is, between 100 and 9999 inclusive. When a valid part number is received, the three-digit code ('A') or the four-digit code ('B') is determined. The part number is printed in the proper format using the partNumFormat manipulator, if the correct code is written.

```
void main()
{
    int partNum;
    char code;
    cout<<"Enter part number - 3 or 4 digits ";
    cin>>partNum;
```

```
        while( partNum < 100 || partNum > 9999)
           {
               cout<<"Part number must be 3 or 4 digits. Please
                enter again: ";
               cin>>partNum;
           }
        if(partNum <= 999)
               code = 'A';
        else
               code = 'B';
        cout<<partNumFormat(code)<<partNum<<endl;
        getch();
    }
```

5. Save the program as **PartNumManipulator.cpp**. Compile and run the program several times. Figure 10-27 shows the output when the user enters a five-digit number, which is not allowed, followed by a four-digit number, which contains the 'B' prefix. Figure 10-28 shows the output when the user enters a three-digit number; the part number includes an 'A' prefix and a leading 0.

Figure 10-27   Output of PartNumManipulator program with a four-digit entry

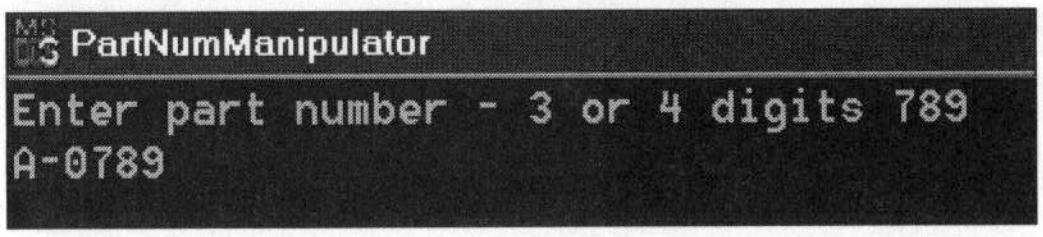

Figure 10-28   Output of PartNumManipulator program with a three-digit entry

UNDERSTANDING COMPUTER FILES

When you store data items in a computer system, you use a **permanent storage device**, such as a disk or a reel of magnetic tape. The term permanent is misleading; a permanent storage device does not store data forever—data can be erased or replaced with new data. Instead, the term permanent is used to contrast this type of data storage with the **temporary data storage** that exists in computer memory. Data items typically exist in memory for only a short time. For example, when you register for a college class, information about the class you want to take, is kept in memory for a few moments while your registration is processed. As soon as you complete the registration transaction, your class data is stored on a permanent device such as a disk. This permanent data is accessed again when the college bills you, prints class lists for your instructors, and prints a final grade.

You can store data on a disk (or other permanent storage device) as a simple stream of characters. However, it is common practice to store data in a **data hierarchy**, which represents the relationships between the sizes of data units that business professionals most often use.

The smallest unit of data that concerns business people is usually the field. A **data field** represents one piece of data, such as a first or last name, phone or Social Security number, or salary. Data fields are created from smaller units of data—for example, a first name might contain 10 characters. However, from a business point of view, individual characters in a name are not as important as the name itself. (Characters also are made of smaller units, called **bits**. Each bit represents a 1 or 0 in memory. However, from a business person's perspective, bits usually are unimportant.)

A **data record** consists of a number of data fields that are logically connected because they pertain to the same entity. For example, your first name, last name, Social Security number, and salary constitute the fields of your record, and your coworkers' records are constructed from the same fields.

A **data file** contains records that are logically related. For example, the company you work for maintains a data file that contains hundreds of records—each one containing all the data fields that pertain to each employee.

 A file that is stored on a disk is not necessarily a data file. You have already created many program files when you wrote your C++ programs. Programmers usually reserve the term "data file" for files that contain data, rather than program instructions.

Often, records within a data file are stored with a space or other **delimiting character** between fields, and a newline between each record. The contents of a typical data file, along with labels for its components, is shown in Figure 10-29. All the data in the figure represents the data file, each row represents a record, and each column represents a field.

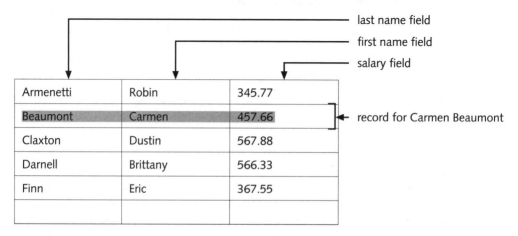

Figure 10-29 A data file containing employee data

SIMPLE FILE OUTPUT

You have used a descendant of the ios class—ostream—and its descendant iostream to produce all sorts of screen output. In C++, when you write to a disk file rather than to the screen, you use a class named fstream, which, like ostream, is ultimately derived from ios. Figure 10-30 shows the relationship between fstream and some other input and output classes.

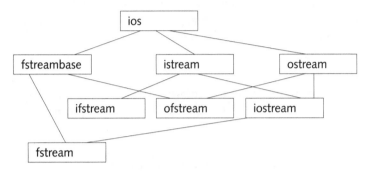

Figure 10-30   The fstream family tree

The fstream class is defined in the fstream.h file, which must be included in any C++ program that writes to or reads from a disk. Figure 10-30 shows that fstream inherits from iostream and its ancestors; therefore you also can use the manipulators that work with screen output for file output.

When you want to perform standard screen output, you use the cout object, a member of the ostream class that already has been instantiated. To perform file output, you must instantiate your own member of the ofstream class. The object has not already been instantiated for you because programs use only one standard output device, but often more than one output file. Therefore, you must create an object with a unique name for each file.

You instantiate an ofstream output file object as you do any other object—by calling its constructor. When you call an ofstream constructor, you can use a filename as an argument. The constructor then will open the file. For example, the following statement instantiates an object named outFile that is a member of the ofstream class:

```
ofstream outFile("Data.txt");
```

The filename "Data.txt" is passed to the ofstream constructor, which then opens the file on the disk. In C++, you do not need a special "open file" statement, as required by many other programming languages.

If a file with the given name does not exist when the ofstream constructor is called, the file is created. If a file with the given name already exists, it is overwritten. The object name outFile is used within the program whenever you want to refer to the file. Your program's internal name for the file object, such as outFile, is not stored on the disk; the disk file is recognized only by the filename passed to your object's constructor.

If you use a filename without a path, the file must exist (or be created) in the same folder as the program that opens the file. If the file is located elsewhere, you can use a complete pathname in the outFile constructor (or with the open() function discussed in the next paragraph). Because the backslash character also is the escape character, you should use two backslashes in any pathnames, for example, `"c:\\DataFolder\\Data.txt"`.

Similarly to how you can declare a variable and later assign it a value, if you don't provide a filename as an argument when you instantiate an ofstream object, and then you create the object, no file is opened. However, you can explicitly open the file later with the open() member function, as in the following pair of statements:

```
ofstream outFile;
outFile.open("Data.txt");
```

Both the ofstream constructor and the open() function are overloaded to accept a second argument you can use if you want to indicate a file mode. Using a **file mode** tells C++ how to open the file. For example:

- ios::out means open the file for output. When you open an ostream object and do not provide a mode, ios::out is the mode by default.

- ios::app means append the file (rather than re-create it)

- ios::ate means position the file pointer at the end of the file (rather than at the beginning)

- ios::nocreate means the file must exist, otherwise the open fails

- ios::noreplace means the file must not exist, otherwise the open fails

An open() operation (whether explicit or through the constructor) can fail for several reasons. For example, the open()fails if you use the ios::nocreate mode and the file does not exist, or if you use the ios::noreplace mode and the file does exist. To check whether an open() has failed, you can try several methods, using the out object itself or its good() or bad() function. For example, the code segment in Figure 10-31 attempts to open a file named Customers.dat to nocreate mode.

You can see from Figure 10-31 that the programmer chose the name outFile for the ofstream object. The values of outFile and outFile.good() both will be non-zero (or true) if the file was opened successfully; the value of outFile.fail() will be non-zero if the file was not opened successfully.

```
ofstream outFile("Customers.dat",ios::nocreate);
if(outFile)
     cout<<"File opened!";
if(outFile.good())
     cout<<"File opened!";
if(!outFile.fail())
     cout<<"File opened!";
```

Figure 10-31   Code that checks whether a file was opened

Instead of coding the filename explicitly within the file definition statement (as in `ofstream outFile("Customers.dat",ios::nocreate);`), you also can store the filename in a string-defined variable, or you can prompt the user for a filename.

The opposite condition can be tested with any of the statements in Figure 10-32. If outFile or outFile.good() has a zero value, or if outFile.fail() has a non-zero value, then the file did not open.

```
ofstream outFile("Customers.dat",ios::nocreate);
if(!outFile)
      cout<<"Open didn't work.";
if(!outFile.good())
      cout<<"Open didn't work.";
if(outFile.fail())
      cout<<"Open didn't work.";
```

Figure 10-32   Code that checks whether a file was not opened

Because you can use the overloaded insertion operator within the ofstream class, once the file is open, you can write to it with a statement such as the following:

```
outFile<<"This is going to the disk";
```

After you have written to a file, you do not need to explicitly execute any sort of "close file" statement when using C++, as you do in many other programming languages. Instead, as with any other object, whenever an ofstream object goes out of scope, a destructor is called and the ofstream destructor closes the file for you. If you want to close a file before the file object goes out of scope, however, you can use the close() function, as in `outFile.close();`.

As an alternative, you can explicitly call the file object's destructor with the statement `outFile.~ofstream();`. The destructor closes the file.

In the next set of steps, you open a file, write your name to it, and close it.

1. Open a new file in your C++ editor. Enter the include statements you need, and begin the main() program by declaring a string to hold your name.

   #include<fstream.h>
   #include<conio.h>
   void main()
   {
        char name[15];

2. Add the statement that declares and opens the output file. If you want to direct your output to a folder other than the root of the a drive, simply substitute the folder path for the a in the statement. Check to ensure that the file opened correctly.

   ofstream out("a:Name.txt");   // change path if necessary
   if(out.fail())
        cout<<"File was not opened.";

3. Continue with the else clause to the if statement when the file opens correctly. Prompt the user for a name, and read it from the keyboard. Echo the name to the screen to confirm it was entered correctly.

```
else
  {
    cout<<"Enter your name ";
    cin>>name;
    cout<<"Name is "<<name<<endl;
```

4. Write the name to the output file. Then end the else clause with a closing curly brace.

```
    out<<name;
  }
```

5. End the program with a call to getch() and the closing curly brace for the main() function.

```
  getch();
}
```

6. Save the file as **WriteNameToFile.cpp**. Compile and run the program. Enter your name at the prompt.

7. Open a text editor such as NotePad, or use your C++ editor. Open the **Name.txt** file in the editor and confirm that your name has been written to the output file. When you run the program using "Ellen" for input as in Figure 10-33, then the text file holding the name looks like Figure 10-34.

 Some operating systems do not distinguish between uppercase and lowercase in a filename. Even though you use the name Name.txt within your program, your operating system might refer to the file as name.txt.

Figure 10-33   Sample run of WriteNameToFile program

Figure 10-34   Contents of Name.txt

SIMPLE FILE INPUT

To read a file from within a program, you can create an object that is an instantiation of the ifstream class. As with ofstream, when you declare an ifstream object, you pass a filename to the object's constructor and the file opens, for example, `ifstream someData("Data.txt");`.

Ifstream and ofstream objects are used in many similar ways. Like the ofstream class, the name of the ifstream object you instantiate can be any legal C++ identifier; the name has no relationship to the name of the file being opened. The file is identified by the filename used as a parameter to the ifstream object's constructor, not by the name of the ifstream object. The open() and close() functions work with ifstream class objects, and many of the file modes, such as ios::ate, can be used as arguments to ifstream constructors or to open() statements just as they are with ofstream objects. Tests such as `if(someData.good())` are allowed as well.

The ifstream class uses the **get() function** to access file data. Therefore, if someData has been instantiated as an ifstream object, then a character can be read from a disk file with the following code:

```
char aChar;
someData.get(aChar);
```

The value of the ifstream object is 0 when it reaches the end of file, so an entire file can be read in and shown on the screen, one character at a time, with the following code:

```
while(someData)
   {
       someData.get(aChar);  // read in a character
       cout<<aChar;  // display character on screen
   }
```

The end of file condition also can be determined by testing the return values of the **eof()**, **bad()**, **fail()**, and **good()** functions. The values of someData.eof(), someData.bad(), and someData.fail() are all true at end of file; the value of someData.good() becomes false at end of file.

As with ofstream objects, when an ifstream object goes out of scope, the file is closed automatically.

In the next set of steps, you read the name in from the Name.txt file you created in the previous set of steps.

1. Open a new file in your C++ editor. Type the include statements you need.

   #include<fstream.h>
   #include<conio.h>

10

2. In the main() function, declare a string to hold the name you will read from the file. Also declare an integer variable you will use to access each name character individually.

```
void main()
{
    char name[15];
    int x = 0;
```

3. Create an ifstream object named in. Use the same path and filename you used to create the Name file in the previous set of steps.

```
ifstream in("a:Name.txt");   // change path if necessary
```

4. Use a loop that continues while input exits. Use the get() function to retrieve one character at a time from the file. The first character is stored in name[0], then you increase the subscript value you use with the name string, so the next character is stored in name[1], and so on.

```
while(in)
{
    in.get(name[x]);  // read in a character
    ++x;
}
```

5. When you created the Name.txt file, the Enter key you used to terminate the name entry was stored with that name. Replace the last character read in with a NULL character.

```
name[x-1] = '\0';
```

6. Use a cout statement to display the name on the screen.

```
cout<<"Name read from the file is "<<name<<endl;
```

7. Add a call to the getch() function and the final curly brace for the program.

```
    getch();
}
```

8. Save the file as **ReadNameFromFile.cpp**, then compile and run the program. If you used the name "Ellen" when you ran the WriteNameToFile.cpp program you created in the previous set of steps, then your output looks like Figure 10-35.

Figure 10-35   Output of ReadNameFromFile program

Using the getline( ) Function

If a file contains data that ends with a newline character, then it's a bit awkward to have a program that uses the get() function to read data from a file because you must discard the newline character. As an alternative, you can use the getline() member function to read input data. The **getline( ) function** takes the form `fileObject.getline(destination, sizeLimit);`, where destination is a declared character string, and sizeLimit is the maximum number of characters you want to store. The getline() function reads file data into the destination location until a newline is encountered, or until the delimiting number of characters is reached; then the newline character is discarded.

In the next set of steps, you write a program that uses getline() to read the name file created in the WriteNameToFile.cpp program.

1. Open a new file in your C++ editor. Type a program that opens the Name.txt file, reads a line of data, and echoes the input to the screen.

```
#include<fstream.h>
#include<conio.h>
void main()
   {
       char name[15];
       ifstream in("a:Name.txt");   // change path if necessary
       // read in a line until newline or 15, whichever comes first
       in.getline(name,15);
       cout<<"Name read from the file is "<<name<<endl;
       getch();
   }
```

2. Save the program as **ReadNameWithGetline.cpp**. Compile and run the program. The output is the same as that shown in Figure 10-35.

The getline() function provides a convenient way to read data records into a program. For example, consider the Employees.txt data file shown in Figure 10-36. The file contains four records with fields storing employees' last names, first names, and salaries. Storing data in this fashion—one data record per line, each record separated with a newline character—is common. Figure 10-37 shows a program that reads the Employees.txt file, and Figure 10-38 shows the output when you run the program. The program reads, displays, and counts records while the end of file condition is not met.

You can use the getline() function with the cin object as well as with an ifstream object.

10

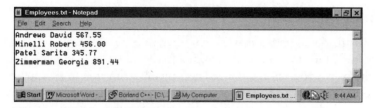

Figure 10-36   Employees.txt file contents

```cpp
#include<fstream.h>
#include<conio.h>
void main()
 {
  char recordIn[40];   // to hold record
  int count = 1;
  ifstream fileIn("a:Employees.txt");
  if(!fileIn)
      cout<<"File not opened"<<endl;
  else
   {
      cout<<"File opened successfully"<<endl;
      fileIn.getline(recordIn,40);      // get first record —
      // up to 40 characters or newline, whichever comes first
      while(fileIn)            // while not end of file
        {
          // display record on screen and add 1 to count
          cout<<"Record #"<<count<<" "<<recordIn<<endl;
          ++count;
          fileIn.getline(recordIn,40);    // get next record
        }
   }
  getch();
 }
```

Figure 10-37   ReadDataFile program

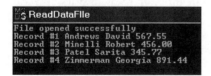

Figure 10-38   Output of ReadDataFile

WRITING OBJECTS TO FILES

It is simple and intuitive to use the ofstream class's overloaded insertion operator to write characters and strings to files. It makes sense, however, that in object-oriented programs you should also be able to write objects to disk files The **write() function** allows you to do just that. The prototype for write() is:

```
ostream& write(char *c, int length);
```

The write() function accepts two arguments: a pointer to a character and an integer. The character pointer points to the address of the argument being written to the disk. If this argument is not a character—for example, if it is a class object—then you must perform a cast on the address of the object to convert it to a character. The second argument to write() represents the size of the object being written.

 Recall that a cast converts one data type to another. You first learned about casting in Chapter 2.

Figure 10-39 shows a Customer class that contains three data members and two functions. It is similar to dozens of classes you previously have worked with.

10

```
class Customer
  {
      private:
            int idNum;
            char last[15];
            char first[15];
      public:
            void enterData();
            void displayData();
  };
void Customer::enterData()
  {
      cout<<"Enter ID number ";
      cin>>idNum;
      cin.get();
      cout<<"Last name ";
      cin.getline(last,15);
      cout<<"First name ";
      cin.getline(first,15);
  }
void Customer::displayData(void)
  {
      cout<<setiosflags(ios::left)<<setw(5)<<idNum;
      cout<<" "<<first<<" "<<last<<endl;
  }
```

Figure 10-39 The Customer class

You can create an array of customer objects, perform the data entry required for the Customers, and write the output to a disk. The format of the statement that writes an object is:

```
outputObject.write((char*)(&object), sizeof(object));
```

The arguments for write() include the address of the object cast to a character pointer, and the size of the object, which can be automatically determined using the sizeof() function. Figure 10-40 shows a main() program that creates five Customer class objects, obtains data values for them, and writes the data to a disk file. A sample run of the program appears in Figure 10-41.

 Whenever you open a file, it is a good idea to check whether the file has actually been opened, and to notify the user if it has not. However, in some of the programs in this book, the check step is left out to keep the examples short.

```
void main()
  {
      const numCusts = 5;
      Customer custs[numCusts];    // declare five Customers
      ofstream dataFile("CustomerFile.dat");
      for(int x = 0; x<numCusts; ++x)
        {
          custs[x].enterData();
          dataFile.write((char*)(&custs[x]), sizeof(custs[x]));
        }
      cout<<"Data entry complete."<<endl;
      getch();
  }
```

Figure 10-40   Writing Customer records to a file

The program in Figure 10-40 executes a for loop numCusts times (five times), performing data entry and writing to the file each time. As an alternative, you might fill the array with data, and then write the entire array to the file with a single write() call. To accomplish this goal, simply move the call to the write() function outside and after the for loop, and then change the two custs objects (custs[x]) references in the write() statement to references to the entire array (custs). Figure 10-42 illustrates this approach, highlighting the references to the array name.

```
MS
DOS Customer
Enter ID number 213
Last name Offenbeck
First name Janice
Enter ID number 345
Last name Reisen
First name Mari
Enter ID number 456
Last name Brewer
First name Kenneth
Enter ID number 587
Last name Kurtz
First name Janet
Enter ID number 682
Last name Bigi
First name Angela
Data entry complete.
```

Figure 10-41 Sample run of Customer program

```
void main()
  {
     const numCusts = 5;
     Customer custs[numCusts];   // declare five Customers
     ofstream dataFile("CustomerFile.dat");
     for(int x = 0; x<num; ++x)
        {
          custs[x].enterData();
        }
     // use the array named custs
     dataFile.write((char*)(&custs), sizeof(custs));
  }
```

Figure 10-42 Writing an array of Customer records to a file

READING OBJECTS FROM FILES

You have used the getline() function with ifstream objects to read in a line of text into a character string. If the line of text actually contains some values that you want to treat as numbers rather than characters, as is true with most data records, then you have to write code to separate the various fields from the character string. It is more convenient to read a data file directly into an array of class objects. You can accomplish this goal with the **read() function**.

The read() function prototype is quite similar to the prototype for the write() function. The prototype or read() is:

```
istream& read(char *c, int length);
```

The read() function requires a pointer to a character, so you must perform a cast when you read an object. The read() function also requires the size of the object being read. To read a Customer class object named customer into an inFile ifstream object, you would write:

```
inFile.read((char*)&customer, sizeof(customer));
```

The program in Figure 10-43 reads in Customer data from the file named CustomerFile.dat and displays each record on the screen. Each record is stored in an object, and each field of each object contains data of the appropriate type.

```
void main()
  {
    const intnumCusts = 5;
    int count = 0, x;
    Customer custs[numCusts];   // declare five Customers
    ifstream dataFile("CustomerFile.dat");
    while(!dataFile.eof() && count < numCusts)
      {
          dataFile.read((char*)(&custs[count]),
            sizeof(custs[count]));
          ++count;
      }
    for(x = 0; x < count; ++x)
          custs[x].displayData();
    getch();
  }
```

Figure 10-43   Reading Customer records from a file

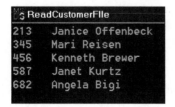

```
ReadCustomerFile
213    Janice Offenbeck
345    Mari Reisen
456    Kenneth Brewer
587    Janet Kurtz
682    Angela Bigi
```

Figure 10-44   Output of ReadCustomerFile program

The program in Figure 10-43 reads in records from the data file until end of file or until the number of records exceeds the number that fits into the array, whichever comes first. The count variable keeps track of the number of records read in. When the array is filled with data records, the records are shown on the screen in a loop that executes "count" number of times.

The program in Figure 10-43 reads a maximum of five records, because the while loop that reads executes only as long as count is less than the numCusts constant. If you want to ensure that all the data records are read (even if there are more than five), an alternative way to code this program involves creating a Customer array with many more elements, and creating a numCusts constant with a correspondingly higher value. Yet another alternative is to dynamically allocate memory for the Customer array.

Instead of reading one record at a time into the Customer array, you can perform one read for the entire array. Figure 10-45 shows a main() program that uses this approach. In the highlighted reference in Figure 10-45, the array name custs is used in the sizeof() function. This tells C++ to read as many bytes as the size of the entire array, instead of just enough bytes to fill one record or one Customer object.

Reading an entire array at one time (instead of reading each element separately) is more efficient. Much of a program's execution time is spent accessing input and output devices.

```
void main()
  {
     const numCusts = 5;
     Customer custs[numCusts];   // declare five Customers
     ifstream dataFile("CustomerFile.dat");
     dataFile.read((char*)(&custs), sizeof(custs));
                         // use the array named custs
     for(int x = 0; x<numCusts; ++x)
       {
           custs[x].displayData();
       }
     getch();
  }
```

Figure 10-45   Reading an array of records

CHAPTER SUMMARY

- The C++ objects cout and cin possess the same traits as other C++ objects—they are members of a class, use inheritance, have access to overloaded operators, and have all other object traits.

- To input data, you can use the extraction operator (>>) after the cin object. You also can use the get() function, which takes either zero, one, two, or three arguments, and returns a reference to the istream class. The get() function leaves unused characters in the input stream. The ignore() function ignores or skips any characters left in the input stream. The getline() function reads a line of text and discards the newline character.

❑ To output data you can use the insertion operator with the cout object. Many of the states of the cout object are contained in a single long integer field, which contains format flags such as ios::left, ios:right, and ios::dec. The setf() function sets these flags; unsetf() turns them off. Other cout functions include width() and precision().

❑ A manipulator function is used to manipulate, or change, the state of the cout object. Any output manipulator function you create should take as an argument an instance of ostream as a reference. It should return the same input argument. This approach allows manipulators to be chained in calls to the cout insertion operator.

❑ Built-in manipulators include endl, newline, setprecision(), setw(), setiosflags(), and resetiosflags().

❑ Creating a manipulator that takes an argument involves writing two functions. The address of the stream and the argument itself must be passed to the manipulator function; this task is handled by the omanip() function, which is defined in the file iomanip.h.

❑ Usually, you store data on a disk (or other permanent storage device) in a data hierarchy in which fields are parts of data records that make up data files.

❑ To perform file output, you must instantiate your own member of the ofstream class. When you call an ofstream constructor, you can use a filename as an argument. The constructor will then open the file. Alternatively, you can declare an ofstream object and use the open() function later. A file closes when: the object goes out of scope; you explicitly call the object's destructor; or you use the close() function.

❑ To read a file from within a program, you can create an object that is an instantiation of the ifstream class. The ifstream class uses the get() and getline() functions to access file data. The value of the ifstream object is 0 when it reaches the end of file.

❑ The write() function allows you to write class objects to files. The write() function accepts two arguments: a character pointer to the address of the argument being written to the file, and the size of the object being written.

❑ You can use the read() function to read a data file into class objects. Each record is stored in an object, and each field of each object contains data of the appropriate type.

REVIEW QUESTIONS

1. cout and cin are _____.

   a. classes

   b. functions

   c. objects

   d. overloaded

2. A sequence of characters used to perform input and output operations is a
_____.

   a. string

   b. stream

   c. flow

   d. parameter

3. The C++ operator used for input with cin is called the _____ operator.

   a. insertion

   b. extraction

   c. inclusion

   d. withdrawal

4. The get() function _____.

   a. takes a reference to a character as an argument and returns a reference to the istream class

   b. takes a reference to a character as an argument and returns a reference to a character

   c. takes a reference to the istream class as an argument and returns a reference to the istream class

   d. takes a reference to the istream class as an argument and returns a reference to a character

5. Any character that terminates data entry is called the _____ character.

   a. delimiter

   b. dummy

   c. parameter

   d. Enter

6. The data entry function that leaves unused characters in the input stream is
_____.

   a. format()

   b. ignore()

   c. getline()

   d. get()

7. You use the ignore() function to _____.

   a. discard whitespace characters entered by the user

   b. skip any characters entered after the user presses the Enter key

   c. skip any characters left in the input stream after a call to get()

   d. read and discard characters when you don't care which character is used

10

8. The getline() function reads a line of text until it reaches _____.

    a. the length used as the second argument

    b. the character used as the third argument

    c. both of the above, that is, whichever occurs last

    d. either a or b, that is, whichever occurs first

9. The arguments such as ios::showpoint that determine the state of the cout object are called _____.

    a. state terminators

    b. delimiters

    c. format flags

    d. final parameters

10. You can combine the arguments to the setf() function using _____.

    a. the bitwise AND operator

    b. the logical AND operator

    c. the bitwise OR operator

    d. the logical OR operator

11. What is the output of the following?

```
cout<<"X";
cout.width(4);
cout<<11;
cout<<22<<"X";
```

    a. X1122X

    b. X 1122X

    c. X 11 22X

    d. X 11 22 X

12. What is the output of the following?

```
cout.precision(3);
cout<<9.8765;
```

    a. 9.9

    b. 9.87

    c. 9.88

    d. 9.876

13. A function that changes the state of the cout object is _____.

    a. a manipulator

    b. an ios operator

c. a format flag

d. an overloaded function

14. Which of the following is a manipulator?

   a. >>

   b. ++

   c. endl

   d. cout

15. Which of the following is NOT a manipulator?

   a. setw

   b. setprecision

   c. flush

   d. width

16. What is the output of the following? `cout<<setw(2)<<5678;`

   a. 56

   b. 78

   c. 57

   d. 5678

17. Which is the correct order from largest to smallest?

   a. field, record, file

   b. file, record, field

   c. record, field, file

   d. field, file, record

18. When you call an ofstream constructor and use a filename as an argument, then _____.

   a. the constructor creates the file

   b. the constructor opens the file

   c. the constructor creates and opens the file

   d. you receive an error message

19. When you create an object with the statement `ofstream oFile("a:\\data\\ document");`, then the object name is _____.

   a. ofstream

   b. oFile

   c. data

   d. document

10

20. If a file named someFile is opened successfully, which of the following is evaluated as true?

    a. someFile

    b. someFile.fail()

    c. !someFile.good()

    d. !someFile

EXERCISES

1. Write a program that allows you to use the keyboard to input the names of 40 friends. Display the names 15 at a time, pausing to let the user press a key before the list continues.

2. Write a program that allows you to enter 10 floating-point values into an array, and then displays each value to an accuracy of three positions.

3. Write a program that allows you to enter 10 floating-point values into an array. The program then should prompt you for the desired precision and then subsequently display each value to the correct precision.

4. Write a program that allows you to enter 10 item stock numbers, prices, and quantities in stock into three parallel arrays. Display all the data in report form, that is, aligned correctly in columns.

5. Create an Item class that contains fields for a stock number, price, and quantity in stock, and functions to set and display each field. Write a program that declares an array of 10 Items. Display all the data in report form, that is, aligned correctly in columns.

6. a. Write a program that lets you enter a five-line limerick and save it in a file.
   b. Write another program that reads the file and displays the limerick on the screen.

7. Complete the following tasks:

    a. Create a class named Book. Data members include the book's title, author, price, and number of pages. Member functions include data entry and display functions. Create an array of 10 book objects. Write data about all of the books to a disk file.

    b. Write a program that reads the Book file and displays Book data on the screen.

    c. Write a program that prompts the user for a minimum number of pages. Read the Book file. Display only Books that contain the prescribed number of pages or more.

8. Each of the following files in the Chapter10 folder contains syntax and/or logical errors. Determine the problem in each case, and fix the program.

    a. DEBUG10-1

    b. DEBUG10-2

    c. DEBUG10-3

    d. DEBUG10-4

CASE PROJECT

You have been developing a Fraction class for Teacher's Pet Software. Each fraction contains a numerator, denominator, a whole number portion, and a floating-point equivalent field. Each Fraction also has access to several functions you have developed. Complete the following three tasks:

a. Although adults are used to working with fractions that are written on a single line with a slash, for example 2/3, children are used to seeing fractions with the numerator above the denominator, and the two separated by a horizontal line, as in:

$$\frac{2}{3}$$

Create a manipulator named primaryForm that formats Fractions so they will appear in this manner. Write a main() program that instantiates several Fraction objects and displays them using the manipulator.

b. As a Fraction drill, write a program that asks a user to create five Fraction objects for which each Fraction value is less than 1/2. Create a disk file that contains the Fractions the student creates.

c. Write a program a teacher can use to review a student's progress. The program reads the Fraction objects created by the student and saved to disk. The program compares each Fraction to 1/2 and displays the Fraction answers that are incorrect using the primaryForm format. Also display a percent correct score for the five student answers.

10

CHAPTER

11

USING TEMPLATES

In this chapter, you will learn:

♦ About the usefulness of function templates

♦ About the structure of function templates

♦ How to overload function templates

♦ How to create function templates with multiple data types

♦ How to create function templates with multiple parameterized types

♦ How to override a function template's implicit type

♦ How to use multiple explicit types when you call a function template

♦ How to use function templates with classes

♦ About template classes and how to create them

♦ About container classes and how to create them

Object-oriented programming provides many benefits compared to traditional procedural programming. You have already used concepts such as inheritance and polymorphism that make a programmer's task easier. In this chapter, you learn to create function templates and container classes. Understanding these concepts also makes your future programming tasks easier by providing new techniques that promote code reusability.

UNDERSTANDING THE USEFULNESS OF FUNCTION TEMPLATES

The concepts involved in the use of variables are basic to all programming languages, and the use of variable names makes programming manageable. If a program should process 1000 employee records, you don't need 1000 different variable names to hold the salaries. When you can label a computer memory location with a variable name such as employeeSalary, the variable can contain any number of unique values, one at a time, during each execution of the program that declares it.

Similarly, creating functions within programs is a helpful feature because functions can operate on any values passed to them (as long as the values are of the correct type). A function that is prototyped as `void compute(int aNum);` can receive any integer value, whether it is a constant (such as 15) or a value stored in another integer variable in the calling function. You can call the compute() function dozens of times from various locations in a program, and it can receive dozens of different integer values. Each integer value, however, will have the name aNum within the compute() function.

In your C++ programs, you have created many functions with a variety of types in their argument lists. Not only have you used scalar types such as int, double, and char in function argument lists, but you also have passed programmer-created class objects, such as Students or InventoryItems, to functions. In each case, the C++ compiler determined the function's argument types when the function was created and compiled. Once the function was created, the argument types remained fixed.

You have learned that you can overload a function to accept different argument lists. Overloading involves writing two or more functions with the same name but different argument lists. It allows you to employ polymorphism, using a consistent message that acts appropriately with different objects. For example, you might want to create several functions named reverse(). A reverse() function might change the sign of a number if a numeric variable is passed to it, reverse the order of characters in a string if a string is passed to it, set a code for a collect call if a PhoneCall class object is passed to it, or issue a refund to a customer if a Customer class object is passed to it. Because "reverse" makes sense in each of these instances, and because such diverse tasks are needed for the four cases of reverse(), overloading is a useful and appropriate tool. When the function name is the same, but the program logic is different depending on the argument, the ability to overload functions is a valuable asset.

Sometimes the tasks required are not so diverse, however, and overloading requires a lot of unnecessary, tedious coding. When the programming logic is the same, writing multiple overloaded functions becomes wearisome. For example, assume you need a simple function named reverse() that reverses the sign of a number. Figure 11-1 shows three overloaded versions of the reverse() function. Each has a different argument list so the function can work with integers, doubles, or floats.

```
int reverse(int x)
  {
      return (-x);
  }
double reverse(double x)
  {
      return (-x);
  }
float reverse(float x)
  {
      return (-x);
  }
```

Figure 11-1   Three overloaded versions of reverse()

The three function bodies in Figure 11-1 are identical. Because these functions differ only in the argument and return types involved, it would be convenient to write just one function with a variable name standing in for the type, as in Figure 11-2. The code in Figure 11-2 shows a highlighted variableType where the type belongs. Although it demonstrates a good idea, this function doesn't quite work in C++. You need to create a template definition.

```
variableType reverse(variableType x)
  {
      return (-x);
  }
```

Figure 11-2   Proposed, but incomplete, variable type function

CREATING FUNCTION TEMPLATES

In C++, you can create functions that use variable types. These **function templates** serve as an outline, or template, for a group of functions that differ in the types of parameters they use. A group of functions that generates from the same template is often called a **family of functions**.

In a function template, at least one argument is **generic**, or **parameterized**, meaning that one argument can stand for any number of C++ types. If you write a function template for reverse(), for example, a user can invoke the function using any type for the parameter, as long as negating the value with a unary minus makes sense and is defined for that type. Thus, if an integer argument is passed to reverse(), it will return a negative integer, and if a double argument is passed, the function will return a negative double.

 C++ also allows you to define macros, which permit generic substitution. Macros are seldom recommended, however, because no type-checking is performed (unlike with a template). Object-oriented C++ programmers rarely use macros.

Programmers often use "function template" and "template function" interchangeably. Technically, you write a function template and it generates one or more template functions.

Before you code a function template, you must include a template definition with the following information:

- The keyword template
- A left angle bracket (<)
- A list of generic types, separated with commas if more than one type is needed
- A right angle bracket (>)

Each generic type in the list of generic types has two parts:

- The keyword class
- An identifier that represents the generic type

For example, the template definition for the reverse() function can be written as shown in Figure 11-3. The first line of code uses the template and class keywords to identify T as the generic class name. Although any legal C++ identifier can be used for the type in the function template, many programmers prefer T (for Template).

```
template <class T>
// T stands for any type — simple or programmer-defined
T reverse(T x)
   {
       return(-x);
   }
```

Figure 11-3 The reverse() function template

Using the keyword class in the template definition does not necessarily mean that T stands for a programmer-created class type, but it may. Despite the class keyword, T can represent a simple scalar type such as int. T is simply a placeholder for the type that will be used at each location in the function definition where T appears.

For clarity, many newer C++ compilers also allow you to replace class with *typename* in the template definition. This substitution makes sense because the template is creating a typename, whether it stands for a programmer-defined class type or a built-in type.

When you call the reverse() function template, as in the following lines of code, the compiler determines the type of the actual argument passed to the function (in this case, a double).

```
double amount = -9.86;
amount = reverse(amount);
```

The compiler substitutes the argument type (a double in the preceding example) for the generic type in the function template, creating a generated function that uses the appropriate type. The designation of the parameterized type is **implicit**; that is, it is determined not by naming the type, but by the compiler's ability to determine the argument type. The compiler generates code for as many different functions as it needs, depending on the function calls that are made. In this case, the generated function is:

```
double reverse(double x)
{
   return(-x);
}
```

 If you have trouble deciding where to use the generic type when you write a function template, first write and test the function using a built-in type such as int or double. When your function works correctly with the built-in type, replace the appropriate type names with the generic type.

You place function templates at the start of a program file, in the global area above the main() function. Alternatively, you can place them in a separate file, and include that file in your program with an #include statement. In either case, the definition of the template class (the statement that contains the word template and the angle brackets holding the class name) and the function template itself must reside in the same source file. When you create a function template, you can't place the template definition and the function code in separate files because the function can't be compiled into object format without knowing the types, and the function won't "know" that it needs to recognize the types without the template definition.

11

USING MULTIPLE ARGUMENTS TO FUNCTION TEMPLATES

Function templates can support multiple parameters. You might, for example, write a function that compares two arguments and returns the larger of the two. Figure 11-4 shows the function template named larger(), which accomplishes this task.

```
template<class T>
T larger(T x, T y)
  {
      T big;
      if (x>y)
            big = x;
      else
            big = y;
      return(big);
  }
```

Figure 11-4   The larger() function template

The larger() function in Figure 11-4 receives two parameters. Within this function, a temporary variable named big is declared. The big variable is the same type as the function arguments. If the first parameter, x, passed to larger() is larger than the second parameter, y, then x is assigned to big; otherwise y is assigned to big. Finally, the value of big is returned. The variables x, y, and big may be of any type for which the greater than operator (>) has been defined, but x, y, and big all must be of the same type because they are all defined to be the same type named T.

The larger() function takes two arguments of type T (whatever type T is). The compiler can create object code for larger(int,int) and larger(double,double), but it will not compile larger(int,double) or larger(double,int). For example, `larger(3,5);` returns 5, and `larger(12.3,5.7);` returns 12.3. However, `larger(3,5.7);` produces a compiler error. Wherever T occurs in the function template, T must stand for the same type.

In the next set of steps, you define a function that displays the smallest of any of three same-type arguments it receives.

1. Open a new file in your C++ editor, and enter the include statements you need for these steps.

   #include<iostream.h>
   #include<conio.h>
   #include<string.h>

2. Write the template definition to use the generic name T.

   template <class T>

3. Write the displaySmallest() function. This function takes three arguments of the same type and determines which value is smallest. The first of the three arguments is assigned to a variable named small. Notice that small is defined to be the same type as the arguments, whatever that type is. If the second argument is less than the small value, replace the small value. Then, if the third argument is less than the small value, again replace the small value. Finally, display the three arguments as well as the small value.

   ```
   void displaySmallest(T a, T b, T c)
   {
           T small = a;
           if(b < small)
                   small = b;
           if (c < small)
                   small = c;
           cout<<"The smallest of "<<a<<" "<<b<<
                   " "<<c<<" is "<<small<<endl;
   }
   ```

4. Write a main() program demonstrating that the function template works whether the arguments are integers, doubles, or characters. Declare three variables of each type, and pass them to the displaySmallest() function.

void main( )
```
{
        int oneInt = 5, twoInt = 7, threeInt = 4;
        double oneDouble = 6.6, twoDouble = 13.7,
                threeDouble = 123.5;
        char oneChar = 'D', twoChar = 'B', threeChar = 'G';
        displaySmallest(oneInt, twoInt, threeInt);
        displaySmallest(oneDouble, twoDouble, threeDouble);
        displaySmallest(oneChar, twoChar, threeChar);
        getch();
}
```

When you write programs, you probably use a function template such as displaySmallest( ) with only one type of argument in each application. The advantage of the function is not so much that you can use it with diverse types within a single program, but that you can use the function in a variety of programs, no matter what types that program uses for its data.

5. Save the file as **SmallestTemplate.cpp** on your Student Data Disk or in the Student Data folder on your hard drive. Compile and run the program. The output in Figure 11-5 shows that the smallest value appears, no matter what types of arguments you use when calling displaySmallest( ).

```
SmallestTemplate
The smallest of 5 7 4 is 4
The smallest of 6.6 13.7 123.5 is 6.6
The smallest of D B G is B
```

Figure 11-5   Output of SmallestTemplate program

OVERLOADING FUNCTION TEMPLATES

You overload functions when you create functions with the same name but with different argument lists. You can overload function templates, as long as each version of the function takes different arguments, allowing the compiler to distinguish between them. For example, you can create an invert( ) function template that swaps the values of its parameters if it receives two parameters, but reverses the sign if it receives only one parameter. Figure 11-6 shows the two versions of the function. The first version receives two reference arguments, locally called x and y. The variable named temp holds x; y is assigned to x, and temp is assigned to y; the result is that the values of x and y are switched. Because the function receives the addresses of the parameters, the values of the variables are switched in the calling program. The second version of invert( ) receives the address of a single argument. When you use this version, the sign is reversed for the parameter.

```
template<class T>
void invert(T &x, T &y)
  {
     T temp;
     temp = x;
     x = y;
     y = temp;
  }
template<class T>
void invert(T &x)
  {
     x = -x;
  }
```

Figure 11-6   The overloaded invert() function template

You must repeat the template definition **template<class T>** for each version of the function. Different versions of overloaded function templates do not need to use the same identifier to stand in for the variable type or class. For example, one version of the invert() function in Figure 11-6 could use T, while the other might use U. The class name is used locally in much the same way that variable names are used locally.

Figure 11-7 shows a main() function that uses the invert() function four times; Figure 11-8 shows the output of this program. When you call invert() with two integers or two doubles, it reverses their values. When you call invert() with a single argument, the function version that reverses the sign of the argument executes.

```
void main()
  {
     int oneInt = -10, twoInt = -20;
     double oneDouble = 11.11, twoDouble = 22.22;
     cout<<"Using invert() with "<<oneInt<<
        " and "<<twoInt;
     invert(oneInt, twoInt);
     cout<<"    results are: "<<oneInt<<" and "
        <<twoInt<<endl;
     cout<<"Using invert() with "<<oneDouble<<" and "
        <<twoDouble;
     invert(oneDouble, twoDouble);
     cout<<"    results are: "<<oneDouble<<" and "
        <<twoDouble<<endl;
     cout<<"Using invert() with "<<oneInt;
     invert(oneInt);
     cout<<"    results are: "<<oneInt<<endl;
     cout<<"Using invert() with "<<oneDouble;
     invert(oneDouble);
     cout<<"    results are: "<<oneDouble<<endl;
     getch();
  }
```

Figure 11-7   A main() function that uses the overloaded invert() function template

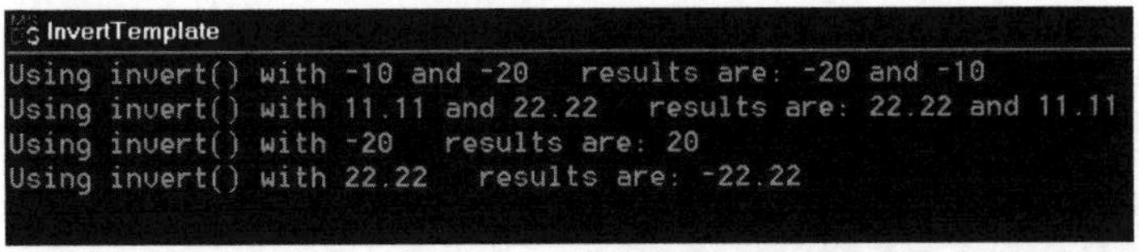

Figure 11-8 Output of InvertTemplate program

In the next set of steps, you overload the displaySmallest() function template to accept two as well as three arguments.

1. If it is not still open, open the **SmallestTemplate.cpp** program. Immediately save the file as **SmallestTemplate2.cpp**.

2. Place the insertion point after the closing curly brace of the displaySmallest() function template, and press **Enter** to start a new line.

3. Type the overloaded version of the function template that accepts two arguments instead of three. This version assigns the first passed parameter to a small variable of the same type. If the second passed parameter is smaller than the first, then the second parameter's value replaces the value of small. The two parameters and the smaller are shown.

```
template <class T>
void displaySmallest(T a, T b)
  {
    T small = a;
    if(b < a)
        small = b;
    cout<<"The smaller of "<<a<<" "<<b<<" is "<<small<<endl;
  }
```

4. Position the insertion point after the last call to displaySmallest that uses three parameters, (`displaySmallest(oneChar, twoChar, threeChar);`), and press **Enter** to start a new line.

5. Add three statements demonstrating that displaySmallest() works with two arguments.

```
displaySmallest(oneInt, twoInt);
displaySmallest(oneDouble, twoDouble);
displaySmallest(oneChar, twoChar);
```

6. Save the file again, then compile and run the program. The output appears in Figure 11-9, demonstrating that the function template has been successfully overloaded.

11

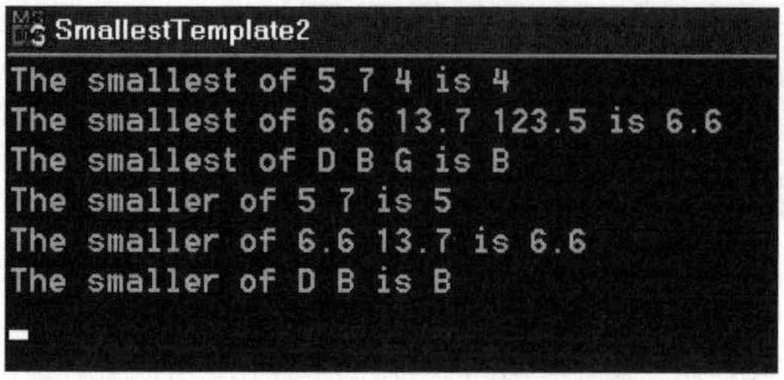

Figure 11-9   Output of SmallestTemplate2 program

USING MORE THAN ONE TYPE IN A FUNCTION TEMPLATE

Like other functions, function templates can use variables of multiple types. For example, a function might receive an integer and return a double, or another function might receive a character and a double and return an integer. In addition to containing a parameterized variable, function templates also can contain multiple arguments and internal variables that are not generic.

Suppose you want to create a function template that displays a value a given number of times. The value could be any type, but the number of times to repeat the value is an integer. It is perfectly legal to include some nonparameterized types in the function argument list, along with the parameterized ones. Figure 11-10 shows a repeatValue() function. The argument value, val, appears with a pound sign and a counter as many times as is indicated by the second parameter, times. The val argument type is generic; the times argument type is not.

When you run the program in Figure 11-10, the output looks like Figure 11-11—the integer displays three times, the double displays four times, the character displays five times, and the string displays six times.

```cpp
#include<iostream.h>
#include<conio.h>
template <class T>
void repeatValue(T val, int times)
  {
      int x;
      for(x= 0; x<times; ++x)
      cout<<"#"<<(x+1)<<" "<<val<<endl;
  }
void main()
  {
      int a = 7;
      double b = 4.5;
      char c = 'C';
      char name[10] = "Alice";
      repeatValue(a,3);
      repeatValue(b,4);
      repeatValue(c,5);
      repeatValue(name,6);
      getch();
  }
```

Figure 11-10 RepeatValue program

```
RepeatValue
#1  7
#2  7
#3  7
#1  4.5
#2  4.5
#3  4.5
#4  4.5
#1  C
#2  C
#3  C
#4  C
#5  C
#1  Alice
#2  Alice
#3  Alice
#4  Alice
#5  Alice
#6  Alice
```

Figure 11-11 Output of RepeatValue program

USING MORE THAN ONE PARAMETERIZED TYPE IN A FUNCTION TEMPLATE

To create a function template that employs multiple generic types, you simply use a unique type identifier for each type. For example, suppose you want to create a whichIsLarger() function that compares two values and prints a message indicating whether the first is larger than the second. The function works when any two parameters are passed, whether or not the two parameters are of the same type. The function template for whichIsLarger() is shown in Figure 11-12. Two generic types, T and U, are defined. The first parameterized type, T, can stand for any type. The second type, U, can stand for the same type, or any other type. Figure 11-12 includes a demonstration main() function that passes a variety of arguments to whichIsLarger(), and Figure 11-13 shows the results.

```
#include<iostream.h>
#include<conio.h>
template <class T, class U>
void whichIsLarger(T val1, U val2)
 {
     cout<<"First is "<<val1<<" Second is "<<val2;
     if (val1  > val2)
         cout<<" First is larger"<<endl;
     else
         cout<<" First is NOT larger"<<endl;
 }
void main()
 {
     int a = 68, b = 20;
     double c = 68.5;
     char d = 'D';
     whichIsLarger(a,b);
     whichIsLarger(a,c);
     whichIsLarger(a,d);
     whichIsLarger(c,d);
     getch();
 }
```

Figure 11-12 whichIsLarger() function and main() program

```
WhichIsLarger
First is 68 Second is 20 First is larger
First is 68 Second is 68.5 First is NOT larger
First is 68 Second is D First is NOT larger
First is 68.5 Second is D First is larger
```

Figure 11-13 Output of WhichIsLarger program

You can see from the program in Figure 11-12 and the output in Figure 11-13 that the function works correctly in recognizing the types of the two parameters, whether or not they are the same. The program successfully compares two integers, an integer and a double, an integer and a character, and a character and a double. The only requirement for the arguments to whichIsLarger() is that T and U are types for which the greater than comparison (>) is valid.

 The value of the character 'D' in ASCII is 68, so when 'D' is compared to the integer 68 and the double 68.5, D is not larger.

 The option of using multiple types in a function template is not available on some older C++ compilers.

EXPLICITLY SPECIFYING THE TYPE IN A FUNCTION TEMPLATE

When you call a function template, the arguments to the function dictate the types to be used. In other words, the compiler deduces the correct types to use within the function template, based on what types the programmer uses in the function call; the determination of the types is implicit. To override a deduced type, when you call a function template you can explicitly code a type within angle brackets immediately following the function name in the function call. You **explicitly** name a type by using the type name. For example, the function call `someFunction<char>(someArgument);` specifies that someFunction's parameterized type will be char, no matter what type someArgument is.

Explicitly specifying a type is particularly useful when at least one of the types you need to parameterize or generate within the function is not an argument to the function. The compiler can deduce function template types only by using the values passed to the function. If the return type of a function must vary independently from the arguments, the compiler cannot deduce this requirement. In this case, you must specify the type within angle brackets.

For example, Figure 11-14 shows a function template named doubleVal(), which accepts an argument, multiplies it by two, and returns it. The return value is the same type as the original argument.

```
template <class T>
T doubleVal(T val)
  {
    val *= 2;
    return(val);
  }
```

Figure 11-14   The doubleVal() function template

The main() program in Figure 11-15 calls the function template three times, using an integer, a double, and a double converted to an integer, respectively. When you examine the output in Figure 11-16, you can see that when the integer 5 is doubled, the result is integer 10, and when the double 6.7 is doubled, the result is 13.4. In the highlighted statement, when the double, 6.7, is passed to the function and the function parameter type is explicitly converted to int, then 6.7 is received by the function as 6, and the result is 12 instead of 13.4.

```
void main()
 {
     int a = 5;
     double b = 6.7;
     cout<<"Using an integer "<<a<<" double is "
         <<doubleVal(a)<<endl;
     cout<<"Using a double "<<b<<" double is "
         <<doubleVal(b)<<endl;
     cout<<"Using a double "<<b<<
         " converted to an int, double is "
         <<doubleVal<int>(b)<<endl;
     getch();
 }
```

Figure 11-15   Program that uses an explicit type for a function's parameterized type

```
DoubleVal
Using an integer 5 double is 10
Using a double 6.7 double is 13.4
Using a double 6.7 converted to an int, double is 12
```

Figure 11-16   Output of DoubleVal program

 You can code empty angle brackets after the function name in a function call to indicate the types should be deduced and not overridden. Using the empty brackets provides clear documentation to anyone reading the program that you intend the type to be deduced. However, using no angle brackets at all achieves the same result.

Using Multiple Explicit Types in a Function Template

You can use multiple explicit types when you call a template function. If you want the return value of a template function sometimes to be the same type as the argument, and sometimes to be a different type, write the function template with two parameterized types. When you use the template function, the two parameterized types, for example T and U, both can stand for the same type, or they can stand for different types. Additionally, you can exercise the option to explicitly name one or both types. For example, Figure 11-17 shows a tripleVal() function that uses two generic types, T and U. The first type, T, must be explicitly coded. The second type, U, can be implicitly deduced from the function argument, or explicitly coded. The main() program in Figure 11-17 uses the function in several ways:

- Explicitly codes int for the T type and passes an integer to implicitly assign the U type

- Explicitly codes int for the T type and passes a double to implicitly assign the U type

- Explicitly codes int for the T type and explicitly codes a double for the U type

- Explicitly codes int for both T and U

Figure 11-18 shows the output of the program in Figure 11-17. The explanation of the output is as follows:

- When tripleVal() receives the integer 22 as an argument, triples it, and returns the integer result, the output is 66.

- When tripleVal() receives the double 8.88 as an argument, triples it to 26.64, stores the result in an integer, and returns the integer result, the output is the truncated result, 26. This is true whether tripleVal() receives 8.88 as a double implicitly or explicitly.

- When 8.88 is explicitly received as an integer, it receives an 8. The output tripled value is 24.

11

```
#include<iostream.h>
#include<conio.h>
template <class T, class U>
T tripleVal(U val)
  {
      T temp = val * 3;
      return(temp);
  }
void main()
  {
      int a = 22;
      double d = 8.88;
      cout<<"Explicit int; int argument: "
          <<tripleVal<int>(a)<<endl;
      cout<<"Explicit int; double argument: "
          <<tripleVal<int>(d)<<endl;
      cout<<"Explicit int, double; double argument: "
          <<tripleVal<int,double>(d)<<endl;
      cout<<"Explicit int, int, double argument: "
          <<tripleVal<int,int>(d)<<endl;
      getch();
  }
```

Figure 11-17   The tripleVal() function and program

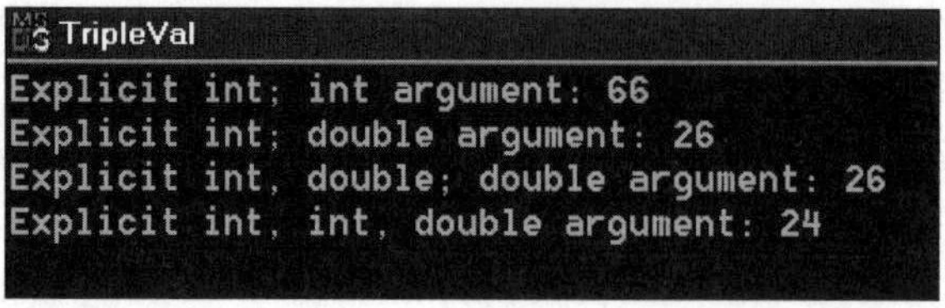

```
⌐⌐ TripleVal
Explicit int; int argument: 66
Explicit int; double argument: 26
Explicit int, double; double argument: 26
Explicit int, int, double argument: 24
```

Figure 11-18   Output of tripleVal program

When you explicitly code multiple types in a template function call, as in tripleVal<int,double>(d), the order is important. The types are assigned in the same order as the generic classes are defined.

USING FUNCTION TEMPLATES WITH CLASS OBJECTS

When programming in an object-oriented environment, you naturally want your function templates to work with class objects as well as with scalar variables. The good news is that function templates work just as well with classes as they do with simple data types. Your only additional responsibility is to ensure that any operations used within the function template have been defined for the class objects passed to the function templates.

As an example, recall the reverse() function template from Figure 11-3 and repeated here as Figure 11-19 for your convenience.

```
template <class T>
T reverse(T x)
  {
      return(-x);
  }
```

Figure 11-19   The reverse() function template

Suppose you develop a PhoneCall class. Its data members include an integer to hold the length of the call in minutes, and a character to hold a code that indicates how the phone call is billed. For example, a phone company might use different codes for a direct-dial call, an operator-assisted call, and a collect call. When you use the reverse() function with a PhoneCall object, the function should signal that you are "reversing" the billing, or setting the billing code to a 'C' for "Collect."

The reverse() function template can "reverse" the value of an integer or double by using the unary minus sign, because you interpret "reverse" to mean "reverse the sign" when you work with numbers. For the reverse() function to work with a PhoneCall object, the unary minus sign must be overloaded to mean "store a 'C' in the billing code field." You must ensure that the unary minus has meaning with a PhoneCall object. That is, when a PhoneCall object is passed to reverse() and becomes known as x, -x must have some meaning.

Figure 11-20 shows a PhoneCall class containing private data members that store the phone number, length of call, and code. The constructor and showCall() functions are similar to many functions with which you have previously worked. The minus sign is overloaded using the operator-() function. The unary minus operator function takes no argument. It sets the code to 'C' for "Collect" and returns a copy of the object that called it.

The binary minus operator used for subtraction would take a PhoneCall argument.

```cpp
class PhoneCall
   {
      private:
            char number[15];
            int minutes;
            char callCode;
      public:
            PhoneCall(char num[], int min, char code);
            void showCall();
            PhoneCall operator-();
   };
PhoneCall::PhoneCall(char num[], int min, char code)
   {
      strcpy(number,num);
      minutes = min;
      callCode = code;
   }
void PhoneCall::showCall()
   {
      cout<<"Call to "<<number<<" for "<<minutes<<
            " minutes. Code "<<callCode<<endl;
   }
PhoneCall PhoneCall::operator-()
   {
      callCode = 'C';
      return(*this);
   }
```

Figure 11-20   The PhoneCall class

The program in Figure 11-21 declares a PhoneCall object and provides initial values for its fields. When you first display the call, as shown in the output in Figure 11-22, the billing code contains the initial value, 'D'. After the PhoneCall is reversed, that is, when its value is replaced with the negative of itself, the billing code becomes 'C'.

```
void main()
 {
     PhoneCall aCall("(715) 234-7643",6,'D');
     aCall.showCall();
     aCall = reverse(aCall);
     aCall.showCall();
     getch();
 }
```

Figure 11-21   Program that declares a PhoneCall object and uses the unary minus

```
 ⌂ PhoneCall
Call to (715) 234-7643 for 6 minutes. Code D
Call to (715) 234-7643 for 6 minutes. Code C
■
```

Figure 11-22   Output of PhoneCall program

The execution of the program shown in Figure 11-22 demonstrates that the reverse() function template can operate correctly on a class object as well as on any simple data type, as long as all operations within the function template are defined for the class objects passed to it. Whether the unary minus is overloaded in various classes for such diverse purposes as to issue a credit on a Customer bill, fire an Employee, or reformat a Disk, the function template class that uses the minus can handle each function call successfully.

In the next set of steps, you create an Inventory class. The class includes an overloaded insertion operator and an overloaded less than operator. With these two operators, Inventory class objects can use the displaySmallest() function templates you created earlier in this chapter.

1. If it is not still open, open the **SmallestTemplate2.cpp** program. Immediately save it as **SmallestTemplate3.cpp**.

2. Delete the main() function, leaving the two function templates you have created—one that finds the smallest of three objects, and one that finds the smaller of two objects.

3. Create the definition for an Inventory class. The class contains fields for stock number and number sold. Functions include a constructor, a member function that is an overloaded < operator, and a friend function that is an overloaded << operator.

class Inventory
{
    friend ostream& operator<<(ostream& out,
        const Inventory &item);
    private:
        int stockNum;
        int numSold;
    public:
        Inventory(const int stknum, const int sold);
        int operator<(const Inventory& item);
};

You can define the operator<() function as type bool instead of int if your compiler supports it. Then use the values true and false instead of 1 and 0 within the function implementation.

4. The Inventory class constructor assigns its arguments to the appropriate fields.

```
Inventory::Inventory(const int stknum, const int sold)
{
        stockNum = stknum;
        numSold = sold;
}
```

5. The insertion operator is overloaded to display an Inventory object's data.

```
ostream& operator<<(ostream &out, const Inventory &item)
{
        out<<"Item #"<<item.stockNum<<" Quantity; "
            <<item.numSold<<endl;
        return(out);
}
```

6. The less than operator takes an Inventory argument and sets a flag variable to 0, indicating false. If the numSold field of the operand to the left of < (the this object) is less than the numSold field of the operand to the right of the < (the passed argument), then the flag variable is set to 1, indicating true. The flag is returned to the calling function.

```
int Inventory::operator<(const Inventory& item)
{
    int flag = 0;
    if(numSold < item.numSold)
        flag = 1;
    return(flag);
}
```

7. Write a main() program in which you declare three Inventory objects. Call displaySmallest() several times, using two or three arguments each time.

```
void main()
{
        Inventory item1(111, 100);
        Inventory item2(222, 200);
        Inventory item3(333, 300);
        displaySmallest(item1, item2);
        displaySmallest(item2, item3);
        displaySmallest(item3, item1);
        displaySmallest(item1, item2, item3);
        getch();
}
```

11

8. Save the program, then compile and run it. The output looks like Figure 11-23. Each call to the function displays the values of the objects involved, and correctly determines the smallest when smallest means lowest number sold. The displaySmallest() function that worked correctly with numbers and characters also works correctly with Inventory objects because each operator used in displaySmallest(), the insertion operator and the less than operator, has been defined for the Inventory class.

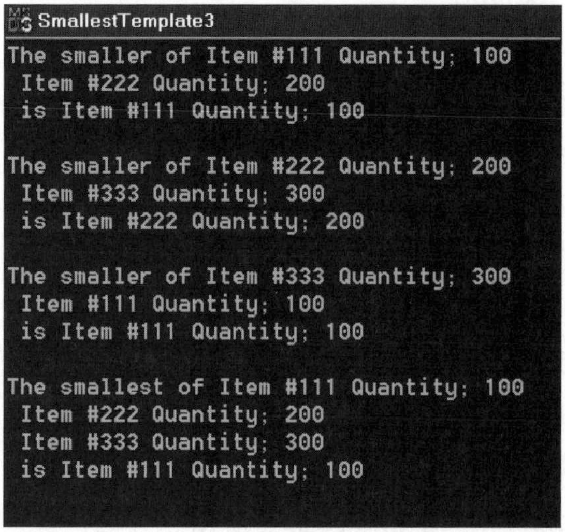

```
SmallestTemplate3
The smaller of Item #111 Quantity; 100
 Item #222 Quantity; 200
 is Item #111 Quantity; 100

The smaller of Item #222 Quantity; 200
 Item #333 Quantity; 300
 is Item #222 Quantity; 200

The smaller of Item #333 Quantity; 300
 Item #111 Quantity; 100
 is Item #111 Quantity; 100

The smallest of Item #111 Quantity; 100
 Item #222 Quantity; 200
 Item #333 Quantity; 300
 is Item #111 Quantity; 100
```

Figure 11-23   Output of SmallestTemplate3 program

USING TEMPLATE CLASSES

Function templates allow you to create generic functions that have the same bodies but can take different data types as parameters. Likewise, in some situations classes are similar and you want to perform very similar operations with them. If you need to create several similar classes, you might consider developing a **template class**, a class in which at least one type is generic or parameterized. The template class provides the outline for a family of similar classes.

To create a template class, you begin with the template definition, just as you do with a function template. Then you write the class definition using the generic type or types in each instance for which a substitution should take place.

For example, consider a very simple Number class that has one data member which can hold any number, a constructor that takes an argument, and a displayNumber() function. The template class definition is shown in Figure 11-24.

```
template<class T>
class Number
  {
      private:
            T theNumber;
      public:
            Number(T n);
      void displayNumber();
  };
// function implementations go here
// - more about this in the next section
```

Figure 11-24   The Number class definition

The class in Figure 11-24 is named Number. Its private data member, theNumber, may be of any type; in other words, theNumber is parameterized. If T stands for double, that is, if theNumber becomes a double, then the Number() constructor takes a double argument. If T stands for int, then theNumber is an int and Number() takes an integer.

Within a program, you can instantiate objects that possess the class template type. You add the desired type to the current class instantiation by placing the type's name between angle brackets following the generic class name. For example, if you want an object named myValue to be of type Number, and you want myValue to hold an integer with value 25 (that is, you want to pass 25 to the constructor), your declaration is:

```
Number<int> myValue(25);
```

To use the Number class member displayNumber() function with the myValue object, you add the dot operator, just as you would with an instantiation of any other class:

```
myValue.displayNumber();
```

If you instantiate another Number object with a double, the display() function is called in exactly the same way:

```
Number<double> yourValue(3.46);
yourValue.displayNumber();
```

An object of type Number might "really" be an integer, double, or any other type behind the scenes. The advantage of using a class template to work with these values lies in your ability to use the Number class functions with data of any type. When you need to write similar functions to display or use data of several different types, it makes sense to create a class template.

11

CREATING A COMPLETE CLASS TEMPLATE

Figure 11-25 shows the class definition for the Number class, along with the implementation of the Number class functions. The code **template<classT>** must appear immediately before the class definition, the constructor function implementation, and the member function displayNumber() implementation. Each of the three must recognize T and understand that it represents a type.

The header for the constructor in Figure 11-25 indicates that the Number constructor belongs to the Number<T> class (whatever T turns out to be), and that its name is Number(). Thus, like all other constructors, the Number constructor shares its class name. This constructor takes an argument of type T, although you also could write a constructor that takes no arguments or other types of arguments. The constructor body simply sets the value of Number's data member, theNumber, to the value of the argument n.

```
template<class T>
class Number
  {
     private:
       T theNumber;
     public:
       Number(T n);
       void displayNumber(void);
  };
template<class T>
Number<T>::Number(T n)
  {
     theNumber = n;
  }
template<class T>
void Number<T>::displayNumber(void)
  {
     cout<<"Number #";
     cout<<theNumber<<endl;
  }
```

Figure 11-25 The Number class

You can see in Figure 11-25 that the definition template<class T> also is required before the definition of the displayNumber() function, so as to identify the T in the class name, Number<T>. The displayNumber() function always displays "Number #" just before the value of theNumber. Even though T is not used within the body of this function, Number<T> is required in the function header to identify the function as a member of the Number<T> class. Remember that for displayNumber() to work correctly, the insertion operator must be defined for the class or type represented by T.

Figure 11-26 contains a main() function that declares three Number objects constructed using integer, double, and character arguments, respectively. Figure 11-27 shows that the displayNumber() function can handle each argument and display it in the Number class format.

```
void main()
  {
      Number<int> anInt(25);
      Number<double> aDouble(3.46);
      Number<char> aChar('K');
      anInt.displayNumber();
      aDouble.displayNumber();
      aChar.displayNumber();
      getch();
  }
```

Figure 11-26   A main() program instantiating three Numbers

Figure 11-27   Output of Number program

The Number class has been created here to help you understand how to create and use class templates. However, it is a stretch to imagine that a business would create the Number class as it stands. If you simply want to construct and print integers, doubles, and characters (and even your own class objects) preceded by "Number #", a generic class is unnecessary, and it is too much trouble to create it. After all, each operation (construction and printing) is already defined for these types, and it is simple to display "Number #" as part of a program. In this instance, creating the class template merely adds a layer of complexity to an otherwise simple task.

However, if extensive print formatting was applied prior to displaying any object, then creating a class template might be worth the effort. Imagine, for example, that a company name and address, followed by a logo, always need to be printed before data, whether the data belongs to the class used for Employees, Customers, or Suppliers. In such a case, it might make sense to create a template class that handles the formatted printing for each of the different type objects. Programmers commonly use template classes for even more generic applications, such as linked lists, stacks, and queues. Such generic classes are called container classes.

11

USING CONTAINER CLASSES

Many C++ compilers come with class libraries called container classes. A **container class** is a template class that has been written to perform common class tasks; the purpose of container classes is to manage groups of other classes. Of course, you always can write your own container classes, but the creators of C++ have already done much of the work for you.

In Java and Smalltalk, all objects derive from the same container class, called Object. This consistently ensures that every object has at least some standard functionality.

A common programming task that is used in a variety of applications is the construction of a linked list. A **linked list** is a chain of objects, each of which consists of at least two parts—the usual components of the object itself and a pointer to another object.

For example, a school might create a Student object with data fields for first name, last name, and grade point average. The school also might want to place Student objects in a linked list based on their registration dates. The first Student in the list would represent the first student to register. The first link in the student linked list consists of two parts: the first Student and a pointer to another Student. When a second student registers, additional memory is allocated to accommodate this Student. The second Student object's memory address is stored in the pointer that belongs to the first student. The second link in the linked list chain holds the second Student object and a pointer to the address of a third student, and so on. The last student's pointer typically holds a dummy value, such as a null character, to indicate the end of the list.

The diagram in Figure 11-28 illustrates a linked list of Students. The first student, Ewa Shannon, is stored at memory address 2000. Besides her Student data, the linked list object holds a pointer to address 2500, where George Martin's Student data is stored. The last Student link, Don Anderson, holds NULL in the linking pointer, because there is no one else in the list.

The school that uses the linked list to link Students in order of registration might want to link Employee objects by Social Security number, InventorySupply objects by item number, and Alumnus objects by a combination of major, year of graduation, and student ID number. Although each of the diverse objects Student, Employee, and Alumnus has a different size, different data members, and different functions, the procedures involved in creating the linked lists are basically the same.

Many linked lists provide more than a pointer to the next logical object. For example, they might contain another pointer to the previous object, enabling the list to be traversed backward as well as forward. Providing this extra link adds complexity to the programming task, but adds functionality to the linked list.

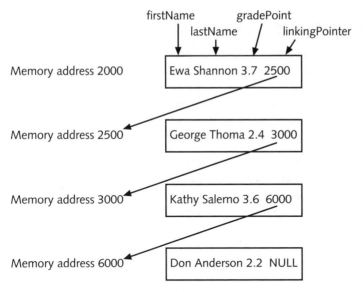

firstName   gradePoint
           lastName   linkingPointer

Memory address 2000   Ewa Shannon 3.7 2500

Memory address 2500   George Thoma 2.4 3000

Memory address 3000   Kathy Salerno 3.6 6000

Memory address 6000   Don Anderson 2.2 NULL

Figure 11-28   A Student linked list

No matter what types of objects are linked, procedures must be developed to establish links between objects and to insert new member objects into appropriate spots within the linked list. The procedures include assigning the correct linking pointer values to the new list members. Other common procedures are deleting a member from the list, reordering a list, and retrieving and displaying the objects from a list. You also might want functions that count the number of items in a list or functions that search through a list for a certain object and pinpoint its position. Each of these functions may prove useful in a linked list, regardless of what type of object is being linked.

A generic class that holds an object and a link, and holds all linked list functions that handle the list's chores, is a useful tool when working with lists, whether they link students, employees, supplies, or alumni. Because a generic class of this type is so useful, the developers of C++ have already created such a container class. Its name is List, and it contains functions such as add(), detach(), and getItems(). The List container class is a template class because the programmers who designed your compiler could not have predicted the exact characteristics of all classes you might create. Even if they could, it would be pointless to develop an Employee linked list class, a Student linked List class, and an InventorySupply linked list class when the "linking" aspects are identical in each case. If you use the List container class, you never have to write your own linked list class, and you can use this tool with any class you create.

Different compilers include different built-in container classes. Indeed, some compilers may not offer any. The more container classes your compiler supplies, the less often you will need to write your own template classes. Nevertheless, it is still beneficial to understand how it's done.

CREATING AN ARRAY TEMPLATE CLASS

When you create an array, you create a list of same-type objects at adjacent memory locations. You perform many standard operations on array data, no matter what type is involved. For example, whether you are working with integers, characters, or Employees, you often want to perform generic tasks such as storing the data into array locations, printing the array, and printing only the first element of the array. Class templates offer the perfect way to create generic functions that accomplish these tasks for any type of array.

You can create a generic Array class with two private data members: a pointer to the beginning of the array, and an integer representing the size of the array. The public functions include a constructor and member functions that show every element in the Array, and show the first Array element only. Figure 11-29 contains the Array class definition.

```
template<class T>
class Array
  {
      private:
          T *data;     // T is the type of the array
          int size;
      public:
          Array(T *d, int s);
          void showList();
          void showFirst();
  };
template<class T>
Array<T>::Array(T *d, int s)
  {
      data = d;
      size = s;
  }
template<class T>
void Array<T>::showList()
  {
      cout<<"Entire list:"<<endl;
      for(int x = 0; x< size; ++x)
          cout<<data[x]<<endl;
      cout<<"--------------------"<<endl;
  }
template<class T>
void Array<T>::showFirst()
  {
      cout<<"First element is ";
      cout<<data[0]<<endl;
  }
```

Figure 11-29   The Array class

The Array class constructor assigns the argument's array address to the Array class array address, and assigns the argument's array size to the Array class member size. The showList() function displays each element of the Array, from element 0 up through one less than size. The last cout statement in the showList() function serves as a separator that shows where the list ends. This statement is part of the function for cosmetic reasons—when you display several lists in a row, the dashed line makes it easy to see where one list ends and another begins.

 Remember that the subscript for any array can hold a value of 0 through one less than the array's size. For example, a 10-element array uses subscripts 0 through 9.

The showFirst() function is even simpler than the showList() function—it simply shows element 0 of the Array.

When you create an Array object, you must supply the beginning address of the array and the size of the array. Assuming you have declared an array such as `int nums[4];`, then you can call the constructor for an arrayOfIntegers with the statement `Array<int> arrayOfIntegers(nums,4);`. The two arguments to the Array object are the name of the nums array and the number of elements it contains.

Instead of hard-coding the size of the array, with a constant such as 4, you can calculate the array size. If you divide the size of an array in bytes by the size of one element of the array in bytes, the result is the number of elements in the array. For example, the following statement serves to calculate the arraySize by dividing the size of nums (the array) by nums[0] (one element of the array).

```
int arraySize = sizeof(nums)/sizeof(nums[0]);
```

You can use the calculated value arraySize in the declaration of arrayOfIntegers, as in the following.

```
Array<int> arrayOfIntegers(nums,arraySize);
```

Figure 11-30 shows a Book class, and Figure 11-31 shows a Client class. Neither contains anything unusual; you have created many similar classes. Each contains some private data, a function that sets values, and an overloaded insertion operator.

11

```
class Book
  {
      friend ostream& operator<<(ostream& out, const Book &aBook);
      private:
          char title[30];
          double price;
      public:
          void setBook(char bookTitle[], double pr);
  };
void Book::setBook(char bookTitle[], double pr)
  {
      strcpy(title,bookTitle);
      price = pr;
  }
ostream& operator<<(ostream& out, const Book &aBook)
  {
      out<<aBook.title<<" sells for $"<<aBook.price;
      return(out);
  }
```

Figure 11-30   The Book class

```
class Client
  {
      friend ostream& operator<<(ostream& out, const Client
       &aClient);
      private:
          char name[15];
          double balDue;
      public:
          void setClient(char Clientname[], double pr);
  };
void Client::setClient(char Clientname[], double pr)
  {
      strcpy(name,Clientname);
      balDue = pr;
  }
ostream& operator<<(ostream& out, const Client &aClient)
  {
      out<<aClient.name<<" owes   $"<<aClient.balDue;
      return(out);
  }
```

Figure 11-31   The Client class

Figure 11-32 shows a main() function that contains several types of arrays. The program in Figure 11-32 is divided into four parts. First, four arrays are created:

- An array named someInts is initialized with three integers.
- An array named someDoubles is initialized with four doubles.

- A two-element Book array uses the Book class shown in Figure 11-30. The two Books receive values through the setBook() function.

- A four-element Clients array uses the Client class shown in Figure 11-31. The Clients receive values through the setClient() function.

Second, a size is calculated for each type of array, and then an Array container object is created using each of the four array types and a correct size value. Third, the Array container class function showList() is called with each Array type. Finally, the Array function showFirst() is called with each Array type. Figure 11-33 shows the output.

```
void main()
{
    int arraySize;
// Declare and assign values to four kinds of arrays
    int someInts[] = {12,34,55};
    double someDoubles[] = {11.11, 23.44, 44.55, 123.66};
    Book someBooks[2];
    someBooks[0].setBook("The Shining",12.99);
    someBooks[1].setBook("Carrie",6.89);
    Client someClients[4];
    someClients[0].setClient("Harris",123.55);
    someClients[1].setClient("Baker",2155.77);
    someClients[2].setClient("Howard",33.88);
    someClients[3].setClient("Silvers",5123.99);
// Calculate size and create Array objects
    arraySize = sizeof(someInts)/sizeof(someInts[0]);
    Array<int> arrayOfIntegers(someInts,arraySize);
    arraySize = sizeof(someDoubles)/sizeof(someDoubles[0]);
    Array<double> arrayOfDoubles(someDoubles,arraySize);
    arraySize = sizeof(someBooks)/sizeof(someBooks[0]);
    Array<Book> arrayOfBooks(someBooks,arraySize);
    arraySize = sizeof(someClients)/sizeof(someClients[0]);
    Array<Client> arrayOfClients(someClients,arraySize);
// Use showList() with each Array
    arrayOfIntegers.showList();
    arrayOfDoubles.showList();
    arrayOfBooks.showList();
    arrayOfClients.showList();
// Use showFirst() with each Array
    arrayOfIntegers.showFirst();
    arrayOfDoubles.showFirst();
    arrayOfBooks.showFirst();
    arrayOfClients.showFirst();
    getch();
}
```

11

Figure 11-32   Program using the Array container class

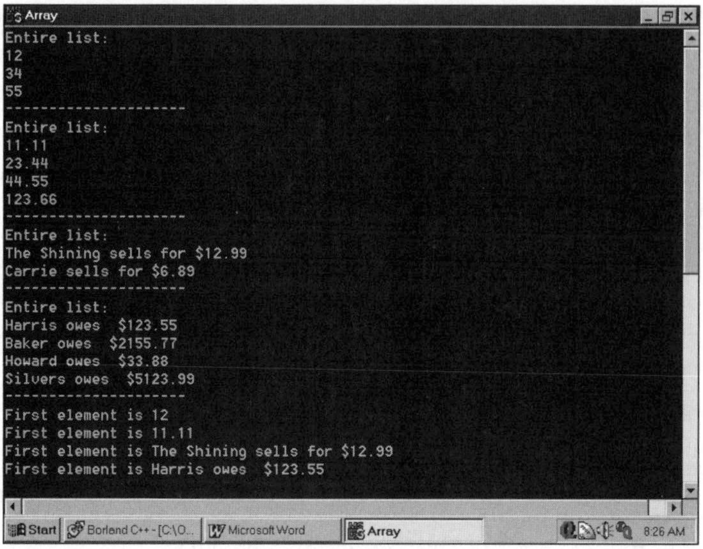

Figure 11-33 Output of Array program

You can see from Figure 11-33 that when you use the showList() function, each list appears correctly no matter how many elements the array contains. With both showList() and showFirst(), each element of each array appears in the proper format, integers and doubles appear in the usual way that they appear within C++, and Books and Clients appear as their overloaded insertion operators were programmed.

If the Array class is carefully constructed, and new member functions are added as needed by various applications, you can handle arrays that are not type-specific. In future programs, whether you create arrays of people, equipment, college courses, or any other items, you will have tried-and-true methods for working with the arrays. Creating useful container class templates takes time, but the subsequent program development process goes more smoothly and is less error-prone.

CHAPTER SUMMARY

- When the logic of several functions is similar, writing the code to overload the functions becomes tedious.

- A function template is a function that serves as an outline, or template, for a group of functions that differ in the types of parameters they use. In a function template, at least one argument is generic, or parameterized. The compiler substitutes an argument type for the generic type in the function template, creating a generated function that uses the appropriate type.

❏ You can overload function templates, as long as each version of the function takes different arguments, allowing the compiler to distinguish between them.

❏ In addition to a parameterized variable, function templates can contain multiple arguments and internal variables that are not generic.

❏ Function templates can have multiple parameterized types; you use a unique type identifier for each type.

❏ When you call a function template, the compiler implicitly deduces the correct types to use within the function template. You can override a deduced type by explicitly coding a type within angle brackets immediately following the function name in the function call.

❏ You can use multiple explicit types when you call a function template.

❏ Function templates work just as well with classes as they do with simple data types—as long as you define all operations for the classes you use within the function template.

❏ A template class is a class in which at least one type is generic or parameterized. It provides the outline for a family of similar classes.

❏ When you create a class template, you use the template definition prior to the class and prior to each function you write.

❏ A container class is a template class that has been written to perform common class tasks; the purpose of container classes is to manage groups of other classes. A linked list is a chain of objects, each of which has at least two parts—the usual components of the object itself, and a pointer to another object. The List container class is an example of a template class C++ developers created for you.

❏ You create container class templates to speed up the development process for applications that require similar tasks.

11

REVIEW QUESTIONS

1. Writing two or more functions with the same name, but with different argument lists is known as _____.

   a. inheritance

   b. overloading

   c. orienting

   d. creating a template

2. Creating a function template is most appropriate when _____.

a. you want a function to take multiple arguments

b. you are writing several functions that take different argument types, but use the same logic

c. you need several functions with the same name, but the logic is different depending on the arguments

d. you want only one version of a function to exist so as to avoid confusion

3. A group of functions that generates from the same template is often called _____.

a. a family of functions

b. a class

c. a polymorphic template

d. an assembly

4. Another term for parameterized is _____.

a. polymorphic

b. template

c. object-oriented

d. generic

5. In the template definition `template<class D>`, D stands for _____.

a. double

b. any programmer-created class

c. any built-in type

d. any class or type

6. The compiler determines the parameterized type in a function template _____.

a. implicitly

b. explicitly

c. duplicitly

d. polymorphically

7. Function templates can receive _____.

a. only one parameter

b. one or two parameters

c. any number of parameters

d. no parameters

8. Function templates _____.

    a. are overloaded automatically

    b. can be overloaded

    c. are never overloaded

    d. can be overloaded, but seldom are in common programming practice

9. A function template argument list can contain _____.

    a. only parameterized types

    b. only nonparameterized types

    c. either parameterized or nonparameterized types, but not both in the same argument list

    d. any combination of parameterized and nonparameterized types

10. You explicitly name a type in a function template call _____.

    a. always

    b. never

    c. to override an implicit type

    d. to overload the function

11. When a function template has two parameterized types, one as the return value, and one as an argument, then _____.

    a. the first type must be explicitly coded

    b. the first type must not be explicitly coded

    c. the second type must be explicitly coded

    d. the second type must not be explicitly coded

12. When you use a class object with a function template, you must _____.

    a. supply a constructor for the class

    b. not use scalar types with the function

    c. define any operation used within the function template

    d. overload the function template

13. A template class is a class in which _____.

    a. at least one type is parameterized

    b. at least one field is not generic

    c. no fields are generic

    d. all types are parameterized

11

14. Which of the following is a template definition?

    a. template<T>

    b. template<class T>

    c. template class <T>

    d. <template class T>

15. To create an Order template class object named backOrder and assign 0 as the argument to the constructor, the proper syntax is _____.

    a. Order backOrder = 0;

    b. Order<int> backOrder = 0;

    c. Order<int> backOrder(0);

    d. Order backOrder<int>(0);

16. When you create a template class, _____.

    a. each of its functions must be overloaded

    b. its functions can receive only a single argument

    c. the list of types the template can use to replace the generic type must be specified in the class header

    d. none of the above

17. A template class that has been written to perform common class tasks, such as linking lists or sorting, is a(n) _____ class.

    a. container

    b. bottle

    c. overloaded

    d. parameter

18. A linked list is usually made up of _____.

    a. two or more objects

    b. an object and a pointer

    c. an object and a function

    d. an object, a function, and a pointer

19. A container class named Sort can sort a list of any type of object in ascending order. Therefore, which of the following must be true?

    a. The Sort class must use the > operator.

    b. Objects passed to the Sort class must have an overloaded > operator.

    c. Objects passed to the Sort class must not have overloaded any operator.

    d. None of the above

20. The advantage to creating container classes is that _____.

    a. you don't have to instantiate objects within a main() program

    b. development time for future classes is reduced

    c. container class code is typically more concise than is code for other classes

    d. unlike other class files, container class files can be included in programs using the #include statement

EXERCISES

1. Create a function template named circleArea(). The function receives an argument representing the radius of a circle, and returns a double representing the circle's area. (The area is computed as 3.14 multiplied by the radius squared.) Write a main() program that demonstrates that the function works correctly with either an integer or a double argument.

2. Create a function template to display a value that is both preceded and followed by 10 asterisks on a line. Write a main() program that tests the function with character, integer, double, and string arguments.

3. Complete the following tasks:

    a. Create a Homework class with fields for the class name, the assignment (for example, "read chapter 11"), and the number of minutes predicted it will take to complete the assignment. Include functions to set the values for the Homework fields, to provide output, and to overload the + operator to add Homework objects' minutes. The result of the addition is a summary Homework object.

    b. Create a function template that adds two values and returns their sum.

    c. Write a main program that tests the function with integer, double, and Homework objects.

4. Complete the following tasks:

    a. Create a distance() function template that accepts two parameters representing two distances from a given point. The function returns the total distance as an integer.

    b. Create a City class with fields for the city name and for the distance from Chicago, the hub city for Amalgamated Airlines. Overload the + operator to sum the distances to produce an integer result.

    c. Write a main() program that declares several integer, double, and City objects, and use the distance() function to compute the distance for several pairs.

       If you use a compiler other than Borland C++, you might receive error messages. See Appendix A for details.

11

5. Complete the following tasks:

   a. Create a function template named average(). It accepts two arguments of the same type and computes their arithmetic average. The average is returned as a double.

   b. Overload the average() function to work correctly with three arguments.

   c. Create a class named CollegeCourse with fields for the course ID (for example, 'ENG 101'), your grade (for example, 'A'), and the credits earned for the CollegeCourse (for example, 3). The CollegeCourse constructor accepts values for these fields as arguments, and calculates a fourth field named honorPoints. Calculate honorPoints as the product of the grade points (4 for an A, 3 for a B, 2 for a C, and 1 for a D) and the credits. Overload the + operator so that honor points for courses can be summed to create a summary CollegeCourse object. Overload the / operator so that a CollegeCourse object's honorPoints can be divided by an integer. Overload the << operator to display the details of a CollegeCourse.

   d. Write a main() program that declares several integers, doubles, and CollegeCourses, and that demonstrates that both versions of average() work correctly with different arguments.

6. Create a class template for a class that holds an object. The template should provide a standard data input function that begins with a generic warning message to enter data carefully. The template also should include a standard output function that issues a generic "Here's the data you requested" message. Write a main() program that tests your template class with an integer and two programmer-designed classes.

7. Create a class template for a class that holds an object and the number of data elements in the object. For example, if an Employee class has two data elements, an ID number and a salary, then the class template holds the number 2 and holds an employee object. Code a standard input function for the object that displays a message on the screen—"You will be asked to enter X items"—where X is the number of data elements. Write a main() program that tests your template class with an integer and two programmer-designed classes.

8. Each of the following files in the Chapter11 folder contains syntax and/or logical errors. Determine the problem in each case, and fix the program.

   a. DEBUG11-1

   b. DEBUG11-2

   c. DEBUG11-3

   d. DEBUG11-4

CASE PROJECT

You have been developing a Fraction class for Teacher's Pet Software. Each fraction contains a numerator, denominator, a whole number portion, and a floating-point equivalent field. Each Fraction also has access to several functions you have developed. Complete these tasks:

a. Create a function template named problem() that accepts three arguments. The first and third arguments are generic values representing values a student will use as an arithmetic drill problem. The middle argument is a character representing a mathematical operation such as '+' or '-'. The problem() function displays the first argument, the operation sign, and the second argument on the screen, and allows the student to input an answer. The function returns the student answer to the calling program.

b. Create another function template named solution() that accepts three arguments. The first and third arguments are generic values representing values, and the middle argument is a character representing a mathematical operation such as '+' or '-'. The solution() function returns the correct answer to the problem.

c. Create a third function template named congrats() that accepts a correct answer. It displays the correct answer and a congratulatory message when a student enters the correct answer to a problem. Display the answer and the message 10 times on the screen cascading to the right. For example, if the correct answer is 27, then the output is:

```
27 Congratulations! Correct Answer!
   27 Congratulations! Correct Answer!
      27 Congratulations! Correct Answer!
```

...and so on, until it appears 10 times.

The function will be used whether the problem needs an integer, double, character, or Fraction answer.

d. Write a main() program that presents a student with at least three integer or double arithmetic problems. Display the problems using the problem() function, and compute the correct answer with the solution() function. If a solution is incorrect, display a brief message, but pass any correct student solutions to the congrats() function.

e. Add three multiple-choice problems to the student drill. The answers are characters—'a', 'b', or 'c'. Display the questions and answer choices with cout statements. If a solution is incorrect, display a brief message, but pass any correct student solutions to the congrats() function.

f. Add three true/false questions to the student drill. The answers are characters—'t' or 'f'. Display the questions and answer choices with cout statements. If a solution is incorrect, display a brief message, but pass any correct student solutions to the congrats() function.

g. Add three Fraction problems to the student drill. Display the problems using the problem() function, and compute the correct answer with the solution() function. If a solution is incorrect, display a brief message, but pass any correct student solutions to the congrats() function.

If you receive compiler errors when compiling these projects, refer to Appendix A to see if the errors are known compiler problems.

11

HANDLING EXCEPTIONS

In this chapter, you will learn:

♦ About the limitations of traditional error-handling methods

♦ How to throw exceptions

♦ How to use try blocks

♦ How to catch exceptions

♦ How to use multiple throw statements and multiple catch blocks

♦ How to throw objects

♦ How to use the default exception handler

♦ How to use exception specifications

♦ About unwinding the stack

♦ How to handle memory allocation exceptions

Most beginning programmers assume that their programs will work as expected. Experienced programmers, on the other hand, know that things often go awry. If you issue a command to read a file from a disk, the file might not exist. If you want to write to a disk, the disk might be full or unformatted. If the program asks for user input, users might enter invalid data. Such errors are called **exceptions**—so-named because, presumably, they are not usual occurrences. The object-oriented techniques to manage such errors comprise the group of methods known as **exception handling**. You learn these techniques in this chapter.

UNDERSTANDING THE LIMITATIONS OF TRADITIONAL ERROR HANDLING

From the time the first computer programs were written, programmers have had to deal with error conditions; errors occurred during the execution of programs long before object-oriented methods emerged. Probably the most popular traditional response to errors was to terminate the program. For example, many C++ programs contain code similar to the code in Figure 12-1. The program uses the **exit() function**, which forces the program to end.

```
int dataEntryRoutine()
{
    int userEntry;
    cout<<"Enter a positive number ";
    cin>>userEntry;
    if(userEntry < 0)
        exit(1);
    // rest of function goes here
}
```

Figure 12-1   A traditional error-handling method

To use the exit() function, you must include stdlib.h, the file that defines it.

In the highlighted statement in the program segment in Figure 12-1, if the userEntry is a negative value, the program in which the code appears is terminated. The exit() function requires an integer argument. It is traditional to use a 0 argument to indicate a program exited normally, and a non-zero argument to indicate an error.

As an alternative to 1 and 0, you can use the constants EXIT_FAILURE and EXIT_SUCCESS as arguments to the exit() function. They are defined as 1 and 0, respectively, in the stdlib.h file.

When you use the exit() function, the program ends abruptly. If the program is a spreadsheet or a game, the user might become annoyed that the program has prematurely stopped working. However, if the program monitors a patient's blood pressure during surgery or guides an airplane in flight, the results could be far more serious. Either way, the user has no idea what caused the program to end.

A slightly better alternative to exit() involves using the atexit() function. The **atexit() function** requires a function name as its argument; this function is then **registered** with atexit(), which means the named function is called automatically whenever the exit() function executes.

Figure 12-2 shows a program that uses the atexit() function to call the printErrorMessage() function, and Figure 12-3 shows a typical execution of the program. When you use atexit() to register a function to execute when exit() is called, the program still ends, but at least the user is provided with information about the abrupt termination.

Although it would be easier to read the function name if the function name were atExit(), that isn't the function name. The name atexit() contains all lowercase letters.

The atexit() and exit() functions do nothing if no error occurs. The function named in the call to atexit() never executes if the program does not exit prematurely.

```cpp
#include<iostream.h>
#include<conio.h>
#include<stdlib.h>
int dataEntryRoutine()
  {
      int userEntry;
      cout<<"Enter a positive number ";
      cin>>userEntry;
      if(userEntry <= 0)
            exit(1);
      cout<<"Thanks!"<<endl;
      return(userEntry);
  }
void printErrorMessage()
  {
      cout<<"You entered a negative number. ";
      cout<<"Program terminated."<<endl;
      getch();
  }
void main()
  {
      atexit(printErrorMessage);
      int entry=999;
      entry = dataEntryRoutine();
      cout<<"You entered "<<entry<<endl;
      getch();
  }
```

Figure 12-2   Program using atexit()

12

```
DataEntryWithExit2
Enter a positive number -5
You entered a negative number. Program terminated.
```

Figure 12-3   Output of DataEntryWithExit2

Functions registered with the atexit() function must be type void and take no arguments.

If you register multiple functions with atexit() within a program, each function will execute in reverse of the registration order.

Although the program in Figure 12-2 works as expected and terminates when the user enters an inappropriate value for userEntry, the program remains somewhat inflexible. A general rule of modular programming is that a function should be able to determine an error situation, but not necessarily take action on it. If the dataEntry() routine is useful and well written, it will be used by many programmers in many situations. Some of these programs (and programmers) might not want to effect such a sudden exit to the program when the user enters an invalid value. Other programs might require that additional tasks be accomplished before the program actually ends. A better alternative is to let a function discover an error, and then notify the calling function of the error so the calling function then can decide what to do about it. This approach provides flexibility by letting the calling function decide whether to carry on or terminate when the invalid data entry occurs.

For example, the function in Figure 12-4 returns a 1 if the dataEntryRoutine() function detects an error, and a 0 if it does not. The calling main() function checks the return value of the function and takes appropriate action, printing an error message or not. However, this error-handling technique has at least two drawbacks based on the following rules:

- A function can return, at most, only one value.

- When a function returns a value, it must return only the type indicated as its return type.

```
#include<iostream.h>
#include<conio.h>
#include<stdlib.h>
int dataEntryRoutine()
  {
      int userEntry;
      int errorCode = 0;
      cout<<"Enter a positive number ";
      cin>>userEntry;
      if(userEntry < 0)
            errorCode = 1;
      cout<<"Thanks!"<<endl;
      return(errorCode);
  }
void printErrorMessage()
  {
      cout<<"You entered a negative number. ";
      cout<<"Program terminated."<<endl;
      getch();
  }
void main()
  {
      int code;
      code = dataEntryRoutine();
      if(code==0)
            cout<<"You entered a valid number"<<endl;
      else
            printErrorMessage();
      getch();
  }
```

Figure 12-4   Program that uses dataEntryRoutine() with error code

First, because a function can return only one value, and the scope of a local variable ends at the end of the block in which it is declared, the userEntry value is lost in the dataEntryRoutine() function in Figure 12-4. The function can return the code that indicates the error status, but if it does, then it can't return the userEntry value as well. (Or, you can rewrite the dataEntryRoutine() so it returns the userEntry, but then the code is lost.)

In the example in Figure 12-4, you could work around the problem of losing one of the values by rewriting the dataEntryRoutine() function so that sometimes it returns the userEntry, and sometimes it returns the error code. For example, the function could return the userEntry if it is not negative, and return an arbitrary error code value such as –1 when the userEntry is negative. However, if you wanted to return the value of userEntry even if it was invalid (negative), you would have no way to indicate the error situation.

As another remedy, you could write the dataEntryRoutine() function so it accepts the address of the userEntry variable from main(). Then the dataEntryRoutine() could alter the actual entry variable instead of a copy of it, and still return an error code. However, allowing functions to access and alter passed variable values violates the general principle of encapsulation, and increases the data coupling of the function.

Second, any error code returned by a function must be the same type as the function's return type. In this case, the data entry is an integer and the error code is an integer, so you could write the dataEntryEntry() routine to return either the valid entry or an error code. However, when you have other functions with a return type of double (or a function that returns an array or a class object), then any error code returned must be the same type, and it simply is not intuitive to think of an error code this way. Of course, the error code could be stored globally, avoiding the return issue. In that case, however, any function could change the error code, and the "feel" of encapsulation and object-orientedness would be lost, and, again, data coupling would be increased.

Fortunately, the creators of C++ have provided you with techniques that circumvent the problems of traditional error handling. The name for this group of error-handling techniques is exception handling; the actions you take with exceptions involve trying, throwing, and catching them.

THROWING EXCEPTIONS

A function can contain code to check for errors, and send a message when it detects an error. In object-oriented terminology, an exception is a message (an object) that is passed from the place where a problem occurs to another place that will handle the problem. This object can be of any type, including a scalar or class type, and a variety of error messages of different types can be sent from the same function, regardless of its return type. In addition, true to object-oriented style, exception handling acknowledges inheritance and can be overridden by the programmer.

The general principle underlying good object-oriented error handling is that any called function should check for errors, but should not be required to handle an error if one is found. The error might need to be handled differently, depending on the purpose of the calling function. For example, one program that uses a data-entry function might need to terminate if the user enters a negative value. Another program might simply want the user to reenter the data. The calling function should have the responsibility of handling the error detected by the function.

When an object-oriented program detects an error within a function, the function should send an error message to the calling function, or **throw an exception**. A throw resembles a return statement in a function, except that the execution of the program does not continue from where the function was called.

You throw an exception by using the keyword **throw** followed by any C++ object, including an object that is a built-in scalar type, such as an int or a double; a nonscalar type, such as a string or numeric array; or even a programmer-defined object. For example, if you write a dataEntry() function in which a negative userEntry represents an error condition, then you can throw an error message exception as shown in Figure 12-5.

```
int dataEntry()
{
    int userEntry;
    cout<<"Enter a positive value ";
    cin>>userEntry;
    if(userEntry<0)
        throw("Invalid entry");
    return(userEntry);
}
```

Figure 12-5   A function that throws an exception

In the dataEntry() function in Figure 12-5, if userEntry is invalid, then a string is thrown (in the highlighted statement) and the execution of the function is finished. Therefore, only valid (that is, non-negative) entries cause the function to continue to execute all the way to the return statement. The string that is thrown is not "returned" from the dataEntry() function; the function has an int return type and so can return only an int. The dataEntry() function concludes in one of two ways: either the error message string is thrown or the userEntry integer is returned.

A function can make more than one throw. Assume, for example, that you need one error message if a value is negative, but a different error message if a value is greater than 12. The function in Figure 12-6 throws two different error messages, based on a userEntry.

```
int dataEntry()
{
    int userEntry;
    cout<<"Enter a positive value less than 13 ";
    cin>>userEntry;
    if(userEntry<0)
        throw("Value is negative");
    if(userEntry>12)
        throw("Value is too high");
    return(userEntry);
}
```

Figure 12-6   A function that throws one of two exceptions

12

Not only can a function make multiple throws, but it also can make throws of different types. Assume you need a function that throws an error message if userEntry is negative, but throws the actual value entered if the user enters a number greater than 12. The dataEntry() function in Figure 12-7 accomplishes this goal.

```
int dataEntry()
  {
      int userEntry;
      cout<<"Enter a positive value less than 13 ";
      cin>>userEntry;
      if(userEntry<0)
          throw("Negative number");
      if(userEntry>12)
          throw(userEntry);
      return(userEntry);
  }
```

Figure 12-7   A function that throws one of two exceptions of different types

When you use the version of the dataEntry() function shown in Figure 12-7, if the user enters a value between 0 and 12 inclusive, the actual value is returned to the calling function when the function ends. If the user enters a negative number, the string message "Negative number" is thrown. If the user entry is greater than 12, the actual number that the user entered is thrown. This does not mean that the number is returned to the calling function; only values between 0 and 12 are returned to the calling function, which presumably continues processing using the value. Instead, any value that is 13 or greater is thrown, or sent, to a different function where it can be caught.

USING TRY BLOCKS

When a function might cause an exception, and therefore includes a throw statement to handle errors, the call to the potentially offending function should be placed within a try block. A **try block** consists of one or more statements that the program attempts to execute, but that might result in thrown exceptions. A try block includes the following components:

- The keyword try
- An opening curly brace
- The code that is tried
- A closing curly brace

For example, a main() program that calls any of the dataEntry() functions created so far in this chapter would place the call to dataEntry() within a try block. Figure 12-8 shows the dataEntry() function from Figure 12-7 and a main() function that tries it.

```
#include<iostream.n>
#include<conio.n>
int dataEntry()
 {
     int userEntry;
     cout<<"Enter a positive value less than 13 ";
     cin>>userEntry;
     if(userEntry<0)
         throw("Negative number");
     if(userEntry>12)
         throw(userEntry);
     return(userEntry);
 }
void main()
 {
     int value;
     try
      {
         value = dataEntry();
      }
     cout<<"Data entry value is "<<value<<endl;
     // rest of the program goes here
 }
```

Figure 12-8   A main() function containing a try block

 When an if or for contains just one statement, curly braces are not required around the statement. With a try block you must include the curly braces, even if only one statement is tried.

12

In Figure 12-8, the call to the dataEntry() function occurs within the highlighted try block. When dataEntry() executes, if the userEntry is valid, then no exception is thrown, and main() executes to the end, using the valid value returned by the dataEntry() function. If the userEntry is invalid (less than 0 or more than 12) then the main() program terminates. This termination result is similar to when you call the exit() function within a program. As a matter of fact, you can call the dataEntry() function without a try block, no ill effects will ensue, and the results will look just like those with an exit() call. If you call dataEntry() without a try block and the userEntry is valid, the program continues; if the userEntry is invalid, the program terminates.

If the dataEntry() function is called from a try block, as in Figure 12-8, then you can deal with the error situation more elegantly and less abruptly than with an exit() call. You handle the thrown exception by catching it.

CATCHING EXCEPTIONS

To handle a thrown object, you include one or more catch blocks in your program immediately following a try block. A **catch block** includes the following components:

- The keyword `catch`
- A single argument in parentheses
- An opening curly brace
- One or more statements that describe the exception action to be taken
- A closing curly brace

For example, Figure 12-9 shows a dataEntry() function that throws a string error message if the user enters a negative number. The main() function in Figure 12-9 calls dataEntry() within a try block. If the user enters a non-negative number during the execution of dataEntry(), then the highlighted catch block in the main() function is bypassed, and the main() function continues with the statement that outputs the entered value. For example, Figure 12-10 shows the execution of the program when the user enters 12.

```cpp
#include<iostream.h>
#include<conio.h>
int dataEntry()
 {
     int userEntry;
     cout<<"Enter a positive value ";
     cin>>userEntry;
     if(userEntry < 0)
          throw("Invalid entry");
     return(userEntry);
 }
void main()
 {
     int userValue;
     try
       {
           userValue = dataEntry();
       }
     catch(const char msg[])
       {
           cout<<"There was an error!"<<endl;
           cout<<msg<<endl;
       }
     cout<<"Value is "<<userValue<<endl;
 }
```

Figure 12-9   dataEntry() function that throws a string, and a main() function that tries it

As with a try block, a catch block must contain curly braces, even if they contain only one statement.

 The catch block header in Figure 12-9, catch(const char msg[]), can be written alternately as catch(const char *msg). The string can be declared using either the array or pointer notation. Additionally, the keyword const is not required for the program to work correctly.

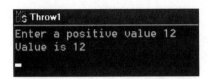

Figure 12-10   Output of program in Figure 12-9 when user enters a positive number

If the user enters a negative number during the execution of dataEntry() in the program shown in Figure 12-10, then the highlighted catch block executes. For example, Figure 12-11 shows the execution of the same program when the user enters a negative number. In this case, the catch block executes, catching the thrown string message. The catch block displays two strings: the first is coded within the catch block, and the second was thrown by the dataEntry() function. After executing the catch block, the main() program continues. The value shown is garbage because in the program, userValue is assigned a valid value only when dataEntry() is completed. The dataEntry() function never comes to a normal end because the error message is thrown before the return statement. To avoid seeing this garbage value, you could take one of several actions:

- Initialize userValue when it is declared in the main() function; its value will change only if the try block is successful.

- Assign a dummy value to userValue within the catch block, as well as within the try block. If the try block is successful, then userValue holds the value entered by the user. If the try block is unsuccessful, then userValue holds the assigned dummy value.

- Declare a flag variable set to 0, then set it to 1 within the catch block to indicate an exception was thrown. Display the value of userValue only when this error flag is off.

12

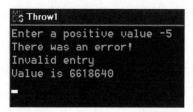

Figure 12-11   Output of program in Figure 12-9 when user enters -5

If you want a catch block to execute, it must catch the correct type of argument thrown from a try block. If an argument is thrown and no catch block has a matching argument type, then the program terminates. However, a catch block is not required to display, or to use in any way, what is thrown. For example, the catch block in the program in Figure 12-10 is not required to display the msg argument. Instead, the catch block could display only its own message, or contain any number of valid C++ statements (including those that call other functions), or even contain no statements at all.

 You cannot include a catch block within a program unless you have a try block. You can, however, have a try block without a catch block, although there would be no reason to do so.

 Calling functions from within catch blocks can be dangerous, especially if you call the function that caused the thrown exception in the first place.

In the next set of steps, you create a passwordEntry() function that asks a user to supply a password. The function takes an integer argument that indicates the maximum legal password size so that any function that calls passwordEntry() can specify its own appropriate size; the function throws the password when the entered password exceeds the size limit. If the password is valid (not too long), then the password is returned to the calling function.

The function could limit password character entry to eight characters by using the getline() function with a limit of 9. Or, the function could allow the user to enter one character at a time and count the characters. However, by allowing even longer passwords to be entered, the calling function gains control over how the passwordEntry() function is used. First, any calling function can send its own appropriate size limit to the passwordEntry() function. Second, any calling function can decide what it wants to do with an invalid password entry.

For example, a calling function might be written to display an error message, to use only the valid portion of the entered password, or to replace the invalid password with a default value.

1. Open a new file in your C++ editor. Type the include statements you will need in this program.

```
#include<iostream.h>
#include<conio.h>
#include<string.h>
```

2. The passwordEntry() function takes an integer argument that indicates the maximum password length and returns a character pointer that contains the address of the password string. The function allows passwords up to 100 characters, and checks to ensure the calling function does not attempt to exceed this limit.

```
char* passwordEntry(int allowedSize)
   {
        const int size = 100;
        if(allowedSize > size)
           {
                cout<<"Password size is too large. Size limit is "
                   <<size<<endl;
                allowedSize = size;
           }
```

3. Once a valid password size is established, declare an array for the password. Then prompt the user for, and accept the password. Accept a password of any length (up to 100 characters), but throw the password if it exceeds the maximum size as requested by the calling program.

```
char password[size];
cout<<"Enter your password. ";
cin.getline(password,size);
if(strlen(password) > allowedSize)
        throw(password);
```

4. As the last step of passwordEntry(), return the valid password when the length of the accepted password is acceptable and the password has not been thrown.

```
        return(password);
   }
```

5. Next, write a main() function that calls passwordEntry(). Declare a constant for the maximum legal password size, and declare a character array that can hold the password.

```
void main()
   {
        const int legalPasswordSize = 8;
        char password[legalPasswordSize + 1];
```

12

6. In a try block, call the passwordEntry() function, and assign its return value to the password array. If an exception is thrown, catch it, display an error message, and use a default value of all asterisks for the password.

```
try
    {
        strcpy(password,passwordEntry(legalPasswordSize));
    }
catch(const char *pswd)
    {
        cout<<"Password is invalid"<<endl;
        strcpy(password,"********");
    }
```

7. Finally, display the password whether it was valid or invalid. Add a call to getch() to hold the output screen if necessary, and close the main() function with a curly brace.

```
        cout<<"Password entered is stored as "<<password<<endl;
        getch();
    }
```

8. Save the program as **Password1.cpp** either in the Chapter12 folder of your Student Data Disk, or in the Student Data folder on your hard drive; then compile and execute the program, entering a valid, eight-character or less password. The output is similar to Figure 12-12. Execute the program entering an invalid password (over eight characters). The output is similar to Figure 12-13.

 When you run or compile the Password1.cpp program, your compiler might issue one or two warnings about the handling of the character array. You can ignore these warnings. Your compiler might also require you to press Enter twice after entering the password.

```
Password1
Enter your password. blueMoon
Password entered is stored as blueMoon
```

Figure 12-12   Output of Password1 program using valid password

```
Password1
Enter your password. blueCheese
Password is invalid
Password entered is stored as ********
```

Figure 12-13   Output of Password1 program using invalid password

USING MULTIPLE THROW STATEMENTS AND MULTIPLE CATCH BLOCKS

Often, several types of errors can occur within a function. You can write a function to throw any number of exceptions, and you can provide multiple catch blocks to react appropriately to each type of exception that is thrown.

For example, you can create a dataEntry() function that throws a string message when the user enters a negative number, but throws an invalid value when the user enters a number that is more than 12. In the example in Figure 12-14, the dataEntry() function throws two types of exceptions—a string and an integer. When a function throws more than one type of exception, then you can write multiple catch blocks as shown in the main() function in Figure 12-14.

```cpp
#include<iostream.h>
#include<conio.h>
int dataEntry()
  {
      int userEntry;
      cout<<"Enter a positive value less than 13 ";
      cin>>userEntry;
      if(userEntry < 0)
      throw("Value is negative");
      if (userEntry>12)
           throw(userEntry);
      return(userEntry);
  }
void main()
  {
      int value = 0;
      try
        {
           value = dataEntry();
        }
      catch(const char* msg)
        {
           cout<<msg<<endl;
        }
      catch(const int badValue)
        {
           cout<<"The number you entered, "<<badValue
               <<", is greater than 12."<<endl;
        }
      cout<<"The value at the end of the program is "
          <<value<<endl;
      getch();
  }
```

12

Figure 12-14   A dataEntry() function that throws two types of exceptions

When you run the program in Figure 12-14, if no exception is thrown, the program bypasses both catch blocks and prints the valid value, as shown in Figure 12-15. If the user enters a negative number, as shown in Figure 12-16, then a string is thrown. In this case, the first catch block executes, and the second catch block is bypassed. If the user enters a number greater than 12, as in Figure 12-17, then an integer is thrown. In this case, the first catch block is bypassed, and the second catch block executes.

```
DataEntryWithThrows
Enter a positive value less than 13 12
The value at the end of the program is 12
```

Figure 12-15   Output of program in Figure 12-14 with valid user entry

```
DataEntryWithThrows
Enter a positive value less than 13 -5
Value is negative
The value at the end of the program is 6618640
```

Figure 12-16   Output of program in Figure 12-14 with negative user entry

```
DataEntryWithThrows
Enter a positive value less than 13 16
The number you entered, 16, is greater than 12.
The value at the end of the program is 6618640
```

Figure 12-17   Output of program in Figure 12-14 with high user entry

Remember, if an exception is thrown, and no catch block matches the type of the thrown parameter, then the program terminates.

In the next set of steps, you modify the Password program so that it throws two types—a string and an integer.

   1. Open the **Password1.cpp** file if it is not still open. Immediately save it as **Password2.cpp** in the same location.

2. Currently, within the passwordEntry() function, if the allowedSized is greater than the size constant, you simply set allowedSize to equal the size constant. Now, you will throw an exception instead. Remove the statement **allowedSize = size;** and replace it with **throw(size);**.

3. To demonstrate that the throw works when a calling function requests that the allowed password size should exceed 100, change the value for the legalPasswordSize in the main() function from 8 to any value over 100, for example, **250**.

4. Within the main() function, insert a new catch block just after the closing brace of the existing catch block, and just before the cout statement that displays "Password entered is stored as ".The new catch block catches an integer, and sets the password to eight X's.

    catch(const int size)
    {
          strcpy(password,"XXXXXXXX");
    }

5. Save the program again (as **Password2.cpp**). Compile and execute the program. The output looks like Figure 12-18. Because the main() program requested a password that is too large, the passwordEntry() function throws the size, and the main() program uses "XXXXXXXX" as the password value. Any other program that uses the passwordEntry() function and requests a size of 100 or less will work as before—either the password will be entered correctly and be stored as the user enters it, or the password entered will exceed the requested limit and asterisks will be stored.

 When you compile the Password2.cpp program, your compiler might issue one or two warnings about the handling of the character array. You can ignore these warnings.

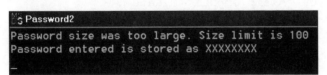

```
Password2
Password size was too large. Size limit is 100
Password entered is stored as XXXXXXXX
_
```

Figure 12-18   Output of Password2.cpp

THROWING OBJECTS

Just as simple variables such as doubles, integers, and strings can be thrown via exception-handling techniques, programmer-defined class objects also can be thrown. This approach is particularly useful in two types of situations:

- If a class object contains errors, you may want to throw the entire object, rather than just one data member or a string message.

- Whenever you want to throw two or more values, you can encapsulate them into a class object so that they can be thrown together.

Throwing Standard Class Objects

Figure 12-19 shows an Employee class with two data fields, empNum and hourlyRate. The insertion operator is overloaded in the same way you have seen it coded in many other classes, but in this Employee class, the extraction operator has been overloaded to throw an exception. As you can see in the highlighted if statement, if either the Employee empNum or the Employee hourlyRate is too high or too low, the entire Employee object is thrown.

```
class Employee
  {
      friend ostream& operator<<(ostream& out,
          const Employee &emp);
      friend istream& operator>>(istream& in,
          Employee &emp);
      private:
          int empNum;
          double hourlyRate;
  };
ostream& operator<<(ostream &out, const Employee &emp)
  {
      out<<"Employee "<<emp.empNum<<" Rate $"<<
          emp.hourlyRate<<" per hour";
      return(out);
  }
istream& operator>>(istream &in, Employee &emp)
  {
      cout<<"Enter employee number ";
      in>>emp.empNum;
      cout<<"Enter hourly rate ";
      in>>emp.hourlyRate;
      if(emp.empNum < 100 || emp.empNum >999 ||
          emp.hourlyRate < 5.65 || emp.hourlyRate > 19.99)
              throw(emp);
      return(in);
  }
```

Figure 12-19   The Employee class

Any program that uses the Employee class can catch the thrown Employee object and handle it appropriately for the application. A few possibilities include:

- A program might assign default values to any Employee whose data entry resulted in an exception.

- A program that tests the accuracy of data entry operators might store caught exceptions just as they are entered and count them.

- A program that is used when hiring Employees for a special assignment that pays more than the usual maximum might ignore the high-end salary violations.

- A program might refuse to accept an Employee with a exception, and force the user to re-enter the values, as in the main() program shown in Figure 12-20.

```
void main()
{
    const int numEmployees = 3;
    Employee aWorker[numEmployees];
    int x;
    for(x = 0; x < numEmployees; ++x)
    {
        try
        {
            cout<<"Employee #"<<(x+1)<<"   ";
            cin>>aWorker[x];
        }
        catch(Employee emp)
        {
            cout<<"Bad data! "<<emp<<endl<<
                "Please re-enter"<<endl;
            --x;
        }
    }
    cout<<endl<<"Employees:"<<endl;
    for(x = 0; x < numEmployees; ++x)
    cout<<aWorker[x]<<endl;
    getch();
}
```

Figure 12-20   A main() program that instantiates three Employee objects

The program in Figure 12-20 declares an array of three Employee objects. Within a for loop, a count is shown, and the data entry occurs within a try block. If the Employee class extraction operator throws an exception, the user is notified that the data entry attempt was invalid, the subscript is decremented so that the user will enter new data in the same array position as the invalid data, and the data entry is tried again. Figure 12-21 shows a typical run of the program. The data entry is tried repeatedly until three valid Employees have been entered; only then are the three valid Employees shown.

```
Employee
Employee #1  Enter employee number 88
Enter hourly rate 12.56
Bad data! Employee 88 Rate $12.56 per hour
Please re-enter
Employee #1  Enter employee number 888
Enter hourly rate 12.56
Employee #2  Enter employee number 889
Enter hourly rate 20.00
Bad data! Employee 889 Rate $20 per hour
Please re-enter
Employee #2  Enter employee number 889
Enter hourly rate 19.99
Employee #3  Enter employee number 890
Enter hourly rate 15.45

Employees:
Employee 888 Rate $12.56 per hour
Employee 889 Rate $19.99 per hour
Employee 890 Rate $15.45 per hour
```

Figure 12-21 Typical execution of the program that uses the Employee class

When you include multiple catch blocks in a program, the first catch block that can accept a thrown object is the one that will execute. When you create a function that throws several types, such as an integer and an Employee, it doesn't matter which catch block you place first. If an Employee object is thrown, the appropriate catch block executes whether it is written before or after the integer catch block. However, if you need to throw both a base and a derived class from the same function, and then carry out different operations when they are caught, code the catch for the derived object first. For example, if you create an Employee class and a child PartTimeEmployee class, catch the PartTimeEmployee object first. The derived PartTimeEmployee object throw will incorrectly match the base Employee class catch if it encounters that catch first because, as a child of Employee, a PartTimeEmployee "is a" Employee.

Throwing Exception Objects

You can create a class that represents an exception. For instance, you might create a class that contains both bad data and a message concerning that data. The class is instantiated only when an exception occurs.

Figure 12-22 shows a Customer class that is similar to many classes you already have worked with. Each Customer holds data fields for a customer number and a balance due, and has access to overloaded extraction and insertion operators that you can use for input and output. The overloaded extraction operator prompts the user for values for the data fields. It allows any Customer number, but checks the entered balanceDue against a highCreditLimit constant that has been set to $1000. The highlighted if statement shows that when the Customer balance exceeds the credit limit, a new object of type CustomerException is created. The CustomerException object has the local name e, and its constructor takes two arguments—the Customer object and a warning string. The newly created CustomerException object is then thrown from the overloaded operator>>() function. Any program that creates a Customer object and uses the operator>>() function within a try block can choose to catch the encapsulated CustomerException object, and use the Customer data, the message, both, or neither as the programmer deems appropriate for the application.

```
class Customer
  {
    friend ostream& operator<<(ostream& out,
        const Customer &cust);
    friend istream& operator>>(istream& in,
        Customer &cust);
    private:
        int custNum;
        double balanceDue;
  };
ostream& operator<<(ostream &out, const Customer &cust)
  {
    out<<"Customer "<<cust.custNum<<" Balance $"<<
        cust.balanceDue;
    return(out);
  }
istream& operator>>(istream &in, Customer &cust)
  {
    const double highCredit = 1000;
    cout<<"Enter Customer number ";
    in>>cust.custNum;
    cout<<"Enter balance due ";
    in>>cust.balanceDue;
    if(cust.balanceDue > highCredit)
      {
        CustomerException e(cust,
            "Warning: balance due exceeds limit");
        throw(e);
      }
    return(in);
  }
```

Figure 12-22 The Customer class

Figure 12-23 shows the CustomerException class. Its data members include a Customer object and a string message, and its constructor requires values for both. The CustomerException class also contains a showMsg() function that displays the details of the Customer object (using the Customer class overloaded insertion operator) and the string message.

 Some C++ programmers often give names that begin with a lowercase x (for exception) to classes that are created specifically to handle exceptions, although this violates the general guideline that class names should begin with an upper-case character.

```cpp
class CustomerException
  {
      private:
          Customer cust;
          char errorMessage[50];
      public:
          CustomerException(Customer aCust, char *msg);
          void showMsg();
  };
CustomerException::CustomerException(Customer aCust,
      char *msg)
  {
      cust = aCust;
      strcpy(errorMessage, msg);
  }
void CustomerException::showMsg()
  {
      cout<<cust<<endl<<errorMessage<<endl;
  }
```

Figure 12-23   The CustomerException class

Figure 12-24 shows a main() program that declares an array of four Customer objects. In this program a loop contains four calls to the overloaded operator>>() function. Because each of the data entry functions is within a try block, the catch block can accept a CustomerException object if the balance entered by the user exceeds the $1000 credit limit. The program in Figure 12-24 accepts the Customer data into the array whether the balance is high or not, but displays the warning message that is part of the thrown CustomerException object for those Customers with a balance exceeding $1000. Figure 12-25 shows the output of a typical execution of the program in which some of the Customers exceed the credit limit and others do not.

```
void main()
  {
     const int numCustomers = 4;
     Customer aCust[numCustomers];
     int x;
     for(x = 0; x < numCustomers; ++x)
       {
          try
           {
               cout<<"Customer #"<<(x+1)<<"  ";
               cin>>aCust[x];
           }
          catch(CustomerException error)
           {
               error.showMsg();
           }
       }
     cout<<endl<<"Customer list:"<<endl;
     for(x = 0; x < numCustomers; ++x)
          cout<<aCust[x]<<endl;
     getch();
  }
```

Figure 12-24   Program that instantiates four Customers

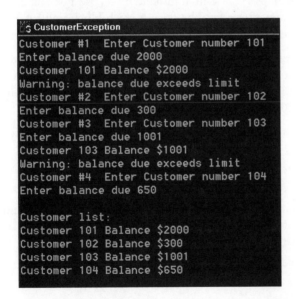

Figure 12-25   Output of typical execution of the CustomerException program

12

When creating a class to hold an exception, make sure that the instantiation of your exception class does not result in the same problem as the original error did. For example, if the original error was caused by insufficient memory, it's probably a poor idea to have the exception class constructor allocate more memory.

USING THE DEFAULT EXCEPTION HANDLER

When any object is thrown with a throw statement, then a subsequent catch block has a usable match if one of the following conditions is true:

- The type of the thrown object and the type of the catch argument are identical (for example, int and int).

- The type of the thrown object and the type of the catch argument are the same, except the catch contains the const qualifier, a reference qualifier, or both (for example, int can be caught by const int, int&, or const int&).

- The catch argument type is a parent class of the thrown argument.

If you throw an argument and no catch block exists with an acceptable argument type, then the program terminates. To avoid termination, you can code a **default exception handler** that catches any type of object not previously caught. You create a default exception handler by creating a catch block with an ellipsis (…) as its argument. If you use a default catch block, it must be the last catch block listed after a try. The default catch block will catch any type of thrown object that has not been caught by an earlier catch block.

In the next set of steps, you demonstrate that a default catch block works as expected. You create an Order class whose data entry function accepts several values and throws a variety of exception types. You decide to handle two types of exceptions with specific actions, and the other types of exceptions with a default action.

1. Open a new file in your C++ editor, and enter the include statements you need for this program.

```
#include<iostream.h>
#include<conio.h>
```

2. Create the definition for an Order class that contains fields for an order number, quantity ordered, and price of each item. Two overloaded operators provide means for input and output. An additional public function is available to set an Order's data fields to zeros.

```
class Order
  {
    friend ostream& operator<<(ostream& out, const Order &order);
    friend istream& operator>>(istream& in, Order &order);
    private:
        int orderNum;
        int quantity;
        double priceEach;
        double total;
    public:
        void zeroAll();
  };
```

3. The zeroAll() function sets each Order field to zero.

```
void Order::zeroAll()
  {
    orderNum = 0;
    quantity = 0;
    priceEach = 0;
    total = 0;
  }
```

4. Add the overloaded operator<<() function that displays an Order's details.

```
ostream& operator<<(ostream &out, const Order &order)
  {
    out<<"Order "<<order.orderNum<<" for "<<order.quantity
        <<" items  at $"<<order.priceEach<<"  Total due $"
        <<order.total;
    return(out);
  }
```

5. The overloaded operator>>() function holds declarations for the Order constants and prompts the user for Order values. After the Order values have been entered, an Order total is calculated by multiplying quantity ordered by price for each item ordered. Begin the overloaded extraction operator implementation as follows:

```
istream& operator>>(istream &in, Order &order)
  {
    const int highOrderNum = 9999;
    const int highQuantity = 50;
    const double highPriceEach = 39.95;
    const double highTotal = 1000.00;
    cout<<"Enter order number - no more than 4 digits ";
    in>>order.orderNum;
    cout<<"Enter quantity ";
    in>>order.quantity;
    cout<<"Enter price per item ";
    in>>order.priceEach;
    order.total = order.quantity * order.priceEach;
```

12

6. Continue the overloaded operator>>() function with a series of statements that tests the validity of each entered value. When the order number is too high, throw a string message. When the quantity or price of an Order is too high, throw the field. When a calculated total is too high, throw the entire Order object. Finally, if no error is detected and nothing is thrown, return from the function.

```
if(order.orderNum > highOrderNum)
    throw("Order number too high.");
if(order.quantity > highQuantity)
    throw(order.quantity);
if(order.priceEach > highPriceEach)
    throw(order.priceEach);
if(order.total > highTotal)
    throw(order);
return(in);
}
```

7. Next, write a main() function that begins by declaring four Order objects and trying data entry for each one.

```
void main()
{
    const int numOrders = 4;
    Order anOrder[numOrders];
    int x;
    for(x = 0; x < numOrders; ++x)
    {
        try
        {
            cout<<"Order #"<<(x+1)<<"  ";
            cin>>anOrder[x];
        }
    }
```

8. Still within the for loop, add several catch blocks. Suppose that in this application you want:

- To force the user to re-enter an Order when the order number is incorrect and a string is thrown

- To issue a warning message when a total is high and an Order is thrown

- To set each field in an Order to 0 if any other errors are detected, and either an integer or double is thrown

Enter the three appropriate catch blocks as follows:

```
catch(char *msg)
  {
    cout<<msg<<"Please re-enter"<<endl;
    --x;
  }
catch(Order orderWithHighTotal)
  {
    cout<<"Order accepted -";
    cout<<"but check credit limit before shipping"<<endl;
  }
catch(...)
  {
    cout<<"Either the quantity or price is too high. Setting all values
    to 0."<<endl;
    anOrder[x].zeroAll();
  }
```

9. Add the closing curly brace for the for loop:}. Then display the four Orders, add a getch() call to hold the screen, and add the closing curly brace for the program.

```
  }
cout<<"Order list:"<<endl;
for(x = 0; x < numOrders; ++x)
    cout<<anOrder[x]<<endl;
getch();
```

10. Save the file as **OrderExceptions.cpp** either in the Chapter12 folder of your Student Data Disk, or in the Student Data folder on your hard drive. Compile and run the program, choosing input values that reflect each of the possible exception situations. Figure 12-26 shows a typical program execution. At the first Order entry prompt, the user enters an order number that is too high, so a string message is thrown. When it is caught, the user is prompted to re-enter the order and the subscript for the Order array is decremented (so the next entry will occupy the position of the Order with the too-high order number). After entering the first order correctly, the user enters the second order with a quantity that exceeds the allowed value. When this error is detected, an integer is thrown. Because the first two catch blocks in main() are coded to accept a character pointer and an Order object, the first two catch blocks are bypassed, and the default catch block executes and sets all the fields in the order to 0.

When the third Order is entered, the quantity and the price are within acceptable limits, but their product exceeds $1000. An Order is thrown and the catch block displays a warning message but accepts the Order. For Order #4, the order number and quantity are acceptable, but the price of the item is too high. The thrown price is a double, so when it is thrown the catch blocks that accept a character pointer and an Order are bypassed. As with the integer, the thrown double causes the default catch block to execute, setting the Order's fields to zeros. Finally, the output shows a summary of the four Orders.

12

```
OrderExceptions
Order #1  Enter order number - no more than 4 digits 12345
Enter quantity 10
Enter price per item 12.55
Order number too high. Please re-enter
Order #1  Enter order number - no more than 4 digits 1234
Enter quantity 10
Enter price per item 12.55
Order #2  Enter order number - no more than 4 digits 234
Enter quantity 400
Enter price per item 14.25
Either the quantity or price is too high. Setting all values to 0.
Order #3  Enter order number - no more than 4 digits 345
Enter quantity 40
Enter price per item 38.50
Order accepted - but check credit limit before shipping
Order #4  Enter order number - no more than 4 digits 456
Enter quantity 15
Enter price per item 42.55
Either the quantity or price is too high. Setting all values to 0.
Order list:    .
Order 1234 for 10 items  at $12.55  Total due $125.5
Order 0 for 0 items  at $0  Total due $0
Order 345 for 40 items  at $38.5  Total due $1540
Order 0 for 0 items  at $0  Total due $0
```

Figure 12-26   Output of OrderExceptions program

USING EXCEPTION SPECIFICATIONS

Any C++ function might throw any type of object. If you don't carefully examine the code within a function, you might not realize how many different types of objects it throws. You can explicitly indicate the exceptions that a function can possibly throw by writing an **exception specification**, which is a declaration of a function's possible throw types. Creating an exception specification provides documentation for later users of the function by indicating what types of errors might possibly be thrown. The user then can plan appropriate catch blocks. If a function throws an error whose type was not listed in its exception specification, then it will produce a run-time error, and abort the program.

You write an exception specification in both a function's prototype and in a function's header immediately after the list of function arguments. Simply write the keyword throw followed by a list of argument types in parentheses. For example, for a dataEntry() function that takes no arguments and returns an integer, and that might throw a character, a double, or an Employee object, you could code the function header as follows:

```
int dataEntry() throw(char, double, Employee)
```

Besides throwing a character, double, or Employee, the function int dataEntry() throw(char, double, Employee) also could throw any object of a class derived from the Employee class.

If you write an exception specification with empty parentheses following throw, you declare that the function will not throw any exceptions. For example, the following dataEntry() function will not throw any exceptions:

```
int dataEntry() throw()
```

Remember that function headers and prototypes that do not include an exception specification list can throw anything (or might throw nothing)—you have seen many such functions throughout this chapter. In other words, if you do not specify the exceptions, then any type exception might be thrown. Once you do specify the exceptions for a function, then only those types listed can be thrown. If you use a throw specification clause with a function, and then throw a type that is not listed, an error will occur and the program will stop prematurely.

If you include an exception specification list with a function, and code a throw type that is not listed, the program will compile and execute if the unlisted type is never actually thrown. For example, if a function specification list does not include type double, but the function throws a double as the result of a negative data entry, and if no user ever enters a negative value, the function still will run correctly. However, if a user does enter a negative value and the double is thrown, then the program will end because double was not included in the specification list.

Be careful when writing an exception specification using a function template because any type might eventually be instantiated. You can't predict what type the function might throw. If you are unsure of what might be thrown, it is safer to leave off the specification list.

12

In the next set of steps, you add a specification list to the OrderExceptions program.

1. Open the **OrderExceptions.cpp** file if necessary. Immediately save it as **OrderExceptionsWithSpecifications.cpp** in the same location.

2. Add an exception specification to the end of the prototype for the overloaded extraction operator function as follows. The specification lists a character pointer, an integer, a double, and an Order object as possible candidates for throwing.

   friend istream& operator>>(istream& in, Order &order) **throw(char*, int, double, Order);**

3. Similarly, add an exception specification to the end of the operator>>() function header.

friend istream& operator>>(istream& in, Order &order) **throw(char*, int, double, Order)**

4. Save the program (as **OrderExceptionsWithSpecifications.cpp**), compile, and run it. It runs as before, but the operator>>() function is more clearly documented because you have specified the types of objects that might be thrown.

In Java, the exception specification list is written using "throws" instead of "throw," and makes more sense grammatically.

UNWINDING THE STACK

When you write a function, you can try a function call and, if the function you call throws an exception, you can catch the exception. However, if your function that calls the exception-throwing function doesn't catch the exception, then a function that calls your function can still catch the exception. A simpler way to say this is that if function A calls function B, and function B calls function C, and function C throws an exception, then if B does not catch the exception, function A can. If no function catches the exception, then the program terminates. This process is called **unwinding the stack**, because each time you call a function, the address of the place to which the program should return is stored in a memory location called the stack. Each time you return from a function, the return destination is retrieved from the stack.

You can picture the stack as a stack of plates. When you stack plates on top of each other, and later want to dismantle the stack, you must remove the last plate stacked before you can remove the previous one. Similarly, when function A calls function B, the computer "remembers" where to return at the end of the function by placing the return location (memory address) in function A at the bottom of the stack. When function B calls function C, the return location in B is placed "on top of" the A address. When function C ends, the top address (the one that returns to B) is retrieved from the stack. When function B ends, the next address (the one that returns to A) is retrieved.

Consider a simple Dog class like the one shown in Figure 12-27. It holds a Dog's name and age, and supports overloaded insertion and extraction operators. In this example, the overloaded extraction operator that provides data entry uses the highlighted if statement to throw the Dog object if the Dog's age is higher than the specified limit.

```
class Dog
  {
     friend ostream& operator<<(ostream& out,
         const Dog &dog);
     friend istream& operator>>(istream& in, Dog
         &dog)throw(Dog);
     private:
         char dogName[20];
         int age;
  };
ostream& operator<<(ostream &out, const Dog &dog)
  {
     out<<dog.dogName<<" Age: "<<dog.age<<" years old";
     return(out);
  }
istream& operator>>(istream &in, Dog &dog) throw(Dog)
  {
     const int highAge = 20;
     cout<<"Enter dog's name ";
     in>>dog.dogName;
     cout<<"Enter age ";
     in>>dog.age;
     if(dog.age > highAge)
         throw(dog);
     return(in);
  }
```

Figure 12-27   The Dog class

Figure 12-28 shows a KennelReservation class that holds information about boarding a Dog. Each KennelReservation includes a kennel number, a month and day for the reservation, and a Dog. The extraction operator implementation includes an exception specification (which is highlighted) indicating that the extraction operator might throw a Dog object. If you examine the operator>>() function code, you cannot find a throw statement. The throw is hidden within the Dog class overloaded operator>>() function. If the Dog class input function throws an exception, it will be passed to the KennelReservation input function. Since the KennelReservation input function does not catch the exception, the exception will be passed on to any function that uses the KennelReservation operator>>() function.

```
class KennelReservation
  {
      friend ostream& operator<<(ostream& out,
          const KennelReservation &res);
      friend istream& operator>>(istream& in,
          KennelReservation &res)throw (Dog);
      private:
          int kennelNumber;
          Dog dog;
          int month;
          int day;
  };
ostream& operator<<(ostream &out, const KennelReservation &res)
  {
      out<<"Reservation for "<<res.dog<<" for "<<res.month
          <<"/"<<res.day<<" for kennel #"<<res.kennelNumber;
      return(out);
  }
istream& operator>>(istream &in, KennelReservation &res) throw(Dog)
  {
      cout<<"Enter kennel # ";
      in>>res.kennelNumber;
      cout<<"Enter month ";
      in>>res.month;
      cout<<"enter day ";
      in>>res.day;
      in>>res.dog;   // call to Dog operator>>()
      return(in);
  }
```

Figure 12-28   The KennelReservation class

Within the KennelReservation function in Figure 12-28, both highlighted exception specifications could be deleted, and the class still would function properly. However, they provide useful documentation. Without the exception specifications, a client who uses the KennelReservation class might be unaware or forget that the Dog class throws an exception. Using the exception specification clause in the KennelReservation input function prototype and header provides a reminder to users that they might want to place the KennelReservation operator>>() call within a try block, and they might want to catch the thrown Dog object.

Figure 12-29 shows a main() function that instantiates a KennelReservation object, and Figure 12-30 shows a typical execution. When the user enters KennelReservation data, Dog data also is entered. When the user's data causes an exception, the Dog input function throws an exception to the KennelReservation input function, which throws the exception to main(), which catches it and prints a message. In this main() program, the Dog is allowed to have a high age, but a warning message is issued. Other client programs that use the KennelReservation class might use a default age or require the user to reenter the age.

```
void main()
  {
      KennelReservation aRes;
      try
        {
            cin>>aRes;
        }
      catch(Dog aDog)
        {
            cout<<"Check age."<<endl;
        }
      cout<<aRes<<endl;
      getch();
  }
```

Figure 12-29   A main() program that instantiates a KennelReservation

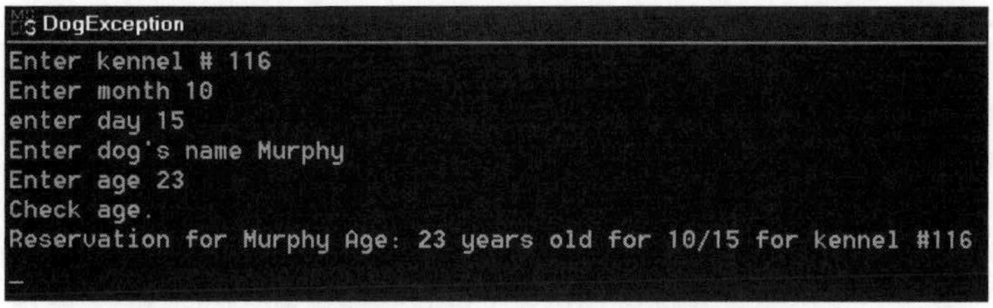

Figure 12-30   Output of DogException program

12

HANDLING MEMORY ALLOCATION EXCEPTIONS

Recall that you can use the operator **new** to allocate new memory dynamically while a program is running. For example, a common place to allocate memory is within a constructor. When you create an object, you often choose to allocate an appropriate amount of memory to accommodate specific data fields. For example, a music store might use a CD class that holds information about each compact disc for sale. Figure 12-31 shows a CD class that uses a character pointer to hold the CD title. CD titles vary dramatically in length, so within the CD constructor, memory is allocated dynamically (see the highlighted statement), allowing just enough room for the individual CD title and the NULL character.

```
class CD
  {
      private:
          char *title;
          double price;
      public:
          CD(const char *name,const double p);
  };
CD::CD(const char *name = '\0',const double p = 0.0)
  {
      title = new char[strlen(name)+1];
      strcpy(title,name);
      price = p;
  }
```

Figure 12-31 The CD class

When you allocate memory, enough memory might not be available. If you use the CD constructor in the class in Figure 12–31 and the new operator fails, the program ends abruptly. If you alter the constructor so that it throws an exception when there is not enough memory to allocate, then your program can choose how to handle the error; possible options include notifying the user of the error and ending the program, creating a different type of object, or abbreviating the CD title and trying the memory allocation again. Figure 12-32 shows a version of the CD constructor that throws an exception. The highlighted statement shows that in this constructor, if a title is 0 (or NULL), meaning that no title has been assigned, then a string is thrown. Otherwise, the assignment of the title and price to the appropriate fields takes place as usual.

```
CD::CD(const char name = '\0',const double p = 0.0) throw(char*)
  {
      title = new char[strlen(name)+1];
      if(title == 0)
          throw("Not enough memory!");
      strcpy(CD::title,name);
      price = p;
  }
```

Figure 12-32 CD constructor that throws an exception

When a CD object is instantiated, the instantiation can be placed within a try block so that the error can be handled. Figure 12-33 shows a try block in which a CD construction is attempted. In this example, the catch block simply displays a message so the user knows the object was not created.

```
try
  {
      CD oneDiskOfMine("Tapestry",8.99);
  }
catch (const char *message)
  {
      cout<<message<<endl;
  }
// rest of program
```

Figure 12-33   A CD construction within a try block

Because an out-of-memory condition causes a problem in any application, the creators of C++ have created an out-of-memory exception handler for you. The **set_new_handler() function** was created to solve the universal problem of insufficient memory. It is defined in the new.h library. You use set_new_handler() by creating a function to handle the error, then passing that error-handling function's name (which is a pointer to the function) to the set_new_handler() function. The function you create to handle the error cannot return any values; it must be type void. Once you have created your error-handling function and your main() program, you must call set_new_handler() within your program with a statement that takes the following form:

```
set_new_handler(nameOfYourFunction);
```

When you write a program that creates a few objects, it is very unlikely that you will run out of memory. To illustrate how set_new_handler() works, in the next set of steps, you create a very large array of some very large objects.

1. Open a new file in your C++ editor. Type the following include statements:

   #include<iostream.h>
   #include<new.h>
   #include<stdlib.h>
   #include<conio.h>

   You need iostream.h for cout, new.h for set_new_handler, stdlib.h for exit(), and conio.h for getch().

12

2. Create a class called BigClass. The class doesn't do anything; it serves no other purpose than to consume a lot of memory. It contains two arrays of 3,000 elements each.

```
class BigClass
  {
    private:
        double someStuff[3000];
        double someMoreStuff[3000];
};
```

3. Create a void function that you can use in the set_new_handler() call. Code the function to display a message, wait for a character input from the user, and exit the program. Recall that programmers commonly use an exit value of 0 to mean normal exit, and use 1 to indicate an error condition. Because this exit is caused by an exception, it makes sense to use 1 as the argument to the exit() function.

```
void noMem()
  {
    cout<<"No more memory"<<endl;
    getch();
    exit(1);
  }
```

4. Write a main() function that demonstrates how set_new_handler() works. Pass the name of the error-handling function noMem to set_new_handler(). Then, set a BigClass pointer named pt1 equal to the beginning address of an array of 30 BigClass objects. If the constructor is successful in allocating memory for 30 BigClass objects, the program prints "First allocation works." Then the program attempts to allocate memory for 30,000 additional BigClass objects. If this construction works, the program prints "Second allocation works." On many personal computer systems, the first allocation works, but the second allocation requires too much memory, and the noMem function executes when the new operation fails.

```
void main()
  {
    set_new_handler(noMem);
    BigClass *pt1 = new BigClass[30];
    cout<<"First allocation works"<<endl;
    BigClass *pt2 = new BigClass[30000];
    cout<<"Second allocation works"<<endl;
    getch();
  }
```

5. Save the program as **BigClass.cpp** either in the Chapter12 folder of your Student Data Disk, or in the Student Data folder on your hard drive; then compile and execute the program. (The program will cause warnings that you can safely ignore.) Depending on your computer, it might take a minute or two to execute. Figure 12-30 shows a typical run of the program on a personal computer. Memory for the first 30 arrays is allocated fairly quickly, and the first allocation message appears on the screen. Then, after about a minute of allocating some of the 30,000 additional arrays, the computer runs out of memory, and the noMem() function is automatically called. Within noMem(), the "No more memory" message appears. After getch(), the program exits, so the display of "Second allocation works" never executes. When you execute the program, if you run out of memory before the first 30 arrays are established, then you should lower the value used for the subscript, and compile and execute the program again. However, if you receive two success messages when you run the program, raise the subscript value for the first array so that it is higher than 30, perhaps to 30000, and try the allocations again. (Don't raise the array subscripts higher than 32,767, because that value represents the highest integer value allowed on most systems.)

Figure 12-34   Output of BigClass.cpp

12

CHAPTER SUMMARY

❏ A popular traditional way to handle error situations was to terminate the program. A superior alternative to traditional error-handling techniques is called exception handling. The actions you take with exceptions involve trying, throwing, and catching them.

❏ The general principle underlying good object-oriented error handling is that any function that is called should check for errors, but should not be required to handle an error if it finds one. When an object-oriented program detects an error within a function, the function should send an error message to the calling function, or throw an exception. You throw an exception by using the keyword **throw** followed by any C++ object. Functions can make multiple throws, and a function can make throws of different types.

❏ When a function might cause an exception, and therefore includes a throw statement to handle errors, the call to the potentially offending function should be placed within a try block.

❏ To handle a thrown object, you include one or more catch blocks in your program immediately following a try block. If you want a catch block to execute, it must catch the correct type of argument thrown from a try block. If an argument is thrown and no catch block exists with a matching argument type, then the program terminates.

❐ You can write a function to throw any number of exceptions, and you can provide multiple catch blocks to react appropriately to each type of exception that is thrown.

❐ Just as simple variables such as doubles, integers, and strings can be thrown via exception-handling techniques, so can programmer-defined class objects. You can throw standard class objects, or create exception classes as a way of encapsulating objects and messages. When you write catch blocks for parent and child classes, code the catch for the derived object first.

❐ You can create a class that represents an exception. The class is instantiated only when an exception occurs.

❐ If you throw an argument and no catch block exists with an acceptable argument type, then the program terminates. To avoid termination, you can code a default exception handler that catches any type of object not previously caught. You create a default exception handler by creating a catch block with an ellipsis (...) as its argument, and place the catch block as the last one listed after a try.

❐ You can explicitly indicate the exceptions that a function can possibly throw by writing an exception specification, which is a declaration of a function's possible throw types. If a function throws an error whose type was not listed in its exception specification, then the function will produce a run-time error, aborting the program.

❐ When you allocate memory, it is always possible that there is not enough memory available, so the creators of C++ have created an out-of-memory exception handler for you called set_new_handler(). You use set_new_handler by creating a function to handle the error, then passing the function's name to the set_new_handler() function.

REVIEW QUESTIONS

1. Errors that occur during a program's execution are called _____.

   a. faults

   b. omissions

   c. exceptions

   d. exclusions

2. Traditionally, computer program error-handling techniques most often resulted in _____.

   a. displaying multiple, confusing error messages

   b. recompiling the program

   c. terminating the program

   d. terminating the programmer

3. A general principle of object-oriented error handling is that a function should _____.

   a. detect an error but not handle it

   b. handle an error but not detect it

   c. both detect and handle errors

   d. not allow errors

4. When a function sends an error message to the calling function, the function is said to _____ an exception.

   a. try

   b. throw

   c. catch

   d. create

5. A throw most closely resembles _____.

   a. an exit

   b. a catch

   c. an output statement

   d. a return

6. You can throw objects that are _____ type.

   a. int and double

   b. any scalar

   c. any class

   d. any

7. Which of the following is true?

   a. A single function can throw both a character and a double.

   b. A single throw can throw both a character and a double.

   c. A single catch can catch both a character and a double.

   d. All of the above are true.

8. Which of the following is true?

   a. You cannot have a try without a catch.

   b. You cannot have a throw without a catch.

   c. You cannot have a catch without a try.

   d. You cannot have a function without a throw.

12

9. When you use a try block, the program _____ throw an exception from a function named within the try block.

    a. might

    b. must

    c. cannot

    d. can also include a catch block that will

10. A catch block can contain _____ argument(s).

    a. no

    b. exactly one

    c. exactly two

    d. at least one, perhaps more

11. A catch block _____.

    a. must not contain an argument

    b. must use any argument it receives

    c. can use any argument it receives

    d. cannot use any argument it receives

12. If an argument is thrown and no catch block exists with a matching argument type, then the program _____.

    a. terminates

    b. continues without problem

    c. displays a warning and continues

    d. uses a default catch block

13. Which of the following is true when you try a function that throws three different types of exceptions?

    a. The program will not compile.

    b. You must provide three catch blocks to react appropriately to each type of exception that is thrown.

    c. You can provide up to three catch blocks to react appropriately to each type of exception that is thrown.

    d. You must provide one catch block with three arguments to react appropriately to each type of exception that is thrown.

14. When a try block contains a function that might throw an exception, but no exception is thrown, then the program _____.

    a. terminates

    b. issues a warning, but continues with statements beyond any catch blocks

    c. continues without incident

    d. uses a default catch block

15. When you include multiple catch blocks in a program, and a thrown object can be accepted by two of them, _____.

    a. the program will not compile

    b. the first catch block will execute

    c. the last catch block will execute

    d. you cannot predict which catch block will execute

16. A primary reason you might create an exception class is to _____.

    a. avoid exception situations

    b. improve program documentation

    c. avoid having to throw and catch objects

    d. encapsulate an object with appropriate error messages

17. A default exception handler catches _____.

    a. any type of object not previously caught

    b. all objects

    c. the first object thrown from a function

    d. the last object thrown from a function

18. The primary reason you use an exception specification is _____.

    a. to allow multiple exceptions to be thrown

    b. as a substitute for catch blocks

    c. to avoid having to use the default catch block

    d. for documentation

19. Functions that contain no exception specification list _____.

    a. can throw string messages

    b. can throw anything

    c. might throw nothing

    d. all of the above

12

20. The purpose of the set_new_handler() function is to _____.

    a. exit a program with insufficient memory

    b. recognize out-of-memory situations, and call a function you specify

    c. allocate new memory for dynamically created arrays

    d. throw memory exception messages to predefined functions

EXERCISES

1. Create a class named RealEstate that has data members to hold the price of a house, the number of bedrooms, and the number of baths. Member functions include overloaded insertion and extraction operators. Write a main() function that instantiates a RealEstate object, allows the user to enter data, and displays the data members entered. The user should receive an appropriate thrown error message if negative values are entered for any of the data members.

2. Create a class named Television that has data members to hold the model number of a television, the screen size in inches, and the price. Member functions include overloaded insertion and extraction operators. If more than four digits are entered for the model number, if the screen size is smaller than 12 or greater than 70, or if the price is negative or over $5,000, then throw an integer. Write a main() function that instantiates a Television object, allows the user to enter data, and displays the data members. If an exception is caught, replace all the data member values with zero values.

3. Create an Inventory class with data members for stock number, quantity, and price, and overloaded data entry and output operators. The data entry operator function should throw:

    ❐ An error message, if the stock number is negative or higher than 999

    ❐ The quantity, if it is less than 0

    ❐ The price, if it is over 100.00

Then perform the following tasks:

    a. Write a main() function that instantiates an array of five Inventory objects, and accepts data for each. Display an appropriate error message for each exception situation. When an exception is detected, replace all data fields with zeros. At the end of the program, display data fields for all five objects.

    b. Write a main() function that instantiates an array of five Inventory objects and accepts data for each. If an exception is thrown because of an invalid stock number, force the user to reenter the stock number for the Inventory object. If the quantity is invalid, do nothing, If the price is in error, then set the price to 99.99. At the end of the program, display data fields for all five objects.

c. Write a main() function that instantiates an array of five Inventory objects and accepts data for each. If an exception is thrown because of an invalid stock number, force the stock number to 999; otherwise, do nothing. At the end of the program, display data fields for all five objects.

4. Create a class named Student that holds a student ID and a grade point average, and contains functions for construction and display. The constructor function should throw a Student object if the ID is larger than four digits or the grade point average is negative or greater than 4.0. Write a main() function to try to instantiate a Student and catch any error.

5. Complete the following tasks:

a. Create a Meal class. Data fields include a string entrée name and a double price. Include a data-entry function that prompts for and accepts values for both data fields, and that throws an exception if the price is less than $5.00 or more than $29.99. Include a public function that returns the Meal price so that you can use it in a calculation in the Party class that you will create in part c of this problem. Also include an overloaded insertion operator to display a Meal's data values.

b. Create an EntertainmentAct class. Data fields include a string act name and a double price. Include a data entry function that prompts for and accepts values for both data fields, and that throws an exception if the price is less than $50.00 or more than $3,000. Include a public function that returns the EntertainmentAct price so that you can use it in a calculation in the Party class that you will create in part c of this problem. Also include an overloaded insertion operator to display an EntertainmentAct object's data values.

c. Create a Party class. A Party contains a Meal, an EntertainmentAct, an integer number of guests, and a total cost. The Party data-entry function prompts the user for Meal, EntertainmentAct, and guest number values. The function also calculates the Party cost, based on the Meal's price times the number of guests, plus the price of the EntertainmentAct.

d. Write a main() function that instantiates at least five Party objects and accepts data for each. When you run the program, provide data that ensures that each type of exception is being recognized. The main() function should catch the exceptions and display an appropriate error message about each.

6. Create a class named Teacher that holds a Teacher's first and last names and the grade level the Teacher teaches. Include a constructor function that uses default first and last names, such as "ZZZZZZ," when no names are provided. Use a character pointer for each name, and allocate new memory based on the sizes of the Teacher's first and last names. In a main() demonstration program, include code to handle any memory allocation errors that occur. Continue to rewrite the main() program until you create enough Teacher objects to cause a memory allocation exception. (*Hint*: You probably will have to create multiple Teacher arrays containing thousands of objects each.)

12

7. Create a Job class that holds a Job ID number and the cost of the Job. Include insertion and extraction operators. Create a JobException class that holds a Job and an error message. When the user enters Job data, if the Job fee is below $250, then create a JobException object and throw it. Write a main() function that declares an array of eight Job objects. If a JobException object is thrown during the data entry for any Job, require the user to enter data for a new Job, and replace the invalid job.

8. Each of the following files in the Chapter12 folder contains syntax and/or logical errors. Determine the problem in each case, and fix the program.

    a. DEBUG12-1

    b. DEBUG12-2

    c. DEBUG12-3

    d. DEBUG12-4

CASE PROJECT

You have been developing a Fraction class for Teacher's Pet Software. Each fraction contains a numerator, denominator, a whole number portion, and a floating-point equivalent field. Each Fraction also has access to several functions you have developed. Complete these tasks:

a. Modify each Fraction class constructor and data entry function (including the operator>>() function) so that it throws an exception whenever a client attempts to instantiate a Fraction with a zero denominator.

b. Write a main() function that declares several Fraction objects. Demonstrate that each of your constructors and data-entry functions correctly recognizes exceptions.

c. Write a main() function that asks the user to enter values for four Fractions. If the user attempts to create a Fraction with a zero denominator, catch the exception, display a message, and force the denominator to 1.

d. Write a main() function that asks the user to enter values for four Fractions. If the user attempts to create a Fraction with a zero denominator, catch the exception, display a message, and force the user to reenter the Fraction values.

e. Write a main() program that asks the user to enter values for four Fractions. If the user attempts to create a Fraction with a zero denominator, catch the exception, display a message, and terminate the program.

13

ADVANCED TOPICS

In this chapter, you will learn:

♦ About the binary system

♦ Why computers use the binary system

♦ How to use individual bits to store data

♦ How to combine bit fields to hold values larger than 1

♦ How to convert a group of bit fields to an integer value

♦ How to use the logical bitwise AND operator with a mask

♦ How to use the logical bitwise OR operator

♦ How and why to shift bits

♦ About recursion

♦ How to use a recursive function to sort a list

The most valuable commodity in a programming environment is the programmers' time. Programmers are paid well to ensure that their systems operate as expected. Programmers concern themselves with two other commodities—computer memory and program run time. In the past, programmers tried to save memory because it was an expensive resource. Over time, the cost of storage has been greatly reduced, but reducing the size of objects is still important, especially when objects are sent over data communication lines. Additionally, speed of operation is important in programs that use many instructions to operate on large quantities of data. This chapter discusses two features of the C++ language that allow programmers to save time and memory within their programs—bit manipulation and recursion.

UNDERSTANDING THE BINARY SYSTEM

Every piece of data stored on every computer in the world is stored as a series of 0s and 1s. This system of storage, called the **binary system**, has been used since the earliest computers were created because it is the cheapest way to store data.

The numbers you are accustomed to using are organized in the decimal system. The **decimal system** is so named because the prefix "dec" means 10 and the decimal system uses 10 digits: 0 through 9. When you use the decimal system and you want to express a value greater than 9, you do not use additional symbols. (Numbers would be too difficult to use if you had to learn thousands of separate symbols, one for each possible value.) Instead, you use an additional one or more of the existing 10 symbols.

The binary numbering system uses only two digits: 0 and 1. When you use the binary system and you want to express a value greater than 1, you do not use symbols other than 0 or 1. Instead, you combine two or more of the existing two symbols.

When you first learned how to construct large values using the decimal system, a teacher probably told you to think of a value such as 321 as having three columns—a hundreds column with a 3, a tens column with a 2, and a ones column with a 1. You can express the value of 321 as 3 times 100, plus 2 times 10, plus 1 times 1. You also learned that for larger numbers in the decimal system, each successive column added on the left is worth 10 times the previous column. In other words, when you analyze a multidigit value, the sequence of column values from right to left is 1, 10, 100, 1000, 10000, 100000, and so on. Table 13-1 shows a few examples of four-digit numbers and how you analyze their values. The columns with leading zeros are shaded because you don't usually use them when expressing a value—for example, you say "14", not "0014". However, you understand that you could use 0s in the hundreds and thousands positions without altering the value of 14.

Table 13-1   Representation of a few decimal numbers

1000s	100s	10s	1s	Decimal Value
0	0	0	0	0
0	0	0	1	1
0	0	0	2	2
0	0	1	0	10
0	0	1	4	14
0	1	0	1	101
0	1	1	0	110
0	3	2	1	321
0	9	9	9	999
1	4	6	8	1468

Constructing values in the binary system works the same way as in the decimal system, except that you have only two symbols to use, so each successive column represents a value only two times greater than the column to its right. The column values for binary numbers are 1, 2, 4, 8, 16, 32, and so on. Table 13-2 shows a few binary numbers and their corresponding decimal values. The values 0 and 1 appear the same way in both systems, but the decimal 2 requires two columns in the binary system because no symbol for 2 is available. Instead, to represent 2 in the binary system you place a 1 in the twos column and nothing in the ones column. As in the decimal system, leading zeros are not required to represent a number, but they are understood to mean that a number is smaller in value than one with more filled column positions.

 When you pronounce a binary number such as 101, say "one zero one" or "one oh one." Do not say "one hundred and one."

You can construct any binary number's decimal value by adding the column values of those columns that contain a 1. For example, Table 13-2 shows that the binary number 10100 contains 1s in the 16s and 4s columns. Therefore, the decimal value of 10100 is 16 + 4, or 20.

Table 13-2   Representation of a few binary numbers

256s	128s	64s	32s	16s	8s	4s	2s	1s	Decimal Value
0	0	0	0	0	0	0	0	0	0
0	0	0	0	0	0	0	0	1	1
0	0	0	0	0	0	0	1	0	2
0	0	0	0	0	0	0	1	1	3
0	0	0	0	0	0	1	0	0	4
0	0	0	0	0	0	1	0	1	5
0	0	0	0	0	0	1	1	0	6
0	0	0	0	0	0	1	1	1	7
0	0	0	0	0	1	0	0	0	8
0	0	0	0	1	0	1	0	0	20
0	0	1	0	1	1	0	0	1	89
0	1	0	0	0	0	0	0	1	129
0	1	0	0	0	0	1	1	1	135
0	1	1	1	1	1	1	1	1	255
1	0	1	0	0	0	0	0	1	321
1	1	0	0	0	0	0	0	0	384

13

When you examine Table 13-2, you see that it quickly takes many more binary digits than decimal digits to represent a value. For example, the value 2 requires only a single digit in the decimal system, but requires two positions in the binary system. The value 321 requires nine digits in the binary system—1s in the columns representing 256, 64, and 1, and 0s in all the other columns.

When you use the decimal system, there is no "highest possible column." That is, you can represent any number, no matter how large, by adding enough columns to support the value. The same is true of the binary system.

The odometer in your car uses the decimal system. After you have driven 9 miles, the column second from the right "turns over" to a 1, and the right-most column becomes 0 again. You can think of the binary system in the same way. After you pass the binary value 1, the column second from the right becomes 1 and the right-most column becomes 0, resulting in binary 10, or decimal 2. After binary 11 (decimal 3), the right-most column becomes 0, forcing the next column from the right to be 0, forcing the third column from the right to be 1. The result is binary 100, or decimal 4.

UNDERSTANDING WHY COMPUTERS USE THE BINARY SYSTEM

Imagine that there are no computers, and that you are the first to attempt to invent an electronic data storage device. You decide to build your storage device from common hardware store supplies, and you want to store values at least up to several thousand. If you need to store a number such as 321, you have several options about the type of hardware to install in your device:

- You can use a huge dial with thousands of settings representing every possible value. Such a device would be very expensive to build and calibrate, and cost perhaps $1000.

- You can use four or five dials with 10 settings each, and use a system similar to the decimal system. For example, to store 321 using four dials, you would set the left-most dial to zero, set the second dial to 3, the third dial to 2, and the fourth dial to 1. Such 10-way switches, like a dimmer switch sold in a hardware store, might cost $40 each. If you used four dials to store each number, you could store values up to 9,999 for $160 per number.

- You can use 15 or 16 two-way toggle switches, like regular light switches on a wall. You could create a code where a specific sequence of ons and offs represents each possible value. Such switches might cost only 15 cents each. If you think of the digit 1 representing On switches, and the digit 0 representing Off switches, then you would be using the binary system. Table 13-2 shows that the value 321 would require at least nine on-off switches. Larger numbers would require more switches, but at 15 cents each, it would cost only $2.25 to store any value requiring up to 15 switches (the decimal equivalent of 32,767). The cost would be many times less than using complicated 10-way switches.

If you use ordinary hardware components, two-way switches are the cheapest. Of course, computers don't use ordinary hardware components; they use circuitry that is far less expensive per switch. However, in the integrated circuits that modern computers do use, two-way switches are still cheaper than any more complex system. For this reason, all computers store values as a series of 1s and 0s. Every piece of data is stored in this fashion—letters and special symbols as well as numbers.

Every computer system uses a code to represent values, although different systems use different codes. Many personal computers use a system called **ASCII** (**American Standard Code for Information Interchange**), in which eight binary digits are used to represent a character. For example, in ASCII, the character A is represented by 01000001. Many mainframe computer systems use a separate code named **EBCDIC** (**Extended Binary Coded Decimal Interchange Code**), in which, for example, the character A is 11000001. Some C++ compilers also support **Unicode**, which is a 16-bit coding scheme. For example, the letter A is stored in computer memory as a set of 16 zeros and ones as 0000000001000001. (By design, this number is the same numeric value as the ASCII code for A.) The reason for using 16 bits is to support all the characters from large foreign alphabets such as Greek, Hebrew, and Chinese. The representation of A using each code is slightly different, but the precise binary code is unimportant. What is important is that each system recognizes an A when it sees one.

Because every computer system uses binary digits to store data, computer professionals have developed a vocabulary with which they can talk about storage. Computer professionals use the term **bit** as shorthand when they refer to a single **b**inary di**git**. Eight binary digits are called a **byte**, which on many systems is the amount of storage required to store a single character such as an alphabetic letter or punctuation mark. Thus, every time you store a letter or other character in a computer system, you actually are storing eight separate digits that represent the character, you are storing one byte.

The left-most bit in a byte is called the high-order bit; the right-most bit is the low-order bit.

USING INDIVIDUAL BITS TO STORE DATA

You have several options for storing the values 0 and 1 within fields in a class you create. For example:

- You can store 0 or 1 in a double field.

- You can store 0 or 1 in an integer field.

- You can store 0 or 1 in a single bit field.

On most computer systems, the 0 or 1 stored in an integer requires less storage than the same value stored in a double. In all computer systems, the 0 or 1 stored in a bit takes far less room than the same value stored in either an integer or a double. When you need to create a field that contains a wide possibility of values, such as an ID number or an inventory quantity, it makes sense to use an integer. When you need to create a class field that might hold only the value 0 or 1 (for example a flag that indicates true or false), you still can use an integer, but you also can use a single bit. The advantage to using a single bit is that you consume far less storage space. Depending on your computer, a single integer might occupy two or four bytes of storage. If you use bits to store true or false information, you can hold up to eight pieces of such information in one byte. That means bits give you the potential to store 16 to 32 times the information you would be able to store in an integer space.

You declare a field to be a single bit by placing a colon and a 1 after the variable declaration. Thus, the declaration `int aFlag:1;` declares a variable named aFlag that occupies one bit of storage. It can hold only one of two values—0 or 1.

For example, Figure 13-1 shows two classes that can hold information about an automobile driver. The information is used to determine insurance premium rates. Each class holds fields for an ID number and several true or false fields, such as whether the driver is male or over 25 years old. The only difference between the two classes is that the DriverUsingInts class uses integers to store the true or false values, and the DriverUsingBits class uses single bits for the same purpose. (The bit designations in the DriverUsingBits class are highlighted.) For simplicity, neither of these classes contains any functions.

```
class DriverUsingInts
  {
      private:
            int idNum;
            int isMale;
            int isOver25;
            int hasPreviousTickets;
            int tookDriversEd;
  };
class DriverUsingBits
  {
      private:
            int idNum;
            int isMale:1;
            int isOver25:1;
            int hasPreviousTickets:1;
            int tookDriversEd:1;
  };
```

Figure 13-1   DriverUsingInts and DriverUsingBits classes

Figure 13-2 shows a main() program that declares one object of type DriverUsingInts and one object of type DriverUsingBits. The program contains three cout statements. The first shows the size of an integer in the computer on which the program is run. Figure 13-3 shows the output on a computer in which integers are stored in four bytes. The other two cout statements in the program in Figure 13-2 display the size of the declared DriverUsingBits and DriverUsingInts.

> Recall that the sizeof() operator is used to show the size in bytes of any object or type.

```
void main()
  {
    DriverUsingInts anotherDriver;
    DriverUsingBits aDriver;
    cout<<"Size of an int on this system is "
        <<sizeof(int)<<endl;
    cout<<"Size of DriverUsingInts is "
        <<sizeof(anotherDriver)<<endl;
    cout<<"Size of DriverUsingBits is "
        <<sizeof(aDriver)<<endl;
    getch();
  }
```

Figure 13-2   Program that declares a DriverUsingInts and a DriverUsingBits

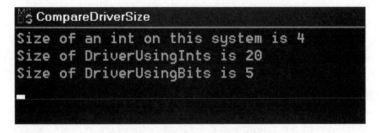

Figure 13-3   Output showing sizes of objects

> If you run the program shown in Figure 13-2, most compilers issue two warnings indicating that the two declared objects, aDriver and anotherDriver, are never used. That's because the demonstration program simply lists the objects' sizes instead of using the objects in any real way. You can safely ignore the warnings.

When you examine the output in Figure 13-3, you see that the DriverUsingInts object requires 20 bytes of storage—four bytes for each of its five integer fields. On the other hand, the DriverUsingBits object requires only five bytes of storage—four bytes for the integer idNum and just one byte for all the other fields added together. In fact, because there are eight bits in a byte, and since only four bits are used for the four flag fields within the DriverUsingBits class, there actually is room to spare. In fact, four additional pieces of information could be stored for a DriverUsingBits object without using any additional memory.

If you use fewer than eight bits as fields in a class, the computer rounds up the storage requirements to the next whole number of bytes. That is, if you store any number of bits from one to eight, you must use an entire byte of storage; if you store nine to 16 bits, you must use two entire bytes of storage, and so on.

When you create a class with several bit fields, some systems place them in order from left to right within a byte; others place them from right to left.

The advantage to storing a piece of data in a bit instead of a byte is the storage space saved. When you write a program that declares a single object, it doesn't make much difference whether the object requires five or 20 bytes of storage. The benefit comes when you store thousands or millions of such objects, or when you transmit those objects across data communication lines. If you are an Internet user, you most likely have been frustrated with the wait time necessary when large objects are sent to you via e-mail, or when you try to download large objects from a Web site. The smaller an object is, the faster you can send it over a network or telephone lines to another user.

When you declare a field to be a bit field, the field type must be int or unsigned int. When a field is type int, it can hold both positive and negative numbers—the left-most bit is reserved to hold the sign and the other seven bits represent the value. When a field is type **unsigned int**, then it must be positive, because no bit is reserved for a sign, and all eight bits are used to store the value. The advantage to using unsigned int when storing bit fields is that when no bit is needed for a sign, more data can be stored. You declare a field to be unsigned int in one of two ways—you can use the type name "unsigned int," or you simply can use "unsigned," which the compiler interprets as "unsigned int."

When you declare bit fields, you can assign values to them in the same way you assign values to ordinary non-bit fields. That is, you can use an integer constant or integer variable that holds a 1 or 0 and assign it to a bit field, and C++ takes care of the conversion. Similarly, the comparison operators, such as == , <, and > work with bits in the same way they work with integers. In the next set of steps, you create a Driver class with two bit fields, and declare some objects that hold values in the fields.

1. Open a new file in your C++ editor. Type the include statements you need to run the program.

   #include<iostream.h>
   #include<string.h>
   #include<conio.h>

2. Create a Driver class that includes an idNum and lastName, and two bit fields that hold gender and age designations. Use the unsigned type for the bit fields. Include a constructor that requires values for all four fields, and a showDriver() function. Notice that the variables in the constructor argument list used to assign

values to the isMale and isOver25 fields are simply integers—they do not have to be any special type of field just because they will be assigned to bit fields.

```
class Driver
  {
    private:
          int idNum;
          char lastName[15];
          unsigned isMale:1;
          unsigned isOver25:1;
    public:
          Driver(int id, char name[], int gender, int older);
          void showDriver();
  };
```

3. Within the Driver constructor, you make all the appropriate data assignments.

```
Driver::Driver(int id, char name[], int gender, int older)
  {
    idNum = id;
    strcpy(lastName,name);
    isMale = gender;
    isOver25 = older;
  }
```

4. The showDriver() function displays all the fields, substituting the strings "Female", "Male", "Not over 25", and "Over 25" for the more cryptic 0 and 1 codes.

```
void Driver::showDriver()
  {
    cout<<"ID #"<<idNum<<" Name: "<<lastName<<" Gender: ";
    if (isMale==0)
       cout<<"Female  ";
    else
       cout<<"Male    ";
    if(isOver25 == 0)
       cout<<"Not over 25";
    else
       cout<<"Over 25";
       cout<<endl;
  }
```

13

5. Write a main() function that declares one Driver object of each type (female and not over 25, female and over 25, male and not over 25, and male and over 25) by using the 0 and 1 codes. Then show the four objects to confirm that the assignments were made correctly.

```
void main()
  {
    Driver firstDriver(222,"Wallace",0,0),
          secondDriver(333,"Parker",0,1),
          thirdDriver(444,"Larson",1,0),
          fourthDriver(555,"Hernandez",1,1);
```

```
            firstDriver.showDriver();
            secondDriver.showDriver();
            thirdDriver.showDriver();
            fourthDriver.showDriver();
            getch();
      }
```

6. Save the program as **Driver.cpp** in the Chapter13 folder of either your Student Data Disk or of the Student Data folder on your hard drive. Compile and run the program. The output looks like Figure 13-4.

```
Driver
ID #222 Name: Wallace Gender: Female   Not over 25
ID #333 Name: Parker Gender: Female   Over 25
ID #444 Name: Larson Gender: Male     Not over 25
ID #555 Name: Hernandez Gender: Male    Over 25
```

Figure 13-4   Output of Driver program

 If you assign a value other than 0 or 1 to a bit field, only the right-most bit is stored. All even numbers contain a 0 in the right-most position, and all odd numbers contain a 1 in the right-most position.

 You cannot use the address operator (&) with a bit field. You can access only addresses of whole bytes or larger objects.

COMBINING BIT FIELDS TO HOLD VALUES LARGER THAN 1

When you want to store a 0 or 1, you can use a single bit. If you want to store larger values, you need more bits. Table 13-2 shows that you need at least two bits of storage to represent the value 2 or 3. Similarly, you need three bits to represent 4, 5, 6, or 7. When you want to store a small value that requires more storage space than a bit, but not as much as a byte or an integer, you simply increase the number following the colon in the declaration of the bit field. For example, `int aField:2;` declares a field that is two bits in size. Within a two-bit field, you can store four values—00, 01, 10, and 11. If you examine Table 13-2, you can see that these four values are the equivalents of the decimal values 0, 1, 2, and 3.

In the next set of steps, assume that you want to include a field within the Driver class you created earlier, and that you allow only three or fewer vehicles per Driver. You could use an integer to hold the vehicle number, but you require only two bits, so you add a two-bit field to the Driver class. Then you can use the new Driver class in a demonstration program.

1. If necessary, open the **Driver.cpp** file. Immediately save it as **Driver2.cpp** in the same location.

2. At the end of the list of Driver class fields (after the isOver25 field), add a new two-bit field that holds the number of vehicles being insured with this Driver.

   unsigned numVehicles:2;

3. Within the public section of the declarations for the Driver class, add a required parameter to the Driver constructor argument list. This parameter holds the number of insured vehicles.

   Driver(int id, char name[], int gen, int older, **int cars**);

4. Change the Driver class constructor implementation to accommodate the new parameter and to assign it to the new numVehicles field.

   ```
   Driver::Driver(int id, char name[], int gender, int older, int cars)
   {
       idNum = id;
       strcpy(lastName,name);
       isMale = gender;
       isOver25 = older;
       numVehicles = cars;
   }
   ```

5. Replace the last line of the showDriver() function. Currently it is cout<<endl;. The new line displays the number of vehicles as follows:

   cout<<"   Driver has "<<numVehicles<<" vehicle(s)."<<endl;

6. Within the main() function, add a number of vehicles to the constructor call for each Driver.

   Driver firstDriver(222,"Wallace",0,0,0),

   secondDriver(333,"Parker",0,1,1),

   thirdDriver(444,"Larson",1,0,2),

   fourthDriver(555,"Hernandez",1,1,3);

7. Save the file as **Driver2.cpp**. Compile and execute the program. The output appears in Figure 13-5. The correct number of vehicles appears with the other information regarding each Driver.

13

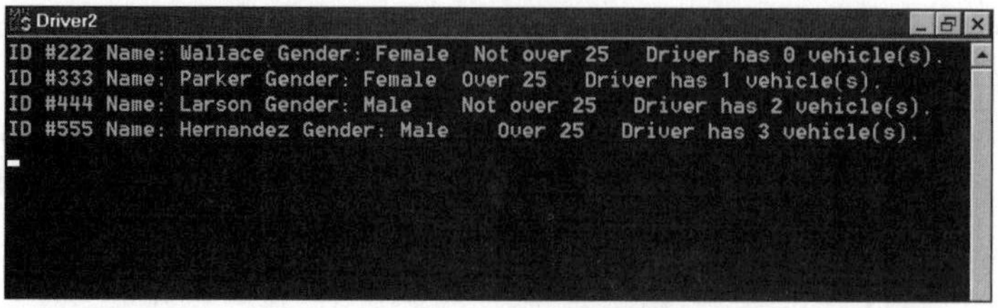

Figure 13-5   Output of Driver2 program

CONVERTING A GROUP OF BIT FIELDS TO AN INTEGER VALUE

For convenience, you can picture a group of bit fields as a single byte or integer. For example, consider the partial Employee class definition shown in Figure 13-6. Besides an ID number, every Employee contains eight yes-or-no fields that indicate Employee attributes, such as whether the Employee is full-time, and whether the Employee requires a deduction for medical insurance.

```
class Employee
   {
      private:
            int idNum;
            unsigned isFullTime:1;
            unsigned deductMedicalInsurance:1;
            unsigned deductDentalInsurance:1;
            unsigned deductLifeInsurance:1;
            unsigned deductUnionDues:1;
            unsigned deductSavingsBonds:1;
            unsigned deductRetirementPlan:1;
            unsigned deductCharitableContribution:1;
   };
```

Figure 13-6   Partial Employee class definition

When you store 0s and 1s in the bit fields for an Employee object, you can think of them as individual fields or as a single unit. For example, Figure 13-7 shows how an Employee who is not full-time and who elects the dental insurance, life insurance, and savings bond options, but no others, appears in computer memory. With 1s representing yes and 0s representing no, the Employee's eight separate flags form the binary number 00101100. (The right-most 0 represents the first field listed within the class—isFullTime.) If you treat this group of flags as a binary number and assign the binary numbering system column values to each column, then the Employee's deduction group value is 32 + 8 + 4, or 44 in the decimal system.

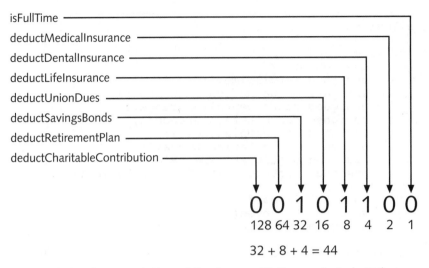

Figure 13-7   Representation of Employee with three selected attributes

Suppose you need to select Employees who have elected the three options—life insurance, dental insurance, and savings bonds—for some purpose. You can use an if statement such as the following to select those Employees and print a message:

```
if(deductMedicalInsurance == 0 &&
      deductDentalInsurance == 1 &&
      deductLifeInsurance == 1 && deductUnionDues == 0 &&
      deductSavingsBonds == 1 && deductRetirementPlan == 0 &&
      deductCharitableContribution == 0)
         cout<<"  Special combination!"<<endl;
```

Alternately, you can use the knowledge that an Employee who elects those three options holds a combined value of 44 in the bit fields, and use a statement similar to the following:

```
if(codes == 44)
    cout<<"  Special combination!"<<endl;
```

Certainly the second option is easier to write, although it is more cryptic. If you use such a technique, then you should document the meaning of the 44 in a program comment. Figure 13-8 shows a complete Employee class, including a convertBitsToInt() function that calculates the combined decimal value of the bit fields that are part of the class.

The Employee class setFields() function prompts the user for an Employee's ID number and for yes-or-no answers to questions regarding the values of each of the bit fields within the class. Because the cin operator uses the address of the variable for which you are reading a value, and because you cannot use the address of a bit, the setFields() function requires a temporary integer object for data entry. The temporary object accepts the input value, which is then assigned to the appropriate bit field.

13

```
class Employee
  {
      private:
          int idNum;
          unsigned isFullTime:1;
          unsigned deductMedicalInsurance:1;
          unsigned deductDentalInsurance:1;
          unsigned deductLifeInsurance:1;
          unsigned deductUnionDues:1;
          unsigned deductSavingsBonds:1;
          unsigned deductRetirementPlan:1;
          unsigned deductCharitableContribution:1;
      public:
          void setFields();
          void showEmployee();
          unsigned convertBitsToInt();
  };
void Employee::setFields()
  {
      int temp;
      cout<<"Enter ID number ";
      cin>>idNum;
      cout<<"Enter 1 or 0 for yes or no ";
      cout<<"to each of the following questions."<<endl;
      cout<<"Is Employee full time? ";
      cin>>temp;
      isFullTime = temp;
      cout<<"Medical insurance? ";
      cin>>temp;
      deductMedicalInsurance = temp;
      cout<<"Dental insurance? ";
      cin>>temp;
      deductDentalInsurance = temp;
      cout<<"Life insurance? ";
      cin>>temp;
      deductLifeInsurance = temp;
      cout<<"Union? ";
      cin>>temp;
      deductUnionDues = temp;
      cout<<"Savings bonds? ";
      cin>>temp;
      deductSavingsBonds = temp;
      cout<<"Retirement plan? ";
      cin>>temp;
      deductRetirementPlan = temp;
      cout<<"Charitable contribution? ";
      cin>>temp;
      deductCharitableContribution = temp;
  }
```

Figure 13-8 The Employee class

```
void Employee::showEmployee()
  {
      cout<<"ID #"<<idNum<<" ";
      cout<<deductCharitableContribution<<
          deductRetirementPlan<<deductSavingsBonds<<
          deductUnionDues<<deductLifeInsurance<<
          deductDentalInsurance<<deductMedicalInsurance<<
          isFullTime;
  }
unsigned Employee::convertBitsToInt()
  {
      unsigned temp;
      temp = deductCharitableContribution * 128
          + deductRetirementPlan * 64
          + deductSavingsBonds * 32
          + deductUnionDues * 16
          + deductLifeInsurance * 8
          + deductDentalInsurance * 4
          + deductMedicalInsurance * 2
          + isFullTime * 1;
      return(temp);
  }
```

Figure 13-8   The Employee class (continued)

The showEmployee() function displays the field bit values for demonstration purposes. A fully developed Employee class probably would contain a more descriptive showEmployee() function that spells out the Employee's status with regard to each of the deduction options.

The Employee class convertBitsToInt() function shown in Figure 13-8 uses the binary system column values to construct an integer from the separate bit fields.

Figure 13-9 contains a main() program that uses the Employee class shown in Figure 13-8. An array of Employee objects is declared and, in a for loop, each Employee is assigned values from the keyboard. The second for loop displays each Employee's values in turn, including the calculated code's value. This program looks for Employees who have selected the dental insurance, life insurance, and savings bond options (but no others), checks each Employee's calculated code against the value 44, and prints a message for the appropriate Employees. Figure 13-10 shows the end of a typical run of the program. You can see from the output that each Employee's bit field values correspond to a decimal number, and that those Employees whose bit field values equal 44 receive the "Special combination!" message.

13

```
void main()
 {
     const int numEmps = 5;
     Employee emps[numEmps];
     int x;
     unsigned codes;
     for(x=0; x< numEmps; ++x)
          emps[x].setFields();
     for(x = 0; x < numEmps; ++x)
        {
          emps[x].showEmployee();
          codes = emps[x].convertBitsToInt();
          cout<<"      "<<codes<<endl;
          // 44 is the code for dental insurance, life
          // insurance, and savings bonds only
          if(codes == 44)
                cout<<"   Special combination!"<<endl;
        }
     getch();
 }
```

Figure 13-9   main() program using the Employee class

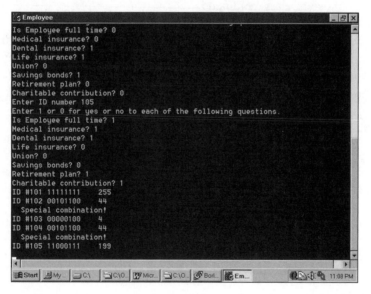

Figure 13-10   Output of a typical run of the Employee program

As an alternative to coding `if(codes == 44)` in the program in Figure 13-9, you could declare a constant such as `const unsigned special = 44;` and then use the if statement `if(codes == special)`.

USING THE LOGICAL BITWISE AND OPERATOR WITH A MASK

Comparing an object's bit fields to a decimal value is efficient when you want to find objects with a specific stored pattern. However, the job becomes more difficult when you want to select objects with multiple possible patterns. Suppose, for example, that you want to find all Employees who carry any type of insurance—medical, dental, or life. The bit values for an Employee with these three deductions and no others are shown in Figure 13-11. Such an Employee has combined bit values that equal the decimal number 14. However, if you want to find all Employees who take deductions for any type of insurance, you cannot just compare the Employee's code value to 14. Many other Employee combinations also contain "on" bits for at least one of the three insurance types, but contain other on bits as well. For example, an Employee who is full-time and takes deductions for all three insurance types, but takes no other deductions, is represented by 00001111, or 15. Another Employee who is not full-time, but takes every possible deduction, including all three insurance deductions, is represented by 11111110, or 254. Additionally, some Employees take the medical insurance option, but not the dental or life insurance. Others take the life insurance only, and so on. There are many numeric combinations for which at least one of the three insurance fields is 1, and it would take many if statements to compare an Employee with every possible valid combination that includes at least one of the three insurance fields.

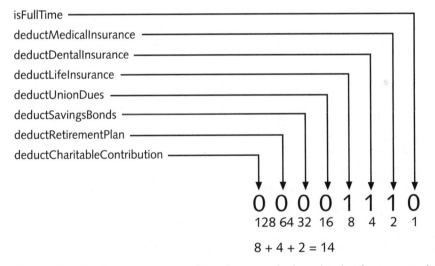

Figure 13-11   Representation of Employee with three kinds of insurance, but no other deductions

C++ provides you with a special set of operators, called bitwise operators, that you can use in situations like the one just described. **Bitwise operators** let you manipulate individual bits of integer or character values. One such operator is the **logical bitwise AND operator**, which is written as a single ampersand (&). You have already used the logical AND operator (without the word bitwise) by placing two ampersands between two boolean expressions.

For example, the following C++ statement prints a message when two conditions are true—gradePoint is at least 3.0, and creditsEarned are at least 30.

```
if(gradePoint >= 3.0 && creditsEarned >=30)
    cout<<"Eligible for honor society";
```

The bitwise AND operator does not compare variable values. Instead, it compares the individual bits of its two operands and produces a result based on the bit values. The result value contains a 1 in any columnar positions where both bitwise AND operands contain a 1; the result value contains a 0 in all other bit positions. For example, suppose value1 contains the bit pattern 10101010, and value2 contains the bit pattern 00001111. Figure 13-12 shows how the expression `result = value1 & value2;` is evaluated.

value1	1	0	1	0	1	0	1	0
value2	0	0	0	0	1	1	1	1
result	0	0	0	0	1	0	1	0

Figure 13-12   Using the logical bitwise AND operator with two values

Figure 13-12 shows that the right-most column of value1 contains 0, and the right-most column of value2 contains a 1. Because both operands, value1 and value2, do not contain a 1 in the right-most column, the right-most bit in the result is 0. Figure 13-12 also shows that value1 and value2 both contain 1s in the column that is second from the right. Therefore, the result field also contains a 1 in its corresponding column. In other words, if both operands contain a 1 in a column, so does the result, and if either or both the operands contain a 0 in a column, so does the result.

The usefulness of the bitwise AND comes in your ability to create a mask. A **mask** is a value whose only purpose is to filter values from other variables. Figure 13-13 shows three possible Employee objects and the result that ensues when you mask their bit values with an insuranceMask set to 00001110. The first two Employee objects shown in Figure 13-13 carry at least one of the types of insurance. Although the results of the logical bitwise AND operation differ for the two Employees, both operations result in a non-zero value. The third Employee represented in Figure 13-13 carries no insurance. When the bit values of this Employee are compared to the insuranceMask with the logical bitwise AND, the result is zero because there are no bit fields for which both the Employee and the mask hold a 1 in the same position.

Consider a multiple choice test for which the test taker fills in bubbles to select answers. To compute a score, you can create a cover sheet with holes that correspond to the correct answers, hold the sheet over the completed exam, and count the number of filled-in bubbles you see. The cover sheet is a real-world example of a mask.

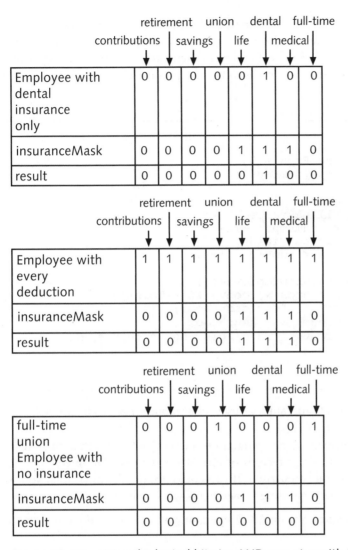

	retirement	contributions	union	savings	dental	life	full-time	medical
Employee with dental insurance only	0	0	0	0	0	1	0	0
insuranceMask	0	0	0	0	1	1	1	0
result	0	0	0	0	0	1	0	0

	retirement	contributions	union	savings	dental	life	full-time	medical
Employee with every deduction	1	1	1	1	1	1	1	1
insuranceMask	0	0	0	0	1	1	1	0
result	0	0	0	0	1	1	1	0

	retirement	contributions	union	savings	dental	life	full-time	medical
full-time union Employee with no insurance	0	0	0	1	0	0	0	1
insuranceMask	0	0	0	0	1	1	1	0
result	0	0	0	0	0	0	0	0

Figure 13-13   Using the logical bitwise AND operator with three Employees and an insurance mask

13

Figure 13-14 shows a program that declares several Employee objects and allows the user to enter values. In the first highlighted statement in the figure, the allInsurance mask is initialized to the value 14, which is the value that indicates true for all three insurance bits. In the second highlighted statement, the mask is used with a bitwise logical AND and with each Employee object to determine whether each Employee has any of the three forms of insurance. When an Employee has none of the three forms of insurance, the result of the mask is a zero, which is interpreted in the if statement as false. Thus, if an Employee carries none of the three forms of insurance, no message prints.

Figure 13-15 shows a typical run of the program. The first two Employees (those with IDs 201 and 202) do not have any form of insurance, and the mask does not identify them as insured Employees. The last three Employees each carry one or more types of insurance. Therefore, their mask results are non-zero; the if expression is evaluated as true, and the insurance message appears.

```
void main()
  {
      const int numEmps = 5;
      Employee emps[numEmps];
      int x;
      unsigned codes;
      unsigned allInsurance = 14;
      for(x=0; x< numEmps; ++x)
          emps[x].setFields();
      for(x = 0; x < numEmps; ++x)
        {
          emps[x].showEmployee();
          codes = emps[x].convertBitsToInt();
          cout<<"    "<<codes<<endl;
          if(codes & allInsurance)
              cout<<"  Has some insurance"<<endl;
        }
      getch();
  }
```

Figure 13-14 A main() program that uses an insurance mask to filter Employee bit fields

Using a mask is convenient. In the program in Figure 13-14, using the mask improves program efficiency; you can select records of Employees who take all three types of insurance by making a single logical comparison. If you could not use the mask, then you would have to make separate comparisons using if statements with each of the three insurance fields.

When you use the logical bitwise AND operator, you can assign the result to a variable, as in the following statement:

```
result = value1 & value2;
```

You also can perform a bitwise comparison and assignment in one operation using &=. The following statement performs a bitwise AND comparison between value1 and value2, and assigns the results to value1:

```
value1 &= value2;
```

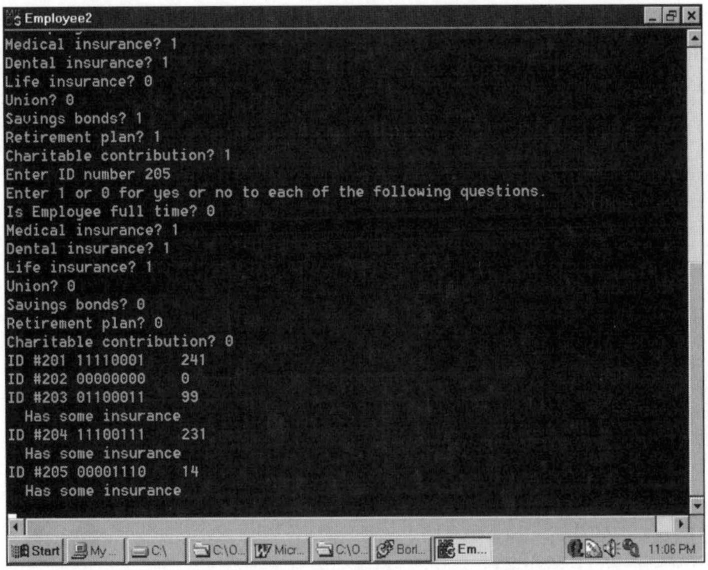

Figure 13-15   Output of Employee2 program

USING THE LOGICAL BITWISE OR OPERATOR

The **logical bitwise OR operator** (|) compares the bits of its two operands, and produces a result in which each bit is a 1 if either of the operand's corresponding bits is a 1. Figure 13-16 shows an example that uses the logical bitwise OR operator. When either or both of the column's bits hold a 1, then the result bit also holds a 1. In other words, the result holds a 0 in a column only if both operands to the logical bitwise OR hold a 0 in the corresponding column.

value1	1	0	1	0	1	0	1	0
value2	0	0	0	0	1	1	1	1
result	1	0	1	0	1	1	1	1

Figure 13-16   Using the logical bitwise OR operator with two values

One way to use the logical bitwise OR is to turn on specific bits within an object. For example, consider objects created from the Employee class in Figure 13-8. Suppose an organization decides to offer two new free benefits, a retirement plan and medical insurance, to all Employees, whether they have previously elected those benefits or not. You can create a mask that holds 1s in those two positions and perform a logical bitwise OR with the mask and an Employee's bit fields. Figure 13-17 shows some possible results. When you use the logical bitwise OR with any Employee and the newBenefitMask that holds 1s in the deductRetirementPlan

13

and deductMedicalInsurance fields, the result contains "on" fields for any options the Employee had originally. Additionally, the result contains on bits in the retirement and medical option fields whether the Employee originally held the benefits or not.

	retirement contributions	savings	union	life	dental	medical	full-time	
Employee with dental insurance only	0	0	0	0	0	1	0	0
newBenefitMask	0	1	0	0	0	0	1	0
result	0	1	0	0	0	1	1	0

	retirement contributions	savings	union	life	dental	medical	full-time	
Employee with every deduction except retirement and medical	1	0	1	1	1	1	0	1
newBenefitMask	0	1	0	0	0	0	1	0
result	1	1	1	1	1	1	1	1

	retirement contributions	savings	union	life	dental	medical	full-time	
full-time union Employee with medical insurance	0	0	0	0	0	0	1	1
newBenefitMask	0	1	0	0	0	0	1	0
result	0	1	0	0	0	0	1	1

Figure 13-17   Possible results of using the logical bitwise OR with an Employee and the newBenefit mask

Figure 13-18 shows a function you can add to the Employee class to assign an unsigned integer's bit values to an Employee's bit fields. If an argument to convertIntToBits() is at least 128, it means the left-most bit in the argument is on, so a 1 is assigned to the deductCharitableContribution field, and the argument is reduced by 128. If the remaining value in the argument is at least 64, then it means the next bit is on, and 1 should be assigned to the deductRetirementPlan field. The procedure continues until each Employee bit field has been assigned its correct value.

```cpp
void Employee::convertIntToBits(unsigned code)
{
    if(code >= 128)
        {
            deductCharitableContribution = 1;
            code -= 128;
        }
    else deductCharitableContribution = 0;
    if(code >= 64)
        {
            deductRetirementPlan = 1;
            code -= 64;
        }
    else deductRetirementPlan = 0;
    if(code >= 32)
        {
            deductSavingsBonds = 1;
            code -= 32;
        }
    else deductSavingsBonds = 0;
    if(code >= 16)
        {
            deductUnionDues = 1;
            code -= 16;
        }
    else deductUnionDues = 0;
    if(code >= 8)
        {
            deductLifeInsurance = 1;
            code -= 8;
        }
    else deductLifeInsurance = 0;
    if(code >= 4)
        {
            deductDentalInsurance = 1;
            code -= 4;
        }
    else deductDentalInsurance = 0;
    if(code >= 2)
        {
            deductMedicalInsurance = 1;
            code -= 2;
        }
```

Figure 13-18   Function that assigns an integer to Employee bit fields

13

```
        else deductMedicalInsurance = 0;
        if(code >= 1)
            {
               isFullTime = 1;
               code -= 1;
            }
        else isFullTime = 0;
}
```

Figure 13-18   Function that assigns an integer to Employee bit fields (continued)

The program in Figure 13-19 establishes a newBenefitMask with a value of 66. The value is set to 66 because an integer with the deductRetirementPlan and deductMedicalInsurance bits turned on has 1s in the columns values at 64 and 2. The program creates an array of Employee objects, and assigns values to each Employee's fields. The second for loop within the program is used to display each Employee's field values, convert the bits to an integer, perform a bitwise OR on the bits with the newBenefitMask, set the Employee's bits with the new value, and display the Employee again. When you examine the end of a typical run, as shown in Figure 13-20, you see that no matter whether each Employee stored 1s in the deductRetirementPlan and deductMedicalInsurance bits prior to the bitwise OR, each Employee contains 1s in these fields afterward.

```
void main()
  {
       const int numEmps = 5;
       Employee emps[numEmps];
       int x;
       unsigned codes;
       unsigned newBenefitMask = 66;
       for(x=0; x< numEmps; ++x)
             emps[x].setFields();
       for(x = 0; x < numEmps; ++x)
           {
             emps[x].showEmployee();
             codes = emps[x].convertBitsToInt();
             codes = codes | newBenefitMask;
             emps[x].convertIntToBits(codes);
             cout<<"    ";
             emps[x].showEmployee();
             cout<<endl;
           }
       getch();
  }
```

Figure 13-19   main() program that turns on Employee bit fields using a bitwise OR

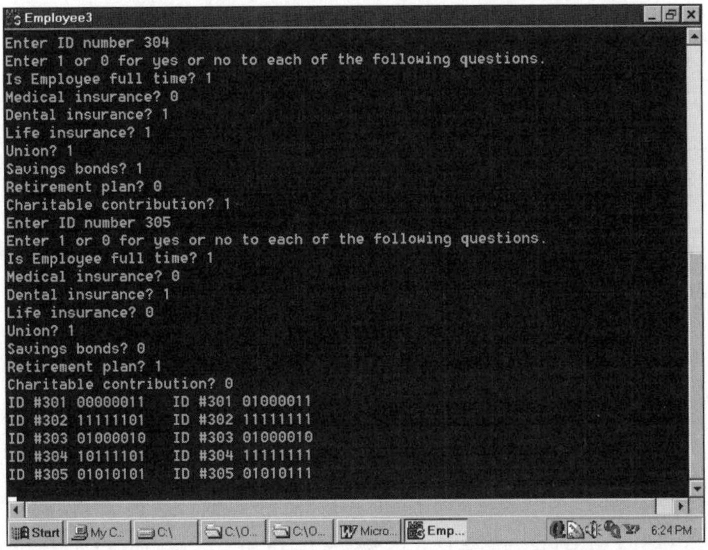

Figure 13-20   Output of a typical execution of Employee3 program

When you use the logical bitwise OR operator, you can assign the result to a variable, as in the following statement:

```
codes = codes | newBenefitMask;
```

You also can perform a bitwise comparison and assignment in one operation using | =. The following statement performs a bitwise OR comparison between codes and the newBenefitMask, and assigns the results to codes:

```
codes |= newBenefitMask;
```

13

SHIFTING BITS

You can use the **bitwise left shift operator** (<<) to shift bits to the left and the **bitwise right shift operator** (>>) to shift bits to the right. Each of these operators requires two operands—the one on the left holds the bits that are shifted, and the one on the right is the number of positions to shift.

For example, Figure 13-21 shows the bit representation of a byte, and the results after shifting one bit to the left, the equivalent of using the expression `result = value1 <<1;`. The bit pattern in value1 represents 46. When each bit is moved one position to the left, the left-most position of value1 is lost and a zero is added to the vacated right-most position in the result. The result value becomes 92—two times the original value of value1.

decimal value	128	64	32	16	8	4	2	1
value1	0	0	1	0	1	1	1	0
result after left shift	0	1	0	1	1	1	0	0

Figure 13-21   Shifting bits to the left

 You left shift in the decimal system when you add a zero to the right of a value. The value 436 becomes 10 times larger, or 4360, when you left shift.

 The bitwise shift operators are overloaded. The << and >> operators are used for input and output as well as for bit shifting.

If you use the expression `result = value1 << 2;`, the result becomes four times value1. For any number n, shifting n bits to the left is the same as multiplying by two to the n power. As with other binary operators, you can shift and assign in one operation using <<= or >>=.

The program in Figure 13-22 shows two ways of multiplying 5 by 2 to the third power. In the first part of the program, a variable named num is set to 5, and a loop is executed to multiply 2 by 2 by 2 to determine 2 to the third power before multiplying by 5 and displaying the answer. In the second part of the program, num is reset to 5 and the bitwise left shift operator performs the same task in one statement. The results, shown in Figure 13-23, are identical. Not only does shifting bits require less code, it also executes much more quickly.

Like the bitwise left shift operator, the bitwise right shift operator provides the same result as dividing by two to the power of the right operand. Again, the advantage is that the bitwise right shift operator works faster and requires less code.

```
#include<iostream.h>
#include<conio.h>
void main()
 {
     int power = 3;
     int base = 2;
     int result;
     int x;
     int num = 5;
     result = base;
     for(x = 1; x < power; ++x)
          result *= base;
     result *= num;
     cout<<"Result is "<<result<<endl;
     num = 5;
     result = num <<= power;
     cout<<"Result is "<<result<<endl;
     getch();
 }
```

Figure 13-22   Program demonstrating bitwise left shift operator

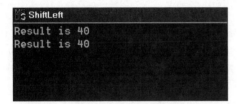

Figure 13-23   Output of Shiftleft program

13

UNDERSTANDING RECURSION

A function that calls itself is a **recursive function**. Many programming languages do not allow a function to call itself, but C++ programmers can use recursion to produce some interesting effects. Figure 13-24 shows a simple example of recursion. In this program, the main() function calls the infinity() function. The infinity() function prints "Help!" and calls itself again (see the highlighted statement). The second call to infinity() prints "Help!"; and generates a third call. The result is a large number of repetitions of the infinity() function. The output is shown in Figure 13-25.

```
#include<iostream.h>
void infinity()
  {
      cout<<"Help! ";
      infinity();
  }
void main()
  {
      infinity();
  }
```

Figure 13-24 An example of recursion

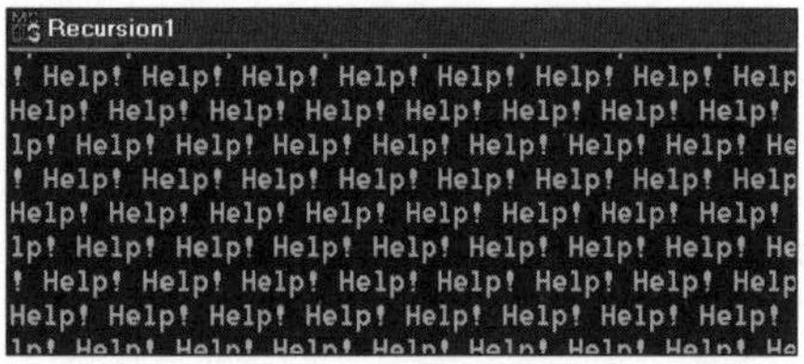

Figure 13-25 Output of Recursion1 program

Every time you call a function, the address to which the program should return at the completion of the function is stored in a memory location called the **stack**. When a function ends, the address is retrieved from the stack and the program returns to the location from which the function call was made.

When the main() program in Figure 13-24 calls the infinity() function, the stack receives the address to which the program should return within main(), but this program never returns to main(). Because infinity() does not execute until its end, it never returns, and the stored address is never retrieved from the stack. Instead of returning, the infinity() function calls another function—itself. When this second function call is made, the new address to which this second call should return also is stored in the stack. You can picture the new return address as being stored "on top of" the first address. However, this address also is never retrieved from the stack, because when this version of the infinity() function executes, it, too, never ends. It executes yet another repetition of infinity() and a third return address is stored in the stack. Because infinity() never reaches its end, and keeps calling another function (itself), eventually the stack overflows with too many stored return addresses, you receive an error message, and the program fails. However, if you can imagine a computer with an infinite amount of memory allocated to the stack, then in theory, this program never ends. Instead, it keeps storing return addresses in the stack, but never retrieves any of them.

Of course, there is no use for a program that never ends. Just as you must be careful not to create loops that can't end, when you write recursive functions, you must provide a way for the recursion to stop eventually.

Figure 13-26 shows a program that calls a recursive function which computes the sum of every integer, from 1 up to and including the function's argument value. For example, the sum of every integer up to and including 3 is 1 + 2 + 3, or 6, and the sum of every integer up to and including 4 is 1 + 2 + 3 + 4, or 10. When thinking about cumulative summing relationships, remember that the sum of all the integers up to and including any number is that number plus the sum of the integers for the next lowest number. In other words, the sum of the digits up to and including 4, is 4 plus the sum of the digits up to and including 3.

The recursive cumulativeSum() function in Figure 13-26 uses this knowledge, so that for any argument, num, passed in that is greater than 1, the function returns a value that is n plus the cumulativeSum() of num –1. The main() program in Figure 13-26 calls the cumulativeSum() function nine times in a loop to show the cumulativeSum() of every integer from 1 through 9. Figure 13-27 shows the output of the program in Figure 13-26.

```
#include<iostream.h>
#include<conio.h>
int cumulativeSum(int num)
   {
       int returnVal;
       if(num == 1)
           returnVal = num;
       else
           returnVal = num + cumulativeSum(num - 1);
       return(returnVal);
   }
void main()
   {
       int num;
       for(num = 1; num < 10; ++num)
       cout<<"When num is "<<num<<
           " then cumulativeSum(num) is "<<
           cumulativeSum(num)<<endl;
       getch();
   }
```

13

Figure 13-26   Program that uses a recursive cumulativeSum() function

```
Recursion2
When num is 1 then cumulativeSum(num) is 1
When num is 2 then cumulativeSum(num) is 3
When num is 3 then cumulativeSum(num) is 6
When num is 4 then cumulativeSum(num) is 10
When num is 5 then cumulativeSum(num) is 15
When num is 6 then cumulativeSum(num) is 21
When num is 7 then cumulativeSum(num) is 28
When num is 8 then cumulativeSum(num) is 36
When num is 9 then cumulativeSum(num) is 45
```

Figure 13-27 Output of Recursion2 program

If you examine Figures 13-26 and 13-27 together, you can see that when 1 is passed to the cumulativeSum() function, the if statement within the function determines that the argument is less than or equal to 1, the returnVal becomes 1, and 1 is returned for output.

On the next pass through the for loop, 2 is passed to the cumulativeSum() function. When the function receives 2 as an argument, the if statement within the function is false, and the returnVal is set to 2 plus the value of cumulativeSum(1). This second call to cumulativeSum() using 1 as an argument returns a 1, so when the function ends, it returns 2 + 1, or 3.

On the third pass through the for loop within the main() function, 3 is passed to the cumulativeSum() function. When the function receives 3 as an argument, the if statement within the function is false and the function returns 3 plus the value of cumulativeSum(2). The value of this call is 2 plus cumulativeSum(1). The value of cumulativeSum(1) is 1. So ultimately, cumulativeSum(3) is 3 + 2 + 1.

Following the logic of a recursive function is a difficult task, and programs that use recursion are error-prone and hard to debug. For these reasons, many organizations forbid their programmers from using recursive logic within their programs. Additionally, many of the problems solved by recursive functions can be solved in a more straightforward way. Examine the program in Figure 13-28. Using a nested loop and no recursive function, this program produces identical output to that in Figure 13-27. The program in Figure 13-28 deals with the same problem in a more straightforward fashion.

```
#include<iostream.h>
#include<conio.h>
void main()
  {
     int num;
     int total, x;
     for(num = 1; num < 10; ++num)
        {
          total = 0;
          for(x = 1; x <= num; ++x)
             total += x;
          cout<<"When num is "<<num<<
             " then the cumulative sum of num is "
             <<total<<endl;
        }
     getch();
  }
```

Figure 13-28   Nonrecursive program that computes a sum

USING A RECURSIVE FUNCTION TO SORT A LIST

It is possible to quickly sort a list using a recursive sorting function. To use this sorting method, you employ a "divide and conquer" technique in which you select a point within a list that represents a middle position, and then divide the list into two sublists. (See Figure 13-29.) Then you swap the positions of pairs of values until all the values in the first sublist are less than the value in the middle position, and all the values in the second sublist are more than the value in the middle position. Subsequently, each sublist is divided in half and rearranged so all the low values are in one sublist and all the high values are in the other. You keep dividing lists into increasingly small sublists until there is only one element in a sublist. At that point, the values are sorted.

13

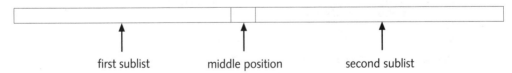

first sublist   middle position   second sublist

Figure 13-29   A list with two sublists

You can solve the sorting problem by breaking down the work into several functions. The simplest function, named swap(), appears in Figure 13-30. This function takes the address of two values, named val1 and val2, as arguments. Then the function reverses the positions of the values. A temporary location holds val1, val2 replaces val1, and the temp value, which was val1, replaces val2.

```
void swap(int   &val1, int &val2)
  {
      int temp;
      temp = val1;
      val1 = val2;
      val2 = temp;
  }
```

Figure 13-30 The swap() function

Figure 13-31 shows the splitList() function. It accepts an array of integers, and two integers representing the starting and ending subscripts in the list. The middle position is calculated by averaging the start and stop values. The middle position and its value are stored, and the middle value is moved to the beginning of the list. Then every value in the list (after the first one) is compared to the first value (which used to be the middle value). If any value is less than the original middle value, the value is exchanged with a value from the other side of the middle; that is, it's exchanged with a value from the other sublist. At the end of the function, the middle value is returned to the middle of the list.

```
int splitList(int nums[], int start, int stop)
  {
      int midValue, midPoint, mid, x;
      mid = (start + stop) / 2;
      swap(nums[start],nums[mid]);
      midPoint = start;
      midValue = nums[start];
      for(x = start + 1; x <= stop; ++x)
          if (nums[x] < midValue)
            {
                ++midPoint;
                swap(nums[midPoint],nums[x]);
            }
      swap(nums[start], nums[midPoint]);
      return(midPoint);
  }
```

Figure 13-31 The splitList() function

The sort() function in Figure 13-32 is the recursive function. It accepts a list of numbers and a start and stop position. As long as start and stop are not the same (as long as start is smaller than stop), the list is split in two and sort() is called twice recursively, using the first half of the list and the second half of the list.

```
void sort(int nums[], int start, int stop)
  {
      int midPoint;
      if(start < stop)
        {
            midPoint = splitList(nums, start, stop);
            sort(nums, start, midPoint - 1);
            sort(nums,midPoint + 1, stop);
        }
  }
```

Figure 13-32   The sort() function

Figure 13-33 shows a main() program that sorts an array of seven integers. It displays the values, calls sort(), and displays the values again. Figure 13-34 shows the output.

```
void main()
  {
      const int numVals = 7;
      int nums[numVals] = {7,2,5,6,4,1,3};
      int x;
      cout<<"At start: ";
      for (x = 0; x < numVals; ++x)
            cout<<nums[x]<<" ";
      cout<<endl;
      sort(nums,0,numVals-1);
      cout<<"At end:    ";
      for(x = 0; x < numVals; ++x)
            cout<<nums[x]<<" ";
      cout<<endl;
      getch();
  }
```

Figure 13-33   main() program that uses sort()

13

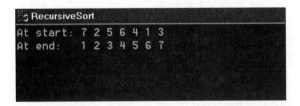

Figure 13-34   Output of RecursiveSort program

The output produced by the recursive sorting program is not remarkable; you can achieve the same results with many other types of sorts that do not involve recursion. Sorts that are written nonrecursively also are easier to understand and debug. However, this sorting function works very well and is an example of a useful form of recursion that programmers some-times employ.

In the next set of steps, you create a recursive drawing function so you can experiment with the way recursion works.

1. Open a new file in your C++ editor. Type the include statements you need for this program.

```
#include<iostream.h>
#include<conio.h>
```

2. Write a recursive draw() function. The function accepts two arguments—a character that is drawn on the screen, and an integer that represents the number of times to draw the character. If the number is greater than 0, the character is output, and the draw() function is called again using a number that is one less than the original number. In other words, the draw() function produces num characters.

```
void draw(char ch, int num)
    {
    if(num > 0)
        {
        cout<<ch;
        draw(ch,num - 1);
        }
    }
```

3. Next, write a recursive display() function. Its three arguments include a symbol to be drawn, an offset number, and a length. If the length is greater than 0, the function calls draw twice. The first time it calls draw(), it passes a space and the offset value to draw(), so draw() produces off number of spaces as output. The second time it calls draw(), it passes the symbol and the length, so it produces len number of sym outputs. After a newline output, the display() function calls itself using the same symbol, but an offset that is two more than the previous offset, and a length that is four less than the previous length. The display() function keeps calling itself until the len variable is reduced to 0 or less.

```
void display(char sym, int off, int len)
    {
    if(len>0)
        {
        draw(' ',off);
        draw(sym, len);
        cout<<endl;
        display(sym,off + 2,len - 4);
        }
    }
```

4. Next, write a main() function that uses the display() function. Initialize an offset variable to 0 and prompt the user for a length and symbol to use as initial arguments to display().

```
void main()
  {
    char symbol;
    int offset = 0;
    int length;
    cout<<"Enter length ";
    cin>>length;
    cout<<"Enter symbol ";
    cin>>symbol;
    cout<<endl<<endl;
    display(symbol, offset, length);
    getch();
  }
```

5. Save the program as **DrawingRecursion.cpp** in the Chapter13 folder of either your Student Data Disk or of the Student Data folder on your hard drive. Compile and execute the program. Figure 13-35 shows the output when the user enters 30 and an asterisk in response to the prompts. The main() function calls the display() function using the asterisk, 0, and 30 as arguments. The display() function calls draw() twice. The first time it uses 0 spaces, and the second time it uses 30 asterisks. Then display() calls draw() two more times using two spaces and 26 asterisks. The third set of calls to draw() uses four spaces and 22 asterisks, respectively. The result is an inverted pyramid.

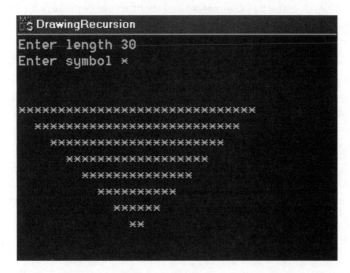

Figure 13-35   Output of a typical run of the DrawingRecursion program

6. Run the program several times using different symbols and lengths until you understand how the two recursive functions operate.

CHAPTER SUMMARY

❏ Every piece of data stored on a computer uses the binary system. The only digits used are 0 and 1.

❏ Computers use the binary system because two-way switches are the cheapest form of storage; most systems store eight bits in a byte. Two popular eight-bit codes are ASCII and EBCDIC.

❏ You can use a single bit for a field that holds a 0 or 1. The advantage is that you consume little storage space. You declare a field to be a single bit by placing a colon and a 1 after the variable declaration.

❏ When you want to store a small value that requires more storage space than a bit, but not as much as a byte or an integer, you increase the number following the colon in the declaration of the bit field.

❏ When you store 0s and 1s in the bit fields for an object, you can think of them as individual fields, or you can think of them as a single unit and assign the binary numbering system column values to each column.

❏ C++ provides you with bitwise operators that let you manipulate individual bits of integer or character values. The logical bitwise AND operator (&) compares the individual bits of its two operands and produces a result with a 1 in any columnar positions where both bitwise AND operands contain a 1, and 0 where they do not. You use bitwise logical operators with a mask—a value whose only purpose is to filter values from other variables.

❏ The logical bitwise OR operator (|) compares the bits of its two operands and produces a result in which each bit is a 1 if either of the operand's corresponding bits is a 1. One way to use the logical bitwise OR is to turn on specific bits within an object.

❏ You can use the bitwise left shift operator (<<) to shift bits to the left, and the bitwise right shift operator (>>) to shift bits to the right. Each of these operators requires two operands—the one on the left holds the bits that are shifted, and the one on the right is the number of positions to shift. For any number n, shifting n bits to the left is the same as multiplying by two to the n power; shifting n bits to the right is the same as dividing by two to the n power.

❏ A function that calls itself is a recursive function. When you write recursive functions, you must provide a way for the recursion to stop eventually. Following the logic of a recursive function is a difficult task, and programs that use recursion are error-prone and hard to debug.

❏ It is possible to quickly sort a list using a recursive sorting function.

REVIEW QUESTIONS

1. The binary system uses the digits _____.
   a. 0 and 1
   b. 0, 1, and 2
   c. 1 and 2
   d. 0 through 9

2. The decimal system and the binary system differ in _____.
   a. the maximum number of columns you can use to represent a number
   b. the meaning of 0 in the right-most column
   c. the number of times larger a column is compared to the column on its right
   d. all of the above

3. The binary number 1100 is equivalent to the decimal number _____.
   a. 2
   b. 12
   c. 14
   d. 1100

4. The decimal number 20 is equivalent to the binary number _____.
   a. 11000
   b. 10100
   c. 1010
   d. 111000

5. The primary reason that two-way switches are used for computer storage is
   _____.
   a. they are the most natural for humans to understand
   b. they are less prone to electrical failure than switches with more settings
   c. they are the cheapest to build
   d. it is simply traditional

6. ASCII and EBCDIC are _____.
   a. computer manufacturers
   b. programming languages
   c. numbering systems
   d. computer codes

13

7. There are _____.
   a. eight bits in a byte
   b. eight bytes in a bit
   c. eight bytes in a character
   d. eight integers in a bit

8. You declare a bit field by placing _____ between the field name and an integer.
   a. a semicolon
   b. a colon
   c. two colons
   d. a space

9. The advantage to storing a piece of data in a bit instead of a byte is _____.
   a. input and output operations are easier
   b. the code is less prone to error
   c. programs are easier to debug
   d. storage space is saved

10. The most common meanings of 0 and 1, respectively, are _____.
    a. true and false
    b. false and true
    c. on and off
    d. yes and no

11. If you declare a character as `char someChar = 'A';`, you can print the address of the right-most bit with the statement _____.
    a. cout<< &someChar;
    b. cout<<&someChar:0;
    c. cout<<&comeChar:7;
    d. none of the above

12. The logical bitwise AND operator is _____.
    a. &
    b. |
    c. <<
    d. >>

13. If byteA contains 10000001 and byteB contains 10100000, then what is the value of byteA & byteB?

    a. 10100001

    b. 00100001

    c. 10000000

    d. 00000000

14. A value whose only purpose is to filter values from other variables is a
    _____ .

    a. cast

    b. queue

    c. sieve

    d. mask

15. You most likely would use a bitwise logical OR to _____ .

    a. make decisions

    b. filter out off bits

    c. turn on specific bits

    d. perform multiplication by powers of 2

16. If someNum = 6, then someNum >>= 1 equals _____ .

    a. 0

    b. 3

    c. 6

    d. 12

17. A function that calls itself is _____ .

    a. recursive

    b. refractory

    c. repulsive

    d. reactionary

13

18. What is the output of the following program?

```
int recursive(int x)
{
    int result;
    if(x == 0)
        result = x;
    else
        result = x * (recursive (x - 1);
    return (result);
}
void main()
{
    cout<<recursive(0);
}
```

a. 0

b. 1

c. 2

d. 4

19. Using the same recursive() function from problem 18, what is the output of the following program?

```
void main()
{
    cout<<recursive(2);
}
```

a. 0

b. 1

c. 2

d. 4

20. What is the output of the following program?

```
int recursive(int x)
{
     int result;
     if(x == 1)
          result = x;
     else
          result = x * (recursive (x - 1);
     return (result);
}
void main()
{
     cout<<recursive(2);
}
```

a. 0

b. 1

c. 2

d. 4

EXERCISES

1. Create a GraduateCandidate class. Include fields for a GraduateCandidate ID number, and last and first names. Also include bit fields that indicate the following:

❑ Has the GraduateCandidate completed 120 credit hours?

❑ Has the GraduateCandidate completed 45 hours in his or her major?

❑ Has the GraduateCandidate paid all campus traffic tickets?

❑ Has the GraduateCandidate paid all library fines?

❑ Has the GraduateCandidate paid all graduation fees?

13

The class includes appropriate functions to set and display all the fields. When you display a GraduateCandidate, include a decision as to whether the GraduateCandidate can graduate. Create a main() program with several GraduateCandidate objects, and demonstrate that your functions work correctly.

2. Create a CustomerProfile class. Each CustomerProfile contains a last name, phone number, and bit fields indicating whether the customer:

- Works full-time

- Owns a home

- Owns a dog

- Owns a computer

- Has a credit card

- Gives to charity

- Subscribes to magazines

Also include appropriate functions to set and retrieve CustomerProfile values. Write a program that allows you to create an array of at least 10 CustomerProfiles, then select homeowners to solicit for home-improvement loans.

3. Using the same CustomerProfile class as in Exercise 2, write a program that allows you to select customers who own both a dog and a computer, so you can send them advertisements about a new pet-oriented Web site.

4. Create a Student class. Include appropriate fields and functions, including eight bit fields that store characteristics of your choice, such as whether the student is a smoker or an early riser. Write a program that creates 10 Student objects. Create another object that stores data about you. Then allow the program to select the most compatible roommates from the array of other Students.

5. Write a recursive function that takes two integers as arguments. The function finds the value of the first integer raised to the power of the second integer. Base your recursive function on the knowledge that for any two numbers x and n, $x^n = x * x^{n-1}$. Write a main() program demonstrating that the function works correctly.

6. Write a recursive function that calculates the factorial of its argument. Base your recursive function on the knowledge that for any number n, the value of n factorial (usually written as n!) is $n * (n - 1) * (n - 2) * (n - 3)....* 1$. Write a main() program demonstrating that the function works correctly.

7. Each of the following files in the Chapter13 folder contains syntax and/or logical errors. Determine the problem in each case, and fix the program.

   a. DEBUG13-1

   b. DEBUG13-2

   c. DEBUG13-3

   d. DEBUG13-4

CASE PROJECT

You have been developing a Fraction class for Teacher's Pet Software. Each fraction contains a numerator, denominator, a whole number portion, and a floating-point equivalent field. Each Fraction also has access to several functions you have developed. Complete these tasks:

a. Create a Problem class for a teacher who wants to test her students on three Fraction features:

   ❏ Adding Fractions that both have a numerator of 1

   ❏ Adding Fractions that have the same denominator

   ❏ Adding Fractions whose sum is less than 1

   The Problem class contains three Fraction objects and three bit fields, each representing one of the above conditions. The Problem class constructor accepts values for two Fractions interactively, and computes the third Fraction object as the sum of the first two. The constructor also sets the bit fields to 1 or 0 appropriately. Write a main() function that instantiates at least 10 Problem objects, prompts the teacher for the type of exercise she is creating today, and displays Problem objects that meet the requested criteria.

b. Write a main() function that declares an array of 10 Fraction objects. Write a recursive sort() function that places the Fraction objects in ascending order.

c. Write a main() function that declares an array of 10 Fraction objects. Write a recursive sort() function that places the Fraction objects in descending order.

13

A CURRENCY MANIPULATOR FOR VISUAL C++

In Chapter 10, you created a currency manipulator that you can use to display a value in currency format—that is, with a dollar sign, a decimal point, and two digits to the right of the decimal. Users of some C++ compilers, particularly Microsoft Visual C++, cannot use the manipulator described in Chapter 10 because of some peculiarities of the Visual C++ compiler. Visual C++ requires you to create a class to create a manipulator with arguments. Figure A-1 shows a Currency class you can use to display a value in currency format.

```
#include <iostream.h>
#include <iomanip.h>
#include <string.h>
typedef char* charp;
IOMANIPdeclare( charp );
class Currency
  {
    private:
      double value;
      static char *szCurrentPic;
    public:
      Currency( double val ) { value = val; }
      friend ostream& operator << ( ostream& os, Currency m );
      friend ostream& setpic( ostream& os, char* szPic );
  };
char *Currency::szCurrentPic;
ostream& operator << ( ostream& os, Currency m )
  {
    cout<<'$';
    cout.setf(ios::fixed |ios::showpoint);
    cout.precision(2);
    cout.width(7);
    os << m.value ;
    return os;
  }
```

Figure A-1 Currency manipulator to use in Visual C++ and the main() function that calls it

```
ostream& setpic( ostream& os, char* szPic )
  {
    return os;
  }
OMANIP(charp) setpic(charp c)
  {
    return OMANIP(charp) (setpic, c);
  }
void main()
  {
    Currency amt = 13.5678;
    cout << setpic( "" ) << amt << endl;
  }
```

Figure A-1   Currency manipulator to use in Visual C++ and the main() function that
calls it (continued)

The class in Figure A-1 is named Currency; any programmer-chosen identifier is acceptable. The Currency class contains a double to hold the value of the currency, and a character pointer used to set the size of the output field. The Currency class holds two friend functions that each return a reference to ostream. Using these friend functions together allows you to display a double in currency format.

This extra level of complexity in creating a manipulator function represents one of a very small number of differences in C++ compilers. For the majority of functions you create, C++ compilers will operate in an identical manner.

Index